Theories of race and ethnic relations

This book brings together internationally known scholars from a range of disciplines and theoretical traditions. In setting out the various theories it demonstrates the range and diversity of approaches to race and ethnic relations current in the field. As well as identifying important and persistent points of controversy, however, the collection also reveals much complementarity and indicates the potential for a multifaceted approach to theorisation.

The theories represented include contributions from the perspective of sociology, social anthropology, sociobiology, and social psychology. These range from the macro-level approaches of the theory of the plural society and Marxian and Weberian forms of class analysis to the micro-focus of rational choice theory, symbolic interactionism and identity structure analysis.

Comparative ethnic and race relations

Published for the Centre for Research in Ethnic Relations at the University of Warwick

Senior Editor
Professor John Rex *Associate Director & Research Professor of Ethnic Relations, University of Warwick*

Editors
Professor Robin Cohen *Executive Director & Professor of Sociology, University of Warwick*
Mr Malcolm Cross *Principal Research Fellow, University of Warwick*
Dr Robin Ward *Head of Ethnic Business Research Unit, University of Aston*

This series has been formed to publish works of original theory, empirical research, and texts on the problems of racially mixed societies. It is based on the work of the Centre for Research in Ethnic Relations, a Designated Research Centre of the Economic and Social Research Council, and the main centre for the study of race relations in Britain.

The series will continue to draw on the work produced at the Centre, though the editors encourage manuscripts from scholars whose work has been associated with the Centre, or whose research lies in similar fields. Future titles will concentrate on anti-racist issues in education, on the organisation and political demands of ethnic minorities, on migration patterns, changes in immigration policies in relation to migrants and refugees, and on questions relating to employment, welfare and urban restructuring as these affect minority communities.

The books will appeal to an international readership of scholars, students and professionals concerned with racial issues, across a wide range of disciplines (such as sociology, anthropology, social policy, politics, economics, education and law), as well as among professional social administrators, teachers, government officials, health service workers and others.

Other books in this series:
Michael Banton: *Racial and ethnic competition* (issued in hardcover and as a paperback)
Tomas Hammar (ed.): *European immigration policy*
Frank Reeves: *British racial discourse*
Robin Ward and Richard Jenkins (eds.): *Ethnic communities in business*
Richard Jenkins: *Racism and recruitment: managers, organisations and equal opportunity in the labour market*
Roger Hewitt, *White talk black talk: inter-racial friendships and communication amongst adolescents*
Paul B. Rich: *Race and Empire in British politics*
Richard Jenkins and John Solomos (eds.): *Racism and equal opportunity policies in the 1980s*

Theories of Race and Ethnic Relations

Edited by
JOHN REX
and
DAVID MASON

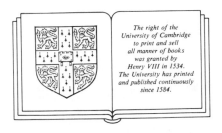

The right of the
University of Cambridge
to print and sell
all manner of books
was granted by
Henry VIII in 1534.
The University has printed
and published continuously
since 1584.

CAMBRIDGE UNIVERSITY PRESS

Cambridge
New York   New Rochelle
Melbourne   Sydney

Published by the Press Syndicate of the University of Cambridge
The Pitt Building, Trumpington Street, Cambridge CB2 1RP
32 East 57th Street, New York, NY 10022, USA
10 Stamford Road, Oakleigh, Melbourne 3166, Australia

First published 1986
First paperback edition 1988

Printed in Great Britain at the University Press, Cambridge

British Library cataloguing in publication data

Theories of race and ethnic relations. –
(Comparative ethnic and race relations)
1. Ethnic relations   2. Race relations
I. Rex, John   II. Mason, David
III. Series
305.8   GN496

Library of Congress cataloguing in publication data

Theories of race and ethnic relations.
(Comparative ethnic and race relations)
Bibliography.
1. Race relations – Congresses. 2. Ethnic relations –
Congresses. I. Rex, John. II. Mason, David (David J.)
III. Series.
HT1521.T47 1986   305.8   86-6126

ISBN 0 521 30573 X hard covers
ISBN 0 521 36939 8 paperback

CE

Contents

Contributors

Michael Banton, *Department of Sociology, University of Bristol*
Gideon Ben-Tovim, *Department of Sociology, University of Liverpool*
John Gabriel, *Department of Sociology, University of Birmingham*
Michael Hechter, *Department of Sociology, University of Arizona*
Richard Jenkins, *Department of Sociology and Anthropology, University College Swansea*
Barbara Ballis Lal, *Department of Social Science and Administration, University of London, Goldsmiths' College*
Ian Law, *Race Relations Officer (Housing), Leeds City Council*
David Mason, *Department of Sociology, University of Leicester*
Marshall W. Murphree, *Centre for Applied Social Sciences, University of Zimbabwe*
John Rex, *Centre for Research in Ethnic Relations, University of Warwick*
John Solomos, *Centre for Research in Ethnic Relations, University of Warwick*
M. G. Smith, *Department of Anthropology, Yale University*
Kathleen Stredder, *Department of Applied Social Studies, Birmingham Polytechnic*
Pierre L. van den Berghe, *Department of Sociology, University of Washington*
Sandra Wallman, *Departments of Anthropology and Geography, University College, London*
Peter Weinreich, *Department of Psychology, University of Ulster*
Harold Wolpe, *Department of Sociology, University of Essex*
J. Milton Yinger, *Department of Sociology, Oberlin College, Ohio*

Preface

JOHN REX

The papers contained in this book arose indirectly from the work of the Research Unit on Ethnic Relations, of which I was Director between 1979 and 1984. Although that Unit was originally founded to do fundamental research in the field of ethnic and race relations, pressures were put on the Unit by its parent body the Social Science Research Council during the years involved to engage more and more in policy-oriented research. It became more and more apparent to me as Director that, if we were not to become simply technocrats researching on the means thought necessary to achieve Government ends and if we were to be able to maintain the independence necessary to look critically at those ends, we needed to have a comparative perspective, and that perspective was in turn dependent upon the understanding of theoretical issues.

On the face of it the development of a universally argued theory and an agreed paradigm for race and ethnic relations research seemed impossible. Not merely were there several disciplines involved, but within the main ones, namely sociology and social anthropology, there seemed to be a number of competing if not warring schools. None the less it was thought worthwhile to try to bring together some of the major internationally known scholars to present their ideas as to possible conceptualisations of the field in order to see whether what appeared at first to be irreconcilable conflict could in fact be replaced by a sense of complementarity.

My own perspective suggested to me that an important starting point would be the confrontation of Marxism, Weberian forms of class analysis and the theory of the plural society. I therefore sought to invite four major theorists from the number in Britain who had defended a Marxist perspective, and others, especially from the USA, who had contributed to the development of plural society theory. I intended myself to defend a Weberian concept of class analysis.

If this was the core of the programme envisaged, however, a number of other theories on different levels of abstraction suggested themselves. I thought that we should confront at the outset precisely this problem of different levels of abstraction and then, against this background, bring in a number of what claimed to be more fundamental types of analysis than the macro-theories of class and pluralism which had been in my mind central. To this end it seemed desirable to look at the paradigms suggested by the theory of rational choice, by social anthropology, by social biology and by social psychology, as well as the micro-sociological approach of symbolic interactionism.

Finally, however, it did seem necessary to look at the question of how the issue of race and ethnic relations looks when there has been a revolutionary transfer of power as in the Communist countries and in post-colonial societies. It also seemed desirable to consider the problems of societies which have in recent times set out to eliminate social inequalities.

The Marxist papers given at the conference were those of Harold Wolpe, who has been especially concerned with the sociology of race and class in his and my native country, South Africa, and of Gideon Ben-Tovim, John Gabriel and their colleagues whose actual paper dealt with the levels of political action to which, as they saw it, a Marxist perspective should lead. Stuart Hall was unfortunately prevented by illness from attending, and it was decided after the conference to invite John Solomos, a member of the Research Unit staff, to contribute a paper which might suggest an overall Marxist perspective.

M. G. Smith, who with J. S. Furnival is generally recognised as one of the founders of the theory of the plural society, gave a paper in which some of the propositions of plural society theory were put to an empirical test, using comparative material from Africa. My own paper on the other hand engaged with plural society theory, arguing that the relationship of the ethnic segments was often a class-like one, and also with orthodox Marxist theory to suggest more flexible concepts of class and class struggle.

To set the whole conference in perspective and to discuss the question of levels of abstraction in sociology we welcomed J. Milton Yinger, whose book on racial and cultural minorities has influenced a whole generation of younger scholars, but we were disappointed that Richard Schermerhorn, who has made one of the most masterly attempts at systematising the study of race and ethnic relations in his book *Comparative Ethnic Relations*, was not able to be with us.

Rational choice theory is a trend of rising importance in social science, including the study of ethnic and race relations, and two of our participants, Michael Hechter from the United States and Michael Banton, were invited to present papers on this theme. Both came, but Banton chose to present a paper on the even more fundamental question of the contrast between Kantian and Hegelian epistemologies in social science. The latter topic was important in that it provided links with my own Weberian paper and with the Marxist papers.

Anthropology was represented, apart from M. G. Smith, by Sandra Wallman who presented her views on ethnicity as a situational factor and demonstrated her approach by referring to her empirical work on networks in two London boroughs. Unfortunately both Fredrik Barth and Abner Cohen were unable to participate, and Richard Jenkins, a former member of the Unit staff, was therefore invited to submit a paper for this volume to set anthropological approaches in perspective.

Barbara Ballis Lal, a student of the Chicago School, reminded us both of the heritage of Robert Park and more particularly of the historical significance of the symbolic interactionist tradition which grew out of the Chicago School but which was above all represented in the work of Herbert Blumer.

Although the conference was primarily attended by sociologists and anthropologists, we were also concerned with the biological and psychological underpinnings of our work. Pierre van den Berghe was invited to argue the merits of sociobiology in this sphere and Weinreich, to talk about empirical research on the question of ethnic identity. Anders Lange and Charles Westin were invited to discuss, more fundamentally, the whole relationship between biological, psychological and sociological explanations. Lange and Westin, whose paper was regrettably too long to be included in this volume, indeed challenged the conference more than did any other speakers to be clear about what it meant by 'theory' and what it regarded as the *explanandum* in ethnic relations.

Then remained the question of race and ethnic relations in situations of political change. On this topic we were disappointed that W. J. Wilson of Chicago was not able to accept our invitation, but we saw Gabriel and Ben-Tovim's paper as dealing with this kind of question. Again we were disappointed that our colleagues Bromley and Koslov from the Soviet Union were not able to participate, but we did have the opportunity to hear an important paper by Marshall Murphree, who is President of the International Sociological Association's Research Committee on Ethnic Minorities and who has studied both minority and development problems in Zimbabwe before and after independence.

A number of other European scholars who did not give papers joined the meeting and the Unit was grateful for their co-operation. They included Andre Köbben and Hans van Amersfoort from the Netherlands

and Yngve Lithman from Sweden. Other English scholars who partici-
pated were Hugh Tinker, Alastair Hennessy, Kenneth Kirkwood, Terry
Chivers and Ceri Peach together with members of the Unit staff.

Being myself a party to the controversies which the book represents, I
did not feel that I could also write an objective Introduction. For this
reason I invited David Mason, whose judicious comments on trends in
the theory of race and ethnic relations had appeared elsewhere, to join
me in editing this book and to write the Introduction. Having assigned
this task to David Mason it would be inappropriate for me to comment at
any length on the papers or on his Introduction. Perhaps, however, I may
be permitted to make three general points.

The first is that I see more coherence in what is written here than
Mason does. As I see it there is considerable ground for agreement and
interchange between the Marxist and pluralist theories and my own. I
also think that many of the other theories discussed are not so much in
opposition to these, but simply at a different level of abstraction. Thus
the rational choice theory, sociobiology and social psychological theories of identity may be seen as explicating some of the macro-concepts
in class theories and pluralist theories. Their publication here may in fact
cause some of the macro-theorists to look more closely at their concepts
to see whether they can be analysed in methodologically individualist
terms. Slightly more difficult to bring into the general debate are the
symbolic interactionist theories and anthropological studies of social
networks. In part the answer may be that there is simply a need for
micro-empirical studies after all the larger political and economic issues
have been disposed of. But there is also another type of claim being made
here and it is important that such theories of race and ethnicity should be
argued about along with the theories which have been referred to above,
some of which might be accused of reifying group concepts.

My second point is that the conference has led me to bring my own
ideas closer to those of M. G. Smith and that there is no way in which I
would wish to agree with the dismissal of pluralist theory in the way
which Jenkins suggests. Indeed I think that if there is one central
organising concept in this field it is that of '*de facto* differential incorporation'. If I have myself emphasised the engagement of racial and ethnic
groups with each other as classes, I do also recognise ethnic estates as an
important element in colonial societies, and would go further, by
agreeing that political and legal structures are as important as economic
ones.

My very last word, however, may seem a surprising one. It is that I am
drawn to the conclusion that race and ethnicity as such, while they may
be a basis on which men affiliate to or are assigned to communal

quasi-groups, are *not* the primary element in what is called racial and ethnic relations. The fact is that the large communal quasi-groups which are called ethnic and racial are the collective entities which are brought together in systems of class, estate, status group domination, caste and individual status striving. What disturbs us about what we call 'race and ethnic relations situations' is very often not the racial and ethnic factor as such but the injustice of elements in the class and status system. Thus it is not surprising that in revolutionary aftermaths the racial and ethnic question declines in importance at least for a time. Thus we find Marshall Murphree telling us that the concern in Zimbabwe is less with race relations than with economic development.

I should like to thank all those concerned with making our conference the success it was and with making this work possible. In particular, however, I should like to thank Ceri Peach for helping us to hold the conference in St Catherine's College and Norman Thornton who handled all the administrative arrangements with very great skill. To our sponsors the Economic and Social Research Council we are grateful for a generous contribution to travel and accommodation expenses.

Introduction. Controversies and continuities in race and ethnic relations theory[1]

DAVID MASON

The papers collected in this volume are, with the exception of those of Jenkins and Solomos, revised versions of papers presented to a conference on Theories of Race and Ethnicity held at St Catherine's College, Oxford, between 19 and 23 March 1984. In convening the conference it had been the aim of Professor John Rex, then Director of the SSRC Research Unit on Ethnic Relations, to bring together in dialogue a number of eminent scholars representing a range of apparently competing theoretical traditions. Part of his object was to test whether there were points of convergence or continuity between theoretical standpoints which might usefully be explored and exploited to the benefit of the subject as a whole.

For a number of reasons, including the inability to attend of some of those originally invited, there is no sense in which the papers collected here can be said to represent every theoretical strand and tendency presently to be found in the field. Nevertheless, the following papers do present the work of a number of the most prolific and influential writers in the specialism. In so doing they raise, collectively and individually, a number of crucial and recurrent themes and points of controversy. It will be the purpose of this Introduction to identify and clarify some of these themes.

The nature of theory

The most obvious starting point for any overview of the volume is the question of theory itself. What do we mean by a theory of race or ethnic relations? It will become clear, even from a brief perusal of the contents page, that the authors assembled here have diverse and often divergent views about the answer to that question, although they do not all consider it necessary explicitly to discuss these issues. For some a theory

1

is little more than a set of working concepts or hypotheses by means of which observations may be classified and ordered. For others a theory is a set of interrelated and structured propositions whose purpose is pre-eminently etiological. For some a social theory needs to be as complex as the phenomena to which it relates, while for others social theory should aim to meet the same criteria of inclusiveness, economy and elegance which is traditionally taken to be the hallmark of theory in the natural sciences. Yet others, while sharing this as an ultimate objective, are content to build towards such an objective by means of smaller steps; what Merton would have called 'theories of the middle range' (Merton, 1968: 39–72). Finally, all of the theorisations represented here involve conceptions of the relationships with other theories. For some the relationship is one of superiority/inferiority, adequacy/inadequacy. For others the question is one of complementarity. It will be convenient to begin our discussion with a consideration of these competing views.

There are, I think, three principal answers presented in this volume to the question: 'What is the relationship between my theorisation and that of others?' They may conveniently be summarised as the 'grand theory', the 'mosaic' approach and the 'pyramid' approach.

According to the grand theory position, the purpose of social theorising is to develop sets of interrelated propositions which approximate ever more closely to an all-embracing theoretical system capable of providing causal explanation of all available observations. Those versions of grand theory which explicitly invoke the natural science model frequently aspire to the derivation of law-like generalisations. Indeed social theories sometimes appear to go further and to imply that they have the capacity to explain as yet unmade observations. To the extent that they do this they are often accused of departing from the natural science model by being, in effect, unfalsifiable. Theoretical systems like Marxism, Freudian psychoanalytic theory and Parsonian functionalism have all been criticised on these grounds.

Whether or not they invoke natural science, however, grand theories share a search for, and typically claim to have found, the underlying basis, deep structure or central dynamic of human social life. Often they are also involved in the search for the origins of this dynamic, although this search is not exclusive to grand theory. Grand theory does not always claim successfully to have established itself in terms of the high goals that it sets itself, but it is distinguished by its claim both that such goals are, in principle, attainable and that it is approaching them. The proper relationship among theories, then, is competitive. One theory is to be preferred to another only if it can be shown to be better; that is, if it explains more observations. In the case of those invoking a natural science model the additional criteria of economy and elegance are also typically invoked. (We should note here that it is possible to argue that the grand theory aspiration is anathema to the natural science tradition. Certainly it is not only grand theorists who invoke these criteria.)

Grand theory in social science does not always follow this model, however. The claim to have discovered the most important dynamic in social life frequently structures the range of questions to which answers are sought. In such cases, theories are to be judged according to whether, and how effectively, they answer such questions. Other questions are relegated to the status of epiphenomena with the assumption that their causation can be traced to the central dynamic even if at present sufficient attention cannot be diverted to this secondary task. In effect such a position involves what Michael Banton in this volume characterises as a meta-theoretical decision. Banton, in fact, implies in his discussion that it is pre-eminently Marxism, with its Hegelian meta-theory, which is thereby restricted in the range of questions which it may, or at least does, address. My own view is that there are myriad opportunities within what Banton calls the Kantian tradition for similarly restricting decisions of a meta-theoretical kind. Thus not only many variants of Marxism but also Freudian psychology and some versions of sociobiology (to name but two) may suffer similar restrictions.

There are hints of grand theory in a number of the contributions in this volume. The various Marxist accounts outlined by Solomos clearly share such an aspiration, while the claims to theoretical superiority of both sociobiology and rational choice theory have more than a hint of grand theory about them, whatever the ambivalence on this issue expressed by van den Berghe and Hechter. Even the apparently more open, revisionist Marxism of Wolpe, by insisting on the privileged status of the mode of production, seems to retain a claim for Marxism as the ultimate grand theory.

What I have, for convenience, called the mosaic approach to theory is one which is probably represented by the majority of the papers in this volume. It is consistent with an ultimate aspiration for grand theory (as expressed by Yinger at the start of his paper), with agnosticism as to its possibility or desirability and with a commitment to cumulative understanding through the complementary examination of social life from a variety of vantage points. This last orientation is not unlike the position of Weber and involves the implication that the complexity and multi-faceted character of social life must be matched by open-mindedness and a willingness to learn from others on the part of the theorist (cf. Freund, 1968). Such a position does not, however, involve the acceptance that all theories are equally adequate. While writers may self-consciously embrace this tradition as an epistemological position, a commitment to theories of the middle range, 'grounded theory' or a more limited search for a conceptual armoury which facilitates research may be an unremarked and taken-for-granted background assumption. Indeed in the present volume the papers by Lal, Murphree and Smith do not explicitly address these issues. What they write, however, would seem to be consistent with their categorisation under this heading, together with the papers by Rex and Wallman.

The pyramid approach to theory, represented in this volume by the work of van den Berghe and Yinger, is in the end difficult to distinguish from the other types listed above. I have separated them out principally in order to draw attention to the facts that each has something to say explicitly about the relationships between different modes of theorising and that each seeks to identify some systematic schema for relating different approaches. Thus van den Berghe invokes the principle of causal distance to identify the roles of different modes and levels of theorisation, while Yinger explicitly discusses the complementarity of different strands of race and ethnic relations theory and endorses the ultimate aspiration for grand theory. Indeed there is a sense in which the positions taken in both of these papers could dissolve into grand theory.

The imperialist tendency in the sociobiological approach is notably strong and the perspective would thus seem particularly to lend itself to grand theory building. This is so despite the ambivalence which van den Berghe exhibits towards such a project (an ambivalence which interestingly, is shared by Hechter). One reason for this affinity with grand theory is the ease with which sociobiology lends itself to the search for the origins of aspects of human behaviour. In the case of the study of race and ethnic relations this is particularly important because of the long-standing question of primordialism alluded to by Yinger. Moreover, since sociobiology appears to combine an approach to the question of origins with an emphasis on the continuity between 'nature' and 'nurture', it is not surprising that it has come to be seen by some of both its opponents and its advocates as providing a 'biological' rationale for racial and ethnic stratification. Indeed it was precisely this that caused Michael Banton during the discussion to ask whether this danger was not too high a price to pay for any advances in understanding which the sociobiological perspective might offer. Van den Berghe's answer, which is spelled out clearly in his paper, was that such a danger could only be a product of misunderstanding, not of the sociobiological perspective itself, and that academics did themselves, and the societies they served, a disservice by subordinating the search for truth to political and ideological pressures of whatever kind. I shall return to the question of the relationship between academic research and political action in due course. For the moment it will be appropriate to consider further the question of origins.

The problem of origins

The problem of origins has long dogged the study of many aspects of human behaviour. It takes on special significance in the field of race and ethnic relations. This is because of the persistence of the question of primordialism. There are several ways in which this question may be approached. One is the position adopted by Yinger who uses the term 'primordial' to refer to that aspect of ethnicity which expresses 'genuine culture' to which a sense of long-standing attachment is experienced. As his paper makes clear, he sees this as only one of a number of sources of ethnic strength. It is, however, redolent of a persistent strand or tendency in the academic discussion of ethnicity which Gabriel and Ben-Tovim have traced to the work of Max Weber. In an important paper they have identified an ambivalence about whether phenotype and/or culture have some independent effect or whether they are mediated by meaning, i.e. represent one of a number of potential bases for action (1979, see especially the discussion of Weber's usage of the concepts of 'race' and 'ethnicity': 191–4). It is this strand which highlights the second way in which the question of primordialism may be approached. It may be summed up in the question: 'Are those forms of human behaviour associated with the racist beliefs and practices characteristic of the history of nineteenth and twentieth-century Europe and its offshoots unique, and hence explicable in terms of some aspect of that history, or are they merely one form taken by a primordial ethnocentricism?' Clearly, if the answer to the second half of this question is 'yes', then not only will there be limits to the capacity effectively to challenge patterns of mutual antagonism founded upon ethnicity and race but also those benefiting from the resultant inequalities will have a powerful ideological excuse for their oppression of others — its 'naturalness'. This brings me to the third way in which primordialism may be approached – from the apparent immutability and naturalness of race as a criterion of differentiation. It is important to note here that, whatever our answers to the questions posed above, the concept of 'race' does have a discernible and traceable history. It is clear that it grew up hand in hand with the scientific exploration of human origins (Banton, 1967; 1977) and that, where it was incorporated into racist theory, it purported to offer an explanation of and justification for the exploitation and subordination of blacks by whites in terms of those origins. It is precisely for this reason that the term 'race' is increasingly questioned as an appropriate analytic category in sociology just as it was earlier in biology (see Miles, 1982).

Paradoxically, given this apparent unanimity across disciplines, M. G. Smith has chosen to incorporate race as one of the central variables in his analysis of pluralism in African societies. By 'race' he means not some loose sociological concept but 'aggregates whose members are objectively distinguished from others by certain gross hereditary phenotypical features' (below, p. 192). Responding to the surprise and unease which this usage evoked among conference participants, Smith has provided, in the revised version of his paper published here, an extended and robust defence of his position. Essentially he argues that the conventional wisdom of modern biology and genetics is a misplaced and illegitimate deduction from the study of monogenetic characters such as blood groups and that it flies in the face of common sense and observation. It is essential to maintain the concept, Smith argues, because 'unlike ethnic identity, racial identity and/or difference is immutable, manifest and *normally* unambiguous in multi-racial societies and contexts' (below, p. 191; emphasis in original). This is not to say that folk ideas of race or ethnicity will necessarily correspond with 'manifest biological differences' (below, p. 191), rather that understanding demands the confrontation of folk concepts with objective evidence.

The point I believe Smith wishes to make here is that it is important not to confuse principles of stratification which have a negotiability from those which do not. Put another way, there are myriad opportunities for boundary crossing and 'passing' where the criteria of group differentiation are capable of being concealed or rendered invisible, and where individuals or groups may in some sense 'choose' whether or not to display or maintain a particular cultural characteristic. By contrast, gross phenotypical differences, such as colour, are difficult, if not impossible, to conceal and can serve as markers of status whether or not other 'cultural' differences are present. Because they have a genetic foundation, they are both permanent and hereditarily transmitted and thus inferior or superior statuses are transmitted across generations. It is because he recognises the power of such markers that Smith wishes to avoid the implication he detects in the claim that such differences are *merely* socially constructed: that they are readily maleable and deconstructed. He rejects the conflation of race and ethnicity, noting that even where a group is culturally indistinguishable from others, phenotypical markers might well serve to differentiate it in terms of rights.

Smith goes on to make a further point. This is that the power and significance of phenotype as marker may well lead to situations in which folk concepts of race grow up, or are invented, in order to justify assigning a peculiarly permanent out-group status to some category of persons otherwise distinguishable only by some more equivocal marker. This is also an important point. In making it, however, I believe Smith has unwittingly carried his argument further than is necessary or sustainable. What is crucial about such situations is that folk concepts of race incorporate not merely presumptions about the immutability of phenotypical characteristics but also the belief that moral and intellectual differences parallel physical variation. The reason the Nazis wished to demonstrate the phenotypical specificity of Jews was in order to sustain an argument that their alleged intellectual, moral and cultural degeneracy was similarly rooted in an immutable biological heritage. It is precisely for this reason that modern biologists and geneticists have challenged the concept of race. Contrary to Smith's implication, they do not deny that phenotypical variation is genetically founded. Rather do they argue that the combination of intra-group variation with the polygenetic basis of phenotypical difference means that it is not possible to develop a scientifically founded racial classification. It is important to recognise and restate this point, I believe, because if we do not we may be forced to conclude, with the racists, that if groups differ systematically in physical appearance, why not also in intellectual capacity and moral worth? The geneticists' argument against this of course is logically the same as the one stated above: namely that the skills and capacities referred to are complexly and polygenetically determined and that there is thus no reason to assume that they all vary simultaneously along a single scale. The fact that this is also true of physical differences means that 'race' can never signify anything more than socially constructed ideal types in terms of which people are categorised.

Put another way, I would argue that the differences cited by Smith are neither objective nor unambiguous. Interestingly, he provides two different lists of 'races'. On page 189 he distinguishes 'Negroes, Asiatic Mongols, Whites (or Caucasians), Australian Aborigines, Amerindians, Pygmies, Bushmen and certain other populations'. On page 192 we are told that 'Altogether, in the African states discussed here, there are five racial categories, namely, Blacks, Whites, Indians, Pygmies, and a residual rather variable category of hybrids.' The difference between these two lists suggests to me that the distinction between 'folk concepts' and 'objective races' is a spurious one. Indeed Smith admits as much when describing his first list as deriving from differences that 'all men remark'. The fact that the two lists differ demonstrates that such distinctions are, indeed, socially contextual, however 'objective' they may appear. Why, we may ask, are phenotypical differences between

Nubians and Zulus not regarded as gross while those between, say, Australian aborigines and pygmies, are? I suspect that the answer is not unrelated to the processes by which such classifications were first developed, processes rooted in European exploration and expansion and in the development of European science. As such there is a strong element of ethnocentrism about them. The fact that they are also not unambiguous is demonstrated by the fact that in all the most rigidly stratified societies in which 'race' is the principal criterion of social placement, it has been necessary to develop complex procedures for classifying the phenotypically ambiguous. (See the example cited by Yinger, below, pp. 21–2. Consider also the example of the system of administrative racial classification in South Africa.) It may be that it is this issue of classification which is crucial and that it is fruitful to follow Jenkins (below, p. 177) in distinguishing groups and categories. Categorisation, he notes, is intimately bound up with power relations and the capacity of one group ascriptively to classify another. It is precisely this process which is at the root of the incorporation of 'race' as a concept implying immutability into the systems of domination conventionally identified as racist. For this reason alone, it seems to me, we should be wary of resuscitating the concept without stronger grounds than those adduced by Smith.

In marked contrast to Smith, Wallman argues that there are no sound grounds for distinguishing the racial as a distinct form of identity. Arguing from the orthodox scientific rejection of the concept of 'race', she suggests that its persistence in folk models allows the anthropologist to see phenotype as 'one element in the repertoire of ethnic boundary markers' (below, p. 229).

Jenkins's discussion of groups and categories is designed to challenge Wallman's conflation. He argues that while ethnicity is more generally concerned with self-identification – 'us' – 'race' is best conceived as a matter of external classification – 'them'. This directly challenges Wallman's implication that the distinction between group and category is not clear-cut: ethnicity may be a matter of both external definition and self-identity. In fact Jenkins makes a similar point in referring both to categorisation in terms of ethnicity and to positive self-evaluation in terms of 'race'. It may be worth noting here that the ideology of *Herrenvolk* which he cites is not the only example of this process. Thus black power or consciousness movements pursue a strategy of resistance through an inversion of the negative categorisations of the racist (cf. Blauner, 1972). This points to a fruitful strand in the anthropological tradition which Wallman describes, namely the conceptualisation of ethnicity as a resource (see also Dhooge, 1981). This is a powerful and important counter to those approaches which see the oppressed merely as powerless victims of domination or, as in some versions of structuralist Marxism, as dupes of system forces over which they have no control. It is crucial to note that even the harshest systems of oppression rarely leave their victims with *no* channels of resistance (cf. Genovese, 1975) and that people do play a role in the making of their own history. Any alternative view must dissolve into either impotent pessimism in the face of oppression or the kind of paternalism of which white liberals are often accused (Blauner, 1972; cf. Rich, 1984).

Having said that, it is important to note that the central focus of Jenkins's criticism of the anthropological approach which Wallman represents is its apparent neglect of asymmetrical power relations. Indeed Wallman admits as much when she argues (below, p. 226) that 'anthropologists are seldom professionally concerned with vertical relations between ethnic groups and macro-state structures, and they rarely undertake studies of social stratification and minority status as such'. Rather are they concerned with 'lateral relations at the micro-level'. The result is that the relationship between identification and categorisation is effectively neglected. Ethnicity may be a resource in the making of a group's history, but the process of categorisation, of which racism is the most striking example in the nineteenth and the twentieth centuries, illustrates that the superior capacity of some groups to define the circumstances under which that history is made is a crucial feature of asymmetrical power relations. Ethnicity is not, therefore, merely a counter resource to some other basis of power chances; it is deeply embedded in the overall power relations of the society, structuring and conditioning, for example, the development and outcome of class struggles. (Compare the discussions in the papers by Rex and Wolpe below.)

Race and class

The race/class debate has been one of the most enduring to be found in the sociological literature in the field. Most often it has been structured around a confrontation between Marxist and non-Marxist scholars in which the latter have argued for an independent causal role for 'race' while the former have insisted that 'race' is merely one manifestation of more fundamental class struggles. There are, in turn, a number of ways of conceptualising the priority of class from this perspective. Some of these are critically reviewed in Harold Wolpe's paper, in which he seeks to argue that the reductionism characteristic of many Marxist treatments of race and ethnicity is as profoundly un-Marxist as the insistence on the priority of racial identity found in the work of some of their opponents. By contrast Wolpe wishes to argue that Marxists must dispense with economistic conceptions of class and the economy and recognise capital accumulation as a social process with economic, political and ideological dimensions. This entails a rejection of any simple opposition between race and class. As he puts it: 'Race may, under determinant conditions, become interiorised in the class struggle' (see below, p. 123).

A number of conference participants had difficulty in discerning what was distinctively Marxist about the analysis offered by Wolpe. How, for example, did it differ from a Weberian approach to these problems? In the revised and extended version published here, Wolpe has implicitly responded to these questions and has made it clear that, although he rejects economic determinism, he still regards the mode of production as having a privileged status; that is to say, the ultimate locus of class struggle is conceptualised as the system of production. In this respect there would seem to remain a gulf between Marxists and Weberians in that, for the latter, class is to be more widely conceived as a category rooted in the market. This is clear in Rex's self-consciously Weberian discussion, where the centrality which he attaches to class relations is explicitly theorised in terms of the relations of employment. A further difference remains. Thus while Wolpe wishes to stress the interpenetration of the political, economic and ideological as determinants of class struggle, Weberians tend to insist on the analytic separation of what Weber called class, status and party. Hence Rex stresses the need to recognise the interplay of political and economic forces in the rise and demise of Empire, particularly with regard to the systems of forced labour to which it gave rise. He draws attention to the creation of estate as well as class relations under such conditions and to the consequences this has for subsequent relations with metropolitan societies following the growth of international migration. The significance of this stress on the need to maintain the analytic separation of class, status and party becomes clear when Rex refers to the possibility that ethnic phenomena may manifest themselves in the absence of any obvious class stratification. Here a theory of ethnicity would be necessary to comprehend the dynamics of the situation. We may go further, however, and suggest that an adequate theory has to provide us with the means to grasp the nature, location and, ultimately, origins of ethnic attachment whether or not we regard it as having been 'interiorised' within class struggle.

Whatever differences remain between Marxists and Weberians on these issues, however, the internal critique of Marxism described by Wolpe, and further attested in the papers by Ben-Tovim *et al.* and by

Solomos, would seem to pave the way for a more fruitful dialogue between theoretical approaches than has sometimes been evident in the past. If these developments were matched by openness on the part of non-Marxists, mutually beneficial results might well ensue. Some hint of the advantages that such a dialogue would offer can be seen in the paper by Murphree.

A special theory?

The class/race debate conveniently draws our attention to a further persistent controversy in the field of race and ethnic relations theory, namely the question of whether a special theory is required to account for the phenomena of racial and ethnic stratification and conflict. Most of the authors here would, I think, answer this question negatively in the sense that they would argue, from their different perspectives, that race and ethnic relations are best conceived as particular instances of more general processes of group formation, boundary maintenance, identity structuring or whatever. At the same time most would recognise the need for at least some minimal conceptual procedures for identifying when ethnic identities are operative. Interestingly, of those represented here, van den Berghe comes closest to offering a special theory. However, even he sees ethnicity as an extension of another principle: nepotism.

Traditionally, the plural society thesis has been seen as the principal example of the attempt to develop a special theory of race and ethnicity. Indeed it is true that it developed as an attempt to comprehend the apparently radically different structures to be found in colonial and ex-colonial societies when compared with their erstwhile Western colonisers. In this respect it offered an important counter to much contemporary Western scholarship which operated with consensual models of relatively homogeneous societies. This was true not only of the dominant theoretical paradigm of the 1950s and 1960s – functionalism – but also of many prevailing political ideologies – liberalism and integrationism. In this respect, although Jenkins is right to suggest (below, p. 181) that there are some theoretical difficulties in identifying what exactly a plural society is, since such a concept appears to imply the possibility of 'monoism', it remains the case that much social theory and popular discourse does indeed assume the existence of such an animal. For this reason alone, the development of the plural society model was a crucially important counter to much of the ethnocentrism which pervaded, and continues to pervade, the discussion of race and ethnic relations. With the development of black resistance in the United States in the 1960s and the growth of ethnically distinct populations in Western European societies, the idea that pluralism denotes a distinct type of society has been increasingly challenged. (We might note that this intellectual challenge has paralleled political/ideological developments such as the 'rediscovery' of ethnicity in the USA and the growth of doctrines of multi-culturalism in Great Britain.) Increasingly those utilising the concept of pluralism have tended to conceptualise it as a variable rather than as a distinct societal type. (See for example the recent volume edited by Clarke, Ley and Peach, 1984).

It seems to me that this last development only exacerbates the problem identified by Jenkins in his contribution, namely the tendency for the notion of pluralism to represent no more than a redescription. It may be that this is an inherent flaw of the perspective. What it does, however, offer in its strong form, as in the work of M. G. Smith, is a reminder that there are indeed differences between societies in which cultural differences result in social segmentation and those in which they do not; between those in which that segmentation gives rise to, or is marked by, *de facto* differential incorporation and those in which it does not; and between those in which that differential incorporation is formally and juridically sanctioned and those in which it is not. The characteristic which makes the South African social formation so odious for many of us is precisely its unique combination of social and cultural pluralism with both *de facto* and *de jure* differential incorporation, the whole founded upon an explicit, if rhetorically ever-changing, racist ideology. To say this is, of course, in no way to minimise the racism we discern in our own societies.

Scholarship and politics

A major theme both in the papers and in the discussion at the conference was the question of the relationship between academic research and political action. There are two possible ways of conceiving this relationship. One is in terms of the constraints placed upon scholarship by political pressure or ideological commitment. The other is related to the question of how academic work can be made to serve political objectives.

In relation to the first conception, the papers by van den Berghe and Banton take up, in different ways, versions of the conventional social science position. According to this view, the search for truth has priority over all other objectives. It is inhibited by all extraneous limitations, including those deriving from political pressure or ideological commitment. Such a position does not exclude political and ideological commitment on the part of the scholar. This commitment can only be pursued, however, by an unerring pursuit of the truth, not by its suppression.

Indeed, van den Berghe goes so far as to argue that academics' only value lies in their ability to challenge deeply held preconceptions of all kinds through their role as the 'court jesters of modern societies'. The difficulty with this position, however, is that court jesters do not have full control over the ways in which their work is interpreted and used. Hence, implicit in Michael Banton's question referred to earlier was the further question: 'Should academics operate a form of self-censorship?'. If the answer is 'Yes' we should note that we may find ourselves on a slope which, like all others, can become increasingly slippery. Where do we, for instance, draw the line between self-censorship for noble reasons and that motivated by fear, self-aggrandisement or political threats? Perhaps in the end the best safeguards against the misuse of knowledge are to be found in an academic community of scholars who maintain what Peter Berger has called 'a militant commitment to reason' (1979: 22). Certainly van den Berghe has not been given, nor would he expect, any quarter from those of his colleagues who find his work variously suspect, dangerous or odious. As his paper makes clear, his own defence of his position is equally robust.

Banton's own approach to this issue reveals the difficulty of any simple distinction between academic purity and ideological distortion. Thus his claim that analysts must make a choice between Hegelian and Kantian epistemologies involves the idea that those opting for the former are restricted by a view of history which predefines the questions they pose while those who adopt the latter stance have a free choice of questions. The argument clearly implies that the example *par excellence* of the Hegelian position is Marxism, of various kinds. Marxism is restricted, so it appears, by a political project derived from or related to a theory of history. Yet Marxists themselves often argue that the very strength of Marxism is precisely the location of research questions in a developmental theory founded on a science of history which also structures their political commitment. Epistemologies which lack this coherence, so they argue, are particularly prone to shifts of fashion, political pressure and ideological manipulation. Yet this openness and flexibility is precisely what Banton sees as giving Kantians their strength and capacity to resist ideological manipulation. In the end I suspect that Banton's dichotomous classification of meta-theoretical options is too simple. The alleged openness of Kantian epistemology to the purely academic selection of research interests does not, even if we grant it, guarantee that academic purity will not be polluted by intrusions ranging from the sinister – political manipulation – to the prosaic – the search for research funds. As John Rex's paper makes clear, the scholar's own biography is frequently a powerful formative influence on research questions.

The above reference to Marxism should not be taken to imply that there is only one variety of this theoretical tradition. Nor would it be correct to imply that Banton himself takes such a view. John Solomos's paper traces the development of the tradition and identifies its varieties and transformations. Two other papers in the volume also deal with Marxist theorisations and represent useful expositions of post-Althusserian positions. Interestingly they both, in different ways, depart from the oft-cited strengths of Marxism referred to above. For Wolpe the starting point of any analysis must be the historical specificity of capitalism and the conditions of its reproduction. The subordination of research questions to political objectives is undesirable not least because political possibilities are conditioned not merely by struggle but by structural conditions.

The paper by Ben-Tovim *et. al.*, by contrast, takes a radically different position. Rather than eschew the political determination of research questions, the authors seek a way out of the strait-jacket of much structuralist Marxism by arguing that research must be harnessed to the struggle for political objectives. In so doing, they seem to depart even more radically from the classical Marxist position. Marx himself, of course, argued for the unity of theory and practice. However, the political project of Marx was clearly derived from an analysis of the capitalist mode of production. The position of Ben-Tovim and his colleagues seems, by contrast, to surrender the definition of their project to the outcome of political debate and struggle among the oppressed themselves and to advocate the orientation of research around that project. As a number of questioners at the conference remarked, there seems to be little to distinguish such a position from the more familiar liberal pluralism (cf. Solomos, below, pp. 97, 105). The problem, as the critics of such pluralism frequently note, is that the power to define is not evenly distributed. What may in such circumstances result is not so much research in the service of the oppressed as manipulation of researchers by minority interest groups or the rule of the mob. The authors would no doubt reply that they are aware of such dangers and are prepared to resist them. The difficulty is that their paper gives no indication of the *theoretical* basis upon which such resistance would be founded; a situation unlikely to be found in classical Marxism.

The relation between scholarship and political action is also discussed in Marshall Murphree's paper. He draws attention to the specificity of the politico-academic contexts in which theoretical and research agendas are drawn up and constrained. In the context of post-colonial states struggling to build national identity and commitment in the service of development these environing influences (the Third World context) are different from those generating the macro-sociological thrust of what he calls the 'international context'. Put another way, the problem for scholars within the Third World context is both to demonstrate their relevance and to make an effective contribution to the development process. The difficulty here is not to be simplistically conceived as the inhibition of academic freedom by states hostile to the idea that ethnic divisions persist, although scholars themselves are aware that ethnic divisions have in the past been exaggerated in simplistic notions of tribalism as part of the ideological fight to preserve white supremacy. Moreover, such alleged divisions continue to be promoted and exploited by those who either wish to undermine the stability of infant states or object to the political complexion of their governments. It is not surprising, in this context, that such governments look with suspicion upon those who draw attention to the persistence of ethnic divisions in the face of nation-building, or that scholars themselves are wary of misinterpretation for political purposes which they do not share. It is one of the strengths of Murphree's paper that he succeeds in demonstrating both the constraints and the opportunities to which such a situation gives rise. In a paper which is an eloquent testimony to the strength of the academic work which can result, he demonstrates how a detailed analysis of the micro-dynamics of ethnicity as a socio-political resource can contribute to the development of policies of nation-building.

Several of the papers do not directly touch on the debate about political involvement at all, although a number of them have clear political implications. Thus, for example, Peter Weinreich's paper on the application of Identity Structure Analysis to Northern Ireland has clear implications for many of the popular and journalistic treatments of conflict in that society. More importantly, both Smith and Wallman adopt positions which, as we have seen, attracted some criticism from conference participants. In Wallman's case this was because of her apparent failure to consider asymmetrical power relations and the role of racism in structuring relations among groups in her research locations. In Smith's case it related to his willingness to accord analytic status to a version of the race concept which it was argued was not scientifically sustainable. Both would, I think, agree with van den Berghe that the search for truth should not be compromised merely because it is open to misunderstanding.

Individualism

Until relatively recently it would have been necessary to note in the introduction to any collection devoted to race and ethnic relations theory the degree to which individualist conceptualisations, associated in particular with studies of prejudice and attitudes, dominated the literature (cf. Zubaida, 1970). As Yinger notes in his paper, this is no longer the case. Indeed, he argues (below, p. 37) that there are grounds for suggesting that individual differences in the tendency to discriminate are now rather neglected in ways that inhibit understanding, even if those adopting such a level of analysis in the past have tended to see it as an exclusive theoretical orientation rather than as part of an interdependent system of explanation. Thus, he argues (below, pp. 26–31) for the inclusion of 'characterological' along with 'primordial' and 'interest' factors in the determination of the strength and nature of ethnic attachments.

This plea for the theoretical integration of individual- and group-centred approaches to the study of race and ethnic relations, whatever reception it might in the past have received from psychologists like the authors of *The Authoritarian Personality* (cf. Yinger, below, p. 38), would clearly receive a sympathetic hearing from Weinreich, the social psychologist contributing to the present volume.

It would be wrong, however, to suggest that a concentration upon individuals 'and their active construction and reconstruction of their social worlds' was limited within the disciplinary boundaries of social psychology. Indeed, an important and influential tradition in sociology – symbolic interactionism – has had this project at its heart. It has been influential not only in sociology but also in social psychology and is, indeed, one of the sources upon which Weinreich draws in developing his Identity Structure Analysis.

The development of the symbolic interactionist approach to race relations within the Chicago School is traced in Barbara Ballis Lal's paper. One of the persistent criticisms of symbolic interactionism is that its stress on individual creativity may be a product of a particular kind of liberal view of American society. Lal, in fact, seeks to show that the tradition, as it developed in the Chicago School, was not blind either to history or to social structure. A similar criticism may, however, also be levelled at another theoretical position represented here: rational choice.

The outlining of a 'rational choice' theory of race and ethnic relations has been an important recent development in the field (Hechter, below, pp. 264–79; see also Banton, 1983). The theory is self-consciously individualistic and 'assumes the theoretical primacy of individual actors rather than of pre-existent social groups' (below, p. 264). According to the theory, individuals act rationally to achieve maximum advantage in relation to their preferences. Thus, to the extent that individual preferences are known, behaviour can be predicted in the face of a given set of structural constraints. To the extent that a significant body of preferences are shared rather than idiosyncratic, the actions of groups can also be predicted. According to Hechter, 'it can be expected that everyone will prefer more wealth, power, and honour to less, because attaining these goods often makes it easier for individuals to attain other (perhaps more idiosyncratic) goals'. Thus the 'law of large numbers allows predictions for the aggregate to be rather precise' (below, p. 269).

There would appear to be a number of difficulties with this approach (see the discussion in Mason, 1982). A crucial one is the assumption of rationality. In order to evaluate the claim that individuals act rationally we need to know what that term encompasses. Does, for example, the predictive power of the theory depend upon the actor's conception of the means–end relationship being the same as the analyst's? If so, is it possible that the convergence between these two conceptions will be weaker the further we move from the Western capitalist societies in which the theory itself was developed? Put another way, is the very conception of 'individual actor' a product of a particular form of social structure, as Durkheim would have insisted?[2] Indeed, far from counterposing individualism and constraint, Durkheim (1964) saw individualism as itself a form of constraint. Thus Hechter's opposition between choice and constraint, in which constraint is ultimately the absence of choice, would have made no sense to Durkheim. For Durkheim both the presence and the absence of opportunities for individual choice represented forms of constraint. A crucial form of this constraint was collective morality or what Hechter would see as shared preferences.

Looked at from this perspective a more interesting question then is: 'Under what conditions do individuals have or not have choice?' This points to the central problem of Hechter's version of rational choice theory: the uncertainty it exhibits about structural constraint. Thus at some points we are told that the theory is reductionist and that individuals and their preferences have priority, while at others we are told that the theory is concerned with the interaction of such individuals' preferences with structural constraints. However, Hechter's conception of structural constraints appears to suffer from all the faults attributed by him to structuralism generally, namely imprecision and an inability to be predictive. More critically, we are never clearly told what the determinants of such constraints are.

As Rex points out in his paper, it is possible to approach these issues from a methodologically individualist position without conceding the atomistic individualism of Hechter's reductionism. Rex argues that the crucial characteristic of methodological individualism, as it is found, for example, in the work of Weber, is that it provides a means of conceptualising the relationship of action and constraint by invoking the actions of hypothetical actors, not by seeking empirically to aggregate the behaviour of individuals. A crucial concept linking individual and structurally centred explanation, he reminds us, is that of 'interest'. Significantly, Hechter's discussion of structuralist accounts of constraint does not consider alternative approaches to the relationship of interest and action to be found in the work of such writers as Lukes (1974).

In the last resort, it may be that my sense of dissatisfaction with the theory lies in its reductionist and imperialist claims in a situation where, by Hechter's own admission, it is unable to satisfy them. Perhaps a less absolutist version of the theory, incorporated into a multi-faceted framework, would ultimately be more fruitful. Such a synthesis would permit the recognition of the significance and scope of individual choice-making – rational or not – in the face of structural constraint without reducing all social action to a matter of individual preferences and gain-maximisation. It would also not make the mistake of counterposing macro-sociology and individualism and thereby imply that a micro-focus must necessarily prioritise individuals. The papers by both Lal and Wallman demonstrate that this is not inevitable, while Weinreich shows that even the individualistic focus of identity analysis cannot dispense with an awareness of the social interdependencies and structural constraints with which individuals are confronted.

Conclusion

At the outset, I suggested that the very diversity of approaches and research problems represented in the papers collected here made the task of constructing an overview rather difficult. This was particularly so because of the variety of different implicit and explicit conceptions of theory itself which were on offer. In attempting to identify and classify these conceptions, I suggested that the flirtation of some authors with grand theory encouraged confrontation and competition rather than a search for dialogue. What a review of the themes and controversies reveals, however, is that there is a good deal of common ground between apparently divergent theorisations, whatever appearances might suggest. Even areas of bitter dispute reveal a good deal of scope for mutually beneficial discourse and suggest that, properly channelled into vigorous academic debate rather than ideological posturing, such disagreements could begin to lay the ground for the better, more inclusive, theorisation urged on us by Yinger.

NOTES

1 I am grateful to John Rex and to Eric Dunning for comments on earlier drafts of this Introduction. Needless to say, I remain responsible for all errors and for the opinions expressed herein.
2 Pierre van den Berghe (this volume) makes a similar point about the assumption of rationality. He argues, however, that the historical specificity of rationality lies in its evolutionary status as one among many adaptive mechanisms.

1

Intersecting strands in the theorisation of race and ethnic relations

J. MILTON YINGER

Social science should continue to dream of grand theory – the remote equivalent of Einstein's search for a unified field theory – but should never forget, if I can press the metaphor, that dreams only hint at reality through symbols of hidden and disguised meaning. The complexity of racial and ethnic relations requires that we examine them from several perspectives. Our dream should be to combine those perspectives, studying their mutual contradictions, identifying their gaps, and examining the effects of their interactions. Only in that way can their value for more general theory and their transferability to other sets of problems be tested.

Some scholars, well represented in this volume, are not comfortable with complex, multivariable explanations of the phenomena of racial and ethnic relations. A few have sought one basic reductionist principle. To Marxists, it is the system of command–obey relationships, particularly in capitalist societies, that is fundamental. Some psychologists emphasise the structure of individual attitudes and identities. Recently van den Berghe has developed what he believes to be a parsimonious theory based on sociobiology: 'ethnic and racial sentiments are extensions of kinship sentiments' (van den Berghe, 1981, 80). They should therefore express the sociobiological principle of inclusive fitness. (How this can be applied to the large, heterogeneous and changing ethnies in modern societies – ethnies that reflect the influence of intermarriage, conversion, adoption and intergroup alliances – is not clear. The principle of inclusive fitness can have, at most, only a highly diluted effect in large and heterogeneous populations.)

Another reductionist approach to the study of racial and ethnic relations is the application of 'rational choice theory', which, like classical economic theory, sees little to be gained by examining the influence of unconscious motives or normative influences. Behaviour is seen as the result of interaction between a set of structural conditions and individual preferences (Hechter *et al.*, 1982; Banton, 1983). (One wonders if the overwhelming dominance of structural conditions, in many circumstances, leave much room for the play of choice, rational or otherwise. It is those conditions – their origins and supports – that are often most in need of analysis.)

Those who focus on one aspect of racial and ethnic relations vary widely in the degree to which they do so for emphasis and as a research strategy or, much less satisfactorily in my judgement, to assert that it is overwhelmingly dominant. Adopting a different approach, it is my aim to examine the way in which several factors can – and need to be – combined into a multi-levelled 'field theory' (Yinger, 1965; Simpson and Yinger, 1985).

The need to clarify our concepts

Theories of ethnic and racial relations both affect and reflect the meanings we assign to key terms. Ambiguities in the meaning of 'race' and 'ethnicity' thus hinder communication and the development of common understandings. Almost no scholars now use the term 'race' to refer to a few, immutable, clearly separate subspecies of *Homo sapiens*, although that may not be far from the modal view of the general public. Complex physiological measurements that go well beyond the gross morphological variables by which races were previously divided, continuous change, as genotypes interact with new environments, and millennia of miscegenation have left earlier conceptions of race in a shambles. At the least we now need to think, with Dobzhansky (1962), not of three or four or five races, but of thirty-four, with imprecise boundaries, and with new ones being formed quite rapidly. Some scholars, emphasising the powerful impact of the social definitions of observable physical differences, recommend either that the term 'race' be set aside (Montagu, 1974) or that it be used to refer, not to a subspecies, but, as van den Berghe puts it (1983, 222), to ' . . . a socially defined group which sees itself and is seen by others as being phenotypically different from other such groups'. Thus he regards race as a special case of ethnicity.

Such a decision has a lot to recommend it. In the United States, for example, persons with one Native American grandparent are legally Native Americans, if they want to be. About eighty per cent of black Americans have some European and/or Native American ancestors. A Mississippi law defining those with 1/32 African ancestry as Negroes was upheld by the courts in 1983, although such persons could thus be identified in most cases only socially. (It should be added that the law was repealed a few months later.)

My own preference is to distinguish between socially defined and biologically defined races. Although the latter mode of definition is of relatively little interest to the social scientist, it is of some significance to the biologist and physical anthropologist. My references in this paper to racial groups will be only to those ethnic groups with a socially defined racial aspect, along with their linguistic, religious, or other cultural aspects.

Of course this decision only complicates the definition of ethnic group or, if we need a noun, of 'ethnie'. In my judgement, we need a definition that recognises the 'thickness' or the salience of the ethnic attachment, since ' . . . it is important to distinguish a sociologically and psychologically important ethnicity from one that is only administrative or classificatory . . . We cannot be content with naming and counting' (Yinger, 1976, 200). An ethnie exists in the full sense when three conditions are present: a segment of a larger society is seen by others to be different in some combination of the following characteristics – language, religion, race and ancestral homeland with its related culture; the members also perceive themselves in that way; and they participate in shared activities built around their (real or mythical) common origin and culture. Ethnicities, it should be noted, ' . . . are never singular, but always exist in systems: one ethnicity implies at least one other . . . ' (Galaty, 1982, 2).

These statements scarcely solve the problem of definition. At times when nationalism is strong (a nation being an ethnic group that claims the right to, or at least a history of, statehood), when governments use ethnicity as a major principle of census-taking and of administration, when cultural divisions create splits within classes, when scholars begin to focus more attention on ancestrally and culturally defined sub-societies, to mention some of the forces at work, then phenomena on many different levels of generality will all be called ethnic groups. Some Asian Americans – persons of Chinese, Japanese, Korean, Indian, Filipino and Vietnamese backgrounds – are beginning to define themselves as an ethnic group. That is also true among some Hispanics in the United States, despite the great diversity between those of Cuban, Mexican, Puerto Rican, Spanish and other backgrounds. Native Americans are probably even more diverse, since they vary widely in language and religion, among other cultural traits; yet their ethnicity is beginning to go beyond its administrative sources to reach into their own organisations and activities (see Trottier, in Keyes, 1981, 271–305).

Moving slightly down the abstraction ladder, we see, in societies with large immigrant populations, a tendency to use the term 'ethnic group' with reference to persons who share a common former citizenship. In the United States, persons of Swiss, Belgian, Mexican or Filipino background may be thought of as ethnic groups, although they vary widely in cultural background.

Thus ethnicity has come to refer to anything from a sub-societal group that clearly shares a common descent and cultural background (e.g. the Oneida Indians or, on a slightly higher level of generality, the Iroquois, the Turkomans in Iran or Albanians in Yugoslavia), to persons who share a former citizenship although diverse culturally (Indonesians in the Netherlands), to pan-cultural groups of persons of widely different cultural and societal backgrounds who, however, can be identified as 'similar' on the basis of language, race or religion mixed with broadly similar statuses (Hispanics in the United States).

These uses of the concept of ethnicity are not entirely different. Nor am I arguing that the meaning of words should not be revised along with changes in the world of experience to which they refer. This great enlargement of the meaning of ethnicity, however, imposes on us the need to be fully aware of the different levels of generality to which it refers in various instances. There is a lot to be learned by seeing similarities embedded in systems that differ greatly. The whale that swims, the lion that runs and the bat that flies have much in common. Powerful theories move up the abstraction ladder; they are relevant to a wide range of data; but they miss the fine detail.

Discussions of 'the ethnic factor' in the United States, for example, that ask whether primordial sentiments or contemporary interests are the more important influence scarcely begin the inquiry. Historical and sociological distinctions must be drawn among at least eight broad categories of groups: Native Americans, Blacks, Northern and Western Europeans, Southern and Eastern Europeans, persons from Asia Minor and the Middle East, Jews, Asians and Hispanics. Even a moment's reflection reveals that each of these categories is very heterogeneous. Each contains several ethnic groups, nations and/or pan-ethnic clusters. And, in turn, each is internally differentiated by class, by rural urban residence, by religion or by other characteristics. Theories that are of value in interpreting group process and individual behaviour at one of these levels are unlikely to be of much value at another level. One can scarcely act or feel 'primordially' as an Hispanic; but those thus defined administratively may find that they have educational, lingual, economic or political interests that cluster more nearly around the Hispanic identity than around any other.

'The one major conviction that emerged' from his study of ethnicity, Epstein remarked (1978, xi), 'was the powerful emotional charge that appears to surround or to underlie so much of ethnic behaviour.' His data richly document this observation. It cannot readily be transferred, however, to the pan-ethnicities or the newly created ethnicities emerging in modern states, often as a result of administrative classification or public labelling.

Ivan Light (1981, 54–86) suggests that we deal with this issue of the range to be covered by the concept of ethnicity by use of the term 'ethnic scope', noting that the boundaries delineating an ethnic group, thus defined, might be continental, national, regional or local in scope. For example, one might think of oneself, and be thought of, simultaneously as Asian, Chinese, Cantonese and from a specific Cantonese locality, in a series of 'nested segments', to use Keyes's phrase. There is a tendency for scope to widen as a result of migration and urbanization.

This is a useful way of recognising the different levels of ethnic awareness. In using the concept of scope, however, one runs the risk of obscuring the changing meaning and the changing sources of ethnic attachments as the circle of identification widens. This may rest, unintentionally, on the desire to protect the belief that ethnicity remains, despite drastic changes in circumstances, a vital force in human affairs. It undoubtedly is a vital force; but I do not think that point is demonstrated by affirming that 'The Common Market and the North Atlantic Treaty Organization are two reflections of a more inclusive level of ethnic awareness in Western Europe' (Light, 1981, 72). One might more plausibly argue that the Common Market and NATO are signs that the power of ethnicity can be overcome when great inter-state interests are involved. If immigrants from numerous countries of Southern and Eastern Europe to the United States, finding themselves in somewhat similar economic and political circumstances, unite in various ways, we gain only a little explanatory power by saying that their ethnic scope has widened. Their ancestors were busily fighting one another. If the sense of a common descent has become a very thin veneer or even completely mythical, then it adds little to a purely 'interest' explanation of political and economic behaviour. The fiction of ethnicity (for example Novak's PIGS) simply disguises the interest basis of some group coalitions. (Of course this says nothing about the wisdom or justice of such coalitions.) In some cases, we will be wiser to refer to 'symbolic ethnicity' (Gans, 1979), 'imagined ethnicity' (Yinger, 1976) or 'pseudo-ethnicity' (McKay, 1982) and seek to discover its causes and consequences. If this suggestion is of value, we face the difficult task of drawing the line between pseudo-ethnicity and ethnicity where the primordial element plays at least some part. Here I want only to note that from my point of view a feeling of common descent, even if it contains a large mythical component, must be found alongside the belief in a shared interest before we should speak of an ethnic factor. To understand the place of ethnicity in human life, we must not be taken in by disguises, however innocent or humane. We have learned to see through such disguises in political and economic life, recognising that not all movements or leaders who proclaim that they are of the people and working for the people in fact fit that description. Similarly, not all ethnic labels are of substantial importance.

Since we are all influenced, in discussing this topic, by our biographies and our societal identities, let me offer a brief comment from the perspective of the sociology of knowledge, posed in the form of question: Is it Americans who are most likely, due to their intergroup situation among other influences, to exaggerate both the existence and the beneficence of ethnicity, even when it is near the line or over the line into pseudo-ethnicity (Gambino, 1975; Novak, 1972); and are they at the same time the most likely to be found among the critics of *The Ethnic Myth* (Steinberg, 1981), of *Ethnic Chauvinism: The Reactionary Impulse* (Patterson, 1977), and to describe *America Without Ethnicity* (G. D. Morgan, 1981)? Although pressure towards nation-states is not entirely lacking in the United States, the kind of pressure in Europe, Asia and Africa described by Anthony Smith is mainly lacking: 'far . . . from being merely transitional phenomena, the nation-state and nationalism have become more firmly entrenched within the world order, even in the most advanced industrial societies. Indeed, within Europe itself, in the industrial heartlands of the West, we are witnessing a resurgence of ethnic nationalism in the wake of an era of massive economic growth . . . Given the chance, most ethnic movements in Africa and Asia would opt for outright separatism' (A. D. Smith, 1981, 4, 138).

In the United States, only among the most disadvantaged minorities do we find such separatist tendencies. Garvey's Universal Negro Improvement Association, the early Black Muslims (now the American Muslim Mission) and some Native Americans have envisaged something approximating to nation-states. These have not, however, been the dominant movements. If we ask under what conditions ethnic groups are most likely to be nationalistic, we might start out with the two-variable model found in Table 1.1 and then note other variables that influence the outcome.

Using only these two variables, Table 1.1 suggests that individuals who migrated freely into a new society (position 1) are least likely to combine with fellow ethnics into a nationalistic, separatist movement; those who collectively have been made members of a society against their will (position 4) are most likely to form or maintain such a movement.

Table 1.1 *Variables Influencing the Strength of Nationalism among Ethnic Groups*

Mode of entry into a society

		Individual	Group
	Entered freely	1	2
Extent of choice			
	Coerced	3	4

These two variables, of course, are insufficient to explain the empirical range. Among the most important other influences that one should add are: the extent of geographical concentration, the degree to which a group is similar in language, religion and race to the dominant group, and the strength of feelings of relative deprivation. This last is especially important in technically advanced societies among groups on the social or geographical periphery that have not kept pace, economically and politically, with the dominant group.

The sources of ethnic strength

After a number of years during which one or another of the several sources of the continuing phenomenon of ethnicity was emphasised as 'basic', most observers now accept the idea that, at least to some degree, both 'primordial' and 'interest' factors are involved or, in Lal's terms (1983), ethnicity expresses both 'genuine culture' and 'stratification phenomena'. Indeed, some argue that material interests are well served by ethnically based movements precisely because, as Daniel Bell put it (Glazer and Moynihan, 1975, 1969), they 'combine an interest with an affective tie'. Cultural symbols are highly flexible and can be rearranged for new purposes while seeming to remain unchanged (Cohen, 1974 c, 39).

On the level of general theory I think it is essential to combine these two factors; but we need also to emphasise that they are not necessarily equal partners. Under some circumstances, feelings of cultural unity and ancestral attachment are the major source. Under other and more common circumstances in the world today, these are only weakly felt; it is the perception of shared interests that is dominant. Puerto Ricans on the United States mainland, for example, are seen as an ethnic group and are treated as one, both officially and informally. Despite class, racial and religious differences among them, they develop organisations and leaders as adaptive mechanisms to deal with their shared circumstances (Herbstein, 1983).

I shall not re-examine here the need, so often and well discussed, to study interest and primordial factors together (see, e.g., McKay, 1982; Lal, 1983; Smith, 1981; Light, 1981, 54–86; Glazer and Moynihan, 1975). For a number of years I have argued that a third influence, analytically distinct from interests and primordialism, should be included, although like the others, its influence varies widely (Yinger, 1976; 1981). We can call it the 'characterological' factor. Those who might seem, by the study of the interest and the primordiality influences, to be equally likely to emphasise their ethnic attachments may vary widely in their feelings and attitudes, because of different individual experiences and tendencies. These will make one person embrace an ethnic identity fervently, while another, similarly placed structurally and culturally, but with different life experiences, will regard his ethnic identity lightly.

Two influences are of special importance in affecting this characterological factor: the sense of being marginal to one's own group and the sense of being marginal to or alienated from the state and the larger society. DeVos and Romanucci-Ross observe that those who personify an ethnic group are often outsiders. Napoleon was a Corsican; de Gaulle's ancestors were Flemings; Atatürk was Anatolian; Marcus Garvey was Jamaican. Such persons '. . . manifest in their own personalities some resolution of previously disturbing internal states, which are also experienced by many other members of the group at large' (DeVos and Romanucci-Ross, 1975, 372–3).

The marginality that other persons feel refers not to their own racial or ethnic group but to the larger society within which they live – particularly with its polity. This may be expressed by a transfer of loyalty – or of its strongest expression – to the racial or ethnic group. In response to a 'support' to 'estrangement' alienation scale (ranging from +100 to −100) that measured trust in government, black Americans shifted, between 1958 and 1972, from a score of +50 to one of −40. (Whites moved from +50 to +8 during the same period.) (See *Newsletter* of the Institute of Social Research, Spring-Summer, 1973; also Schwartz and Schwartz, 1976; Clemente and Sauer, 1976.) We should not forget that this is a summation of a set of individual scores. Among some Blacks, trust remained high. It was the most alienated, however, who were most likely to shift to a 'black nationalist' perspective. This statement is difficult to document directly. Perhaps a study of name preferences among black Americans in the Detroit Area Study can serve as a useful index. These preferences were compared with the respondent's alienation scores – measures of the level of distrust of dominant institutions, as shown in Table 1.2.

Table 1.2 *Name preference by alienation score among black respondents*

	Preference (N)	Per cent	Mean alienation score
Afro-American	21	5.5	6.1
Black	144	38.0	5.1
Negro	89	23.5	4.0
No preference (volunteered)	80	21.1	3.8
Coloured	45	11.9	3.6

(From Schuman and Hatchett, 1974, 84)

Those with high alienation scores were significantly more likely to prefer 'Afro-American' or 'Black' – designations that are more expressive of 'nationalistic' sentiments.

The interest, primordial and characterological levels of analysis of racial or ethnic identity are highly interactive. We need, however, to keep them analytically separate, because they can vary independently of each other. Such an identity will be at a maximum within a group when there is a widespread perception that their shared and individual interests can thus better be served, when the reality and/or the mythology of an ancestral culture is strongly felt and when significant numbers of individuals are alienated from the state – that is, feel powerless within it (although not powerless in general), do not trust it, hold its values and policies in low regard.

These factors can be visualised in three-dimensional social space as shown in Figure 1.1. Although some locations within that space may be empirically unlikely, it seems wise to leave open the possibility of unusual combinations of influence from interest, primordialism and character. The 'surprising' discoveries of high levels of ethnic identity even when primordial attachments seem virtually lost may indicate a combination of high levels of perceived interests interacting with a high proportion of alienated persons – perhaps as a result of strongly felt relative deprivation (Williams, 1978, 59–64). Such deprivation, it should be emphasised, is often with reference not to one's individual situation but to the situation of one's group relative to others (Pettigrew, 1978, 32–7).

In our efforts to understand the sources of the continued or renewed strength of ethnic attachments, we need to look at the situation from several very different perspectives. This will lead us to ask: Who benefits most when ethnicity plays a prominent part in the ways in which interests

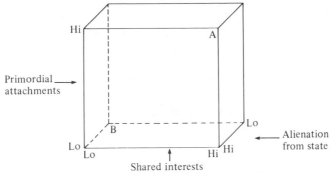

(At point A all 3 factors are at a maximum, at point B at a minimum)

Figure 1.1 The three sources of ethnic strength in urban societies

are pursued? In some societies, dominant groups have seized upon the use of ethnic differences as a less costly way to manage conflict and to distribute rewards than is the open recognition of class differences. An ethnic group may be 'paid' for its political loyalty; otherwise potentially disruptive minority leaders may be contained by absorbing a few into the middle and even higher levels of authority in the dominant institutions. Eduardo Mondlane, the first President of Frelimo, once told me that he could have moved quite readily into high office in what was then Portuguese East Africa had he seen himself as *assimilado* and accepted Portuguese sovereignty. When such tactics succeed, as they did not with him, what seems like mobilisation of an ethnic group on its own behalf must also be recognised in part as a deflection toward pursuit of individual status improvement through co-optation. Cynics will say that this is mere tokenism; optimists will say it is the entering wedge. I suspect that both of these things are true, but that we do not yet know fully the conditions which lead to one or the other assuming greater importance.

Sometimes the emphasis on ethnic or racial distinctiveness comes primarily from the recently comfortable, as a way of trying to protect their gains. For them, a social bond is preferable to a class bond. At other times, those who have suffered at the hands of the dominant group, but who now see some new opening, some opportunity for resource mobilisation not previously available, are more willing to emphasise their racial or ethnic identity as a stratagem for group improvement (Steinberg, 1981).

It is true that ' . . . ethnicity emerges as the basis for collective action when there are clear advantages attached to ethnic (versus religious, kinship, class, or some other) identity' (Olzak, 1982, 254). What this does not tell us is for whom there are clear advantages. Ethnic and racial groups are internally differentiated by age, sex, education, skill and other variables. Individuals differ in their definitions of group boundaries, in the strength of their identity, in their priorities (goals) and in their preferred policies (means). What helps men may hurt women; what helps the young may hurt the old; what helps the skilled may hurt the unskilled. We cannot be content with analysis at the racial or ethnic group level alone. On the whole, the least advantaged in the various groups involved are also the least aided by emphasis on ethnicity.

The internal sources of strength or weakness of ethnic attachments cannot, of course, be separated from the interactions with and the influences of the surrounding society. The effects of demographic, economic, political and cultural forces are mixed in most settings. Some tend to draw the boundary between a racial or ethnic group and the larger society more sharply, thus reinforcing any inclinations towards separatism. Other influences obscure the boundaries and in the limiting case wipe them out. Under some circumstances, other lines of differentiation that cut across racial and ethnic boundaries are strong. When a state is under outside threat, citizenship may be the dominant identity. In some states, cultural diversity is produced by several cross-cutting influences. 'India is the model entry: religion, caste, and language provide interlocking, interacting, and distinctively separate bases for politically relevant identity groups' (Young, 1976, 97). Or, particular economic, political and cultural forces may give special relevance to class distinctions. Rapid social change that affects men and women or young and old differently may create age-graded, generational forces and women's movements with reciprocal men's movements, that blur both class and ethnic boundaries (Kasschau, 1977; Joseph, 1983).

Although I shall not be discussing such cross-cutting forces, I want to emphasise that attention to the influences that accentuate racial and ethnic distinctions is inevitably an abstraction from the larger empirical picture. Perhaps these influences can best be seen by looking out at the societal and state setting from the perspective of the members of a non-dominant group. They perceive, or at least experience, a number of both assimilative and dissimilative forces, some increasing and others decreasing the salience of their membership in a racial or ethnic group. Extending the set of variables discussed in connection with Table 1.1, I have listed several of these forces in Table 1.3. We can think of them as variables that should help us to study the effects of intergroup contact comparatively. The influence of each one can be judged, of course, only with 'other things being equal'.

Table 1.3 *Variables that affect the salience of racial or ethnic group membership*

Tend to increase salience	Tend to decrease salience
1 Large group (relative to total population)	Small group
2 Residentially concentrated by region and community	Residentially scattered
3 Short-term residents (high proportion of newcomers)	Long-term residents (low proportion of newcomers)
4 Return to homeland easy and frequent	Difficult and infrequent
5 Speak a different language	Speak the dominant language
6 Different religion from majority	Share majority religion
7 Different race	Same race
8 Entered the society by forced migration or conquest	Entered voluntarily
9 Come from culturally different society	Come from culturally similar society
10 Attracted to political and economic developments in land of origin	Repelled by those developments
11 Homogeneous in class and occupation	Diverse in class and occupation
12 Low average level of education	High average level of education
13 Experience a great deal of discrimination	Experience little discrimination
14 Resident in a society with little social mobility	Resident in open-class society

(Adapted from Yinger, 1984)

Racial and ethnic divisions and discrimination

One could probably develop a theory of racial and ethnic relations that was not simultaneously a theory of discrimination, of dominance and oppression, of inequality. I believe it to be true, however, that such relations are overwhelmingly tied to stratification systems. I shall be discussing them from that perspective. (For a fuller discussion, see Simpson and Yinger, 1985, chaps. 3–5, on which the next several paragraphs are based; see also Rex, 1981.)

During the several decades in which the study of racial and ethnic relations has occupied an important place among social scientists, theoretical disagreements have often rested on the different levels of analysis from which they proceeded. Rather than seeing these different levels as part of an interdependent system, the tendency in many cases has been to emphasise one level as fundamental.

(1). Prejudice and discrimination, to some of the early observers (for example Sumner and Giddings), were expressions of ethnocentrism, of 'dislike of the unlike'. They were cultural phenomena. In almost all societies, if not in all, each new generation is taught 'appropriate' beliefs regarding other groups (LeVine and Campbell, 1972; Brewer and Campbell, 1976). Often there are reciprocal ideologies held by oppressed groups that describe the 'morally repugnant qualities' of the oppressors (Kuper, 1974). Turner and Singleton (1978) note the tendency to 'ignore the impact of culture' in recent studies of ethnic oppression. It seems likely, however, that discussion of the primordial element in ethnic identity has brought culture back into analyses to some degree, for primordialism almost always has a negative pole (ethnocentrism) as well as a positive pole (attachment). Recent studies of stereotyping have documented how the socially derived 'pictures in our heads' affect our behaviour toward the members of other ethnic and racial groups (Hamilton, 1981).

Cultures are scarcely unambiguous, of course, in their systems of norms and values related to racial and ethnic relations. Myrdal's classic analysis of *An American Dilemma* (1944) was built around the idea that white Americans were culturally trained both for an egalitarian and open society and for a racially stratified society. Gordon has recently described what he sees as a new American dilemma, a clash of values in which ' . . . proponents of both sides can claim in good faith to derive their respective positions from standard moral and religious systems, one side emphasising principles of equal treatment and individual meritocracy, the other principles that call upon group compensation for undeniable past injustices' (Gordon, 1981, 181). He refers to these as 'liberal pluralism' and 'corporate pluralism' respectively. The former emphasises individual rights, the pursuit of which is not to be affected in any way by racial or ethnic identity. It does not stipulate segregation, but neither does it formally promote integration. The latter formally recognises racial and ethnic entities: ' . . . patterns of political power and economic reward are based on a distributive formula which postulates group rights and which defines group memberships as an important factor in the outcome for individuals' (Gordon, 1981, 183).

I find Gordon's distinction too sharp. Some support corporate pluralism as one desirable element because they believe that without it liberal pluralism is a sham, tending to freeze everyone in his or her current position. If you start twenty metres behind, equal opportunity will scarcely allow you to win a hundred-metre race.

(If I may add a personal 'aside', I am uncomfortable with both the forms of pluralism that Gordon describes and would prefer a third variety, which might be called 'remedial pluralism' – an indication of the need for persistent and probably long-term 'corporate' activity, in his sense of the term, to make certain that 'liberal' pluralism is not simply a mask for privilege. Somewhere Tawney wrote that the watchwords of liberals become, in new settings, the watchwords of conservatives. Or, one might say, radicals fight the revolutions, conservatives write the constitutions. In America today, the 'new dilemma' that Gordon discusses is the old conflict of liberty versus equality. Since I see a significantly greater degree of equality as essential for an increase in liberty for those with modest power and income, the current call for 'colour blindness', the opposition to affirmative action, and the claim that all that is needed is equal individual access to opportunity seem to me to support not democratic pluralism but the perpetuation of present unequal status structures.)

(2). A second level of analysis – and the one that today is most likely to be emphasised as basic – sees inter-racial and inter-ethnic relations, with their accompanying patterns of dominance and oppression, as expressions of the struggle for power, income and prestige. Those who agree on this emphasis nevertheless disagree on the structural causes. I will here only suggest the range of views by commenting on five perspectives.

The Marxist interpretation is that capitalist societies create 'racism' to assist exploitation. Defenceless workers yield more surplus value; they cannot obtain in wages the total value of their labour (Nikolinakos, 1973; Cox, 1948). 'The Negro people are oppressed because the rulers of our society find it highly profitable to oppress them' (Doxey Wilkerson in Aptheker, 1946, 8). Of course this leads one to wonder why ethnic and racial inequalities have persisted in Communist states (Connor, 1979).

In recent years, powerful new insights into ethnic and racial relations have been attained by building on Marxist thought, but developing a much more flexible and empirically based analysis. A prominent illustration of this approach is the concept of 'internal colonialism' (see, e.g., Blauner, 1969; Clark, 1965; Carmichael and Hamilton, 1967; Hechter, 1975; Karlovic, 1982; Barresa, 1979; Smith 1981, 29–35; Stone, 1979). The term is part political slogan and part analytic tool. It is scarcely surprising, during a period when more and more 'external' colonies were winning independence, that not only analysts but also internal minorities and their supporters should declare: We are colonies too. 'The dark ghettos', Kenneth Clark wrote (1965, 11), 'are social, political, educational and – above all – economic colonies'.

In the most ambitious scholarly application of the concept of internal colonialism, Hechter (1975) argues that in Britain even extensive industrialisation and urbanisation, social and physical mobility, the growth of literacy and political participation did not succeed in bringing the Celtic fringe or periphery into the core of British national development. Once a cultural or racial group has established dominance it is often able, according to internal colony theory, to maintain ' . . . a cultural division of labour: a system of stratification where objective cultural distinctions are superimposed upon class lines' (Hechter, 1975, 30).

We are given new insights by being encouraged to see cultural and racial relations within the framework of an internal colony model. Those insights will be clearest if we explicitly recognise that we have moved up the abstraction ladder. We are now comparing dominance patterns within states with those between states. When we study order or family rather than genus or species, to use biological classificatory terms, we downplay differences in order to focus our attention on similarities. The question is, how large are the differences we are omitting from the analysis; and how much are we led to exaggerate the similarities? Are we simply moving from species to genus or from species to order? Are we comparing lions and tigers or bats and whales?

I do not intend, by this way of stating the problem, to suggest that I have a clear answer with respect to the colony model. My guess is that both external and internal colonies differ enormously among themselves. The most deprived of the internal and the least deprived of the external colonies may be quite similar; the least deprived of the internal and the most deprived of the external may be very different in their relationships to the dominant groups.

It is essential, as we move up the abstraction ladder, that we be aware of the differences we are leaving out and the similarities we may be inclined to exaggerate (Glazer, 1971; Moore, 1976). Applications in America, for example, tend to make internal colonies appear to be more homogeneous in class and culture than they are. Buchanan has recently shown (1983) that the 300,000 Haitians in the New York metropolitan area have a variety of class identities and attitudes that cut across and influence the ethnic status they are assigned in common in the United States. The colony model can also deflect attention from the domination over lower classes within the core. It sometimes tends to overlook the processes of integration of core and periphery that can go on alongside the colonisation process and in some conditions reverse it.

We need a general theory of internal colonialism but also theories applicable to more specific kinds of conditions, to deal with such questions as these: How are the patterns of domination affected by the political and economic systems within which they are found, comparing, for example, Marxist and capitalist societies (Karlovic, 1982)? Which kinds of core–periphery splits can be healed and which ones may actually grow along with the growth of parity?

Segmented, or dual, or split labour market theories also emphasise class conflict, but with a more complex picture of the forces at work than one finds in most orthodox Marxist interpretations (Cain, 1976; Marshall, 1974; Bonacich, 1972, 1976). In its simplest form, a split labour market is one with three classes: capitalist, cheap labour and higher-priced labour, the two latter often drawn from different racial or ethnic groups. The outcome of their interaction is not uniform across situations. When higher-priced employees are especially powerful, they can drive the cheaper labour out of the market, or block its entrance; or they can win a kind of compromise with employers under which they get a monopoly over the best jobs. Finally, under such conditions as high demand for labour, political democracy and a low ratio of minority workers, higher- and lower-priced labour may combine, economically and/or politically, in an attempt to reduce the power of employers.

In large and complex labour markets, all of these processes may be going on at once. In the United States it has been and still is difficult for agricultural workers to get adequate wages, first because of the large number of vulnerable black Americans and more recently because of the availability of equally vulnerable Mexican Americans or of undocumented aliens. At the same time, it has been difficult for the children of these workers to enter the skilled labour market because, to put it very simply, of poor educational opportunities and because apprenticeships are tightly controlled by those already in the trades. Difficult, of course, does not mean impossible. Segmented labour market theory, like the theory of internal colonialism, is a valuable analytic tool; but it can also be a hindrance if we forget that in focusing on one level it leaves out of the picture many aspects of the total economic, political and cultural situation.

Classical and neoclassical economic theories also seek to explain racial and ethnic inequalities primarily by reference to economic forces – in their case, to the operation of the 'market'. One can scarcely quarrel with the assertion that workers with fewer skills in a market demanding more and more skills will receive lower wages and have higher rates of unemployment. When we ask, however, why there should be significant differences in skill levels between racial and ethnic groups, or why those differences are growing or declining, we have to go beyond the market for an answer, to study the political, moral, attitudinal, demographic and technical influences on the market. Some of these have been recognised by neoclassical economists, so that attention to non-economic motives (Arrow, 1971), legislative influences (Stiglitz, 1973) and monopolistic conditions (Thurow, 1969) has been added to their analyses (see also Tobin, 1965; Becker, 1971). These extensions, however, scarcely give one an adequate explanation of the persistence of intergroup inequalities. By focusing on the market and assuming 'other things to be equal' one can attain elegant interpretations in the abstract world of one's creation; but the rough-hewn real world will be understood only by the addition of other levels of analysis.

The model of the 'market' that one thinks most accurate, let me add, has strong implications for policy choices. 'If one thinks of labor markets as fairly competitive, then minimum wage legislation not only results in unemployment of low-skilled workers, but eliminates the strong competitive forces that would naturaily have led to the alleviation of economic discrimination among these workers. If one thinks of all capitalists conspiring together to exploit workers of low skills (many of whom may belong to particular groups in the population), then minimum wage legislation is an important element in the reduction of exploitation' (Stiglitz, 1973, 294–5). The usual situation is mixed, so that the effect of minimum wage legislation, as of other economic policies, is problematic.

I shall mention only one other theory of discrimination and prejudice that is concerned with the economic level, although it shades off toward the personality level of explanation that I shall refer to below. In sharp contrast to the Marxist interpretation and for the most part to the internal colony model, although more readily reconciled with segmented labour market and classical market theories, Gunnar Myrdal (1944) challenges the view that the upper classes of the dominant racial and ethnic groups, having the most to gain, are most antagonistic to the interests of lower-status groups. He is referring to Black–White relationships in the United States, but his interpretation can readily be generalised to racial and ethnic relationships in other settings. Myrdal pays far more attention to the fears and attitudes of lower-class Whites than to the economic interests of the powerful. When the feedbox is empty, says a Swedish proverb, the horses bite each other.

Many other observers have picked up this theme, documenting, at least on the level of attitudes, the greater tendencies toward authoritarianism and racial antagonism among the least well-off members of the dominant ethnic or racial group (Lipset, 1959; Nunn, Crockett and Williams, 1978; A. W. Smith, 1981).

I will not discuss here the serious problems of measurement and interpretation of this relationship (see Jackman, 1981; Jackman and Senter, 1980), but want only to emphasise the need to distinguish carefully between prejudice and discrimination, between attitudes and words on the one hand, and actions on the other. If the powerful members of the dominant group are the chief defenders – not without exceptions, of course – of the whole institutional structure by which minority racial and ethnic groups are exploited, then their more polite verbal behaviour may be of relatively little importance.

Had he been talking more directly about the efforts to monopolise certain skills and opportunities, rather than about attitudes and the displacement of aggression, Myrdal's interpretation could be seen as a version of segmented labour market theory: 'Our hypothesis is that in a society where there are broad social classes, and in addition, more minute distinctions and splits in the lower strata, *the lower class groups will, to a great extent, take care of keeping each other subdued*, thus relieving, to that extent, the higher classes of this otherwise painful task necessary to the monopolization of the power and the advantages' (Myrdal, 1944, 68).

In a similar argument, Murray Kempton has remarked (*New York Review of Books*, 2 February 1982, 8) that '. . . the genius of our politics is the art of distracting the resentments of a cheated middle class and letting them fall upon a worse-cheated lower class' – or, in terms of our interest, on ethnic and racial minorities. Kempton was referring to American politics, but I imagine that he would by no means limit his remark to the United States.

I hope it is more than simple eclecticism to say that I find evidence to support each of the five macro-social or economic theories of ethnic and racial relations. They are mutually limiting but not mutually contradictory. None can be exclusively true, but each can help to account for patterns of domination and inequality in complex societies.

(3). Nevertheless, even when added together they do not make up an adequate theory of ethnic and racial relations. I have indicated the need to take culture into account. A third level of analysis, previously overemphasised by some scholars and now rather neglected, deals with individual variation in the tendency to discriminate. On this level, attention should be directed to the study of the processes by which individuals are socialised, the nature of their self-regard, the wants and values instilled by society and the degree to which they are able to fulfil those wants and realise those values (see Bagley and Verma, 1979; Bagley *et al.*, 1979; Ehrlich, 1973; Simpson and Yinger, 1953 [1985]). In trying to answer some kinds of questions it makes very little difference, for example, if some slave-owners were especially cruel and others relatively humane. It is the slave system that must be examined. For other kinds of questions, however, we need a microscope rather than a telescope; we need to see in clear detail the tendencies of particular individuals involved in an encounter across a racial or ethnic line. Social scientists who direct their attention wholly to 'the big picture', to structures of power, to the macro-social patterns, are sometimes inclined to overlook the micro-social dramas in which the tendencies of particular landlords, employers or police officers are the crucial facts for those with whom they are interacting.

Unfortunately, this level of analysis has been developed primarily by persons who regard it as fundamental, not as part of an interdependent system. Their exaggerations, found in such major works as *The Authoritarian Personality* (Adorno, Frenkel-Brunswik, Levinson and Sanford, 1950) and the hundreds of studies which led up to and followed that volume, are partly responsible for the opposition to and neglect of analysis of individual variation in tendencies to discriminate (for a thoughtful re-evalution see Altemeyer, 1981). More to the point for our discussion here, however, is the inclination of many scholars simply to prefer some other level of analysis, equally incomplete by itself despite its analytic power. For a rich understanding of the empirical situations, rather than the abstract world of our models, we must combine micro-social, macro-social and cultural levels (Yinger, 1983).

Recent research has moved beyond the *Authoritarian Personality* type of analysis to document the ways in which widely shared, if not universal, tendencies of individuals affect interactions among the members of racial and ethnic groups (as well as among members of other groups). The research is demonstrating the need for continued use of a micro-social or social psychological level of analysis to complement the structural and cultural levels. To understand what is going on in the day by day encounters in London or Birmingham or New York or Moscow it is not enough to study possible segmented labour markets or structures of power that govern the control of surplus value. On the individual level, '... persons will tend, where possible, to notice and distort the characteristics of others in the direction of their current motivational states' (Backman, 1981, 241). Most personal encounters involve 'status organizing processes', '... in which evaluations of and beliefs about the characteristics of actors become the basis of observable inequalities in face-to-face social interaction' (Berger, Rosenholtz and Zelditch, 1980, 479). Studies of these processes have shown how equal status interaction among persons of different races can be promoted by experimentally modifying the expectations of both the dominant and the minority group members. The modifications have been attained by training the minority group members in skills that are deemed valuable in themselves and relevant for other activities that contradict the expectations of all concerned (see e.g., Cohen and Roper, 1972).

Conclusion

Little doubt remains that almost all contemporary societies are multi-ethnic (Said and Simmons, 1976). There is scarcely less doubt that they will continue to be so for the foreseeable future. That observation, however, is only a starting point for analysis, because the strength of ethnic attachments – which is the crucial fact – varies widely. An earlier thesis that modernisation, in its various meanings, would break such attachments is now countered with its antithesis: sub-societal, culturally and ancestrally defined groups persist; they may even be strengthened by the competitive forces released by modernisation (Olzak, 1982).

Support for this antithesis comes not only from a flood of observation and research but also from ideological perspectives. Many members of currently favoured ethnic and racial groups and their scholarly spokesmen declare: See what groups A, B and C have done despite earlier levels of discrimination and deprivation similar to those now faced by groups demanding special privileges. (With reference to the American experience, Lieberson's *A Piece of the Pie: Blacks and White Immigrants since 1880* (1980) skilfully refutes this contention.) They find it more congenial to emphasise a 'cultural' factor than to examine the structures of discrimination that work in their favour. Paradoxically, aggrieved groups are also more and more willing to accept this definition of the situation: discrimination is focused on us because we are different. We affirm our difference; and we demand group-oriented remedies that do not require us to assimilate to a society that treats us so badly.

In my view, neither the assimilationist thesis nor the persistence-of-ethnic-difference antithesis is adequate. We may be ready for a synthesis that recognises the wide variation and explores the conditions under which societies fall along various points on the range. In some societies, the lines separating ethnic groups are thin; assimilation has been extensive; intermarriage is quite common. 'Affective ethnicity' based on self-identification and support for cultural pluralism continues (Pettigrew, 1978, 30–1), but cross-cutting memberships and contacts predominate. In other situations, it is the society itself and its state that are precarious. Ethnic and racial identities are the most powerful, even though they may be new clusterings that have emerged out of the conflicts of the modernisation process (see, for example, Young, 1976).

We shall not be able to develop a powerful theory of ethnicity until we recognise this 'ethnic continuum', as Cohen calls it. David Parkin (in Cohen, 1974c, 147) illustrates that continuum well:

At one end of the continuum we have highly corporate
political groups such as the Hausa of Ibadan, whose
considerable political autonomy is accompanied by a trading
monopoly, preferred residential segregation, and religious and
cultural exclusiveness. At the other end are ethnic groups, or
rather categories, whose members recognize and interact
among themselves by reference to their cultural affinity but
who do not otherwise hold significant corporate interests in
common.

The extent to which groups are excluded from or brought into the
solidarity of the 'terminal' community of a society (Geertz, 1973,
255–310), that is, are accepted into that community and accept it as
pre-eminent, is another continuum that is to some degree correlated
with the ethnic continuum and to some degree cuts across it. From the
perspective of individuals, the terminal community is the widest solidary group with which they feel significant integration. Alexander
(1980, 7) speaks of the inclusion process '... by which previously
excluded groups gain solidarity in the "terminal" community of a
society'. This concept leads us to one of the basic questions in a theory
of ethnicity: What are the conditions under which newly encountered
or newly created or otherwise excluded groups are brought within that
solidarity? And what are the consequences of various degrees of inclusion for social inequality, for cultural homogeneity/heterogeneity and
for inter-societal relations?

We scarcely have time to think about that question before an even
larger one demands attention. If we think of the world – this small
spaceship, indeed, this crowded lifeboat – as the terminal community,
which groups are included within its solidarity, which ones excluded?
How are the circumstances and the policies within societies involved in
this most vital inclusion/exclusion process? What lessons, if any, have
we learned about the consequences of sub-societal solidarities and
cultural variation that can now be applied to the world situation?

I have been attempting to emphasise the need to be acutely aware of
the level of abstraction on which we are working in any given piece of
research, lest we mistake our analytic statements for descriptions of the
empirical world. Such awareness is particularly necessary if we seek to
apply our studies of racial and ethnic relations within societies to
inter-societal relations. It should be clear by now that the nation-state,
the culturally homogeneous polity, is a rare phenomenon and is likely
to become ever more rare. States are thus prefiguring the world situation. The ways in which ethnic and racial groups are included in or

excluded from full participation in the life of societies will strongly influence our ability to build a world order in which similarities are not coerced and differences do not divide and the inequalities bequeathed to us by history are effectively curtailed.

2

Epistemological assumptions in the study of racial differentiation

MICHAEL BANTON

Looking back on 1948 with the advantages of hindsight, it can be seen that the publication in that year of Oliver C. Cox's *Caste, Class and Race* was an event of much greater significance than was appreciated at the time. Cox's challenge to what he called 'the new orthodoxy' of Robert Park and Ruth Benedict, with whom he associated Lloyd Warner and Gunnar Myrdal, was the opening salvo in an exchange of fire that may have reached its climax in the 1970s. In this paper I seek to clarify the nature of the dispute and to describe some of the ways in which it has developed. If there is a simple illustration of the difference between the two positions it is that Park would probably (like his contemporary Malinowski) have asked students 'what is your problem?', whereas the question for Cox and his successors is 'what is *the* problem?'.

Cox's dissent

What distinguished Cox's philosophy of social science can best be seen in his statements about how the phenomena of racial relations are to be defined. Early in the section of the book devoted to race he sets out to eliminate certain concepts that he believes to be commonly confused with that of race relations. One of the concepts to be eliminated is that of racism, because studies of its origin substitute 'the history of a system of rationalization for that of a material social fact' (1948: 321). He does not state this explicitly, but it can be deduced that in his view material social facts can be understood only as features of historical constellations. He concluded that 'probably the crucial fallacy in Park's thinking is his belief that the beginnings of modern race prejudice may be traced back to the immemorial periods of human associations' (1948: 474). According to Cox, Park failed to appreciate the differences between the social formations of classical antiquity and of modern capitalism. Something quite new took place when Europeans appropriated territory in the New World and created a system of social relations based upon the principles of capitalism. For this system to develop, labour was required. The system could grow more rapidly if that labour, or a large section of it, could be bought and sold just like any other commodity and the labourers treated as chattels rather than as people. A supply of labour was found in Africa which could be marketed in this way since Africans were physically distinctive and could therefore be made subject to special laws. If white workers could be persuaded that black workers were different, then they might not perceive that the true interest of all workers lay in their taking common action against their exploiters. The 'material social fact' was therefore a complex system of relations which would develop in a historically predictable manner.

In 1948 Cox understood 'racism' to 'refer to a philosophy of racial antipathy', though more writers at that time seemed to define it as a doctrine, dogma or ideology according to which race determined culture. I discussed its use as a concept in that sense in an address published in 1970. Cox commented privately on my address: 'if racism is not societally based – an emanation of a given society – it is not anchored in time and space. We become concerned with an historical study of intellectual usage ... racism ... can be dead only if changes in the society itself demonstrate it'. This suggests that, if not in 1948, then at a later date Cox was willing to regard 'racism' rather than 'race prejudice' as an appropriate name for 'the socio-attitudinal facilitation of a particular type of labour exploitation' (1948: 393). It is not a distortion of Cox's line of thought if, in accordance with a meaning that the name has acquired in the last twenty years, it is said that in Cox's view racism was a new phenomenon that was part and parcel of the growth of capitalism.

At one point Cox writes that

> we may think of race relations as that behaviour which
> develops among people who are aware of each other's actual
> or imputed physical differences. Moreover, by race relations
> we do not mean all social contacts between persons of
> different 'races', but only those contacts the social
> characteristics of which are determined by a consciousness of
> 'racial' difference. Two people of different 'race' could have a
> relation that was not racial. (1948: 320)

This reads like the kind of definition found in orthodox sociology and suggests that Cox had not completely liberated himself from the position he was attacking. As can be seen from other parts of his book, things were to be defined not by the parties' consciousness but by their functions

in the social order: 'race relations . . . are labor–capital–profits relationships; therefore, race relations are proletarian–bourgeois relations and
hence political–class relations' (1948: 336). In such circumstances it is to
be expected that people will become conscious of actual or imputed
physical differences, but the object of study is a complex of relations
existing on different levels (productive forces, relations of production
and ideological forms) located in a historical sequence.

For Park, the phenomena of race relations had many facets, and
presented many problems to the social scientist. Racial differentiation
occurred in an ecological context as different human groups competed
for resources. It could also be studied in terms of prejudice, as an
expression of the consciousness of a group seeking to defend a privileged
position; in terms of social distance, as members of such a group
regulated the kinds of relations they would enter into with varying sorts
of non-members; in terms of personality, for example, the effect of
occupying a socially marginal position; and so on. There were as many
problems as there were useful ways of looking at the evidence. For Cox,
there was one inclusive problem, the historical fact of racial differentiation; the sociologist's conceptual framework had to be adjusted to
grasp the object of study and to reveal the principles which explained its
changing character. The opposition between these two views is at root
epistemological. For the intellectual tradition in which Park stood,
knowledge grows from the ordering of evidence within the concepts
defined by a theory; for Cox, knowledge was revealed in history to those
who understood its dynamics.

Two epistemologies

In a recent book (1983: 88) I followed Sir Karl Popper in calling these two
views 'philosophical pluralism' and 'philosophical monism'. I have since
come to appreciate that this nomenclature is idiosyncratic; it confuses
some readers because in philosophy the debate between pluralism and
monism relates to the number of substances in the world. Ernest Gellner
(1977) has contrasted the same two epistemologies in a pyrotechnic
address entitled 'Positivism Against Hegelianism', but these two names
do not make a true pair, while the first of them has some associations
which will predispose some readers against any doctrines attributed to it.
Perhaps the least unsatisfactory solution is to call the two epistemologies
'Kant-inspired' and 'Hegel-inspired'.

The first line of thought has its origins in Kant's contention that all
known or knowable objects are relative to a conscious subject. In the
Critique of Pure Reason Kant referred to experiments conducted by

Gallileo, Torricelli and Stahl which taught all students of nature a crucial lesson:

> Accidental observations, made in obedience to no previously thought-out plan, can never be made to reveal a necessary law, which alone reason is concerned to discover. Reason . . . must approach nature in order to be taught by it . . . not in the character of a pupil who listens to everything the teacher has to say, but of an appointed judge who compels the witnesses to answer questions which he has himself formulated . . . Hitherto it has been assumed that all our knowledge must conform to objects. But all attempts to extend our knowledge of objects by establishing something in regard to them *a priori*, by means of concepts, have, on this assumption, ended in failure. We must therefore make trial whether we may not have more success in the tasks of metaphysics, if we suppose that objects must conform to our knowledge (1929: 20, 22).

To do this would be to learn a lesson from Copernicus:

> Failing of satisfactory progress in explaining the movements of heavenly bodies on the supposition that they all revolved round the spectator, he tried whether he might not have better success if he made the spectator to revolve and the stars to remain at rest. A similar experiment can be tried in metaphysics, as regards the *intuition* of objects. If intuition must conform to the constitution of the objects, I do not see how we could know anything of the latter *a priori*; but if the object (as object of the senses) must conform to the constitution of our faculty of intuition, I have no difficulty in conceiving such a possibility. (Kant, 1781: 21)

Kant went on to maintain that all our knowledge begins with but does not wholly derive from experience. We do not know objects as things in themselves, but we know about them because we have concepts which we can use to make nature answer our questions. A simple modern illustration would be that of the grid that is used in the construction and interpretation of maps. Co-ordinates are imposed on the map like a net and the location of any point can be determined by reading off the numbers on two dimensions. Our concepts are like that net. In this fashion a sociologist can work out suitable measures or definitions of racial consciousness, prejudice, etc., and use them to examine behaviour. The research worker can then make statements about what he or she has examined without claiming to have grasped their essential nature as 'things in themselves'.

The intellectual tradition in which Marx stood drew upon the epistemology of Hegel, who thought he had gone beyond Kant. In his *Logic* (1830: 73), Hegel wrote:

> According to Kant, the things that we know about are *to us* appearances only, and we can never know their essential nature, which belongs to another world we cannot approach ... the true statement of the case is rather as follows. The things of which we have direct consciousness are mere phenomena, not for us only, but in their own nature; and the true and proper case of these things, finite as they are, is to have their existence founded not in themselves but in the universal divine Idea.

Where Kant looked to natural science, Hegel looked to history and to religion. He maintained that the world of objects is not only related to a conscious subject but can be only the revelation or manifestation of an intelligence that works and comes to self-knowledge through man. Humanity was advancing to self-knowledge by discovering God's purpose in history: the gradual realisation of human freedom. Our knowledge of objects is increased when that knowledge can be subsumed in our understanding of how the world is developing. Thus where traditional logic was, and still is, based upon a law of contradiction according to which A cannot be both A and not-A, Hegel uses his dialectic to maintain that knowledge is itself developing so that the assertion of A evokes its negation; this is not the negation of A as a totality but a negation only of some claim for A (its particular content) and therefore it produces a revision or synthesis which is an improvement. 'It is ... a higher, richer concept than that which preceded; for it has been enriched by the negation or opposite of that preceding concept, and thus contains it, but contains also more than it, and is the unity of it and its opposite' (Hegel, 1812–16: 191).

Marx claimed to have turned Hegel right side up, but, according to John Plamenatz, Marx misunderstood Hegel's position. In Hegel's view 'social existence would not be *social* nor change social *dialectical* unless the beings involved in them had consciousness in the sense that only men have it – unless they could think conceptually and their ideas and their behaviour continually affected one another' (Plamenatz, 1975: 84, 449). The nature of Marx's debt to Hegel is a more complex problem than some of Marx's own statements would suggest. What matters for present purposes is the epistemological argument, advanced by Hegel, that though there is a knowledge originating in the conscious subject there is a more comprehensive knowledge to be obtained by locating observations in an understanding of human development. According to Roy Edgley, Marx's philosophical arguments can best be understood if they are seen as relating to different levels of reality. Marx's views concerning certain of these should be acceptable to authors employing a Kantian epistemology (and may, indeed, have been so at earlier times): for example, both schools may agree in criticising the 'assumption that the cognitive relation is one in which the knowing subject directly confronts the material object, his or her thought passively reflecting that object'; both can agree that 'knowledge and beliefs are actively produced and . . . are social and historical products'. Marx wrote about the way appearances of reality may misrepresent it and of the need to understand why these appearances follow particular paths in diverging from the truth (Edgley, 1983: 267–8, 283). Those who stand in the contrasting tradition also accept the tasks of studying folk concepts and popular consciousness, and of explaining how they reflect the social conditions of historical time and geographical space.

By asking analytical questions students can attain one kind of knowledge (sometimes called 'positive knowledge') which is relatively independent of the observer's personal biases. The clearest examples are provided by natural science. There is another kind of knowledge, differing in degree rather than in kind, which has a wider focus and is synthetic. Thus students believe they know about how their society has changed in the past and is destined to develop in the future, and about how people's understanding of these changes is influenced by the position in which they themselves stand in relation to the processes in question. For Marxists, these kinds of knowledge, though existing on different levels, are comprehended in one science which is materialist and practical. For Kantians, there are essential differences between logical relations and real relations (Edgley, 1983: 294), between deductive explanation and historical explanation, between laws of social change and the philosophy of history, between positive knowledge and ideological or philosophical knowledge. The issue is whether the subject–object relation affects the kind of knowledge that can be attained at every level or whether at the most general level it can be transcended by the categories of a unified science.

Orthodox social scientists seek sharp definitions that enable the research worker to make systematic observations which, because they are related to theories, permit an accumulation of knowledge. For them, objectivity resides in the use of techniques which permit individual observers to transcend the subjectivity of their perceptions and agree that certain of their observations are matters of fact. Those who stand in Hegel's shadow claim that their knowledge is validated by history. By locating phenomena in their scheme of historical change they learn the true nature of things and define them according to their reality. When asked to prove to the sceptic that their understanding of historical change is correct, they retort that the sceptic's class interests may prevent him from perceiving the reality underlying the realm of appearances.

The relevance of this philosophical distinction can be seen by considering Cox's arguments about the difference between racism and anti-Semitism. He maintains that in North America the dominant group or ruling class does not like the Jew. It is willing to like him if he ceases to be a Jew and voluntarily becomes like the generality of society. That same group or class likes the Negro provided he stays contentedly in the place allotted to him, where he can be easily exploited. It wants the Negro to cease trying to become like the generality of society. Thus, says Cox, anti-Semitism is a form of social intolerance, whereas race prejudice is a social attitude propagated so that the exploitation of either the group or its resources – or both – may be justified (1948: 393, 401). Other writers, and particularly social psychologists, argue that prejudice is, in origin, a disposition on the part of individuals who displace their own frustrations onto scapegoats. Those whites who are prejudiced against blacks are likely to be prejudiced against Jews also. So racism and anti-Semitism have much in common. A parallel can be drawn with the debate about black racism. Those who, with Cox, see racism as a historical complex facilitating the exploitation of blacks by whites believe that it is nonsensical to describe anti-white prejudice among blacks as black racism; the behaviour is to be understood as a reaction to the racism of the dominant group. Indeed Cox (1948: 380) declares that to study the prejudices of subordinated groups is to make the tail wag the dog. Those who, with the psychologists, study attitudes will say that similar or identical attitudes are expressed by individuals who have different complexions and that the attitudes have to be understood for what they are. To maintain that people with dark complexions cannot, by definition, be racist is, they object, itself a kind of prejudice or racism.

Cox has been criticised by contemporary Marxists for his economism, that is for envisaging the economic base as directly determining the ideological forms within which people conceptualise social issues. His critics believe that in between revolutionary periods ideological forms may be relatively autonomous and develop in their own ways. Yet on the topic with which this paper deals Cox was a representative of the Hegelian epistemology. He believed that the *explanandum* (that which is to be explained) was racism as a material social fact, and that the only satisfactory *explanans* (or explanation) was a historical one, showing it to be a predictable outcome of a particular system of labour exploitation. Other sociologists who have been attracted by the panoramic sweep of the Marxist philosophy of history have experienced a tension between that longer view and the criteria of proof to be used in short-term analyses. Many have moved away from a Hegelian epistemology and, with the Kantians, would assert that they too seek sharp definitions that will help them improve their theories; some speak of a 'positivist Marxism'. How far such movements can go without losing all right to the name 'Marxist' is a subject of debate, for Marxism has traditionally sought not knowledge for its own sake but only sufficient knowledge to enable the leaders of the proletariat to identify the best way forward. Others could discuss these trends better than I can. My contention is that despite its deficiencies (on which see Miles, 1980) *Caste, Class and Race* was historically important as the starting point for Marxist analyses of race relations. Some of the contrarieties of the recent past (like the differences between the two ways of defining racism) cannot be properly understood unless they are located in the two philosophical traditions I have tried to describe. The opposition between the followers of Park and the followers of Cox is now declining, in that sociologists on both sides of the divide have incorporated into their intellectual traditions lessons learned from their challengers. The alignments of the parties to the debate shifts constantly so that descriptions are soon out of date. Therefore the fairest kind of nomenclature is a historical one which identifies the traditions by reference to the two philosophers.

Fact and value

Most sociologists would now agree that there is no distinctive class of social relations to be identified as racial relations. The assumption that there was such a class was a product of racial consciousness that developed among white people in the United States and North-Western Europe in the latter part of the nineteenth century. The theory of permanent racial types advanced in the 1850s made a crucial contribution to this consciousness. It presented racial differences as stemming from objective zoological characters which, on the social level, gave rise to particular subjective perceptions and reactions. The main advance of recent times has been the recognition that though there are objective physical differences they serve on the social level only as social signs. Skin colour, facial structure and hair form acquire sign values which vary over time and from one situation to another; they are taken as indicators of people's social position, temperament and allegiance.

Though these sign values change, there can be stable patterns, as in the white view of blacks that Cox sees as a material social fact. Cox locates this view in a conception of historical development which in turn defines white prejudice as an obstacle to the progressive forces in society – and therefore as evil. Most writers in the Kantian tradition also condemn racial prejudice, but the difference between the two forms of argument is vital. The Kantians seek a definition of prejudice which they can use in their research to differentiate certain kinds of attitude or statement. As individuals they may express disapproval of particular expressions of prejudice, but in doing so they make a moral judgement that can be distinguished from the judgement that leads them to favour a particular definition. The Hegelians regard this as subjective; they claim to discover the moral nature of something as an objective quality by ascertaining its place in history. They recognise that the material social fact changes over time but identify a continuity that is grounded in social and historical function.

Particularly in the first half of the twentieth century, racial differences were often described in terms of superiority and inferiority. Now it is more usual to hear the argument that (in the words of a British Member of Parliament) 'the whole question of race is not a matter of being superior or inferior, dirty or clean, but of being different'. Martin Barker (1981: 20–1), noting the shift, maintains that just as the earlier kind of representation has been described as racist, so must the more recent one, and that there is now a racism linked to a theory of human nature: 'Human nature is such that it is natural to form a bounded community, a nation, aware of its differences from other nations. They are not better or worse. But feelings of antagonism will be aroused if outsiders are admitted.' That there is such a theory seems beyond question, but whether its use in particular arguments is worthy of praise or blame requires separate consideration. It is also necessary to consider whether it is a new form of an earlier argument or a distinctive one. Barker does not do this. He trades on the assumption that there was a recognisable entity known as racism and generally regarded as evil to imply that because the new argument has some features in common with the previous one it is a new form of it with the same moral status. (That it is new should not be taken for granted; Barker himself contends – controversially – that much of it can be found in the work of David Hume.) That important issues are at stake can be seen from the way in which Barker (1981: 14–16) discusses what he calls 'the argument from genuine fears'. He quotes statements by parliamentarians about such fears to contend that this argument is used only with the political purposes of restricting minority rights and playing upon majority prejudices. Thus 'the argument from genuine fears is a central weapon in the Tory argument. It was the chosen conceptual implement that enabled the theory of the new racism to step forward when needed.' Believing the fears to have been generated to serve a particular end, Barker feels free to ignore their other features. To someone who does not share his presuppositions, it is as if he refused to acknowledge that the fears may indeed be genuine.

It is sometimes thought that the realm of fact can be clearly separated from that of value, and the distinction between the two has indeed been traced back to Kant's *Critique of Pure Reason*, but such a claim is open to many objections (for an excellent review, see Ginsberg, 1963). Statements of fact and value are often closely related, but nevertheless there are advantages in many circumstances in attempting to keep them apart and in trying to examine such interrelations as exist rather than jumbling them together with the excuse that strict separation is impossible. The ways in which value judgements about racial prejudice have affected the definition of what is to be studied have been illuminated by Frank Reeves (1982). He shows that if prejudice is seen as an expression containing a descriptive, evaluative or prescriptive sentence referring to a member of a racial group (or to the group as a whole) then it can be distinguished from negative affective states, but to qualify as a prejudiced evaluation it must be regarded by some audience as morally, legally or factually unjustified. In other words, judgements of value cannot be excluded from the conventional definition of prejudice. However, by using the techniques of economic analysis it is possible to distinguish the value judgements of the people being studied from those of the student.

This alternative approach treats prejudice against contact with members of a racial category as a preference that has to be compared with other likes and dislikes. It is a taste for a particular kind of social relation which may be either positive or negative, just as consumers have positive and negative tastes for different kinds of goods in the shop. Some tastes, such as those for pornography, gambling and carousing, may be considered evil, but there is a demand for these things that will be satisfied unless the penalties are very high. To take an extreme case, sometimes people want their spouses killed. They may offer money to others to commit murder and may find people willing to accept such a contract, indicating that tastes which are almost universally condemned can still be satisfied in the market. This approach can be used in the study of racial prejudice and of attitudes towards immigration. Take, for example, the speech by Mr Enoch Powell published in *The Guardian* for 9 November 1981 in which he maintained that the British were losing their sense of nationhood and referred to 'a Britain which has lost, quite suddenly, in the space of less than a generation, all consciousness and conviction of being a nation: the web that binds it to its past has been torn asunder'. Later in that speech he touched upon the practice by which men and women in the British Empire were made British subjects and upon the British government's reluctance to introduce new laws 'until the presence of a common status where there was no common nationhood had produced in the cities of England a concentration of other nationals who asserted the contradictory claim to belong – and yet not to belong – to this nation'. He continued; 'so far our response has been to attempt to force upon ourselves a non-identity and to assert that we have no unique distinguishing characteristics: the formula is "a multi-racial, multi-cultural society". A nation which thus deliberately denies its continuity with its past and its rootedness in its homeland is on the way to repudiate its own existence.'

Anyone who shares Mr Powell's sentiments must place a high value upon his or her identification with a distinctive community stretching over the centuries and moulded by the experiences associated with the possession of a common territory. People of different appearance and customs cannot belong as of right to such a community but must earn their membership by the slow processes of assimilation. To require those who feel like this not to discriminate, in any circumstances, against those with whom they cannot identify, is to require them to deny emotionally important inclinations. They may have little difficulty in refraining from discrimination in formal and imperial situations, but they want no intimate contact, and their sense of social satisfaction (or welfare as the economists conceive it) is reduced by what they perceive as an immigrant take-over of parts of their homeland.

Other white people will have different tastes and it is perfectly possible to study their distribution. Older people are more likely than young to place a high value upon identification with a historic community. That taste might well be at its lowest among university students. Probably they would place a relatively high value upon cultural diversity and believe that in a multi-racial world Britain would be a better society if it reflected some of the differences outside its boundaries and, internally, had come to terms with physical variation by overcoming racial prejudice. Another category of white people might regret the loss of physical homogeneity in the nation's population but believe that attempts to remedy this by repatriation would run counter to far more fundamental values.

Appearance as a boundary sign

Enoch Powell's objection is not to the granting of citizenship to people of a different appearance. It is an objection to the granting of citizenship to people who do not belong, and do not seek to belong, to the nation. Because he deals with only limited aspects of a complex set of relations he seems to imply that a physically different appearance is to be taken as a sign of not belonging. In so doing he evokes sentiments associated with fundamental elements in British culture, ones which seem indeed to have their parallels in all known cultures. This is one version of the view criticised by Martin Barker, but Barker overlooks the variables that intervene between human nature and social boundaries. Human nature requires culture, for human potentialities cannot develop without it, but they can develop within quite different cultural frameworks. Cultures differ both in content (for example, the ways in which relationships of descent are traced) and in the richness of their texture (the variety of norms of conduct and the extent to which they are interrelated). All cultures, and particularly the rich ones, make life more meaningful for human beings, but just as they bring benefits so they entail costs. In rich cultures there is a diversity of norms which stipulate how people should behave and can therefore be seen as imposing constraints upon their freedom. The greater the diversity of norms, the harder it is for a stranger to gain acceptance as a new member of the society. By their activity in sharing the values that make their lives meaningful, people mark themselves off and unintentionally designate others as non-participants in their cultures, groups, cliques, sets, etc. A culture is not bounded like a geographical unit. It is internally divided in ways that relate to different kinds of activity. Some activities concern the centres of power in social relations; some are felt by individuals to touch upon intimate aspects of their lives; some activities are peripheral to power, and some carry only a low emotional load. In industrial societies people spend much of their time in situations constructed by technological requirements, such as the rules for driving automobiles in traffic; these are not invested with much cultural significance and therefore they do not operate in important ways to exclude people who want to belong to communities. So, rather than speak of bounded communities, it can be helpful to recall the notion of social distance associated with the names of Robert Park and Emory Bogardus and think of a community as a series of concentric circles. A newcomer who respects the wishes of those who already belong, and who is willing to modify his (or her) own behaviour, can gain entry in the outer circle and move inwards.

In traditional working-class neighbourhoods in England, people created a measure of human dignity and self-determination by building their own highly structured culture. It was founded upon distinctions of age, sex and marital status; upon norms about the use of the various parts of the house; upon the cycles of the week, the calendar, and the phases of the individual's lifespan; upon the division between work and leisure, and so on. Among the year's events were festivals when people did things they would normally consider improper, when, for example, they engaged in conspicuous consumption or ignored workaday values – as by laughing over the vulgar postcards associated with the seaside holiday. The behaviour that typifies such occasions has, according to Bernice Martin, misled sociologists into seeing working-class culture as characterised by the desire for immediate gratification, in opposition to the postponed gratification of the middle classes who invest for a better future standard of living. In her experience the way of life of the traditional working class is a culture of control. She sees the behaviour expected on festive occasions as reflecting and reinforcing an underlying order that is defined by a series of boundaries with ritual supports. Like many other observers, she notes how important in these neighbourhoods is the distinction between those people who are respectable and those who are rough. To become, and remain, respectable, a household's income had to be carefully protected against the masculine temptations of drink and gambling; the roughs were the people who could not or would not accept the disciplines of boundary that made the control possible. As she says (1981: 62):

> The rituals in the working class culture of control were the foundations of such dignity and independence as they were able to wrest from a hard environment. The control was not merely external, societal coercion; it was the control which the individual could actively exercise over his own conditions of life. Those who could not or would not exercise this control were infinitely more coerced by circumstance than were those who embodied controls in their own life-style. The Protestant ethic may have been the precondition of entrepreneurial capital accumulation, but this distinctive proletarian culture of control was the prerequisite of the organized labour movement and of the perhaps uniquely British tradition of the inherent dignity of manual labour.

A richly textured culture made possible only by the exercise of such controls leaves room for immigrants and strangers provided they accept the legitimacy of the system and enter it from the bottom. As they meet the conventional expectations, so they can work their way up. Other studies have shown that English people, when assessing claims to status, make fine distinctions between patterns of speech, so it is hardly surprising if they draw comparable inferences from physical features like skin colour. To start with it may not be respectable to have a dark skin, but in the course of time such an association will weaken and the values of respectability will triumph over those of complexion because the former provide a comprehensive and flexible set of criteria for evaluating everyone's claims whereas colour does not. Some of the African seamen who had settled in Britain before 1939 understood the expectations of the native working class and tried to meet them. Many of the West Indian and especially the African settlers who came after the war were of a different mind. When, in the late 1950s, the older residents of the neighbourhoods in which they settled complained that immigration resulted in a decline in standards, liberally minded commentators (themselves mostly middle-class) were unsympathetic. They replied that these neighbourhoods were declining anyway. The settlement of immigrants was a proof of it rather than the cause. These commentators would not acknowledge that, even apart from the question of colour, the entry of residents who did not share the local values of respectability was bound to occasion a loss of amenity for those who would not or could not join the migration to the suburbs.

Two later sociologists, Annie Phizacklea and Robert Miles (1980: 169), who carried out a survey in Willesden (West London), were struck by the way in which the English respondents expressed a 'sense of loss, of being left behind in a decaying area which has been taken over by the "coloureds"'. They maintain that working-class racism is best understood in terms of the political economy of the city in a capitalist society. As the processes of production change, so certain industries decline and with them the inner city neighbourhoods in which a population of skilled and semi-skilled workers gave an extra boost to the cultivation of respectability. Thus racist sentiment is exacerbated by capitalist decline. The link between this thesis and the Hegelian tradition is discussed in the next section. What should be noted here is that an explanation of the attitudes of one generation alone is weak. The older generation may remember what things were like before the immigrants arrived, but their attitudes are not always transmitted to the next generation. The attitudes of the younger people will be related to the circumstances of their lives as well as to those of their parents' lives. Bernice Martin discusses the behaviour of members of an East London gang who had been involved in the murder of a Pakistani. Their racial attitudes seem, more than any other of their views, to have resisted the influence of their liberal youth leaders and to have persisted as they grew older. Looking back a little later, one of the gang members was concerned to explain and defend their racialism. He deplored the influx of coloured people because it changed his neighbourhood and its way of life by confounding the equation of territory with appearance and by upsetting the boundaries; 'I think a geography book when showing people of all nations, Chinese should be yellow, Nigerians black and Europeans white. Your friends in the Bethnal Green bookshop think we should all be black. Black is beautiful, shit' (Martin, 1981: 144). Martin relates this to David Lockwood's distinction between the traditional proletarian and the deferential traditional cultures within the working class. In the former, she says, it is not only classes that are seen as antagonistic categories but also races, sexes, and every kind of territorial unit. Those brought up in that culture are much more likely to use violence in maintaining what they regard as the proper boundaries than are the deferential traditionals who are more ready to regard the various social categories as interdependent. Moreover, Martin is able to show that such an interpretation fits other features of the proletarian youth culture of the 1960s, such as the conflicts between the mods and rockers and between the skinheads and hippies, the hostility towards those schoolmates who studied seriously, and the skinheads' hatred of the privatised new working class. Without in anyway condoning them, she contends that 'Paki-bashing' and racial prejudice can be better understood if they are seen as manifestations of a culture which sanctifies boundaries and anathematises mixed categories of all kinds. This interpretation parallels the Freudian conception of prejudice as a displacement of tensions generated within the personality by the frustrations of socialisation. The cultural analysis suggests that the frustrations may be generated by cultural controls and that they are displaced onto those who do not belong, who do not accept the same disciplines, and who may, by their very presence, raise doubts about whether the struggles of those who do belong are really worthwhile. Such an analysis seeks to account for the preferences held by individuals. It treats racial prejudice not as a unitary phenomenon but as a name for a set of multi-faceted observations.

Historical and positive knowledge

The central issues are those of the nature of historical knowledge and its relation to positive knowledge. Hegelians believe that humans can attain a reliable knowledge of the way historical change occurs. They use this knowledge as a meta-theory to identify the important problems on the level of positive knowledge and to determine how these should be conceptualised. Kantians accept that everyone seeking positive knowledge will work with some philosophy of social science, but deny that the study of history can yield knowledge which is as secure as positive knowledge; positive knowledge is of use in the interpretation of the historical record and, conversely, a historical perspective can illuminate studies of the present, but historical interpretation is necessarily shot through with subjective perceptions.

Phizacklea and Miles, though critical of Cox's work in other respects, are at one with him in seeing capitalism as developing in accordance with definite principles, one of which is class struggle. The tendency of native white workers to categorise immigrant workers as competitors rather than comrades modifies the course taken by class struggle. The native workers mark off the immigrants as competitors with lesser claims to scarce resources, utilising physical differences to do so. The overriding concern of Phizacklea and Miles is with this differentiation within the working class (they identify black migrant labour as a class fraction and write mostly of racial categorisation, but this is the means by which differentiation is achieved). The ways in which the parties talk about the differentiation do not provide reliable criteria for defining it. The differentiation has to be comprehended in its totality and the only way to do that is to uncover its place in the historical process.

Since they believe that it is this differentiation which matters, anything which is part of it, whether causal or not, gets swept into their definition of racism. Because the markers used by whites to identify and conceptualise blacks and Asians are physical ones, they are more appropriately called racial than, say, national. Any reference to a physical market to differentiate people then counts as racist. The authors are thus led to the conclusion that at least seventy-five per cent of their total sample (industrial plus residential) held racist beliefs. The remaining twenty-five per cent was made up of those persons who made no such reference during the course of the interview. From a Kantian standpoint the decision to use such a definition may seem unwise, but there can be no *a priori* objection to it. Nevertheless the decision creates its own difficulties, even for the authors. The first of them is quite unexpected. They count as racist anyone who refers to blacks or Asians as different, but they themselves refer to them as differentiated. Presumably, they do not consider themselves as racist. Is it not possible that some of their respondents were referring to blacks and Asians in the same way as they do? In which case, why call them racist if the authors are to be exculpated? What distinguishes the two kinds of statement?

Second, by defining racism as a kind of differentiation irrespective of its cause, Phizacklea and Miles are unable to banish either the reader's worries about its causes or their own. At the outset they define racism as negative beliefs 'which identify and set apart another group' as if these were causes, but their coding of answers is less strict. Phizacklea and Miles do not claim that racism is caused by the decline of the neighbourhood but that when decline is experienced and people feel powerless 'a scapegoat is truly manna from heaven' (1980: 22, 169), a view which implies that the underlying drive towards racism is psychological. Their rationale justifies their neglect of middle-class racism, though, there could be a connection which might help explain those elements in working-class racism which are common to English people of different classes.

Thirdly, it is notable that many of those who assert that Asians get preference say that it is the government or the local council which favours them. Phizacklea and Miles quote four statements to this effect, but there are more.[1]

> 'We don't think ["the race thing"] is important, not in this area ... what is wrong is not the council. I think it's just possibly the government when they allow them to come into the country and they just turn round and put them up in a hotel and then give them a council flat.' (English male, 318)

> 'Some people get favoured ... we had a lot of Uganda Asians come over here and straight into a house.' (Asked, 'Do you think it's the people in the greatest need?') 'Yes. It probably is.' (English man, 320)

> 'It's not the people's fault that come here. It was the government at the time.' (English woman, 418)

> 'I'm not against coloured or anything ... I know they have to have somewhere to live when they come over here but there are still a lot of people waiting for places and I can't understand why they are given preferences over us.' (English woman, 419)

Many of the interviews were conducted shortly after a much-publicised incident early in May 1976 in which two families of Asian refugees from Malawi on arriving at Heathrow were temporarily housed by the local council in a four-star hotel at a cost of £600 per week per family.

Why should the council act in a way that is considered to show preference to immigrants? The key lies in the rules by which council officials have to operate, as some of those interviewed understood. In the course of his description of housing allocation David J. Smith (1977: 246–7) writes:

> homeless families are normally given a high priority in terms of time (they must be rehoused quickly) but a low priority in

terms of quality of accommodation. Families displaced by
clearance are always given a high priority in terms of timing
and quality. Waiting list applicants are commonly given a low
priority in terms of timing but a high priority in terms of the
quality of accommodation offered.

Many of those interviewed in Willesden thought these priorities were not
quite right. Presumably the weights to be given to the different criteria
are matters on which reasonable people can reasonably differ. Yet it
seems that if anyone criticised the priorities he or she was inevitably
recorded as holding a racist belief. As the authors acknowledge, this
means that those West Indian respondents who thought that the rules
favoured Asians were also classified as racist.

Phizacklea and Miles could have restricted their definition of racism to
beliefs which cause or actively maintain racial differentiation, as opposed
to passively reflecting it. Inspection of the interview schedules for the
residential sample (which recorded a higher incidence of racist belief than
the industrial sample) suggests that the proportion counted as holding
such beliefs would have been reduced to a maximum of twenty-five per
cent. The interviews were not very highly structured (for good reasons)
and so coding was dependent upon the exercise of personal judgement;
this means that any quantitative representation of the responses is
subject to a substantial margin of error.

These, however, are minor criticisms relative to the more important
issue of how differentiation in the working class (or classes) is to be
understood. In traditional working-class communities there were many
forms of differentiation (and they have not all disappeared). The men
were particularly conscious of the differing degrees of prestige attaching
to jobs of varying skill; they respected craftsmanship, reliability and
experience; they expected newcomers to prove themselves and, if they
could, to work themselves up to a higher position in others' eyes. The
women were the guardians of respectability, as discussed earlier. These
two hierarchies were interrelated; both gave rise to patterns of continuous differentiation. Phizacklea and Miles set out to study a third
pattern of differentiation in isolation from the other two; they assumed it
to be discontinuous and did not look for continuities. Therefore they
could make no use of scraps of contrary evidence, such as the English
woman who said:

'There are far too many immigrants in this area. It's not a
question of colour because Asians I don't mind at all, in fact I
feel they are an asset to the locality because they are a very

cultured people; they keep themselves to themselves; they are quiet; and they embrace a lot of the qualified positions like doctors. Quite unlike the other lot . . .' (407)

In the interviews with the residential sample there is more evidence of the status struggle than of any awareness of a class struggle.

'I know you have bad and good coloured people and also white people. Here they are all mixed together.' (English man, 309)

'If I had small children I wouldn't want to bring them up in this area. I certainly wouldn't want them mixing with a lot of the children here because for one thing their language is absolutely appalling.' (English woman, 404)

'I hear girls coming home from that school swearing at married women.' (English woman, 409)

'Really the coloured families around here are very nice; on some of the other estates they aren't so nice.' (English woman, 418)

Though they may not be aware of it, respondents like these who are concerned about social status are making use of a continuous scale of differentiation which enables them to assess the claims to respectability of people irrespective of their ethnic origin.

A comparison

The research by Annie Phizacklea and Robert Miles was conducted from the SSRC Research Unit on Ethnic Relations. At the same time, also from that Unit, another study was conducted of ethnic relations in Battersea, South London, by a team under the leadership of Sandra Wallman. Her study paid very careful attention to the history of the borough, discovering the way in which its particular character was moulded and reflected in some of its political figures; it examined the demographic history of a locality that was the object of more detailed research; but rather than extracting from historical knowledge any criteria of what is significant in the present it used this knowledge to assess continuities over time. The focus, for both the historical and the contemporary research, was upon the way in which individuals used ethnic categorisation in the daily business of life. Living in the locality was seen as a matter of balancing a household economy and getting along with the neighbours. How, the research team asked, was this affected by differences in ethnic origin?

Apart from the historical investigation, the team looked at the way in which a special community was created when, about the time the research started, a locality of 500 households got itself officially designated a Housing Action area. This committed the local council to the improvement of the housing in the locality; it means a substantial input of valued resources, and it boosted the residents' sense of belonging to a distinctive community. 446 households, more than one-third of which were of ethnic minority origin, were involved in an intensive self-study of their activities, including their use of local amenities, their contacts with kin and friends, their organisation of household tasks and their economic activities. The analysis of local involvement concluded that ethnic origin had less effect than age, family cycle, work commitments and social class. When asked about any plans they might have for moving, just two per cent made explicit reference to ethnic or social difference: the whites among them objected to the presence of too many blacks, and the blacks to the presence of racially prejudiced whites (Wallman, *et al.*, 1982: 121). Here there is a point of contact with the Phizacklea and Miles study, revealing a very different social pattern. Wallman and her co-authors made no use of any concept of racism.

It was found that many more whites than blacks obtained work by learning of opportunities through friends, but it was the locally born whites who benefited and ethnic origin did not of itself keep anyone out of the information system. The work patterns of 'ethnic South Londoners' and Caribbean-born South Londoners of long standing were very alike. A follow-up survey found that 'men born outside South London are almost twice as likely to be unemployed as those born in it; and men who have lived in South London for one to five years are three times as likely to be unemployed as those resident for more than five and less than ten. These probabilities are largely independent of colour' (Wallman *et al.*, 1982: 182–3).

Wallman concluded, first, that the population of Battersea was mixed in a way that left plenty of scope for ethnic solidarity or discrimination, but ethnic origin had little bearing on the business of livelihood. Battersea had 'always' considered outsider status to be more a matter of newness to or non-involvement in the area than of colour or foreign origin. Secondly, neither colour, language nor ethnic origin were central or persistent local issues. 'Those most often cited are: faceless bureaucrats, ambitious politicians, people who ... leave large rubbish by the dustbins, have noisy and frequent parties' (Wallman *et al.*, 1982: 186).

Neighbouring came first. 'Thus: a Newcastle man, three years resident, with a wife from the other side of London, is called a "foreigner" by a Jamaican woman resident of ten years standing who clearly is not' (Wallman *et al.*, 1982: 187). Those who resided in the locality when it was designated a Housing Action Area belonged: 'ethnic ratios and affiliations are beside the point'.

What a contrast with Willesden! Some difference was to be expected, because Battersea has been subject to less drastic and less rapid change. Some of the difference between the impressions of ethnic relations left by the two books may derive from the personal orientations of the two teams, especially since it is these orientations which influence the selection of the research question and that in turn leads to the adoption of particular research methods. Yet in all probability the most important differences lie in the size and nature of the areas studied. The designation of the nine small streets in Battersea as a Housing Action Area created circumstances favourable to the growth of community feelings which were absent from the Willesden locality. Indeed, it was their absence that many of the Willesden respondents lamented. Studies conducted by the Department of the Environment (Burbidge, 1981) support the claim that the standard of housing management can make a very substantial difference to the quality of life on an estate; this is of great significance to harmonious relations between people of different ethnic origins. From a sociological standpoint an important consideration is that community sentiment encourages (and is indeed dependent upon) the development of a continuous scale for appraising entitlement to social status.

Conclusion

My first and overriding thesis is that much of the dispute and mutual incomprehension in recent theoretical writing about racial and ethnic relations derives from the differences between two contrasting sets of epistemological assumptions. I may not have described these assumptions accurately enough, or have allowed sufficiently for developments within each tradition (for example, the ways in which Phizacklea and Miles have carried forward Cox's mode of analysis), or found satisfactory names for the two outlooks. But I hope to have established that there are important differences in the selection and definition of *explananda*, and in the criteria of explanation, that cannot be understood apart from their philosophical presuppositions.

Writers who stand in the Kantian tradition believe that knowledge grows most rapidly if research workers are free to select the *explananda* that interest them in the context of their own intellectual heritage, developing the theories that appeal to them. They seek definitions which will help them improve the explanatory power of those theories. Writers in the Hegelian tradition derive their criteria of what to study and how to study it from their understanding of history. They seek definitions which grasp the true nature of the objects in question. There is more dispute about how to formulate research questions than about what constitutes a satisfactory answer to a question, and it is pertinent to note that the dispute about appropriate questions is greater among sociologists than among those who study inter-group relations from the vantage points of social psychology, human geography and economics.

The opposition between the two epistemologies is particularly sharp with respect to the values of research workers. To Kantians it appears as if some Hegelians, and particularly the Marxists, use sociology to advance their political views; they bring into their work what to others appear value-laden concepts (for example, of oppression) so that their writing has what seems to be a hortatory and unacademic tone. Such criticisms appear to the recipients either to miss the point or to be evidence of a wilful attempt to avoid consideration of the most important issues. They reply that in such circumstances it is difficult to stage any proper debate. In the course of time this conflict may be resolved by the reformulation of questions suggested by the Hegelian view so that they can be tested by the methods developed within the Kantian tradition – but to my critics this conclusion will appear only a reiteration of my epistemological assumptions.

NOTE

1 Dr Annie Phizacklea has very kindly allowed me to read transcripts of interviews with the residential sample. She, Robert Miles, Theo Nichols, Edo Pivcevic and David Watson have also commented on this paper in draft.

3

The role of class analysis in the study of race relations – a Weberian perspective

JOHN REX

The study of race relations, in common with a number of other politically charged areas in the social sciences, seems beset by feuds and conflicts of a quite theological intensity. Thus such approaches as plural society theory, rational choice theory, sociobiology, Marxism, Weberianism, the anthropological theory of ethnicity and psychological theories of identity all seem to be making imperialist demands to command the whole field to the exclusion of all other theories.

Closer investigation of these theories, however, reveals that they are in fact in large measure complementary. First, they may be dealing with different kinds of problems, as, for example, when Marxist writers deal with the question of class and race in South Africa (e.g. Wolpe 1976), while M. G. Smith deals with the forms of incorporation of ethnic groups in plural colonial and post-colonial societies (1965, 1974) and Barth deals with the problem of 'boundary-maintenance' when Pathans come into contact with other groups (1969a). Second, they may be looking at problems from the perspective of different social science disciplines such as political sociology, which is likely to be concerned with the macro-relation of groups within a social system, or cognitive anthropology, which deals with the belief systems of ethnic groups, or social psychology, which may be concerned with the role of identity concepts within the personality system. Finally, they may operate on different levels of abstraction so that theories range from macro-theories about the relations between groups and institutions to what appear to be individualist theories, but which, in fact, may actually serve to explicate group concepts on the macro-level in terms of the meaningful action of hypothetical actors. Theories differentiated in all of these ways will be seen, when they are carefully explained, not to contradict but to complement one another.

It is in this spirit that this paper seeks to draw attention to the value of an emphasis on class analysis as an approach to some of the major problems of race relations. In its first part it seeks to do this merely by describing what some of these problems are and what their role has been in shaping my own general approach to race relations questions. In the second part it seeks to place class analysis within a more general and systematic theory. To do this it has to indicate what its relationship is to other theories with rather different *explananda*, thus pointing to a more broadly defined field, and also to relate the collectivist and structural issues which the term 'class analysis' normally suggests to underlying conceptual problems which are best stated in terms of methodological individualism.

Obviously I do not accept some of the distinctions made in this volume and elsewhere by Michael Banton (1983), who seems at times to equate class analysis with what he calls a 'Hegelian' as distinct from a 'Kantian' approach to social science. I actually share most of Banton's preferences for Kantian social science (Rex 1982b), including his rejection of Hegelian reifications of the concept of class. But Weber, who was certainly a Kantian, by no means turns away from class analysis, including among other groups differentiated by property ownership, groups with differential relations to the means of production (Weber 1968, vol. 1, ch. 2). My argument against Banton would be that the form of class analysis advocated here is not only fully Weberian and Kantian but is also capable of the sort of methodologically individualist explication to which his version of rational choice theory appears to point.

Before taking up these theoretical points in more detail, however, I have devoted the first part of this paper to a biographical account of the development of my own theoretical concerns in the field of race relations. I have done this not out of self-indulgence but in the hope of avoiding misunderstanding. Very often in this kind of field, if one states issues purely in the abstract, one's readers are likely to take one to be referring to a quite different subject-matter or problem. Thus what I say here might not be applicable to all instances where different ethnic groups are neighbours or to all cases of immigration. It is relevant to certain instances which have seemed to me to be politically important, however, and my hope is that my theoretical responses to these particular situations might, if clearly understood, have much wider if not universal application.

Four theoretical encounters with the field of race relations

The four situations in which I have had to formulate my own theories of race relations have been (a) the problem of white racial supremacy in

South Africa, (b) the argument which developed among British and American social scientists in the 1950s and 1960s about 'the plural society', (c) the attempt of the various agencies of the United Nations to define the problem of 'racism' and hence, by implication, the field of 'race relations', and (d) the need to conceptualise the structural problems involved in entry of 'colonial' immigrants to the metropolis.

(a) Conceptualising race relations in South Africa

My starting point in the sociology of race relations was as a child, a student and a politically engaged democrat in South Africa. As I saw it, the kind of conflict between racial groups which formed the daily stuff of my political existence there could only be adequately comprehended as one of class struggle. That is to say the relations of conflict between Bantu[1] and white at least (those between these groups and Indians and coloureds being more complex) resulted not primarily from perceived physical or cultural difference but overwhelmingly from the fact that whites were engaged in the exploitation of Bantu labour.

If it is 'Marxist' to say that these group formations, and the actions and forms of consciousness to which they led resulted from the differential relationship of the groups concerned to the means of production then my position was Marxist. Bantu workers typically worked in unfree conditions and because of the power controlled by whites had little control over the means of production, thus being subject to ultra-exploitation. Whites controlled the means of production or, if they were workers rather than entrepreneurs, were protected from ultra-exploitation by trade unions, by welfare provisions and, above all, by their control of what van den Berghe has called a '*Herrenvolk*' state.

But immediately this has been said it must be added that a 'class-struggle' model of South African society did not conform to a classical Marxist model. There were white workers as well as black and there were divisions of a class-like kind between white and black. The black (Bantu) workers had been conquered militarily and they lived in effect in two societies, one that of the town, the mine and the factory, the other the peasant society of the so-called reserves. Finally, on the white side, the behaviour of capitalist entrepreneurs was considerably constrained even if it was sometimes facilitated by the state. On all these matters a Marxist approach had either to be considerably revised or at least specified in order to account for the peculiarity of this capitalist instance.

On the question of the divided working class, it seemed to me obvious that the class position of a mine-worker in a compound (who may be taken as an extreme 'ideal type') was different from that of a free white worker. Coming from the poorer sections of the latter group myself, I could see that my own kin and community were able to defend real privileges against competition from all other groups differentiated from them by skin colour. Parliament, the state and the police were on their side. I could not easily accept therefore the claim made by white Marxists that these differences were a matter of false consciousness only and that there was a long-term inevitability about united class action by white and black workers.

In order to account for this difference I suggested (Rex 1973) that one must take into account the fact that the Bantu had been subject to military conquest. Thus there was in the South African case a factor which was extraneous to Marxist analysis, namely the availability to the whites both historically and contemporaneously of physical coercion. Franz Oppenheimer (1975) seemed as important in the analysis of this situation as Karl Marx and it seemed that one had to agree with Herbert Blumer that capitalism always took advantage of those essentially political circumstances in which it found itself (Blumer 1965b).

The existence of the economy of the reserves and the commuting of Bantu workers from this to the obviously capitalist economy of the cities led some of my contemporaries to talk about the co-existence of two modes of production. I could not accept that formulation myself, because it did seem to me that the whole system was a single capitalist one. None the less I did argue that this was a different type of capitalist system from that known in Europe, enjoying as it did the advantages both of labour discipline in the mines and factories akin to that available to slave masters and of lack of responsibility for the reproduction of the labour force (Rex 1973).

Finally there was the question of the state. True, the South African state had been quite explicitly designed by Cecil Rhodes and Smuts to facilitate the exploitation of labour, but Smuts's party had eventually been defeated by a coalition of white workers and farmers, which had considerably restricted the functioning of capitalism. One did not have to accept the liberal interpretation of history which came to hold that the state was an archaic product of the frontier mentality to see that it represented class forces of a non-capitalist, albeit white kind. (This polarised debate has been well presented by Harrison Wright (1977).)

These 'revisionist' positions quickly produced opposition from Marxist theorists. On the one hand, they suggested that I had failed to understand that the crucial issue under the heading of 'relation to the means of production' was that of the extraction of surplus value and that this occurred in the employment of white as well as black workers. On the other, they suggested that I had caricatured Marxism, and that a good Marxist analysis could readily be introduced to take account of racism, the existence of interpenetrating modes of production and the relative autonomy of the political.

Harold Wolpe, who is a South African Marxist and my contemporary, has now come to the view that the existence of divisions within the working class is something which can be explained through a complex and elaborate application of the theory of surplus value. For those of us who question the theory in any case, of course no such elaborate subsidiary hypotheses are necessary. Empirically, however, we agree on the fact of a racially divided working class (Wolpe 1976).

Stuart Hall, starting from the issues posed by Wolpe's disagreements with me, has taken on board many of the criticisms which I have made of Marxist analysis, arguing that the structural issues which I raise are not incompatible with a more sophisticated form of Marxism. In particular, he believes that the Althusserian notions of structures in dominance and of the articulation of different modes of production in social formations are able to explain from a Marxist perspective most of the issues which I have raised in relation both to South Africa and to the Caribbean (Hall 1979a).

It would seem then that current Marxist opinion is not so much opposed to what I have said about the South African situation as critical of me for dissociating my analysis from Marxism. For my part, I am not particularly concerned about how my work is labelled provided that we can agree on structural issues. All that I would say is that I would wish to pursue a class analysis whether or not the labour theory of value is regarded as having ultimate validity.

My South African experience, however, has left me more inclined to conceptualise my class analysis in terms of Weberian concepts. Specifically, Weber used the concept of capitalism in both a wide and a narrow sense. In the wider sense it involved both the capitalism peacefully oriented to market opportunity (including free labour markets) and 'adventurer' or 'booty' capitalism which he saw as being characteristic of imperialism, while in the narrow sense it was confined to the former. I find these notions useful in that what seems to me to be involved in South Africa is not so much a society which articulates two modes of production as one in which a modern capitalist state is marked by strong elements of surviving booty capitalism. So far as the status of relatively unfree black labour is concerned I believe that it is best understood in terms of a typology of labour which can be derived from Weber's *General Economic History* (1961) and from his writings on agrarian institutions in the ancient world. Finally, it seems to me that the much more flexible notion of classes being generated wherever there is differential control of or access to property seems to have provided a basis for the understanding of the divided South African working class.

There are, of course, many respects in which the discussion so far has been simplistic. It has concentrated almost entirely upon the white–Bantu relationship and it has spoken as though class is the sole basis of the relationship between these groups. Clearly, in so far as the relations between coloured and Indian or between Bantu and white are class relations, they are relations of a more complex and secondary kind. Moreover, cross-cutting class formations there has to be some classification of groups according to their linguistic, religious and other cultural characteristics, and any of the groups mentioned and discussed as though they were classes might be sub-divided on the basis of these criteria. In addition, it has to be noted that members of the non-white groups vary in the degree to which they have become acculturated to the dominant white culture. Pierre van den Berghe has dealt with these questions very well in his *South Africa: A Study in Conflict* (1965). None the less it must be pointed out that analysis in terms of cultural, or for that matter of status, differentiation is subsidiary to and does not replace class analysis.

Finally, one other point needs to be noted. This concerns the subjective consciousness and the organisational forms which occur among those who have the same objective class positions. On this matter both the Weberian and Marxian traditions tend to be rationalistic in that they assume that these forms of social bonding will arise *de novo* among members of a class. In fact, where other bonds of an ethnic and cultural kind already exist, these will pre-empt the formation of new bonds. In the South African case ethnicity provides the basis of class bonding to a greater degree than almost anywhere else. One does not have to preach to a Bantu mine-worker that he should have bonds with his fellow Bantu miners. He has them already and puts them to use in a class context.

(b) The plural society debate

To anyone whose primary political and sociological experience has been in South Africa the dominant paradigm of North American and Western European sociology, namely functionalism, appears strangely irrelevant. Clearly we are not talking there of a shared normative order or a simple system of functionally related institutions. The emphasis has to be on groups in conflict. This criticism, however, cannot be directed at the theory of the plural society as it is developed by Furnivall (1939) and Smith (1965). Thus when I first encountered Furnivall I wrote an article (Rex 1958) welcoming it as the way forward towards a conflict model. As I saw it, the work of Furnivall, as well as that of Malinowski, in his *The Dynamics of Culture Change* (1965) and Myrdal in his famous methodological appendices to *An American Dilemma* (1944; see also Myrdal 1958), pointed in this direction.

There is no need in this context to summarise the work of Furnivall or Smith on the plural society in Indonesia and the Caribbean. What is important here is to notice the account which each gives of the way in which the separate ethnic groups or cultural segments are related to each other. For Furnivall the groups are held together by 'the market place', and, though this is something of a metaphor for the whole of economic life, it does suggest commercial rather than productive or employment relations. For Smith the one shared institution is the political one. What I have felt bound to ask is whether it would not be better to look at the point at which conflict most usually arises, namely in the business of employment relations and production.

I am sure that both Furnivall and Smith would say that they included such relationships under the heading of 'the market place' or 'the political institution', but it is important that this point should be spelt out, for it is precisely the relations of employment which give rise to class formation and conflict. What I have tried to do therefore is to emphasise that the ethnic groups and segments in their models have at least some of the character of classes. The East Indians of Guyana, for example, have at their core a group of indentured labourers, while the Afro-Caribbean population is descended from freed slaves.

I have suggested (Rex 1981) that the best way to approach the study of a multi-racial, multi-cultural society is to look at its mode of production and at the conflicting interests and relationships which this generates. Usually this means looking at what Weber saw as the typical institutions of booty capitalism, such as the slave plantations, latifundia, purchasing and marketing companies and tax-farming. These provide the basic framework within which one ethnic group exploits another. Cultural difference is then activated as a means of pursuing the interests of the various groups.

A crude focus on the mode of production, however, is inadequate as a basis for the analysis of colonial society if the concept of mode of production is narrowly interpreted. Clearly such groups as secondary traders, white settlers (as distinct from the 'plantocracy'), coloureds, freed slaves and poor whites, missionaries and administrators do not have their position defined directly by their relationship to the core productive institutions. Rather they have a functional role in relation to the social system as a whole. Often these roles are performed by culturally closed groups who have unequal legal rights. It seems appropriate to refer to these groups not as classes, but as colonial estates.

I have also suggested that this analysis of colonial society in terms of classes and estates describes only the first phase of the constitution of colonial societies. The process of the supersession of the institutions of colonial booty capitalism by a more liberalised capitalism allows more movement between groups and a tendency for ethnic classes and estates to be replaced by classes of the 'Marxist' kind. None the less such class formation is profoundly affected by the historic colonial legacy. The new classes are still marked by ethnic bonding and sometimes their operation is still affected by ideas and structures derived from the older colonial economic order. Thus trade unions and political parties are formed on an ethnic basis, and sometimes, despite a person's class position in the modern order, he may still be placed and have his rights defined by his ancestor's position under colonialism.

To say this is not to say that the plural society theory has nothing to commend it. On the one hand it emphasises the fact of cultural and institutional differences between classes and estates. On the other it draws attention to many problems of the detailed process of social change which are overlooked in an analysis in terms of the dynamics of the mode of production. Marxists who speak of determination and of 'structures in dominance' could readily accept this.

(c) Defining racism

Since the 1939–45 war had involved racialist oppression, the United Nations and its agencies felt called upon in the post-war world to look systematically at the problem of race relations in all contexts. They began this task, however, in a profoundly idealistic way. Since racial oppression had been *justified* in terms of biological ideas, it was assumed that the correction of these ideas would of itself alter structures. When, however, biologists concluded that racial differences had no relevance to the political differences and conflicts among men, sociologists were called upon to look at the structural contexts in which racist ideas flourished. My own thinking about race and ethnic relations was stimulated by participating in these discussions.

One response to the impasse created by the biologists' disavowal of responsibility was to say that the differences said to be racial were better described as 'ethnic', and there was something to be said for this, in that quite obviously the issue of concern was not simply that of groups distinguished by phenotype. Unfortunately, too often, when this line was taken, ethnic differentiation was treated as a benign phenomenon. What was left out was the element essential to the understanding of racism, namely that ethnic groups sometimes had identities imposed on them to restrict their mobility and to facilitate their exploitation and oppression.

Some anthropologists, stressing that ethnicity was situational, emphasised that it was 'a resource' but left out of consideration its role as 'a liability' allowing the justification of oppression in ethnic or racial terms (Wallman 1978b).

I suggested (Rex 1983c) that there were in fact two interesting areas of study. One was that of ethnicity as a source of difference and as a means of collective organisation in non-exploitative, non-oppressive situations. The other was that of situations in which one ethnically or racially defined group exploited or oppressed another. It was the second which was of political as well as academic importance.

What I argued was that there was a distinguishable group of structural situations which had three characteristics. These were:

(1) that there was a situation of severe conflict, oppression or exploitation going beyond that which was normal in a free labour market

(2) that this conflict, oppression or exploitation occurred not simply between individuals but between groups, so that it was not possible for an individual having particular phenotypical or cultural characteristics to leave his group and join another

(3) that this system of conflict, oppression or exploitation was rationalised or justified in terms of some sort of deterministic theory which had often been of a biological sort.

I said that it was situations of this kind which were commonly referred to as race relations situations.

This attempt to define the field was criticised from a number of different points of view. First, it was suggested that it left out intercultural situations which were not marked by exploitation and oppression. Second, it was argued that it did not include many race relations situations as commonly understood and included others of a non-racial sort. Third, some argued that it failed to make an adequate distinction between race and class.

So far as the first objection is concerned, I accept that what it says is true. My argument, however, is that it is worthwhile separating out situations of group exploitation as a special field, because they have important characteristics of their own which they do not share with situations of benign ethnicity. On the second point I am quite happy to divert attention away from phenotype as such to that group of situations which, whether it rests upon phenotypical or upon cultural differences, actually involves exploitation and oppression. It seems to me that in the relatively peaceful relations between black and white members of the Parisian bourgeoisie there is little to interest a student of race relations as I understand the subject, while, on the other hand, the essentially ethnic relations of Northern Ireland actually have much in common with black–white relations in other countries.

I do think, however, that there is a distinction to be made between the sort of situations which I am grouping together and what are normally thought of as class situations. I have in mind here the fact that the group relations to which I refer are marked by some use of force. This is a crucial difference. I do not say that exploitation does not occur in free labour markets, but it does seem to me that one is dealing with something sociologically different when relations between employer and employee involve the use of force. Of course it can be said that at the outset of the industrial revolution in Britain the situation of the working class was very like that which my three criteria of a race relations situation suggest. I accept this and do not really mind if such phases of development of metropolitan capitalism are seen as structurally of the type which I am discussing. On the other hand, the historic moment of force in such an industrial nation did lead on to the creation of a situation in which there was 'free labour' in which workers were exploited in the labour market.

What I sought to do having established a first definition of 'race relations situations' was to go on to list the possible historical circumstances in which such situations might occur (Rex 1973). Originally I suggested that these included (1) frontier situations, (2) slave plantations and post-plantation societies, (3) situations of severe class conflict, (4) estate and caste systems, (5) status systems, especially in post-plantation societies, and (6) situations of cultural pluralism. These were all, of course, colonial situations. I also went on, however, to refer to situations in metropolitan societies, including complex systems of urban stratification, pariah situations and scapegoat situations.

This listing of possible contexts of race relations situations was relatively unsatisfactory and unsystematic and not perhaps faithful to my general definition. It does, however, bear some relationship to the much more systematic attempt by Schermerhorn (1970) to describe what he calls 'repeatable sequences of interaction between subordinate ethnics and dominant groups'. These are (1) the emergence of pariahs, (2) the emergence of indigenous isolates, (3) annexation, (4) migration and (5) colonisation, including under (4), (a) slave transfers, (b) movements of forced labour, (c) contract labour transfers, (d) reception of displaced persons and (e) admission of voluntary immigrants. Some of these situations, according to Schermerhorn, lead to 'racism' and some to pluralism.

Subsequently my own attempts (Rex 1981) to systematise the contexts of race relations situations have been rather more systematic and have rested upon the notion of an imperial and colonial system (in the widest sense, 'mode of production') developing and changing over 400 years and having consequences for the stratification of both colonial and metropolitan societies. This imperial system, I have suggested, has generated numerous class and ethnic groups which, whatever sources of conflict there are which arise from sheer cultural difference, find their dynamic in the fact that the groups concerned have differing degrees of power in a complex economic and political order.

This is, of course, a somewhat more 'Marxist' approach than that of, say, Schermerhorn. It is therefore perhaps appropriate to say that I now think that while the economy and the polity provide the dynamic for inter-group relations, actual bonding of the groups internally depends upon cultural factors. The multi-faceted class struggle between groups is also an ethnic struggle. If I were to use Althusserian language I might perhaps say that race and ethnicity provide a structure in dominance (Hall 1979a). Like Althusser, however, I would still want to keep in focus the economy (and the polity) which is determinant 'in the last instance'.

(d) Colonial immigrants and metropolitan societies

Much of my own research has been concerned not with colonial societies but with the fate of two dark-skinned immigrant groups in the metropolis (Rex and Moore 1967, Rex and Tomlinson 1979). In these studies I have had to develop a more specific model which seeks to relate the position of the immigrant minorities to an ongoing system of classes within a capitalist welfare state. As a part of a larger totality, however, I see these studies as exploring race relations studies at the metropolitan end of an imperial economic and political system.

The situation in Britain in the 1950s and 1960s was one in which politics had been structured in terms of class solidarity and class struggle to a much greater extent than was the case in North America (Rex 1979). This was above all expressed in the fact that the major forms of political mobilisation were to be found in the Conservative and Labour Parties. None the less there was little evidence of a 'hegemonic' working class. What seemed to me to have happened was that, as a result of working-class pressure, certain basic rights of workers had been conceded and that there was at least a temporary consensus about the desirability of full employment, a partially planned economy, the recognition of trade unions with the right of collective bargaining, and the acceptance of minimum standards of welfare in the sphere of unemployment benefit, housing and education. T. H. Marshall had suggested that these developments had made the allegiance of working-class people to 'citizenship' much more important than their allegiance to class (1950). I saw the consensus as more fragile and as depending upon the continued existence of class-consciousness and independent political organisation within the working class (Rex 1961).

The situation in other societies was, I recognised, different from this. In the United States, for example, there was a more open, individualist and less class-based society in which individuals depended less upon welfare rights won through class struggle and much more upon the achievement of economic independence through the acquisition of property. In that situation Gunnar Myrdal (1964) had suggested that the position of the American urban poor and, particularly, the black American poor was that of an 'underclass' who were continually unemployed and increasingly unemployable, who lived in a culture of poverty and a tangle of generationally transmitted pathologies.

My own suggestion in the British case was that the crucial empirical question was that of how far the new dark-skinned minorities enjoyed the rights which the working class had won in the welfare state; specifically, I wanted to know whether they had the same access to housing, employment and education. These questions could not, of course, be answered in either/or terms. None the less I concluded that there was a denial of access to housing, producing quasi-ghettos, that the minorities were partially confined to the least acceptable jobs and that there was increasing segregation in inferior schools. To some extent, therefore, I saw them as constituting an underclass in the specifically British sense of those who did not benefit from incorporation in the welfare state.

There was a much more important reason, however, why I saw the need to modify Myrdal's conception of the underclass (Rex and Tomlinson 1979). This was that the groups concerned were not simply some kind of rotting mass. They developed forms of group consciousness and organisation of a class-like kind and struggled for their own rights sometimes within the working class and sometimes against it. In Marxian terms they might be said to form not simply an 'underclass in itself' but an 'underclass-for-itself'. Organisations like the Indian Workers' Association and groups expressing 'black consciousness' seemed to me to be expressions of class interest as surely as trade unions and the Labour Party were expressions of the class interests of the mainstream working class.

Pierre van den Berghe has challenged this notion, suggesting that the groups concerned are 'ethnies' rather than classes (van den Berghe 1981). My reply to this is that I think that the dynamic of their situation derives from their class position, even though when it comes to organisation, consciousness and social bonding, new bonds formed on the basis of sheer class interest are not necessary, because they already exist in the ethnic organisation of those concerned. This complicates matters somewhat in that the pursuit of present class interest is often coupled with a continuing concern with the politics of the homeland and the larger question of the class interests of the group in the larger imperial system. It does not mean, however, that class is not still a central dynamic factor.

Before leaving this topic, I should perhaps add that the situation in Britain has been fundamentally altered in the late 1970s and the 1980s. There is now mass unemployment, working-class power has been undermined and the whole welfare state deal called into question. In that situation the class position of the ethnic minorities is fundamentally altered. Many British working-class people now find themselves in the same position as that held by the minorities in the 1950s and 1960s. It is not that the minorities are no longer an underclass. Rather, many British people have been forced into an underclass position. Two things are therefore likely to occur. One is that there will be more emphasis upon sheer class struggle, with all of the deprived and the unemployed being forced into united action, black and white together. The other is that some of the declassed whites may seek to act against and in competition with minority groups.

Finally, I should like to add that white behaviour in these circumstances is not simply to be construed as a result of racism or of the legacy of the colonial past. What whites are doing is basically to pursue their economic interests. Something of what Frederick Johnstone (1976) suggests in the South African situation is true here. The capitalist class has created basic distinctions between employed and unemployed. Within that framework the white workers fight for their own interests against their black fellow workers (though Johnstone is of course referring to the behaviour of the whites in employment).

Class theory and race relations theory

The account which I have given of these four political and intellectual encounters does not, of course, of itself constitute a sociological theory. It does not, as an established theory or a set of hypotheses fit to be established as a theory should, start with a set of abstract concepts, parsimoniously stated, from which propositions can be developed which can be tested against events in the real world and used subsequently to explain the world. What has now to be done therefore is to show how far the structures and processes referred to in these encounters are part of a more general structure and a more general process of change. Having done this, it will be necessary to ask whether this structure and these processes sufficiently explain all the kinds of problems normally dealt with under the heading of 'race relations' or whether there are other areas closely related but requiring a different kind of explanation. Finally it will be necessary to ask whether the theory of class on the macro-level requires explications in terms of a more elementary and perhaps more fundamental conceptual system. Ultimately a general theory of race relations could be said to start from this elementary and fundamental level, the equivalent of atomic theory in physics, but the explanation of concrete historical situations would be in terms of macro-concepts such as 'social class'.

The first question which we have to face then is: Can the processes referred to in the four cases which I have mentioned be reduced to a more general process? Three of them referred to specific historical situations and the fourth (the attempt to define racism) remains on a relatively descriptive level, indicating the empirical features of a race relations situation but not showing why such situations should occur. How then can we be more systematic?

Race relations theory and the world and imperial systems

I think that one possible systematic starting point from which such situations could be explained is to be found in the work of Immanuel Wallerstein (1974) and his notion of a world economic system. I would, myself, be inclined to narrow Wallerstein's focus to look not simply at one world economic system but at the various world empires of the European states. Within each of these empires I would suggest that groups of individuals have been placed in different relationships of access to and control of the political apparatus and are united or divided by the interests which they are forced by their situations to pursue. True, the resultant groupings are bonded by ethnicity. It is this that gives them their strength as compared with simple classes formed *ab initio*. This does not mean, however, that ethnicity and cultural differences are the sole or the main basis of the dynamics of their interaction.

Within this overall framework I would suggest that we need to consider separately the structure and dynamics of post-colonial society and that of metropolitan societies in so far as they involve the relations between colonial immigrants and their own class systems. Marxian theory would, of course, wish to go further than this and to consider the economic laws which underlie the operation of the system as a whole and thus has led some of those who write about the world economic system and the political economy of development to concentrate their attention on the class struggle in the metropolis as the main or the only ultimate source of change.

I confess that on this level I am an agnostic. I do not have any great confidence that the world capitalist system will as a result of the crisis move forward dialectically towards some new kind of order from which the class struggles generated by capitalism will disappear. But, in any case, if we are talking about the immediate historical world, we have to look not simply at that which is 'determinant in the last instance' but at structures presently in dominance. Those structures are classes and groups in conflict, which define themselves and are defined in ethnic and racial terms, but which also engage in a kind of class struggle resulting from their immediate relation to the means of production and its supporting political apparatus.

In colonial and post-colonial society the kind of social system which we are talking about is not, however, one of class struggle of a simple sort. The attempt to conceptualise it in classical Marxist terms is hopelessly inadequate. We have to take account of the fact of labour exploitation which involves varying degrees of unfreedom and the use of force. Arising from this we have to recognise the role of the polity as well as the economy and considerably to stretch, if we are to use it at all, the concept of the 'mode of production'. We have to recognise that legal inequality and differences in the history of different groups produce something like an estate system. And, finally, recognising that this colonial system is partially challenged and penetrated by a new *laissez-faire* type of capitalism, we have to see the way in which groups which were generated by the older colonial order are projected as interest-groups or classes into the present.

Obviously, in dealing with colonial societies I use the term 'class' in an extended sense. I refer to any group of individuals having common interests as a result of its relationship to the economic or political apparatus; I do this because I believe that groups with a shared relationship to the political structure have common interests generated by their position and that they must bargain with other groups in something like the way in which classes in the socio-economic sense do, particularly when they pass from the stage of individual competition and bargaining to collective bargaining. Alternatively, one might say that once classes develop the capacity for collective action they become more like politically defined estates.

Possibly, however, this merging of classes and estates under the single term 'class' is confusing. What we have is a system of class struggle surrounded by and resting in an estate system. I have tried in another essay (Rex 1981) to deal systematically with this problem. M. G. Smith (1974), on the other hand, deals with the problems in another way. He sees most colonial societies and post-colonial societies as being characterised by the differential 'incorporation' of ethnic groups or segments. This is to my mind an acceptable formulation which draws attention to the political structure which is the estate system. What it perhaps fails to do is to show how this estate system is related to the class system which arises where groups have not only different legal statuses but also different relationships to the means of production.

Some critics of my own ideas on this point have suggested that it is quite wrong to place emphasis upon class analysis in situations like that in South Africa. They argue that a person's position there is not determined by his relationship to the means of production but depends rather upon his political status which also determines his relationship to the means of production. Against this I would say that, though relations to the means of production are secondary, once political status determines a position in the production system, it is the production system which generates patterns of conflict of interest and gives rise to collective actions. Black workers in South Africa, that is to say, are assigned to production roles as a result of the political system, but having been so assigned operate as a class.

Finally, at the metropolitan end of the imperial system, we have the emergence of a new and more recent type of race relations situation. Race relations problems arose in the colonial world because of the penetration there of the metropolitan capitalist system. But now we also face relatively large-scale migration from the colonial world to the metropolis. What we are concerned with is the penetration of classes from the colonial world into the class system of the metropolis itself. Thus a Sikh peasant from the Punjab, or an artisan or small-scale farmer from Jamaica, may be seen as moving within the total imperial class system to the relatively privileged and well-rewarded position of worker or small shop-keeper in Britain. I have sought to emphasise in my work that in such circumstances groups may be thought of as classes both within the metropolitan system which they are seeking to enter and in relation to the wider imperial system.

The limitations of class analysis

It may be pointed out that even though the above analysis is relevant to many of the situations generated by capitalist imperialism, it by no means covers non-capitalist societies; nor does it cover those situations in which ethnic groups interact in non-economic contexts.

So far as the first of these objections is concerned, my own view would be that the level of analysis suggested here does apply to all complex societies, and just as much to socialist as to capitalist ones. In fact what happens in socialist societies is the subordination of allocation through the market to allocation of a political kind. In terms of the analysis suggested here such political allocation systems are just as capable of generating both estate and class differences as is a capitalist system. It is perfectly possible in a socialist system for ethnic groups to be given specific roles within the political and the productive system and for them consequently to have interests to defend.

There are, however, certainly some types of situation which the kind of class theory which I have been suggesting does not cover. It is obviously the case that ethnic groups do sometimes interact on a non-competitive basis. They may simply be neighbours with differing cultural systems or they may be groups sharing a common oppression and not competing with one another. In these cases there is obviously interest in considering the processes whereby boundaries are maintained between the groups even though they interact and even though individuals may move from one group to the other. This is the sort of problem which Wallman discusses in another paper. What I have said here is not in conflict with her work. I would simply make the point that it is no more capable of providing a comprehensive theory of ethnic relations than the theory outlined here. My theory leaves out non-competitive situations. Hers leaves out the crucial elements of economic and political conflict.

Apparently more difficult to deal with is Banton's handling of the question of group boundaries in his *Racial and Ethnic Competition* (1983), for while he does not confine himself to situations of inter-group competition and bargaining it is in his discussion of these that he raises the question of boundaries. But there really is no conflict between Banton's position and that outlined here. Clearly the action of classes and estates involves boundary-maintaining processes which are an essential part of the strategy of such groups. This is quite unlike what occurs in an open status system in relation to what Cox (1948) calls social class as distinct from economic and political class.

Banton's 'rational choice' account of group competition places him on the same side as myself and against those who hold that ethnicity is primordial (Geertz 1963b). In fact one might go further and say that the theory adopted here is more open to some notion like primordiality than Banton's. What I am claiming is that whereas there is a problem for Marxist theory in showing how classes-in-themselves become classes-for-themselves, i.e. bonded, organised and collectively conscious agents, the existence of common ethnicity of a 'primordial' kind gives the class-in-itself (i.e. the group with the same relation to the means of production) an immediate basis for action. Whether or not this ethnicity can be regarded as being adequately explained as 'primordial' may be questioned. All I wish to say is that there is no reason why one should not recognise that class formation may be facilitated by the existence of ethnic identities having their origins other than in the relations of production. Class theory can and should be supplemented by the theory of ethnicity. At the same time, the theory of ethnicity should recognise that collective ethnic organisation may often lie dormant and only become activated by the emergence of shared interests.

What I am saying, in summary, is that class theory taken by itself does have considerable limitations. There may be purely ethnic situations where there is no conflict of class interest. People may be assigned to class positions on the basis of racial and ethnic markers. And, finally, the formation of classes-for-themselves may be greatly facilitated by, if it does not actually require, something like ethnic bonding. But to make these points is by no means to say that the elements which are given centrality in class theory, namely the relationship of groups to the means of production and to the control of political and legal power, are not among the most important in the theory of race and ethnic relations.

Methodological individualism and the explication of group concepts

In some of its versions (Hechter 1983) rational choice theory claims uniquely to embody the principles of methodological individualism. This, however, would appear strange in that the Weberian type of class analysis advocated here can clearly be called 'methodologically individualist'. Indeed, Popper, who popularised the term 'methodological individualism', clearly saw Weber's work as meriting this label. Methodological collectivism is characteristic of the theoretical enterprise of Durkheim and of some forms of Marxism. There is no sign of it in the sort of analysis which is suggested here.

There are, however, certain features of methodological individualism, in the sense in which that term may be used to characterise the work of Weber, which distinguish it from the economistic sort of rational choice theory which is now often advocated. Methodological individualism is *methodological*; that is to say it does not imply that all social situations can be reduced empirically to the action of masses of individuals. What it argues is that the apparently 'external' constraints of actions which confront a rational choosing actor are themselves capable of being construed as the action of other individuals. Banton, with his emphasis upon competition, is apparently fully aware of this. Other writers like Hechter seem less so.

The key notion which connects explanations on the individual level with structural explanation, however, is that of 'interest'. What Marxist and some other structural forms of explanation rightly suggest is that the realisation of actors' aims may be dependent upon their relationship to other actors organised in a particular way and to the external world. That is to say, the actors have an 'interest' in the world being organised in that way. And we may also say that, given such relationships, actors may be compelled or at least constrained to act in particular ways and that their action is not sufficiently understood simply by considering their own individual performance schedules.

With this said, however, the degree to which choices are constrained will depend upon the level of patterns of relations to social structure and the material world. In the politically important cases which we have discussed here (or at least in the white supremacy case and the case of the colonial and post-colonial plural society) the actions of individuals are very constrained indeed, at least for the oppressed groups. There may, however, be cases in much more open societies in which all individuals have some measure of choice as to whether they align their actions with those of their group or merely free-ride on the gains which it makes, as Hechter suggests. The important difference between the theory advanced here and that of Hechter is that I am suggesting that constraint of choice is the more frequent case, at least in what we call race relations situations.

Banton's theory appears to be much closer to my own in that he recognises the importance of markets in the structuring of social interaction. He does seem to me, however, to share the 'optimistic' assumptions of exchange theory under which outcomes are mutually beneficial to the parties involved. My own pessimistic assumption is that the collective bargaining of groups in the market is likely to lead, especially when those groups are racially and ethnically distinguished, to conflict on the political level. When the sanctions which individuals use against each other go beyond the threat to go to another supplier we have to move from rational choice theory to conflict theory.

Perhaps my main conclusion is that there is great value in deepening the understanding which is gained from macro-explorations through the development of systematic explication of class and group concepts on the methodologically individualist level. I would see the appropriate theory on that level however as being conflict theory, rather than rational choice theory.

Van den Berghe (1981) of course suggests that the appropriate ultimate explanation should be in terms of conflict theory but that the conflict is ultimately determined by a biological law of nepotism. I beg leave to be agnostic on this. In any case it seems to me that van den Berghe in practice, when he is creating the groups to which nepotism applies, envisages precisely the kind of patterning of political and economic interests which is suggested here.

What is perhaps most surprising when one considers the relation of a class theory of racial and ethnic conflict to other theories outlined here is that they are very often complementary. Class theory is useful – perhaps it is the most centrally useful theory – in approaching major problems of race and ethnic relations. There is no reason, however, why it should not take its place within a more systematic theory.

NOTE

1 Although the term 'Bantu' has become discredited politically because it was used in a racist way, its use to distinguish those of South Africa's people who speak Bantu languages remains not only convenient but also correct.

4

Varieties of Marxist conceptions of 'race', class and the state: a critical analysis

JOHN SOLOMOS

1. Introduction

It is a commonplace that the reliance of Marxist theory on the pivotal concepts of mode of production and class, along with the preoccupation with general models of historical development, has precluded Marxists from making a significant contribution to the study of racial and ethnic divisions within capitalist society.[1] The relative absence of a substantive discussion of these questions within the texts of classical Marxism seems to add weight to the assertion made by Frank Parkin that, as a form of social analysis, Marxism is incapable of dealing with such divisions short of subsuming them under more general social relations (production- or class-based) or treating them as a kind of superstructural phenomenon (Parkin 1979a and b).

This commonplace assertion seems to be contradicted, however, by the increased interest among a number of Marxist theorists in clarifying the complex forms of non-class (even if class-related) forms of division and oppression that are characteristic of late capitalist societies, including racial and ethnic divisions, but also gender, national, regional, religious and locality-based divisions.[2] Indeed, over the last decade in particular, a wide variety of Marxist conceptualisations of race, class and the state have emerged, including a substantial body of theoretical studies which attempt to develop a more precise and systematic understanding of racism in capitalist society as rooted in the dominant social relations and power structures (Genovese 1971, Nikolinakos 1973, Hall 1977, 1980b, Gabriel and Ben-Tovim 1978, Sivanandan 1982, Miles 1982, Centre for Contemporary Cultural Studies 1982, Brittan and Maynard 1984). In addition a number of Marxist-inspired historical and empirical studies of specific forms of racist structures in different societies have been published over the years, including the USA (Reich

1981, Fox-Genovese and Genovese 1983, Marable 1984) and South Africa (Wolpe 1980, Burawoy 1981).

The existence of these theoretical and empirical studies does not, of course, mean that the criticisms of writers such as Frank Parkin can be dismissed. Many of the problems which they highlight within Marxist discourse, especially economic determinism and theoretical abstraction, are still to be found in much of the mainstream of Marxism, which continues to treat racism as little more than an irritant to the smoother structures of historical materialism (see Ben-Tovim *et al.* in this volume for more discussion of this point). Racism remains an inadequately theorised concept within the terms of both sociological and Marxist theory. The remainder of this paper will, first, discuss some of the most important attempts to develop a critical understanding of the inter-relationship between race, class and the state in contemporary capitalism. Second, I shall attempt to develop an alternative framework for analysing racism which builds upon the strengths of recent contributions, particularly in relation to the need to ground a theory of racism in the broader framework of political economy. The paper concludes with a few remarks about the implications of Marxist analyses of racism and the state for political practice, particularly in relation to anti-racist struggles.

2. Origins and foundations

It will be helpful to clear away some preliminary points before proceeding. Although this paper addresses the question of a Marxist analysis of 'race' and racism in capitalist society, it would be quite mistaken to think of contemporary Marxism either as unified or as composed of a unified set of dogmas. This is an assumption that is too often made in the race relations literature, on the grounds that the substantial difference between a Marxist approach to *race* and other approaches lies in the reliance by Marxists on an economic determinist explanation for the emergence and reproduction of racism. Consider the following remarks from Frank Parkin's critique of Marxism and its analysis of class:

> On current evidence one could be forgiven for concluding that
> the preferred Marxist response to the fact of racial or
> communal strife is to ignore it. Not one of the various
> reformulations of class theory ... makes any serious attempt
> to consider how the division between blacks and whites,
> Catholics and Protestants, Flemings and Walloons,
> Francophones and Anglophones, or between indigenous and
> immigrant workers affects their general analysis. It is

especially difficult to see what kind of explanation could in any
case be expected from those formulations which draw heavily
upon the conceptual storehouse of political economy. Notions
such as the mode of production make their claims to
explanatory power precisely on the grounds of their
indifference to the nature of the human material whose
activities they determine. To introduce questions such as the
ethnic composition of the workplace is to clutter up the
analysis by laying stress upon the quality of *social actors*, a
conception diametrically opposed to the notion of human
agents as *träger* or 'embodiments' of systemic forces. (Parkin
1979b, p. 625)

As a statement in support of the thesis that it is impossible to combine a
Marxist analytic framework with a serious analysis of racial and/or ethnic
divisions this passage suffers from several problems. First, it takes only a
limited degree of knowledge about recent Marxist debates to see that
Parkin's main assertion, that the explanatory power of the concept of
mode of production depends on an indifference to the role of social
actors, is contradicted by the vast body of literature (on class, the state,
the labour process and political economy) which has attempted to argue
the centrality of human agency to any rounded Marxist explanatory
model.[3] More than this, the thrust of recent Marxist writings on class and
the state has been informed by the need to take on board the insights
derived from feminism, and this has further broadened the parameters of
what Parkin calls the 'conceptual storehouse of political economy'
(Sargent 1981, Gilroy 1982).

More fundamentally, perhaps, there is little to support Parkin's
assertion that 'the preferred Marxist response to the fact of racial or
communal strife is to ignore it'. On the contrary, a sizeable and growing
body of theory and research in the area of race and ethnic relations is
based on or draws some inspiration from Marxism. While it may be true
that much of the recent debate about class and the state does not say
much that is of direct relevance to the question of race, it is strictly
speaking not the case that recent Marxist writings ignore divisions within
classes or the role of non-class political organisation. The substance of
the work of authors such as Nicos Poulantzas, Manuel Castells,
Guglielmo Carchedi and Erik Olin Wright recognises the reality of such
divisions and the role that they play in processes of class formation and in
political struggles.[4] What is even more clear from these debates is that it
is quite mistaken to see Marxism as a monolithic set of assertions or to
assimilate it wholesale into some notion of economic determinism or

class reductionism. Rather, it is best viewed today as consisting of a spectrum of competing schools of thought ranging from economic determinism to more sophisticated explanatory models which fully recognise the centrality of human agency and collective action (Wright 1980).

This view of Marxism as heterogeneous contradicts the oft-stated assertion (which Parkin repeats) that the Marxist approach to racial and ethnic divisions can be identified according to the basic principles of reducing 'race' to class, and the explanation of the origins of racism as coterminous with the rise of capitalism. Such a view of the Marxist contribution to the study of racism is seemingly supported by the close association between the class/race model developed by Oliver C. Cox in his study of *Caste, Class and Race* (first published in 1948) and some more contemporary contributions to the analysis of racism (Sivanandan 1982). Although this is not the place to develop a critical discussion of Cox's analysis of class and 'race', it is important to point out that his work is by no means seen by contemporary Marxists as an adequate analysis of the complex historical determinants of racism or of the relationship between racism and capitalist social relations (see e.g. Gabriel and Ben-Tovim 1978, Miles 1980). Moreover, as Eugene Genovese (1971) has pointed out, Cox's work was very much the product of his time, in that he was familiar with a Marxism that had not yet been influenced by the work of Gramsci and other 'Western' Marxists or by the experience of racial conflict that took place during the 1960s.

If Parkin's dismissive attitude towards Marxism does not hold on the grounds which he suggests, this is not to say that a coherent and fully fledged analysis of racism has been produced from a Marxist perspective. Far from it. Cox's study, though not self-consciously written as a Marxist analysis, is still widely considered as *the* Marxist analysis of this question (see Banton, this volume), largely because it is the most substantive study which attempts to utilise concepts such as class and exploitation in order to explain the role of 'race' and racism in capitalist societies. Other studies written from a Marxist perspective have tended to limit their analysis to abstract theoretical exegesis, or to analyse the experience of one particular society in isolation. Cox's attempt to combine theory with a comparative analysis of racism thus stands out as a unique contribution, whose status as a classic sociological analysis is acknowledged by even his most severe critics.

There can be no question here of attempting critically to analyse the contribution of Cox to a Marxist analysis of racial and ethnic divisions, which is a theme in any case of other papers in this volume and of a growing debate within Marxist circles (Gabriel and Ben-Tovim 1978,

Miles 1980, 1982). It needs to be pointed out, however, that the model of Marxism with which Cox was familiar was based on the conceptual baggage of 'base' and 'superstructure' and an instrumental view of the state as the agent of the capitalist class (Cox 1948, p. 321). This adherence to such views runs counter to the main tendency of contemporary Marxist analysis, which in fact has evolved a number of competing schools of thought, and whose central concern is to question the tenability of the classical base–superstructure model as a conceptual framework (P. Anderson 1983). In relation to the question of class, for example, Adam Przeworski has pointed out that the traditional separation between the economic definition of classes and the political and ideological determinants of class-formation is in fact quite misleading when it comes to the concrete analysis of the contradictions that arise either within or between social classes. Przeworski argues, and here he expresses a view shared by most neo-Marxist writers, that it is not possible to separate the 'objective' analysis of class from the totality of economic, ideological and political relations which organise, disorganise and reorganise social classes as a result of class struggles and historical transformations (Przeworski 1977; but see also Wright 1980).

It would be quite mistaken, therefore, to see recent Marxist writings on the question of race and class as deriving from Cox as such. In some cases Cox's work does form one starting point, but only one among many. It can be argued that equally important influences on recent Marxist writings on 'race' are the works of neo-Marxist writers such as Louis Althusser and Nicos Poulantzas, the criticisms levelled at economistic Marxism by such writers as John Rex and Edna Bonacich, and the works of feminist writers. All of these influences are evident in the approaches discussed below, although this does not mean that they do not also rely on the conceptual apparatus of classical Marxism and to some extent on the pioneering work of Cox and others (Gabriel and Ben-Tovim 1978). The argument developed in this paper, therefore, will be that there is not one approach to the question of race and class from within the Marxist tradition but rather several approaches. The equation of a Marxist approach with the work of Cox, or with a simple form of economic and class reductionism, is both mistaken and woefully out of date in the context of recent debates about the nature of the state, class and racism. In order to substantiate this point I would like to move on to a critical analysis of three of the most important Marxist approaches to race, class and the state.

3. Neo-Marxist approaches to 'race', class and the state

Within the broad spectrum of recent Marxist or Marxisant approaches to 'race', class and the state it is possible to detect a wide variety of theoretical models, historical analyses and political arguments. Even though using similar theoretical reference points, either to classic texts by Marx and Engels or to the works of more contemporary Marxist thinkers such as Nicos Poulantzas, a number of fairly distinct schools of thought have emerged over the last decade. Each of these schools lays a claim to the work of Marx, either as a source of inspiration or more directly as a general theoretical framework within which any analysis of racism in capitalist society must be located. The complexity of recent debates cannot be adequately analysed within the limits of this paper, but for heuristic purposes I shall discuss three important models that constitute various dimensions of recent Marxist debates on 'race', class and the state: the relative autonomy model, the autonomy model and the migrant labour model.[5] There can be no question here of attempting a general survey of all the literature that could be classified as falling into these models. Rather the limited objective of this paper is to raise some theoretical problems concerning all three approaches and to make some suggestions for an alternative formulation.

(a) Relative autonomy model

Within the last decade, one of the most important and influential redefinitions of the Marxist analysis of 'race' and racism has been developed by a number of studies originating from the Birmingham Centre for Contemporary Cultural Studies (CCCS).[6] The works which have emanated from CCCS over this period are heterogeneous in approach, substantive issues and political inclination but are unified through a common concern with developing an analysis of racism which fully accepts its relative autonomy from class-based social relations and its historical specificity in relation to the laws of motion of capitalist development. Although it would be unwise to label this body of work as a 'school' of thought with a coherent and fully worked out framework of analysis, there does seem to be some justification in Brittan and Maynard's view (1984) that there is a distinct CCCS approach to such issues as racism, sexism and more generally intra-class divisions. Moreover, the theoretical and political controversy which surrounded the publication of *The Empire Strikes Back* in 1982 has resulted in a number of critical articles which question both the theoretical and the political linkages between recent CCCS texts and Marxism (Young 1983, Miles 1984a).

The origins of the Centre's concern with racism can be dated back to the early 1970s, when a number of research students and its then Director, Stuart Hall, became involved in a project which was concerned with explaining the development of 'moral panics' about the involvement of young blacks in a specific form of street crime, namely mugging.[7] The context of this study was the environment of cities such as Birmingham, where sizeable black communities had grown up and established their own specific community, cultural and political practices. This in turn led to the development of ideological and political responses from within local communities, from the local state and its agencies and from the institutions of the central state. The research carried out by the CCCS team, which was eventually published in 1978 as *Policing the Crisis* (Hall *et al.* 1978), took as its central concerns the processes by which 'race' came to be defined as a 'social problem' and the construction of 'race' as a political issue which required state intervention from both the central and the local state. There is no space here to discuss the rich and complex analysis which Hall and his associates developed of this period or the subsequent discussion of these issues by other authors.[8] Suffice it to say that the concrete historical analysis on which *Policing the Crisis* is based provided a materialist basis for what has subsequently become known as the 'CCCS approach' to 'race' and class and has continued to exert a deep influence on the work of younger researchers at the Centre. This is best exemplified by the jointly produced volume of the CCCS Race and Politics Group, *The Empire Strikes Back: Race and Racism in 70s Britain* (1982).

Before moving on to discuss the more recent work of the Centre, however, it is important to understand the core concepts developed by Stuart Hall and his colleagues in the earlier phase. A purchase on the distinctiveness of this approach can be gained through Hall's programmatic statement of his position in a paper significantly titled 'Race, Articulation and Societies Structured in Dominance' (1980b), which had been widely read and discussed even before it was published. Hall's starting point is clear enough, in that he attempts to develop an analytic framework which locates racism in historically specific social relations while allowing for a degree of autonomy of the 'racial aspects' of society. He makes this clear when he argues that:

> There is as yet no adequate theory of racism which is capable of dealing with both the economic and the structural features of such societies, while at the same time giving a historically concrete and sociologically specific account of distinctive racial aspects. (Hall, 1980b, p. 336)

From this starting point he engages in a dialogue with a number of sociological analyses of 'race', particularly the work of John Rex, and with the analyses of class ideology and the state which developed under the influence of Althusserian Marxism. At the core of this dialogue are two fundamentally important questions. The most important of these focuses on the relationship between racism and the structural features of capitalist society and asks 'How does racism function within capitalist social relations and how is it produced/reproduced?' The second question points to a related but more concrete set of concerns about how racism is actually constituted in specific societies or institutions, asking 'How does racism influence the ways in which class, political, gender and other social relationships are actually experienced?' While the concerns of Hall and his associates in *Policing the Crisis* are somewhat different from those of the authors of *The Empire Strikes Back*, for example in relation to the analysis of black youth cultures and the role of the state, they generally agree on the importance of locating the relative autonomy of racism at a macro-level and on the centrality of racism in relations of power and domination in post-war Britain (Hall 1980a, CCCS 1982, chapters 1 and 8).

Hall's reconceptualisation of racism hinges upon a reappraisal both of Marxist concepts and of some aspects of the work of sociologists of 'race'. In relation to the first he is particularly concerned to draw out the implications of the reconceptualisation of ideology and the state in contemporary Marxism for the analysis of racism. The bulk of his main theoretical paper on the subject begins by supporting John Rex's critique of reductionist Marxist analyses of racism, particularly in relation to South Africa, but then goes on to argue that the emergence of a critical theoretical paradigm within Marxism allows for a more adequate analysis of racism within the context of Marxist theoretical and historical research. Drawing upon studies of imperialism, dependency theory, the state and ideology, he argues:

> A new theoretical paradigm [has emerged], which takes its fundamental orientation from the problematic of Marx's, but which seeks, by various theoretical means, to overcome certain of the limitations – economism, reductionism, 'a priorism', a lack of historical specificity – which beset certain traditional appropriations of Marxism, which still disfigure the contributions to this field by otherwise distinguished writers, and which have left Marxism vulnerable and exposed to effective criticism by many different variants of economic monism and sociological pluralism. (Hall 1980b, p. 336)

While conceding the criticisms made by Rex (1973, 1983c) and others of a simplistic 'Marxist' analysis of racism, Hall wants also to argue that a more critical and multi-dimensional materialist analysis of the phenomenon is possible.

In establishing this possibility he himself suggests three principles as the starting point for a critical Marxist analysis of racism. First, he rejects the idea that racism is a general feature of all human societies, arguing that what actually exist are *historically specific racisms*. Though there may be features common to all racially structured societies, it is necessary to understand what produces these features in each specific historical situation before one can develop a comparative analysis of racism. The second principle is that, although racism cannot be reduced to other social relations, one cannot explain racism in abstraction from them. Racism has a *relative autonomy* from other relations, whether they be economic, political or ideological. This *relative autonomy* means that there is no one-way correspondence between racism and specific economic or other forms of social relations. Third, Hall criticises a dichotomous view of 'race' and 'class', arguing that in a 'racially structured' society it is impossible to understand them through discrete modes of analysis. 'Race' has a concrete impact on the class consciousness and organisation of all classes and class factions. But 'class' in turn has a reciprocal relationship with 'race', and it is the articulation between the two which is crucial, not their separateness (Hall 1980b, pp. 336–42).

Hall's own writings on this subject have been fairly limited and programmatic so far, and have moved little beyond the three principles suggested above. They have been influential, however, in the development of subsequent Marxist studies of racism, partly through the popularised and revised form of his ideas which can be found in *The Empire Strikes Back*, produced collectively by the Race and Politics Group of CCCS in 1982. Although written at a distance from some of the concerns to be found in the Centre's earlier work on 'race' and from Hall's theoretical sources, this volume took as its starting point a theme already made familiar by Hall and his colleagues, namely that the political construction of 'race' as a problem in contemporary Britain represents an integral aspect of how the British state is attempting to manage the current 'organic crisis of British capitalism' (CCCS 1982, chapters 1 and 8). Drawing particularly upon the work of a number of authors who have attempted to reconceptualise the role of the state in relation to racism (e.g. Carchedi, Sivanandan, and Castells), the authors of this work attempt to rework Hall's earlier studies and to provide a more concrete analysis of the relation of 'race' to British decline during the 1970s.

The Empire Strikes Back can be said to mark a change from the previous works of the Centre on 'race' in at least three senses. First, it argues that previous sociological and Marxist accounts of race relations represent a body of work which has done little to further our knowledge of racism and which can even be seen as reproducing ethnocentric or common-sense views of 'race' (CCCS 1982, chapters 2 and 8). This mode of critique is in fact quite different from Hall's critical, but by no means unsympathetic, treatment of the works of 'sociologists of race' and their relationship to Marxism. In addition it links up with a more fundamental line of critique emanating from authors such as Cedric Robinson (1983), who sees the central concepts of Marxism as 'Eurocentric' and fairly limited in their applicability to 'racially structured' societies.

The second divergence relates to the greater emphasis placed on the role of 'state racism', or the role of state activity in reproducing racism. While elements of this analysis can be traced back to the work of Hall and his associates (Hall *et al.* 1978), there is a sharper focus in *The Empire Strikes Back* on the concrete ways in which the state intervened to manage 'race' throughout the 1970s, in ways which were detrimental to the interests of black communities. This is achieved at a general level through an analysis of the growth of 'authoritarian statism' and 'popular racism' within the context of deep-seated crisis:

> The parallel growth of repressive state structures and new racisms has to be located in a non-reductionist manner, within the dynamics of both the international crisis of the capitalist world economy, and the deep-seated structural crisis of the British social formation. (CCCS 1982, p. 9)

It is also achieved through an emphasis on the ways in which racism structures different areas of social life, notably education, policing, youth policy and also the position of black women in the labour market (Solomos *et al.* 1982).

This in turn links up to a third area, namely the attempt to reconceptualise the complex relationship between 'class' and 'race'. In the concluding chapter of the book, Paul Gilroy mounts a sustained critique of both Marxist and sociological analysis of 'race' for failing to deal adequately with the autonomy of 'race' from 'class'. In so doing he questions the view of the working class as a continuous historical subject, particularly since such a view cannot deal adequately with the ways in which blacks can constitute themselves as an autonomous social force in politics or with the existence of 'racially demarcated class factions' (Gilroy 1982, p. 284). The theoretical basis of this critique can be traced back to the work of Hall, although it also draws some of its inspiration from previous studies at the Centre of working-class culture (Hall *et al.* 1980) and from the more recent debates about class theory within Marxism (see e.g. Przeworski 1977). This is exemplified by the combination in Gilroy's work of a model of determination which gives *class struggle* as opposed to *class structure* a degree of determinacy, and a view of black workers as racially structured. The difficulties which this position entails are made explicit when Gilroy argues:

> The class character of black struggles is not a result of the fact that blacks are predominantly proletarian, though this is true. It is established in the fact that their struggles for civil rights, freedom from state harassment, or as waged workers, are instances of the process by which the working class is constituted politically, organised in politics. (Gilroy 1982, p. 302)

Referring specifically to those excluded from employment, particularly the young black unemployed, he posits that there may be various types of struggles which mobilise them politically, not all of which bear a direct relationship to 'objective' conditions. It follows that 'the privileged place of economic classes in the Marxist theory of history is not to be equated with an a priori assertion of their political primacy in every historical moment' (Gilroy 1982, p. 303).

It is also of some relevance to note, in relation to the above point, that *The Empire Strikes Back* includes some of the most sustained treatments of the place of gender in the dialectic of 'race' and class (see the chapters by Hazel Carby and Pratibha Parmar). Along with the work of Annie Phizacklea on migrant women (Phizacklea 1983), it constitutes an isolated attempt in this field seriously to analyse the role of gender in the articulation of racist ideologies.

Perhaps the most notable absence from the Centre's work on racism is a serious analysis of the political economy of racism. Apart from a rudimentary and limited study by Green (1979), and some minor references in both *Policing the Crisis* and *The Empire Strikes Back*, this remains a serious gap in the Centre's work. It becomes particularly critical in the context of the oft-repeated criticisms made of mainstream sociological studies of 'race' for not taking account of the broad economic and social determinants of racism. The emphasis on the relative autonomy of racism seems to have led to a neglect of the economic context of racial structuration, or at the least to a de-emphasis on the role played by the 'economic' in the narrow sense. This is a point that will be discussed later, particularly in relation to the migrant labour model.

There are a number of other aspects of the Centre's work on racism which can be fruitfully discussed (see Freedman 1983–4). Here I have tried to highlight the broad contours of the contribution it has made to a Marxist analysis of racism and to mention some of the ambiguities and tensions that arise. Before taking up the problems to which this model gives rise, it is necessary to outline the other two models.

(b) Autonomy model

Recently some Marxist theorists have argued that there is a need to go beyond the notion that racism is a 'relatively autonomous' social phenomenon and to break more definitely from the economic and class-reductionist elements in Marxist theory. Thus a major theme in the influential writings of John Gabriel and Gideon Ben-Tovim,[9] who have developed a theoretical perspective which specifically emphasises this point, is that the bulk of neo-Marxist theory on racism is still based on implicit, if not explicit, economic and class-reductionist assumptions. They are particularly critical of the 'relative autonomy' model, which they see as defective from both a theoretical and a political perspective. From a theoretical angle they see the dichotomy between capitalist social relations and 'race' as merely another way of reproducing a more sophisticated form of class-reductionism, under the guise of the nebulous concept of relative autonomy. This in turn is seen as supporting a deterministic analysis of political struggles against racism and thus allowing little room for anti-racist political strategies to be effective rather than symbolic (Gabriel and Ben-Tovim 1979, Ben-Tovim *et al.* 1981a).

Contrary to the bulk of recent Marxist writings on racism, which take capitalist social relations and class relations as a starting point, Gabriel and Ben-Tovim argue that racism can best be understood as the product of contemporary and historical struggles which are by no means reducible to wider sets of economic or social relations. This leads them to take as their starting point the various struggles, local and national, political and ideological, which go into the social construction of 'race' in specific situations (Gabriel and Ben-Tovim 1978). Yet it would be too simplistic to see their position as one which holds that racism is not in some way related to wider social relations. A number of their papers on anti-racist struggles do in fact show how wider structural constraints do play a role in limiting the effectiveness of such struggles (e.g. Ben-Tovim *et al.* 1981a). What they do argue, however, is that there is no way of determining what these limits are, outside of specific struggles and historical situations.

The consequences of this position are that there is no *a priori* reason to see racism as the product of class or economic relations, and that the only way to overcome the traditional dilemma in relation to the 'base/superstructure' model is to eschew any attempt to analyse racism outside of its own ideological conditions of existence (Gabriel and Ben-Tovim 1978). In opposition to the preoccupation of the CCCS studies with the linkages between 'race' and class, and more concretely with the articulation between capitalist crisis and the development of racism, Gabriel and Ben-Tovim suggest that the starting point of a Marxist analysis should be the ideological and political practices which work autonomously to produce racism. Rejecting all forms of reductionism they argue that:

> Racism has its own autonomous formation, its own contradictory determinations, its own complex mode of theoretical and ideological production, as well as its repercussions for the class struggle at the levels of the economy and the state. (Gabriel and Ben-Tovim 1978, p. 146)

In this view, the ideological level is primary, since it is only after the ideological production of racist ideologies that they intervene at the level of the economy and of political practice. In effect, Gabriel and Ben-Tovim attempt to push beyond the constraints of the relative autonomy model by questioning the viability of any attempt to situate 'race' in terms of class. The 'autonomy' of racism lies precisely in its irreducibility to any other set of social relations, since any attempt to account for racism in terms of external relations entails a reductionist argument (Ben-Tovim *et al.*, this volume).

Moving a step beyond this formal critique of reductionist Marxism, supporters of the autonomy model would also argue that their analysis provides a more relevant guide to the complex political realities of racist politics and anti-racist struggles (Ben-Tovim *et al.* 1981a). Starting from the position that the state as an institution is not monolithic but the site of constant struggles, compromises and administrative decisions, they argue that the most important task of research on 'race' is to highlight the political and ideological context in which anti-racist struggles occur. Referring to the need for struggles to change institutionalised racism as a 'long march through the institutions', with the overall objective of bringing about 'positive and democratically based political and policy changes to secure the elimination of racial discrimination and disadvantage' (p. 178), they question the usefulness of the notion of relative autonomy when confronted with the complexity of political struggles against racism.

This last point is important in understanding the coherence of the analysis developed by Gabriel and Ben-Tovim, since they self-consciously see their theoretical work as linking up with political practice. There is no space here to discuss the detailed and rich analysis they have made of the political context of anti-racist struggles in Liverpool and Wolverhampton. Suffice it to say that the development of their approach, from the early formal critique of traditional Marxist views of 'race' and class to their more recent preoccupation with the local politics and racism, reflects their actual political involvement in anti-racist politics.

Another way of making this point is that although they would agree with Hall that 'race' and 'class' form part of a complex dialectical relation in contemporary capitalism, they would question the usefulness of interpreting this relationship in terms of the 'relative autonomy' of racism. Ultimately they see a contradiction in arguing that racist ideologies have a certain autonomy from material relations, while also holding on to the principle that it is these relations which determine 'in the last instance' the degree of autonomy. More fundamentally, they seem to be arguing that even the work of Hall and his associates, with its explicit disavowal of determinism, supports an implicit base/superstructure model.

Given their insistence on the irreducibility of 'race' to class, and the political conclusions they draw from this position, it may not be surprising that Gabriel and Ben-Tovim do not spend much time discussing the degree of determinancy which state power and class relations have in relation to racial structuration. Their version of the 'extended' as opposed to the 'monolithic' state does have a rather pluralistic ring about it, at least as regards their discussion of the role of race relations legislation and the role of the local state. Their dual strategy of attrition against racism, both within and outside the state apparatuses, is predicated upon the premise of the primacy of struggle over all other levels of determinancy (Ben-Tovim *et al.* 1981a, and Ben-Tovim *et al.*, this volume). But this seems to push the agency versus structure argument in the direction of a voluntarist theory of political change, and one which ignores the centrality of the distinction between the appearance and the reality of political struggles (Connolly 1981). Moreover, there seems to be a heavy emphasis in their approach on the importance of policy-oriented research as a tool for anti-racist struggles. The lack of policy-relevance is one of the weaknesses they highlight in other Marxist approaches in this field.

The ambiguities of the autonomy model relate as much to political issues as to straightforward theoretical questions. The work of Gabriel and Ben-Tovim can also be read, however, as a theoretical innovation in the sense that it breaks quite fundamentally with the main concern of other Marxists working in this field, namely the search for a non-reductionist and historically specific analysis of racism. For Gabriel and Ben-Tovim the search for a more plausible model of determination leads into a cul-de-sac, and they have responded by rejecting all forms of determination outside of struggle.

(c) Migrant labour model

The third explanatory model which has been used by recent Marxist writers, especially by Robert Miles and Annie Phizacklea,[10] takes a radically different starting point from the other two approaches outlined above. Arguing on the basis of a critical reinterpretation of classical and neo-Marxist theories of class, the state and ideology, Miles and Phizacklea construct a theoretical model of racism which prioritises the 'political economy of migrant labour' as opposed to what they call the 'race relations problematic' (Miles 1980, 1982, Phizacklea and Miles 1980, Phizacklea 1984). The substance of the difference between this approach and the previous two is that throughout their work Miles and Phizacklea seek to prioritise the role that class and production relations play in the reproduction of racism. This position has recently been clearly stated by Phizacklea, who argues:

> If social scientists continue to use the term 'race' . . . because people *act* as though 'race' exists, then they are guilty of conferring analytical status on what is nothing more than an ideological construction. Our object of analysis cannot be 'race in itself', but the development of racism as an ideology within specific historical and material contexts. (Phizacklea 1984, p. 200)

This quotation is from an article which bears the title 'A Sociology of Migration or "Race Relations"?'. In a similar vein Miles argues that the work of some Marxists (notably that of Sivanandan and the authors of *The Empire Strikes Back*) shares a common terrain with the 'race relations' problematic of John Rex, because they both 'attribute the ideological notion of "race" with a descriptive and explanatory importance' (Miles, 1984a, p. 218).

Central to this position is the notion that racism can only be understood by analysing it in relation to the basic structural features of capitalism. This is linked to a related point, which has been repeatedly made by Miles and Phizacklea, in relation both to the sociology of race relations and to other Marxist studies of racism. Their work carefully eschews any reference to 'race' except in inverted commas, because they see 'race' as itself an ideological category which requires explanation and which therefore cannot be used for either analytical or explanatory purposes (Miles 1982, 1984a, Phizacklea 1984). The reason for their insistence on the distinction between 'race' and racism becomes clear through their reliance on what they call 'the process of racialisation' or 'racial categorisation' (Miles 1982, pp. 153–67, Phizacklea 1984). Broadly speaking, this concept posits that 'race' is a social construction which attributes meanings to certain patterns of phenotypical variation. This process of attributing meaning to 'race' results in a reification of real social relations into ideological categories and leads to the common-sense acceptance that 'race' is an objective determinant of the behaviour of black workers or other racially defined social categories. As evidence of this confusion Miles and Phizacklea cite the example of how black workers are not analysed in terms of the social relations of production but as a 'race apart' (Phizacklea and Miles 1980, Miles 1982), the ways in which politicians and governments have utilised the category of 'race' in order to obfuscate the reality of racism (Miles and Phizacklea 1984), and at a more concrete level the way in which the use of the idea of 'race' to interpret the 1958 riots deflected attention away from the actions of racists against blacks and from the role of the state (Miles 1984b). Precisely because they conceptualise 'race' as an ideological reification, and one which can do little to challenge common-sense images of 'race', they suggest two main programmatic conclusions: (a) that 'race' cannot be the object of analysis in itself, since it is a social construction which requires explanation; (b) that the object of analysis should be the process of 'racialisation' or 'racial categorisation', which takes place within the context of specific economic, political and ideological relations.

In rejecting the descriptive or analytical value of 'race' as a concept Miles and Phizacklea insist on the importance of racism, and the discriminatory practices which it produces, as the crucial factor in the formation of what they call a racialised fraction of the working class, and of other classes (Phizacklea and Miles 1980, Miles 1984a, pp. 229–30). This has been interpreted as a way of reiterating the role of class determination as opposed to 'race', or the use of an economistic version of Marxism to analyse the position of black workers in Britain (Gilroy 1982). In addition, it has been argued that the emphasis that Miles and Phizacklea put on 'class' as opposed to 'race' serves to underplay the role that black struggles play in unifying people who ostensibly occupy different class positions (Parmar 1982).

In rejecting these criticisms Miles has recently attempted to clarify the starting point of his work, and its relationship to the work of CCCS and Gabriel and Ben-Tovim (Miles 1984a). Rejecting the view that his work, along with that of Annie Phizacklea, asserts the primacy of class over 'race', he goes on to argue that his model is grounded in the notion that internal and external class relations are shaped by a complex totality of economic, political and ideological processes. As regards the role of racism in this complex totality he develops a definition of racialisation which differentiates between the economic and the political/ideological determinants. Miles explains:

> The 'race'/class dichotomy is a false construction.
> Alternatively, I suggest that the reproduction of class relations
> involves the determination of internal and external class
> boundaries by economic, political and ideological processes.
> One of the central political and ideological processes in
> contemporary capitalist societies is the process of racialisation
> ... but this cannot, in itself, over-ride the effects of the
> relations of production. Hence, the totality of 'black' people in
> Britain cannot be adequately analysed as a 'race' outside or in
> opposition to class relations. Rather, the process by which
> they are racialised, and react to that racialisation (both of
> which are political and ideological processes), always occurs in
> a particular historical and structural context, one in which the
> social relations of production provide the necessary and initial
> framework within which racism has its effects. The outcome
> may be the formation of racialised class fractions. (Miles
> 1984a, p. 233)

What is important about this redefinition is that it (1) locates racism as a process of ideological construction, and (2) prioritises the 'effects' of the relations of production. The substantial difference between the migrant labour model and the two previous models lies precisely in the emphasis it places on the ways in which migrant labour is included or excluded in terms of the relations of production.

In the later works associated with this approach the model of 'racialisation' gains an added dimension through comparative references to the experience of migrant labour in other advanced capitalist societies. This is seen as providing added proof as to the limited nature of the race relations approach (Phizacklea 1984). Another area in which Miles and Phizacklea have shown a growing interest is the role of political discourse and ideologies, particularly in relation to the construction of 'immigration' and 'race relations' as a political problem (Miles and Phizacklea 1984).

Miles's critique of the approach encapsulated in *The Empire Strikes Back* is a succinct statement of this difference of approach. Distinguishing between the liberal and the radical sociology of 'race' relations, he identifies the work of John Rex as representing the former and the work of CCCS (1982) as representing the latter. He does so on the ground that both liberal and radical sociologists of 'race' share the same terrain, i.e. they both hold that 'race' is a real political phenomenon with its own effects and determinate relationships, but they are distinguished by the latter's attachment to Marxism (Miles 1984a, p. 218). As a starting point, therefore, Miles argues that while all variants of the sociology of 'race' accept the equivalence of class and 'race' as analytic concepts, the Marxist position should be that production relations provide the historical and structural context within which racialisation occurs. Although he accepts that in some respects the CCCS authors question the validity of 'race' as an analytic concept, he makes the point that this critique is undermined by their emphasis on the importance of cultural as opposed to production relations. It is this 'silence on production relations' that leads the CCCS authors, according to Miles, to ignore the material and political basis of racism within the working class (Miles 1984a, pp. 228–30).

Both of these issues are of some significance, since they highlight a point often repeated by Miles and Phizacklea in their empirical research, namely that blacks are not a 'race' apart which has to be related to class but 'persons whose forms of political struggle can be understood in terms of racialisation within a particular set of production (class) relations' (Miles 1984a, p. 230). At any particular time racism can have an autonomous impact, but its effects will be limited by the wider sets of capitalist social relations.

The migrant labour model diverges drastically from the work of Gabriel and Ben-Tovim, although perhaps less so from the work of Hall or the authors of *The Empire Strikes Back*. Although it is clearly arguing against a simple reductionism, to the economic or other levels, it also consciously avoids the 'silence on production relations' which it sees as characteristic of the CCCS school. What is at issue in the migrant labour model is not 'race' as such but the racialisation of a specific migrant population in the historical context of post-1945 Britain.

4. A critique and an alternative framework

As argued above, the basic problem confronting any Marxist (and perhaps non-Marxist) account of the complex relations between 'race', class and the state is to be found in the very nature of 'racism' in contemporary capitalist societies. From the brief survey of the competing approaches to this question in neo-Marxist discourse it should be clear that there are at least two problems which seem to defy resolution. First, the question of the 'relative autonomy' or 'autonomy' of racial and ethnic categorisations from economic and class determination. Second, the role of the state and the political institutions of capital societies in the reproduction of racism, including the complex role of state intervention in many countries to control immigration, to manage 'race relations' and, more broadly, to 'integrate' racial and ethnic groupings into the 'wider society'. Finally, it must be remembered that few Marxist writers have ventured beyond theoretical and macro-level analysis, resulting in a mode of analysis that points to contradictions and struggle but says little about the concrete historical and contemporary experience of racism at the level of everyday life and human agency.[11] This has meant a notable failure to push Marxist analysis beyond the theoretical understanding of racism towards the practical understanding of how to overcome it, a point noted elsewhere in this volume of Ben-Tovim and his co-authors.

Before venturing into a discussion of these implications, however, I want to reiterate that it is far too simplistic to see Marxism as essentially a determinist theory of social development, whether from an economic or a class perspective. Given the wide currency which is still given to such a view of Marxism within the race relations literature (see e.g. Jeffcoate 1984), and the tendency to search for an essentialist theory of racism in some Marxist writings, it may be as well to note that numerous schools of thought within Marxism have been established precisely in opposition to a determinist interpretation of Marxist theory. Many of the most challenging Marxist studies of the state, ideology, social class and specific historical events over the last two decades have attempted to develop an analytic framework and empirical analyses which question deterministic models of politics and society (Wright 1980, Anderson 1983, Jessop 1982, 1983). Moreover, there is by now a sizeable body of empirical and historical studies which have relied on Marxist analytic concepts in order to analyse specific aspects of advanced industrial societies (Anderson 1983, Burawoy and Skocpol 1983). Taken together these two bodies of literature bear ample witness to the vitality and complexity of neo-Marxist theory and to the futility of trying to construct an analytic framework of racism which is acceptable to all Marxists. What follows therefore are some suggestions which are meant to draw together strands of argument which were developed in the previous sections and to open up questions for debate.

Now, if the arguments developed above are accepted, one must ask what kind of theory of racism is possible within a Marxist framework if each kind of racism has to be analysed in relation to its historical and socio-political context. Bearing in mind the critical observations about the three analytic models discussed above, I want to draw briefly on a point first made by Stuart Hall and his colleagues and recently taken up by a number of other authors, namely that in post-1945 Britain:

> Race is intrinsic to the manner in which the black labouring classes are complexly constituted . . . Race enters into the way black labour, male and female, is distributed as economic

agents on the level of economic practice – and the class struggles which result from it into the way the fractions of the black labouring class are constituted as a set of political forces in the 'theatre of politics' – and the political struggle which results; and in the manner in which the class is articulated as the collective and individual 'subjects' of emergent ideologies and forms of consciousness – and the struggle over ideology, culture and consciousness which results. This gives the matter of race and racism a theoretical as well as a practical centrality to all the relations and practices which affect black labour. *The constitution of this class fraction as a class, and the class relations which inscribe it, function as race relations. The two are inseparable. Race is the modality in which class is lived. It is also the medium in which class relations are experienced.* (Hall *et al.* 1978, p. 394, emphasis added)

This reconceptualisation of the class–'race' dialectic is certainly awkward, and represents a programmatic statement rather than a fully worked-out framework of analysis. But it has the merit of focusing on racism as a specific social relation and on the need to analyse the historical conditions which make distinctions based on 'race' and ethnic origins an important issue in a specific society. In addition it serves to highlight the weakness of the accusation that Marxist accounts of the 'race'–class dialectic are necessarily deterministic. There is, however, a degree of obfuscation in the argument that 'race' and class relations are inseparable, since this tells us little about the specificity of either, or of the historical processes which produce this complex structure in dominance.[12] In the end the approach suggested by Hall, and by subsequent CCCS work, does little to show the specificity of racism, or to analyse the 'work' which racism accomplishes (Hall *et al.* 1978, p. 338). It merely suggests ways of reworking the categories of Marxist analysis in such a way as to account for the complex reality of racial categorisation in contemporary capitalism, and it does not tackle thorny problems in the definition of 'relative autonomy'. It has thus been criticised for being too abstract and ahistorical in its analysis of the role of black labour in Britain and of migrant labour more generally.

In considering this problem the work of Gabriel and Ben-Tovim suggests the most straightforward resolution. Arguing that the choice between 'determinism' and relative autonomy is a false one, they go on to reject the whole idea of a 'society structured in dominance' because they see it as introducing a base/superstructure model by the back door. By implication they argue that the central question is not the relationship between racism and the wider social totality but the conceptualisation of racism as the object of struggle in historically defined conditions (Ben-Tovim *et al.*, this volume). Another resolution is suggested by the work of Miles and Phizacklea. They reject the problematic of 'race in itself' and concentrate their analysis on the development and reproduction of racism as an ideology based on specific political, economic and ideological relations (Miles and Phizacklea 1984, Phizacklea 1984). In essence this second approach sees attempts to analyse the 'interrelationship between race and class' as based on the false premise that these two categories have the same analytical significance, while in fact racism is but one of the means which transform the positions occupied by class fractions in capitalist societies (Miles 1984a, pp. 228–9).

The work of the autonomy and migrant labour schools, like that of CCCS and Sivanandan, does indeed raise the questions which remain unclear in much of the Marxist discussion of 'race' and class. But they all do so within fairly limited parameters, and they have by no means exhausted the potential for a more rigorous formulation of the theoretical problems confronting a Marxist analysis of racism. What follows are some tentative suggestions about how to build upon and move beyond the parameters of recent debates.

It is not my intention to develop a fully fledged alternative framework for dealing with the issues raised in the previous discussion. Rather, the limited objective here is to draw out some of the implications of the criticisms made above for a critical analysis of the dialectic of 'race', class and state. I want to concentrate, particularly, on the problems which arise in trying to utilise a Marxist analytic framework for explaining racism, by outlining a conceptual model which holds that: (a) there is no problem of 'race relations' which can be thought of separately from the structural (economic, political and ideological) features of capitalist society; (b) there can be no general Marxist theory of racism, since each historical situation needs to be analysed in its own specificity; and (c) 'racial' and 'ethnic' divisions cannot be reduced to or seen as completely determined by the structural contradictions of capitalist societies.

In broad outline these three propositions are meant to establish the interconnectedness of racism with wider social relations, while allowing for a degree of autonomy and discontinuity. This in itself does not take us very far in establishing the actual nature of discontinuities in an empirical sense, and indeed this is perhaps impossible without comparative and national studies of different kinds of racism. But it seems to me to be important that the three propositions remain interlinked, because short of this it is only possible to achieve a one-dimensional analysis of racism and not the dialectical and dynamic approach which Bonacich

(1980) rightly identifies as the basic feature of Marxist approaches to 'race'.

Nevertheless, it should be clear from the above discussion that all three propositions are essentially contested among Marxists. While propositions (b) and (c) can be said to have a wide currency in one form or another, there is much dispute about (a), whether at a macro-level or through specific debates about the relationship of 'race' and class. Gabriel and Ben-Tovim would dispute the relevance of point (a) in relation to a concrete analysis of racist ideologies. The problem remains, however, that economic and social conditions do play a role in structuring racism as an ideology and as a set of practices in specific institutions. If this is accepted, and to some extent even Gabriel and Ben-Tovim accept that there are limits on the effectiveness of struggles against racism, then the question arises of how one conceptualises the relationship between ideologies and social structures. Is it simply a question of an eclectic combination of autonomous levels in a specific situation? Or do economic, political and ideological relations exercise some determining influence on the expression of racist ideologies?

The fundamental problem with abandoning the relative autonomy model is that of avoiding the trap of a simple pluralism, which sees 'race' and class relationships as completely separate. This is why it seems to me that it is important to insist on the complexity of 'determination in the last instance', while accepting that there is some form of determination of racism by other social relations. For example, within the context of economic decline and political crisis-management during the post-war period, can one really talk of the complete autonomy of racism? Or can one separate out the political meanings which are attached to 'race' today from the actions of successive governments in defining and redefining the immigration/'race' issue during the last four decades? Or can one understand the long-term patterns of inclusion and exclusion of black workers in the labour market without an analysis of the restructuring of British industry during this period?

For these reasons alone there are grounds for questioning whether a pluralistic version of Marxism is any more adequate in analysing the contradictions of racial structuration than pluralistic theories have been in their analysis of capitalist societies (Meiksins Wood 1983, Connolly 1981). Additionally, however, there seems to be little possibility that the autonomy model can capture the complexity of power relations or adequately analyse the historical context in which racism has become entrenched, in different societies and at different times, at all levels of the social formation. In this sense I am less worried about the distance Gabriel and Ben-Tovim have travelled from classical Marxism than about the fact that their model does not seem to be able to analyse the development of racism except through the ever-present concept of 'struggle', which is not located in any social context.

Perhaps one way of dealing with the issue of determinism may be through a strict application of proposition (b), namely that there can be no general theory of racism. It is precisely on this point that there hinges the possibility of further advance in Marxist theory, since it focuses attention on the contexts in which racist ideologies develop and are transformed, or on what Gilroy has called 'the construction, mobilisation, and pertinence of different forms of racist ideology and structuration in specific historical circumstances' (Gilroy 1982, p. 281). But the application of this position has led to the emergence of more problems, since few Marxists have actually analysed processes of racial structuration at the level of actual societies. The example of South Africa is one which has attracted most attention (Wolpe 1980, Burawoy 1981), along with some aspects of racism in contemporary Britain. This had led to a tendency to produce more refined concepts without approaching the more thorny questions relating to their applicability to actual concrete situations (Rex 1981).

The unsettling nature of the encounter between contemporary Marxism and 'race' is far from reaching a conclusion. This is reflected in the numerous either/or kind of formulations which have been summarised and criticised above; for example do we talk of 'race' or class, 'race' or racism, autonomy or relative autonomy, 'race' or migrant labour'? This type of debate is prominent in the early stages of theoretical discussion, when there is uncertainty about the exact nature of differences and agreements across the main contestants. The further development of debate, however, would require greater specification of the social relations of racism in specific societies, and its interconnections with class and non-class aspects of social reality (Resnick and Wolff, 1982). Once the question is defined in this way it also becomes clear that, although it is important in a specifically Marxist framework to establish some degree of determination, Marxian theory is also radically anti-determinist.

It needs to be said that there are numerous aspects of recent debates which have not been fully covered in the above discussion. All three theoretical models, for example, are closely linked to differing assessments of the role of the state, of politics and of the possibility of anti-racist struggles. The role of autonomous black political struggles in relation to class-based political action remains a central area of dispute, as does the issue of the role of state intervention in the area of 'race relations'. Many of these issues are also the object of lively discussion outside of Marxism (Rex 1981). These are questions, however, which need to be addressed separately, since they relate to more specific assessments of the political economy of contemporary Britain.

5. Conclusion

This paper has tried to locate the position of 'race' in Marxist discourse and to assess the adequacy of the various theoretical approaches to its study in capitalist societies. While much of the recent literature written from the various perspectives analysed above hardly merits the designation of a 'Marxist theory of race and ethnic relations,' it clearly represents a large and growing body of work. I have tried to argue that Marxist theories of 'race' are heterogeneous in approach, though it can be argued that they are unified through a common concern with (a) the material and ideological basis of racism and racial oppression, however it may be defined, and (b) the role that racism plays in structuring the entire social, political and economic structures of societies. In other words, the basic level of agreement between the various Marxist approaches is that they accept that there is no race relations problem as such, that there is no problem of racism which can be thought of as separate from the structural features of capitalist society.

Equally important, however, are the differences in approach which have become evident over the last decade within the broad spectrum of Marxist writings on racism. It is in this context that we can best appreciate the studies discussed above. Whatever their theoretical deficiencies and analytic weaknesses, the overall effect of Marxist contributions in this area has been to redefine the problem of 'race' in capitalist society in a way that makes theoretical and political debate more open and challenging. They have focused attention on the history and contemporary reality of racism in capitalist society, and its complex economic, political and ideological preconditions. By questioning the adequacy of both traditional Marxist and non-Marxist treatments of racism, and by emphasising the need for linking theoretical analysis to anti-racist politics, these studies have in their different ways helped reinstate the idea that racism is no mere epiphenomenon but a social construct resulting from the complex social relationships and economic and political structures of capitalist societies (Hall *et al.* 1980, Freedman 1983–4, Miles 1984a).

But the interest of these studies is not restricted to the field of Marxist theory and politics. For the problems with which they have been grappling occur in similar forms in non-Marxist social and political theory. For although the basic starting point of Marxist approaches to this question may be said to differ markedly from the various non-Marxist approaches, there can be little doubt that many of the substantive analytical problems are actually quite similar. This is not to say that the specific theoretical and analytical divergences between the two sets of approaches are not important, for they clearly are. What is at issue, however, is the adequacy of the explanations they offer about the role of racism in contemporary capitalist societies, the role of the state in reproducing or countering racist practices, and the adequacy of the political conclusions they draw about how to overcome racism. Because the Marxist approaches have focused on the social relations that produce and reproduce racism, they have touched upon issues which are of concern to non-Marxist theorists, namely the origins of racist ideologies and institutions and the role of political power relations. In so doing, recent Marxist analyses may well open up possibilities for broadening out the debates about 'race', class and the state in potentially fruitful directions.

Perhaps in the long run this will be seen as one of the main achievements of recent Marxist debates on racism. The kinds of question which they raise about theory and anti-racist politics open up the possibility for reflective discussions of the role of racism in contemporary societies and the strategies for overcoming it. The theoretical and political self-consciousness which the approaches discussed above show are a fundamental challenge to both traditional Marxism and rival problematics within the social sciences, and one which deserves to be taken up across a variety of disciplines. In addition, however, they have provided an extra impetus to attempts to link academic research to questions of practice, particularly in relation to political struggles against racism. In so doing they have posed questions beyond the limits of traditional Marxist class analysis and have pointed to the need for a deeper analysis of non-class forms of domination.

If this brief sketch of the content of recent Marxist debates on 'race', class and the state is accurate, there are many questions about the specificity of racism which have been inadequately theorised. But recent debates have at least opened up the possibility of a more dynamic and accessible Marxist contribution to the analysis of racism. Whether this possibility is realised depends on the success of attempts to broaden the horizons of current Marxian conceptions of the dynamics of advanced capitalism. Along with gender, racism remains one of the key axes on which this reconceptualisation has to take place, both at the level of theory and at that of practice.

NOTES

1 Apart from the work of Parkin, which is discussed below, see Forsythe 1979, Stone 1977, Bonacich 1980, Brotz 1983, Banton 1983.
2 It is not possible to discuss these issues specifically in the context of this paper, but valuable and provocative overviews of all of them can be found in Wright 1980, Sargent 1981, Resnick and Wolff 1982 and Cottrell 1984.
3 The dialectic of 'agency' and structure in Marxist thinking is usefully discussed in Gintis and Bowles (1981), where it is argued that there are usually two opposing tendencies in Marxist writing, one based on a commitment to structural determination and another committed to a notion of practice. They themselves suggest a resolution in terms of a unified conception of structure and practice.
4 A useful and challenging discussion of the political context of their analysis can be found in Jessop 1982. But see also Meiksins Wood 1983.
5 This threefold classification is imposed and reflects an assessment of the main tendency in each body of work. There are no doubt other models which can be usefully discussed, or other points on which these three approaches could be sub-divided. Nevertheless for the purposes of this presentation this classification seemed most appropriate. See also Bonacich 1980, G. Morgan 1981 and Omi and Winant 1983.
6 A somewhat broader overview of the Centre's work on this can be found in Freedman 1983–4. On the work of the Centre more generally see the edited volume, *Culture, Media and Language*, by Hall *et al.* 1980, and Johnson 1983.
7 The concern with racism can be traced back further in terms of Hall's own work, but the impact of '*race*' on the Centre's project dates from this period and therefore predates Hall's more theoretical studies of racism and social relations.
8 A fuller discussion of this point can be found in Solomos *et al.* 1982.
9 Throughout this paper I refer to the work of Gabriel and Ben-Tovim, though in fact much of their work has been carried out with a number of other researchers associated with their work in Wolverhampton and Liverpool. On the theoretical origins of the criticisms which this model develops in relation to relative autonomy see Cutler *et al.* 1977–8, Hindess 1984, and more generally the work associated with Barry Hindess and Paul Hirst.
10 In a recent paper Phizacklea argues that there are links between this position and the broader tradition of the sociology of migration which has developed in both Europe and the USA (Phizacklea 1984).
11 The relative absence of historical awareness and specificity from much of the Marxist debate on racism has been noted, from rather different angles, by Rex 1981, Bonacich 1981a and 1981b, Miles 1982, Robinson 1983, and Brittan and Maynard 1984. What is surprising, however, is that despite this awareness few attempts have been made to redress the balance and develop historically based analyses of racist ideologies and practices.
12 This is a problem discussed from a different perspective by G. Morgan 1981 and Green 1979. For an interesting American perspective see Omi and Winant 1983.

5

Class concepts, class struggle and racism

HAROLD WOLPE

Introduction

In this paper my object is to draw on the theoretical implications of recent internal critiques of Marxist theory with a view to advancing some propositions, in a perhaps more explicit form than hitherto, relevant to the analysis of social structures and conflicts in capitalist societies in which racism is salient.

Before proceeding further, it is important to make quite explicit that throughout this paper the use of the term 'racism' refers, first, to a process of categorisation in which real or supposed physical[1] differences serve to ground invidious conceptions of social differentiation and, second, to social practices in which the placing of individuals or groups unequally in the social structure entails, as an essential element, those physically based categorisations. That is to say, 'racism' refers to discriminatory practices in which a socially constructed notion of 'race' is implicated.[2]

In order to specify the issues which are to be discussed, the paper begins with a recapitulation of the old debate between class-based and race-based theories of social structure and conflict in capitalist social formations in which race is pertinent. Paradoxically, both these competing theories depend for their construction, in opposite ways, on notions of class,[3] which, while often different, none the less share the common property of being conceived of economistically. In one case, an economistic conception of class is the foundation of a theory which attributes racism to economic interests in the economy; in the other case, it is precisely *because* class is assumed to be a purely economic concept that it is held to be irrelevant to the explanation of the presence and processes of racism, itself, in turn, conceived of as a phenomenon outside and independent of the economy. In both cases, class as an economic relation and racism as a non-economic relation are defined as standing in an entirely external relationship to one another.

So long as these positions are held, it seems clear that there can be no escape from the limitations of the accounts of racism which are found in the literature. In these accounts, racism is explained either as an external effect of capitalist economic relations or as the autonomous effect of race (whether conceived of as socially constructed or primordial) and, in this event, if class is held to be relevant at all, class and race are treated as two entirely autonomous systems. The limitations of the reductionism entailed in the first two approaches and of the dualism of the third approach has been widely discussed and will be touched on briefly below. Here the main purpose has been to stress that the source of these limitations lies in the reductionist conception of class common to these approaches.

In this paper, it will be argued that the way out of this impasse requires, to begin with, the abandonment of economistic conceptions of class and, hence, of the reductionism and dualism to which they give rise. This opens the way to a reformulation of the concept of class struggle such that under specific, contingent conditions race can (indeed must) be understood as a form of that struggle, as internal to it. And this will be so, under the specified conditions, whether that struggle is confined to the sphere of the economy or becomes generalised to the sphere of politics. It must be emphasised, however, that to say this is not, at the same time, to imply anything about the *cause* of the 'interiorisation' of race in the class struggle.

Furthermore, it also does not follow that because race, under certain conditions, may be interiorised in the class struggle, all conflicts which centre on race are, therefore, to be conceived of as class struggles. On the contrary, it will be argued that struggles focusing on race may take on a form in which class is not interiorised within them. Yet, and this is the crucial point, from a Marxist standpoint, the question that has to be posed in relation to these struggles is: in what way and to what extent do forms of organisation and struggle about race have consequences for the class structure; or, to put this more accurately, do they tend to sustain or to undermine the conditions of existence and reproduction of the fundamental classes of capitalist society – capital and labour – and the relations between them?

The reductionism of race relations theory

Characteristically, in race relations theory, race is conceived of as the irreducible constituent and determinant of social structure and relations

– and this is so whether race is regarded as primordial or otherwise given, or as socially constructed. From this viewpoint, the fundamental unit of analysis is the racially defined individual, and the social structure is composed of a plurality of racially defined and hierarchically placed orders or groups.

In the most extreme variant of this approach starting from the notion 'race', a theory is constructed in which (a) individual subjects, and the racial orders or groups they constitute, owe their formation, their unity and their homogeneity to a single origin – racial attributes, and (b) the social relations within and between these groups are similarly governed by racial categories – that is, the interests of racial groups are derived from and are formulated in terms of their racial attributes.

Quite clearly there are numerous variations on this theme in the race relations literature.[4] Nevertheless, whatever the complexity of the arguments, they demonstrably rest on an assertion which attributes an autonomous and irreducible determinancy to race in one of two ways; either race is conceived of as a real biological division of human groups which, directly, has social effects; or, more frequently, the biological divisions are said to be *the* foundation of socially constructed categorisations which then function to establish relations of dominance and subordination and forms of inequality.

This line of analysis has been subjected to wide-ranging and trenchant criticisms which it is unnecessary to repeat here.[5] For present purposes it is sufficient to emphasise one feature of this approach which has not been brought to the surface in the critical literature.

As I pointed out above, for race relations theory the effect of race is to produce a structure of racial inequality. This, indeed, is why race relations analysis is thought to be important. The relationship between racially defined groups and individuals involves, however, of necessity, even within these extreme versions of race relations theory, a description of their economic, political and status characteristics – characteristics which are normally thought of as belonging to class analysis. Indeed, conflicts between racial groups are precisely seen to be over these class factors. Thus, the reduction of inequality to race has, curiously enough, the unintended outcome for race relations theory of producing a simple identity between racial groups and class position. Yet, class analysis is thought to be irrelevant, since the single determining factor is attributed to race. Van den Berghe (1967: 267), for example, makes the point explicitly:

> Social classes in the Marxian sense of the relationships to the means of production exist by definition, as they must in any

capitalist country, but they are not meaningful social realities. Clearly, pigmentation, rather than ownership of land or capital is the most significant criterion of status in South Africa.

Robert Miles, in *Racism and Migrant Labour* (1982), has remarked that race relations theory

> assumes, but does not attempt to demonstrate, that the predominant active element in the conjuncture is a categorisation by reference to physical variation, and in so doing must lead to monocausal explanation. In other words, by labelling a situation as one of 'race relations', one is implicitly denying that any other force can have an equal or predominant effect. To anticipate a later argument, this approach means that if one labels the participants in a process as 'races', and their interaction as 'race relations', then one is denying either that they occupy a class position or that their class position is of significance to the situation and process.

Accurate as this is as a characterisation of the versions of race relations theory which explicitly deny the relevance of class and/or stratification, is it of equal applicability to the body of literature which, while still based on the principle of race, nevertheless does explicitly acknowledge the pertinence of class? This latter literature, instead of merely denying the significance of class, concentrates upon the way in which the class–race relationship is formulated. The purpose of the discussion which follows is to show that, by starting from an inadequate, economist conception of class, the attempt to accord an autonomous weight to race and, at the same time, to recognise the relevance of class leads to contradictory and incoherent 'resolutions' of the theoretical problems involved. The point may be briefly illustrated through a discussion of the work of Kuper (1974) and Heribert Adam (Adam and Giliomee 1979). Although written from different theoretical positions, their work none the less shares common difficulties which are also widespread in the literature.

Kuper's starting point is quite unequivocal: within Marxist theory, the concept of class is an economic category, and the 'catalyst' of social transformation is to be found in the economy. Consequently, that theory is unable to illuminate racially structured societies:

> My initial assumption was that theories of revolution derived from the analysis of conflict between social classes in racially homogeneous societies might not be very illuminating when applied to situations of revolutionary struggle between racial groups. Indeed, I would argue more positively that the

> theories may be quite misleading in the context of racially
> structured societies. (Kuper 1974: 200)

The correct approach is to recognise that race and the economic give rise
to distinct orders:

> In some critical respects relevant to conceptions, class
> structures and racial structures constitute different systems of
> stratification, however much they may overlap. (61)

And again:

> At the level of theory ... the concepts of race and class are so
> very different, that it is difficult to understand the justification
> for the introduction of class concepts as the crucial variable,
> outside the dogma of the universality of the class struggle.
> (224)

Kuper, however, accepts the great importance of 'economic factors' in
racially structured societies and, indeed, that 'wherever there is racial
stratification there is also economic stratification' (200).

This poses the problem of the relationship between class and race.
Kuper says:

> There is need to develop a set of propositions concerning the
> interrelations of economic and racial stratification ... The two
> main variables would relate to economic development and
> stratification on the one hand, and to racial structure on the
> other. (199)

The difficulty which Kuper faces in his attempt to develop these
propositions flows directly from his insistence that class and race, or,
more broadly, the economic and the political, constitute two entirely
separate orders in the society. This, I will show, leads into an incoherent
position.

Kuper attempts to establish the separateness of the class and racial
orders in the following way:

> The essence of the distinction is that class structures are
> intrinsic to interaction in the society, whereas racial structures
> are in some measure extrinsic, or have a point of reference
> outside of the interaction ... To be sure, the racial structure is
> also constituted by the interaction, but the *racial differences*
> which are socially elaborated, *have preceded the interaction*.
> (61; emphasis in the original)

> *race ... constitutes an independent basis for power ...* In the
> case of the subordinate racial minority, race is an independent
> basis for exclusion from privilege, and economic and political
> deprivation flow from that exclusion. Hence the situation
> encourages perceptions of race as the crucial factor in social
> discrimination. (61–2; my emphasis)

The obvious question that arises from this formulation is: how is it
possible to conceive of race as an 'independent basis' for the acquisition
of political and economic power without specifying the conditions
(including the structures of political and economic power) which make it
possible for race to operate in that way?

Kuper deals with this question by the confusing statements both that
racial differences have an independent significance (that is, presumably,
have causal efficacy – why else his insistence on their independence of
class?) in producing social inequalities and that race has no causal effect
whatsoever:

> *The racial divisions are viewed as phenomena in their own*
> *right, and accorded structural significance. There is, of course,*
> *no suggestion that the racial difference gives rise to the plural*
> *society; or that it has any causal significance.* Plural societies
> are generally established by conquest, followed by the
> expropriation of resources, and the exploitation of labour ...
> But peoples do not establish domination over each other
> because they are of different race, but in the pursuit of quite
> concrete interests in power and other resources.
>
>   The foundation, then, is the inequality of the racial groups
> in the access to the means of power. This infrastructure is the
> basis for a superstructure of inequality, as the original political
> inequality is extended to other institutions and structures. The
> elaboration of inequality is most marked in the economy and
> in education. In the economic sphere, it is the relationship to
> the means of power which appreciably defines the relationship
> to the means of production ... (269; my emphasis)

On inspection of the above passages, it is quite clear that the
contention that race and class are two quite distinct social orders which
are simply externally related gives way to the argument that there are,
rather, two different paths to unequal political and economic power – an
economic path and a political path based on race. On what possible
grounds can it be further argued that the resulting entities (whether they

be rich or poor, or owners or non-owners of means of production) do not constitute class or class fractions which have a particular socially defined racial composition?

Kuper simply does not deal with this problem, and nor can he, except by insisting that classes which acquire power (including means of production) on the basis of race are racial entities and by ignoring their place in the class system. Thus, he can speak of the 'ruling' and 'subject' races and can argue that this relation of subordination–domination is organised around control of the means of economic and political power and, yet, escape from the implications of this for his attempt radically to separate class and race by the simple expedient of invoking race to the exclusion of class. And this despite the fact that at various points he *ad hoc* recognises that racial groups may be internally divided into classes and that classes themselves may be racially fragmented.

He is forced to deny the class content of his analysis because he defines this as economic and race as non-economic and he is unable to provide the theoretical means for articulating the two orders. The path to the formation of classes is through the economy; the path to the formation of racial groups which acquire or are dispossessed of economic means is via the political on the basis of race. We do not have to accept Kuper's simplistic dichotomy between the political and the economic to hold that, within a social formation, there may well be alternative paths to class formation and that this may result in the internal fragmentation of a class on the basis of racial categorisations. This result may be due to something which Kuper cannot recognise: class struggles conducted through the medium of racial discourses. Thus it would seem that Kuper has no means of dealing with situations of the type in which workers, who are categorised as white, strike against white capitalist employers in order to protect their occupational monopolies against workers defined as black. In Kuper's terms, is this a racial or a class struggle?

He does recognise that class and race may 'overlap', but, none the less, he insists throughout, as I have already pointed out, that race cannot at all be explained in terms of class:

> At one extreme, racial and economic divisions tend to co-incide, as in the initial stages of colonial domination. At the other extreme, perhaps purely hypothetical, there has ceased to be stratification by race, and racial differences, though present, are no longer salient in a system of stratification based on differences in economic status. Between the two extremes fall those societies in which both racial and economic stratification are present, but do not fully coincide. This is the

more general case in the contemporary world, and the one
with which I deal in the present chapter. (200)

But if race and class do coincide (even if not fully) how can it be argued
that theories of class struggle are misleading and irrelevant? Furthermore, whether race and class do or do not coincide may be quite
irrelevant to the pertinence of class struggle. Once Kuper acknowledges
the *coexistence* of racial structures and class structures, it is not open to
him *merely to assert* that race is both independent and dominant to the
exclusion of class.

For Heribert Adam in *Ethnic Power Mobilized* (1979), a racially
structured society must be understood as 'a synthesis of the interplay
between ideology and economy' (50). Unlike Kuper, he assigns to class
an explicit importance in the structuring of the society and he rejects the
emphasis on 'racism and prejudice' which, he says, dominates the
literature. This then poses for Adam the question of how to relate class
and race, but because of the theoretical inadequacy of his position he is
only able to slide from an economistic reductionism to an unexplained or
conjectural account of the autonomy of race.

He begins by locating race in relation to the economy, that is to class,
as follows:

> labour, capital and markets, while never sufficient as
> monocausal explanations, do determine the organizational
> needs from which ethnic ideologies *emanate* and with which
> they dialectically interact. (x; my emphasis)

Later in the book he elaborates this:

> In summary, Marxist analysis succeeds in penetrating beyond
> the symbolic structures with which groups interpret their
> changing reality. By not taking such ideological expressions as
> given or 'primordial' innate sentiment, the changing function
> of cultural identity can be discerned. The decoded symbols
> mostly reveal class interests hidden behind the proclaimed
> ethnic unity. Thus Marxist analysis can pinpoint the
> constituents of ethnic agitation. But this is where the
> usefulness of class analysis usually ends. (50)[6]

The reason why class analysis loses its usefulness at this point is because it
is unable to explain the process of ethnic mobilisation

> by which mere particularistic interests become a common
> cause ... Adherents mobilize for sacrifice, group action, and
> the promise of a better future in the name of a common bond

> (language, religion, race, ancestry, sex) . . . intragroup
> conflicts are portrayed as minor . . . Class conflict, for
> example, is subjugated to the propagated need of group unity.
> (61)

It is to be noted from the above passages that race, or in this case ethnic, mobilisation necessarily stands outside of, masks and cuts across class relations – the latter are economic and entail economic interests, whereas race and ethnicity relate to something else. But if class cannot account for or explain this, what does? Earlier Adam argued that 'ethnic ideologies emanate' (x) from the economy. Now, however, he ascribes them to an apparently universal 'utopian yearning' or 'longing' for 'harmonious and secure human relationships' (62). Why this should lead to *ethnic* solidarity is not explained. Be that as it may, at the same time ethnic attachments are said to change according to changing circumstances (including changes in class relations?) and to serve new goals (implying an instrumentalism?) and, yet, to persist *if* a need for ethnicity is perceived. Thus:

> But what happens if the situational context . . . changes so that
> racial beliefs no longer serve the group interest but amount to
> an obstacle for new goals and strategies? *The concept of ethnic*
> *mobilization suggests that because racial sentiments are not*
> *acquired biological dispositions of individuals and groups they*
> *can be adjusted and discarded according to changing*
> *circumstances . . . ethnic and racial mobilization depends on its*
> *suitability and expediency in a specific sociopolitical*
> *environment in permanent flux . . .* To consider racial
> perceptions as immutable qualities ignores their changing
> functions. Ethnic attachments persist, but only as long as they
> serve a purpose . . . Above all it depends on whether there is a
> perceived need for ethnic identification and how mobilizers
> capitalize on these needs. (63; my italics)

Ethnic identification, then, stems from universal yearnings outside of the economy, and yet it persists as an instrument serving particular, changing goals, including economic interests. But this is merely to repeat the problem – the relationship between race and class – without offering a coherent theoretical means to deal with it. As I have already argued, the difficulty stems, in an important respect, from the utilisation of an economistic conception of class. It is this, as I shall try to show later, which leads to an overdrawn and inadequate formulation of the race–class opposition.

Class reductionism

A contrast with the race-based and race reductionist theories discussed above is provided by class-based theories which are derived from Marxist theory. The contrast lies in the fact that, in this approach, the central role in the structuring of the society is attributed to class relations, rather than to race relations. Classes are not discrete entities; they are defined in terms of relations of production and cannot be conceived of outside those relations. Thus, in capitalism, for example, the capitalist class is concep-' tually constituted in its relation to the working class. That, fundamental, relation is a relation of exploitation – the capitalist owners of the means of production organise the workers in a labour process to produce surplus value which the former appropriate.

The problem with reductionist Marxism[7] is not this starting point but rather the path which is then followed. The fundamental error lies not in the fact that classes are first defined *abstractedly* in terms of relations of production but in the fact that it is then assumed that the abstract economic content of that definition is carried over into the concrete and that classes are formed, unidimensionally, as concrete social forces expressing that economic content.[8] Hence, the classes and the individuals who inhabit them owe their formation, their homogeneity and their unity to a single, economic, origin.

Clearly, this provides the foundation for a conception of given, objective class interests. The interests of the unitary classes derive directly and entirely from the concept which defines them – the concept of the place they occupy in the relations of production – and these given interests govern all social relations, including the ideological and political superstructure. At the level of the superstructure, economic interests take on ideological and political forms. The latter are generated by the economic relations and the economic interests they embody. Thus, to the extent that conflicts in the political and ideological superstructure focus on race relations, these are nothing other than the (mystified) form of the economic class struggle determined by the clash of economic interests.

Obviously, the problem which arises for a reductionist class theory is how to explain why the class struggle takes on the form of a struggle over race relations, and here the theory has little to offer since it assumes that the explanation is that this emanates directly from the economic relations of the classes in the economy. The theory cannot explain the diverse ideological and political forms which arise on the basis of capitalist relations of production or, indeed, within the capitalist economy itself. It merely invokes the notion of false consciousness and attributes the salience of race to the machinations of the ruling class which deploys it to divide the working class. The theory, therefore, allows no space for the possibility that a complex combination of conditions may contribute to the racial content of the class struggle in the political and, indeed, also in the economic sphere.

But this has important consequences, since race is then left unexplained or is treated in an *ad hoc* and/or a functionalist manner. Therefore, the specific conditions in which racial categorisations come to provide the content of class struggles and/or the basis of organisation of interests in a manner which both cuts across class divisions and yet may serve to sustain, amend (for example, racialisation or deracialisation) or undermine them, are neglected.

In recent years, in an attempt to escape from the weaknesses of this line of argument, a Marxist literature has emerged which has been concerned with the development of non-reductionist concepts of class, ideology and politics. It is not my intention to survey this literature here; rather, as I indicated earlier, I want to use aspects of it to advance a theoretical position which departs from both the reductionist and the dualist perspectives outlined above. The essential starting point for this is a non-reductionist concept of class.

A non-reductionist Marxist conception of class

It is, of course, the case that the theoretical starting point for a Marxist analysis of a social formation is the economy – the mode of production – and the classes that are defined in the concept of the particular mode. Does it follow that, because the economy is privileged in this way, an economism is necessarily entailed? That is to say, is the argument that the social relations and processes of production are central to the characterisation and explanation of a social formation to be construed as meaning that the 'economic', abstractly defined as a 'purely' economic sphere, is determinant?

In the analyses discussed above, this was precisely what was assumed and here I want to argue that this assumption, and the difficulties which were identified as following from it, have their roots in a conflation of different levels of abstraction such that a highly abstract economic *concept* of class becomes transformed into an economistic or reductionist *determinant* of the concrete.

By conflation of levels of abstraction I mean a mode of analysis comprising two elements. First, as I suggested above, an abstract concept, in this case class, is made also to be an *empirical description* of the concrete form in which the class exists. Thus, for example, the concept of the capital class as owners of the means of production and of labour-power as the class of direct producers which is exploited in the process of production is assumed to exhaust the characterisation of the classes and their relations in the concrete. As they are defined, so do these phenomena exist. Second, however, since classes and the relations between them exist as 'purely' economic entities due to the conflation referred to, it follows, if primacy is given to classes and class struggle, that the 'purely' economic is assigned a determining role not only in the economy but in the structuring of all social relations.

Viewed in this way, privileging the mode of production does entail, simultaneously, an essentialism – all social phenomena are merely an expression of the economic essence of class – and a corresponding failure to view the concrete as the outcome of multiple determinations, as Marx expressed it in the 1857 Introduction to *A Contribution to the Critique of Political Economy*. This provides the key to an alternative, non-reductionist approach.

It has already been implied that the concept of the relations of production provides a necessary but not sufficient basis for the analysis of classes and class struggles. It is a necessary basis in two senses. First, because it points to and defines, in terms quite specific to Marxism, a terrain of analysis, the mode of economic production and reproduction. Second, that terrain includes the 'places' where the classes are, as it were, brought into existence – the productive enterprises – and the relations between them established. Clearly, without capitalist enterprises, there could be no capitalist or working class.

But, at this level of abstraction, both capital and labour are, necessarily, conceptualised as unitary and homogeneous classes and the relation between them as an undifferentiated relation of exploitation. It is precisely for this reason that the abstract concept does not provide a *sufficient* basis for analysis. For, while at one level classes must be conceived of as unitary entities, concretely, to the contrary, their internal unity is always problematic. In the sphere of production and exchange, classes exist in forms which are fragmented and fractured by politics, culture, ideology and, indeed, the concrete organisation of production and distribution itself. A class, that is, is constituted, not as a unified social force, but as a patchwork of segments which are differentiated and divided on a variety of bases and by varied processes. It is true that a more or less extensive unity may be brought about when, for example, a trade union movement or a working-class party is able to articulate the demands of different fractions of the working class and to win their support in the sphere of production and exchange. Similarly, when representative organisations articulate demands as class demands in the political sphere (whether these demands relate to state politics or to the sphere of the economy), the unification of a class or class fractions as social forces may occur. But, and this is the fundamental point, that unity is not given by the concept of labour-power; it is constituted through practices. One might say that class unity, when it occurs, is a conjunctural phenomenon.

There are at least two important conclusions which follow from this argument. The first of these is that, once we reject the notion that classes are formed as simple economic unities, we must also reject the so-called class-theoretical approach which conceives of classes as entities with pre-given economic interests, which, acting out of these interests, constitute the social formation. On the contrary, classes, defined by the relations of production, are formed as social forces by heterogeneous conditions which they are implicated in producing. At the concrete level, then, social classes are simultaneously economically, politically and ideologically shaped.

The second important point which emerges relates to the meaning to be given to the notions of class conflict and class consciousness. In the literature, class consciousness and conflict are said to exist when 'class issues' are involved. But what are class issues? If classes are defined as economic entities, then class issues, it seems, must relate directly to the economic elements that define classes – presumably the relations of production, wages and the like. Therefore, from this standpoint, class consciousness and class conflict can only be, in some sense, purely economic. Thus, race, for example, must be excluded from and opposed to class.

If, by contrast, it is accepted that classes are formed, even in the sphere of production, simultaneously through politics, economics and ideology, then race may well become the content, under specific conditions, of the class struggle. As Stuart Hall (1980b: 341) has observed:

> Race is thus ... the modality in which class is 'lived', the medium through which class relations are experienced, the form in which it is appropriated and 'fought through'.

Capitalism, class struggle and race

A major conclusion which follows from the above discussion is that it is not possible to make a concrete analysis of the relations and processes within the economic sphere of a capitalist social formation as if they were subject to 'purely' economic determinants and calculation. The mode of production is privileged, but the economy is *not* autonomously formed. This is not to argue that it is unimportant to analyse the conditions of the economy in economic terms. Analyses of rates of profit, the nature of technological innovations and the 'technical' division of labour these give rise to, the level of the balance of payments, rates of interest, investment patterns, labour distribution, unemployment figures and so forth are obviously of great importance. They provide an account of one set of conditions which are quite indispensable to an understanding of the economic sphere and which provide a context for, pose issues for and set limits to struggles within that sphere as well as in the terrain of state politics.

However, and this point is crucial, these conditions of the economy are the *outcome* of relations and processes which are in no sense purely economic, even when they occur in the economic sphere. Thus, for example, if the rate of profit depends in part on the rate of exploitation, then the former will be the outcome of political, economic and ideological determinants to the extent that, in the struggle for wages, economic calculation will incorporate considerations of status, gender and race, contingent upon the power and character of political, employers', trade union and other organisations. Or, again, attempts by management to introduce new technology which would have radical effects upon the division of labour and would threaten certain jobs may be obstructed by workers, struggling to protect their employment, who become mobilised around interests defined in gender, religious or racial terms.

The process of capital accumulation, then, is a social process entailing, within the sphere of production and exchange, economic, political and ideological determinants. It follows from the non-economistic conceptions of class and the economy which have been outlined above that the simple opposition between race and class must be rejected. Race may, under determinant conditions, become interiorised in the class struggle.

In making this point, however, it is necessary to distinguish between the different spheres in which these struggles occur, the relationship between these spheres and the effect of this upon the content of these struggles.

First, it is essential to note that the 'politics of production' (Burawoy 1985) and politics in the sphere of state politics occur in terrains which are structured in radically different ways and that this has significant effects upon the nature and content of the struggles conducted within them. What differentiates the struggles within these diverse spheres is that they are mediated by distinct institutional and organisational matrices which structure their form and, in large measure, their content. Burawoy (1985: 253–4), formulates the point as follows:

> we must choose between politics defined as struggles regulated by *specific apparatuses*, politics defined as struggles over

certain relations, and the combination of the two. In the first, politics would have no fixed objective, and in the second it would have no fixed institutional locus. I have therefore opted for the more restrictive third definition, according to which politics refers to struggles within a specific arena aimed at a specific set of relations.

Thus, in the sphere of production, the apparatuses of management, trade unions, the organisation of the labour process and so forth structure class struggles over relations in production (the labour process) and over relations of production (the relations of exploitation). In the political sphere, on the other hand, state apparatuses and the relations between them (for example, judiciary, executive and legislature), political parties and so forth structure the mode of struggle for state power. Burawoy's formulation is, however, too restrictive, for it is clear that the objectives of political struggles in the different arenas may not be as clearly segregated as is suggested by his formulation. The objectives of struggles in the sphere of state politics may include attempts to impose a specific regime of control within productive enterprises; by contrast, to the extent that relations in and of production are believed to be sustained by the state, production politics may make state power its objective. None the less, the apparatuses within each sphere will continue to structure the form in which these struggles occur.

In the sphere of production, individuals are allocated to positions in the production relations. In so far as this allocation takes place on the basis of racial and gender categorisations, the result is the formation of classes or class fractions which are characterised both by the place they occupy in those relations *and* by these categorisations. Thus, individuals and the classes they form are constituted by a complex of 'factors' of which position in the relations of production is a *sine qua non*.

Regarding this process Miles (1982: 185) says:

> the process of racialization (which occurs at the level of ideological relations) has effects on, but is also structured within and by, economic relations. By this I mean that although the process of racialization has an independent effect on production relations in so far as, for example, it directly assists in the allocation of persons to positions in those relations, it does not in itself determine the existence of the positions. The existence of the positions is determined by the mode of production.

The last sentence seems to reintroduce an economic reductionism which Miles is at pains to avoid in his book. To ascribe the existence of economic positions simply to the mode of production overlooks the fact that, at least in so far as the focus is on relations *in* production, the labour process, the positions themselves are the outcome of class struggles which are infused with political and ideological content. Be that as it may, Miles's formulation appears to pose the question of the 'origins' of racialisation in the economy, but he, correctly, refuses this question and, instead, argues that the concern should be not to establish the origins of racism but rather

> to explain the generation and reproduction of racism. By the former notion I mean that we should trace the conditions for and the manner in which certain ideas and arguments were and are articulated by certain groups (conceived of as classes or class fractions). In saying this, I make no assumption that these ideas are necessarily novel. Rather, the concern is with the fact that they have appeared and given social support in a given context. By the latter notion, I mean that we should trace the conditions under which these ideas are repeated and spread beyond the group that articulated them. (102)

Reformulated in the terms which have been the focus of this paper, the question which arises concerns the effects of the relationship between the sphere of production (or more generally the economy) and the sphere of state politics on racialisation or de-racialisation in either arena. Once we abandon the iron law of economic reductionism, it is possible to recognise that the relations between the sphere of production and the sphere of state politics may be complementary, contradictory or both. The point can be illustrated by two examples.

It can be shown that over a long period in the development of capitalism in South Africa, the structures of racial domination in the political sphere provided a legal framework and coercive state apparatuses enabling racial structures and practices to be imposed within production. In recent years, a restructuring of the division of labour, white labour mobility, the struggles of the black workers in the factories and other changes have begun, in part, to erode the dominant and monolithic character of racial categorisations in the economy. One effect of this has been to set up pressures for changes in the political sphere which emanate from the economy. So far, in the political sphere, these pressures have generally been resisted: over one or two issues – for instance the recognition of black trade unions and the abolition of job reservation – the state has yielded; but elsewhere – for instance in the tricameral parliament and on the issue of urban black representation –

although the form has been altered, the imposition of racial categorisations continues.

Racialisation of one sphere may become the condition for the same process to occur in another sphere, as, for example, in the case of colonial rule. Here, the establishment of administrative structures over already existing and spatially separated 'tribal' communities, and the subordination of indigenous law, politics and culture and so on, provide the political, ideological and legal foundations for the racial positioning of subjects in the arena of production as capitalist production develops. In this case, by contrast with the first illustration, pressures for change may originate in the political sphere with the anti-colonial national liberation struggles. The success of the struggle may result in the more or less rapid de-racialisation of the political sphere, yet, despite this, change may be resisted in the economy and may occur more erratically and much more slowly.

It was argued earlier that the relations which become the object of contestation and the mode in which that contest is conducted within the different spheres is mediated by their particular institutional and organisational structures. At the same time, the relations in one arena may become the object of struggle in the other, but the form of struggle will be conditioned by the specific institutional and organisational matrices of the latter. For example, in the political sphere, parties and organisations with particular class social bases and articulating specifically class interests may struggle to maintain or eliminate the racial positioning of subjects in the relations in or of production and to secure or undermine the conditions external to production which may sustain the racial positioning. In this event, the racial struggle is simultaneously and directly a class struggle.

Does it follow from the fact that *class interests may entail race* that, therefore, race should be considered *only* as an element in class formation and class interests? This seems to be the conclusion of a rather ambiguous formulation by Miles (1982):

> What will be argued is that the analytical problem is to locate the place and impact of what I shall term the process of racial categorization on class relations. This process is an ideological process and has its own determinate effects on political and production relations and, hence, the constitution of and struggles between classes. (4)

> And what of the conceptual fate of 'ethnic relations'? There can be no place for it as a distinct area of investigation per se

for the reasons argued above. However, a place has to be found for the notion of 'ethnic group' in so far as one must recognise the sense of common identity amongst groups of people who wish to recognise and maintain their cultural differences vis-à-vis others. This phenomenal process has real political and ideological effects on, inter alia, the development of class struggle and the formation of class consciousness. But, equally, one must recognise that the persons who constitute a group which is formed and identified on this basis also have a position in essential relations. That is, they have a position in production (and, thereby, class) relations. It is this fact that 'ethnic relations' studies cannot recognise, account for and assess the significance of. (71)

The ambiguity in this argument lies in the fact that, on the one hand, a place has to be found for the notion of 'ethnic group' (despite his contention earlier in the book that race – and in this respect ethnicity is no different – has no analytical utility), yet, on the other hand, there can be no room for it as a distinctive area of investigation *because* the individuals who constitute the group are, simultaneously, class subjects. It is, of course, true that individuals, whatever their ethnic position may be, also have a class position (as van den Berghe, for example, recognised). But merely to state this appears quite simply to invert van den Berghe's denial of the pertinence of class and thus to reduce all relations to class relations, and in a manner which simply conflates the sphere of production with the political sphere.

The point is, however, that classes and class fractions are directly constituted and reconstituted in the sphere of production through economic, political and ideological processes which operate through the changing institutional and organisational apparatuses of production. In so far as struggles over the economy, in the sphere of state politics, intrude on the economy, they are mediated precisely by those apparatuses which constitute the capital–labour relation.

By contrast, in the political sphere, despite the fact that individuals do not shed their class positions, none the less the institutional and organisational structure does not operate directly to constitute classes within that sphere, although it may serve as a condition of the reproduction of classes in the economy. As Poulantzas (1971) argued, the political structure, law and ideology function to categorise individuals as citizens, legal subjects and so on, but not as class subjects. This may be too sweepingly stated, but none the less the integration of class position with other positioning categorisations may occur, in the political sphere, in a mode in which class position is more vulnerable to subordination. That is to say, the location of class subjects in the political sphere may take place in such a way that racial positioning and hence racial interests become dominant.

In the sphere of production, the class basis of politics tends to be clear enough even when racial positioning is the dominant issue – thus, as I indicated earlier, struggles here take place on the basis of organisations whose membership is drawn from a class or a fraction of a class, and the question of racialisation relates directly to positions in production.

In the political sphere, the situation is not so clear, but, nevertheless, the politics of race may take on a class form. This will occur when organisations, drawing their membership explicitly from a particular class or classes, conduct their struggles in terms of discourses in which class-belonging is an important ingredient. Naturally, the content of that struggle may vary – at one pole racialised fractions of a class may struggle politically to defend or improve their positions in the division of labour through state intervention in the economy and/or through the protection of supportive political conditions; at the other pole, the struggle to end racialised class relations may entail the attempt to abolish those relations as such rather than the attempt to de-racialise them.

But what of the situation in which (a) the social basis of an organisation or a mass movement is not restricted to a particular class but incorporates, as it were at random, a range of different classes and (b) that organisation or movement, in its struggles and discourses, defines the issues exclusively in racial terms? In this situation there is a discursive isolation of racial categorisations from class relations, and, although it may be argued that the linkage between race and class in fact persists (for example, the individuals do not lose their class positions), yet as I argued above there is an institutional and organisational foundation for the expression of racial interests.

The racial structure has been conceived of, by some writers, as an ideological phenomenon – it is produced by ideologies of self-identity and by the identification by others of individuals as bearers of that identity. But it is necessary to understand the development of these identities as the product of a complex intersection of various institutional, organisational and other conditions and processes. What these are is, of course, a matter for empirical analysis. Historically, they have involved, *inter alia*, conquest and the political subordination of people who have come to be categorised in racial terms, the imposition of colonial administrative structures on existing 'tribal' units, ghettoisation and so forth.[9]

The crucial issue which arises is whether it is possible to analyse the production of these entities without being forced into a class or race reductionism or a dualist position. Clearly, simply to recognise that the racial 'segments' comprise individuals who also have class positions does not take the argument very far. The argument in this paper allows a number of propositions to be stated by way of conclusion.

First, the racial order, including 'corporate' racial groups, has to be analysed as the outcome of multiple determinations of which the operation of an economy characterised, in an non-economistic way, by the capital–labour relation and the structure of state power are essential elements – the account cannot be reduced to race, although the process of racial categorisation cannot be reduced to 'pure' economy.

Second, conversely but inseparable from this, the decisive question for a Marxist analysis is how, in what way and to what extent do the reproduction, transformation and disintegration of the racial order serve to maintain or undermine the relations of capital accumulation? Thus, for example, the racial structure may facilitate, through political mechanisms, the capacity of a petit-bourgeoisie to become a racialised fraction of capital. Again, the preoccupation with race may serve to confine political struggles to changes *within* the existing system.

These are rather obvious examples but, in fact, the analysis of the effects of politics which is confined to race on the fundamental relations of the social formation is extremely complex. But that such an analysis is indispensable to an adequate account of racially structured societies, and hence to political practice, is the necessary conclusion of the argument in this paper.

NOTES

1 For the purposes of this paper it is unnecessary to draw a distinction between the terms 'race' and 'racism' as used here and terms such as 'ethnicity', 'nationalism' and 'tribalism'. Although the latter terms do not necessarily entail the use of notions of biological difference, none the less, given that 'race' is here used in the sense of a social categorisation, the theoretical arguments addressed in the paper apply, in principle, to other social categorisations. Obviously, important differences do arise at the level of concrete analysis.
2 Miles (1982) contends that 'race' is not a theoretical concept capable of grounding a theory of race relations. He argues that race is to be thought of under the concept of ideology.
3 A great deal of the race relations literature uses the concepts 'class' and 'social stratification' interchangeably. Clearly, however, the Marxist conception which insists on class as designating a *social relation* and the notion of an hierarchical ordering of strata in stratification theory are quite different (see Ossowski 1963). However, it is unnecessary to pursue the point here, since,

despite the loose use of the terms 'class' and 'stratification', in the critique of class-based explanations of racism, race relations theory normally has in mind, however imprecisely, some version of the Marxist conception of class. Consequently, in what follows, I will use only the term 'class'.

4 See, for example, Simpson and Yinger 1985, Schermerhorn 1970, Cashmore and Troyna 1983, Rex 1983c, Miles 1982, Kuper and Smith 1969.
5 See, for example, Miles 1982, Wolpe 1970, Hall 1980b.
6 The similarity of this argument to the 'false consciousness' argument of reductionist versions of Marxism is patent, yet, curiously enough, Adam rejects such a position on the same page!
7 There is an extremely large literature written from this perspective, but since my purpose is not to review this literature or, indeed, to draw out much of value in it, it is sufficient to refer by way of example to Cox 1948, Davies 1979, Legassick 1974.
8 This is discussed more fully below, pp. 120–2.
9 See Bates 1973, Kuper and Smith 1971.

6

A political analysis of local struggles for racial equality

GIDEON BEN-TOVIM, JOHN GABRIEL, IAN LAW, KATHLEEN STREDDER[1]

I Introduction

The analysis of local politics and struggles for racial equality which makes up this paper[2] has been developed on the basis of our involvement in local politics. The raw data of our political experience have been accumulated through our participation in and contact with local organisations (e.g. Community Relations Councils, anti-racist groups and the Labour Party), our contact with local officers and politicians, including our roles as members of formal local committees, and our involvement in local campaigns. Our research has been carried out in Liverpool and Wolverhampton over a six-year period, although our involvement in local politics in both areas dates back considerably beyond this. More specifically, our work has included campaigns to secure and implement an equal opportunity policy with Liverpool City Council and to alter racist housing allocations and management structures in the Council and major local Housing Associations; in Wolverhampton it has included race-related political interventions in the fields of education and youth provision.

In making sense of our political experience we have worked within and at times consciously outside a number of traditions and positions within the social sciences. A brief acknowledgement of these may serve to locate the analysis which follows. The first of these concerns the relationship between research and politics. Although prevailing academic wisdom does advocate such a distinction, most authors in the field of race relations do nevertheless align themselves to a particular value standpoint, e.g. the promotion of racial harmony, the elimination of racial discrimination or the deracialisation of labour. However, despite the instrusion of value judgements in this way into race relations research, very little attempt is made to develop the implications of these value positions in any systematic way. In the main, political including policy recommendations, where they appear, remain somewhat hollow and gestural, devoid of political context and failing to contribute in any significant way to the realisation of these recommendations.

Our research, in contrast, has focused on concrete struggles over racial inequalities. Our direct involvement in those struggles has facilitated the production of knowledge and of a process of research which takes account of local conditions and contributes to change as directly as it can, in the light of these conditions. Although this has not ruled out the possibility of producing objective research evidence (e.g. surveys and case studies of institutionalised racism), what we have done is to allow local conditions to dictate research priorities and to use research findings to press for institutional change. Our intervention has served to facilitate and maximise our political analysis.

The tendency towards academicism (which the above distinction between research and politics in our view implies) is all the more surprising in the case of contemporary Marxist analysis, given the latter's commitment to social transformation. Instead of vindicating itself in terms of its contribution to political practice, much contemporary Marxist writing appears content to establish its fidelity to a particular interpretation of classical Marxism and to establish the ideological purity of its own position. Those internecine wranglings with academic bedfellows, Marxists and non-Marxists alike, are facilitated moreover by a misplaced reliance on Marxist economic theory at the expense of the development of an analysis along the lines of Marx's own political texts. The latter are rooted in an analysis of class forces and prospects for socialist and communist organisations as well as of the (highly complex) role of the state and its implications for struggle, e.g. the *Civil War in France* and the *18th Brumaire of Louis Bonaparte*. Our analysis will clearly depart from these texts in terms of content and level of analysis (civil war in Britain in the 1980s is neither a reality nor, for most, a realistic prospect). Nevertheless the idea of integrating theory and practice through an analysis of a highly specific and complex set of historical conditions (i.e. a conjuncture) within the context of a broadly based set of socialist objectives is consistent with the analysis undertaken in this paper, i.e. of local struggles aimed to secure greater equality, justice and power for racial minority communities.

The study of race itself has thrown up a variety of perspectives, many of which are brought together in this book. Each develops its own analysis in terms of a particular conception of race and of the nature and source of racial inequality. In contrast to many positions found within this book and elsewhere in the field, we choose to focus on the politics of racial inequality and on the role played by political forces in both reinforcing those inequalities on the one hand and seeking to reduce them on the other. We are not concerned, therefore, with exploring race relations in terms of culture or in terms of biological differences where those are said to manifest themselves in intelligence or (in the case of sociobiology) in innate tendencies to compete and discriminate on racial grounds. Nor do we wish to explain race relations or racialised labour in terms of class inequalities, capital accumulation and patterns of migration. This is not to suggest that race does not have a cultural or class dimension or even a symbolic significance attached to biological 'differences' (e.g. colour). Our concern with these perspectives is the secondary role assigned by them to the analysis of politics and political intervention. At most politics becomes a kind of residue, what is left (for manoeuvrability) once the determining factors, i.e. culture, biology or the economy, have exerted their influence.

In focusing on the political dimension of inequality we do not believe that we are entering some kind of autonomous sphere, where action takes over from structural constraints. On the contrary, our analysis will establish a formidable set of limiting conditions which make political advance at best slow. What prospects there are for advance, however, are not assisted in our view by a knowledge of 'immigrant culture' unless an analysis is developed of the implications of minority community rights and demands for institutional provision and of how such provision can be secured. Nor is the struggle for racial equality advanced very much by theories that racial discrimination and conflict are biologically inevitable. On the contrary, such arguments can only serve at best to legitimate political inaction and abstention and at worst to reinforce existing inequalities. Even if we were to accept that competitive and discriminatory behaviour results from genetic adaptation (which we do not), the latter must itself develop in response to environmental conditions. These conditions are by no means fixed but are contingent on a complex interplay of factors, including politics. Consequently the analysis and development of politics can in principle serve indirectly to influence forms of adaptation and hence work to reverse rather than merely acknowledge these genetic factors which supposedly give rise to racial discrimination.

Finally we are not convinced that an analysis of racism and/or racial inequality which takes economic laws of capital accumulation, migration, declining rates of profit etc. as its starting point can contribute very much to the struggle for racial equality. The economy does have a place in the political analysis of race, but its role should not usurp the significance of the political processes to which it is subject, i.e. as an

arena of struggle in which policies and practices with regard to investment, employment and management that serve to reinforce racial
inequalities can be set against forces within the labour movement or the
anti-racist movement which seek to redress them.

Our conception of politics therefore is not restricted to formal govern-
mental institutions but refers to a mode of analysing institutional
structures and relations in general. Within these institutional contexts, it
focuses on sites of struggle and conflict the outcome of which cannot be
predicted. The contingent character of those struggles rules out the
possibility of constructing a general theory of politics and/or the state.
Power can no longer be conceived in terms of fixed quantities ascribed to
individuals on the basis of some preconceived hierarchy of the state.
Instead we need to establish those conditions which make the exercise of
power possible (e.g. law, control over policy administration, access to
material resources, prevalent ideologies) and the struggles which ensue
around those conditions. The development of an analysis in this way has
implications for how we review reforms and policy initiatives. These are
the tangible outcomes of those struggles and, however gestural they
might appear, they have the potential to provide the means for further
advance. They serve to redefine those conditions referred to above and
hence help to create the balance of opposing forces. In this paper
therefore we shall conceive race policy initiatives neither as necessarily
tokenistic nor as correct solutions to problems but rather as resources
whose outcomes depend on the mobilisation of forces for and against
racial equality.

Although there exist numerous possible contexts for undertaking the
kind of political analysis developed in this paper, our own context is
necessarily limited in focus. First it is primarily local, since conditions in
the late 1970s and early 1980s have offered considerably more scope for
political interventions in this arena than at central level. Our statuses as
provincially based professionals and local activists have also shaped the
focus of our analysis. Moreover those struggles in which we have been
most actively involved have centred in and around local government,
since this has been where local anti-racist forces have devoted much of
their energies of late. This can be understood in part in terms of the
relatively greater opportunities for access and intervention provided by
local government and hence the increased prospects of some limited
advance.

Our analysis begins with a consideration of one overriding experience
of local governments from the standpoint of local organisations. This
experience can be encapsulated in the notion of marginalisation. The
means by which the process of marginalisation operates is linked to those

conditions referred to above which in turn provide the basis for the exercise of power. We consider examples of these conditions in the second part of the paper. We have also argued in this Introduction that those conditions are in part defined through and as a result of struggle. The role of anti-racist forces in helping to contain and redefine those conditions through pressure for political including policy reforms will be considered in the third part of this paper.

II Local politics and struggles for racial equality in Liverpool and Wolverhampton

(1) The process of marginalisation

One primary and pervasive experience of local organisations which take up the issues of racism and racial equality with local government is that of marginalisation. One effect of this experience is to push anti-racist forces away from the centre, towards the periphery of local politics (cf. Ouseley 1984). Not surprisingly, then, struggles against racism have become struggles within and against marginalisation. The process of marginalisation can be identified by a close examination of three forms of relation between local government and local organisations.

(i) Marginalisation through consultation

Governments, both central and local, of all political complexions have attached, at least nominally, some significance to the involvement of local communities in local decision-making. Race-related policies and policy documents have, albeit sometimes ambiguously, laid stress on the need to consult minority communities. The reality of consultation, however, in our view can hardly be said to represent a significant advance in terms of an extension of local democracy. On the contrary, and almost without exception, the variety of consultative measures in which we have been involved or which we have observed close at hand have served to emphasise inequalities between consultors and consulted. This has been the case irrespective of the particular form of consultative measure.

Committees, located within local government structures, have become an increasingly popular form of local consultation. These sometimes have statutory status, as do the Race Relations Committees in both Wolverhampton and Liverpool. At other times they are created in response to a particular issue or crisis, have only informal links with the existing committee structure and thus take on a semi-statutory status. In each of these cases, however, elected representatives, sometimes attended by local officers, sit alongside representatives of local organisations, and overall the committee has a brief or remit.

Although statutory and semi-statutory committees would appear to provide the 'best' opportunity for consultation to involve serious dialogue and responsible action on the part of local City Councils, the experience of local organisations on Liverpool's Race Relations Liaison Committee demonstrates the circumstances of community powerlessness even at this level. Devoid of any rights or sanctions, the Black Caucus of the Race Relations Liaison Committee has witnessed formal decisions regularly ignored, or directly opposed, in the Policy and Finance Committee or, in some cases, in the leadership caucus of the Party Group, from which the Black Caucus is excluded.

This process, which included the rejection of a million-pound DOE grant-aided sheltered housing scheme for the ethnic elderly, culminated in the appointment by the Labour Group of a Principal Race Relations Adviser despite massive objections by the black representatives on the appointment committee. These objections were based on the appointee's total lack of relevant qualification and experience and on his stance on racial inequality which he subordinated to the more general issue of urban deprivation and class inequality. The ensuing boycott of this appointment by local authority unions and black organisations led to the suspension of the Race Relations Liaison Committee and the previously legitimated black representatives and groups were branded by the Labour leadership as an 'unrepresentative faction' (*Black Linx* 1984).

A second form of consultation is the variety of one-off public meetings organised by local authorities in response to the increasing demands by community groups over the last decade. These include day conferences, seminars, workshops and exhibitions on a range of issues (e.g. mother-tongue teaching or policing practices) and are viewed by members and officers of the local authority as consultative exercises, in so far as they are concerned with community-linked issues. The fact is, however, that most often they fail to provide the opportunity for the exchange and development of ideas, let alone for the making of policy. On the contrary, they are more likely to create a false consensus and a context in which dissension and conflict are covertly, if not openly, discouraged; and recommendations, statements of intent and even written reports which emerge from them are likely to be disregarded.

A third form of local consultation is the *ad hoc* meeting which involves politicians and officers on the one hand and representatives of local organisations on the other. This obviously differs from the committee in that it has no statutory status and therefore is subject not only to termination at the discretion of the elected representatives but also to their whim and will for the nature, aim and action of the meeting. Consultations in Wolverhampton with the local Council for Community Relations over funding arrangements under Section 11 provide a clear example of the problems encountered here. The differences in power between the political and officer leadership on the one hand and WCCR on the other manifested themselves in such things as control over the agenda and the direction of the discussion; control over the information that was to be made available; control over those decisions that are negotiable and those that are not; and, ultimately, the power of veto.

(ii) Anti-racism as extremism

The absence of any genuine forms of participatory machinery has encouraged alternative kinds of community response to emerge. In Wolverhampton, for instance, the absence of adequate forms of consultation over Section 11 provoked black organisations to write a letter of complaint to the Home Office, to threaten a boycott of local elections, and in one instance to stand an independent candidate against the incumbent Labour Party member. Such actions were dismissed as naïve and extreme by local Labour politicians, although they were nevertheless predictable given the failure of local organisations to have any effect on the Local Authority.

In the case of the appointment of the Principal Race Relations Adviser in Liverpool black groups were forced to undertake a variety of protests (a sit-in, a disruption of a Council meeting, a march and a regular vigil outside the municipal offices). These actions were used by the Labour Group to label, isolate and undermine the opposition that was mounted in this way, through slurs of 'self-appointed leaders', using 'alien' methods of protest, encouraging 'violent' activities and 'dividing the working class'.

It is not only the various kinds of reaction described above which attract labels of extremism and fanaticism. Equally unacceptable is the content of anti-racist arguments, which is often dismissed as hysterical, outrageous or pure fanaticism. Anti-racist arguments are described in these ways because they fall outside local bureaucratic definitions and interpretations of race problems (e.g. those which explain race problems in terms of cultural differences). These official definitions, articulated by principal officers and administrators, have become deeply embedded in professional policy and practice. Their respectability and apparent neutrality often serve both directly and indirectly to legitimate local popular racist opinion.

Anti-racism, since it challenges the prevailing norms inherent in institutional policy and practice, is thus inevitably regarded as extreme.

This is particularly the case in so far as local organisations are encouraged to resort to direct action, protest, accusation and demonstration. In our experience there is a tendency for politicians and professionals to capitalise on the extremities of anti-racism and to use them as a pretext for inaction rather than responding systematically to the principles underpinning anti-racism and the struggle for racial equality

In Wolverhampton, the 'turban case' involving Mr Noor, a leading member of the Indian Workers' Association (GB), provides a good example of some of the above points. A Sikh pupil was sent home from a local school by the head teacher for wearing a turban. In the protest following the incident, the head teacher's actions were described, by Mr Noor, as racist, and the allegation was printed in the local *Express and Star*. It was this allegation which provided the basis for a libel suit which was successfully filed against Mr Noor with damages of £50,000.

Mr Noor might have won this case had it been commonly accepted that actions which effectively discriminate against racial groups can quite legitimately be described as racist. The head teacher, then, in preventing the pupil from conforming to personal religious requirements, would have been guilty of indirect discrimination at the very least. The official view however was that Mr Noor had over-stepped the bounds of reason and that his allegation of racism constituted a gross aspersion on the character of a local head teacher whose contribution to multi-cultural education was officially well-regarded. Linked to this, and working against him, was Mr Noor's reputation for making 'outrageous' remarks on race issues, with the case being popularly presented as a battle between the forces of 'extremism' and moderation.

Mr Noor's struggle, although not successful in itself, was part of a broader more successful struggle to put institutionalised racism on the political agenda. In common with the broad strategy pursued by anti-racist organisations he sought to bring terms like 'racism' from the extremes or margins of political debate into official argument. That racism has become increasingly acknowledged not only in judicial decisions but also in policy documents, committee reports and ministerial interventions must in part be attributed to community struggles like Mr Noor's.

(iii) Funding cultural initiatives

There is a tendency on the part of local authorities to restrict race relations initiatives to one-off, high-profile measures rather than to develop a sustained, mainstream-oriented programme of action. This tendency is in part a reflection of trends within central government philosophy and funding policies. In particular, inner city initiatives including the Urban Programme and more recently *Policy for the Inner Cities* (Cmnd 6845) have provided a framework within which funds have, somewhat ambiguously, been made available for meeting the special needs of minority groups. The term 'ethnic group' becomes significant in this political context, since resources are thus linked to ethnic (or cultural) differences or needs (cf. Stewart and Whitting 1983).

Inner city policies have been directed on a selective basis to those geographical areas of highest social need, including both Liverpool and Wolverhampton. Resources have thus been allocated to fund a range of local centres and projects for Afro-Caribbean, Asian and Chinese communities. In general the funding of these centres and other limited project initiatives provides confirmation that measures are being taken by the two local authorities, a fact which may be expedient in the aftermath of street conflicts or 'riots'. At the same time such funding can serve to divert attention away from racial inequalities which are institutionally generated and/or maintained through mainstream provision. The failure to link these *ad hoc* cultural initiatives to any kind of participation in formal political processes has further served to immunise local institutions from more fundamental and sustained pressure from local organisations and groups. Not only are cultural initiatives expedient, visible and non-threatening through their isolation. They are also relatively cheap, particularly for local authorities who are able to claim approximately seventy-five per cent of the total cost of their programmes etc. from central government.

The inconsistencies in Liverpool City Council's relationship with the Chinese community illustrate some of these points. The Council funds a Community Centre and some Centre staff, and gives high-profile support to the Chinese New Year celebrations. Yet despite the Council's success in winning Urban Programme and Section 11 funding for the establishment of a Chinese Social Work Unit in the Social Services Department, great resistance was mounted by leading Labour politicians to support for the potentially more significant policy-oriented Unit.

(2) Conditions which serve to marginalise anti-racist forces

(i) Local political ideologies
We have suggested above that power in social relations could be analysed in the first instance in terms of those conditions which create the potential for its effective exercise. In this section we shall identify a number of such conditions, the first of which has been the prevalence of a particular form of racial ideology, which has been referred to elsewhere as 'colour-blindness' (Ouseley 1982b), so called because it fails to acknowledge the

specific dimension of racism and racial inequality and consequently resists any attempt to tackle racism independently of the patterns of urban deprivation or class inequality. Its strength lies in its compatibility with various shades of political opinion and its consequent accommodation within certain brands of liberalism, conservatism and socialism as well as the universalistic ('a-political') ideologies and practices of public administration and its practitioners. Each of these broader ideologies in turn is able to justify action, or more strictly in the case of colour-blindness inaction, through a defence of the supremacy of individual rights, national interest or class struggle over the needs, disadvantages and rights of racially defined groups.

What binds the threads of colour-blind ideologies therefore is the absence of racism (except when it is defined in the very narrow sense of overt and conscious discrimination). What varies is the justification for the absence which may in our experience be anticipated in various ways, including assertions that to raise the question of racism is divisive, an incitement to racial discord or an invitation for a 'white back-lash', or that the problems attributed to black people are shared with the white population, the working-class, or all in the inner cities.

This failure to acknowledge the specific dimensions of racism is linked in terms of its policy implications to various forms of resistance to positive action: thus special provision, e.g. for ethnic elders or Asian girls, has at times been opposed in the name of a commitment to integrated facilities, despite the exclusion of black people from such provision or its unsuitability for particular minorities. Positive action has also been dismissed on the basis of opposition to 'preferential treatment', however much existing practices are shown to favour the indigenous white population.

Thus the whole spectrum of political ideologies may each appeal to conventional forms of reason and morality which in so far as they continue to prevail serve to undermine the force and credibility of anti-racist politics. The latter has thus the formidable task of forging links with positions which appear broadly incompatible at one level (e.g. conservatism, liberalism, socialism) but which converge in the common refusal to acknowledge the specific character of racism and racial inequality along with the policy implications which follow from this acknowledgement.

(ii) Legislation and central policy initiatives

The relationship between those conditions which serve to marginalise anti-racist forces can be regarded as both mutually supportive and at times inconsistent. In other words we do not regard them as some kind of chain of cause and effect; nor do we regard one condition as more significant than the others. Central policy initiatives, including legislation, can under certain conditions be used both in support of and in opposition to political ideologies, such as colour-blindness, operating at a local level.

In general, central policy initiatives add up to a patchy, somewhat inconsistent framework comprising laws, policy statements, directives, circulars, reports, regulations and consultative machinery. In so far as race has become an issue centrally, it has been confined to a number of special policies which have served to reinforce overtly negative (as far as black people are concerned) formulations of the race problem (e.g. policies on immigration and policing). It has also provided an extremely loose, permissive and ambiguous framework within which positive policies need or need not be developed locally (e.g. the Urban Programme or the Race Relations Act with its non-directive support for 'positive action' initiatives). Finally, the 'special' nature of these initiatives has left a whole range of policy fields untouched in terms of providing directives, regulations and terms of enforcement for the development of positive initiatives at a local level.

Section 11 of the 1966 Local Government Act exemplifies all three of the above characteristics. Section 11 was not in terms of its inception a measure designed to redress racial injustices or to promote racial equality. It was more a form of financial compensation paid by central government to certain local authorities for (staffing) expenses arising from the settlement of immigrants and from associated 'problems' within their local areas (Young 1983). In this sense then Section 11 serves to reinforce negative views of black people and to make understandable and legitimate local hostility at their presence. The absence of any positive framework for the specific allocation of the monies available allowed local authorities to claim funding for staff salaries without developing special job responsibilities or even, for the most part, identifying holders of Section 11 posts. Finally, even if Section 11 had been used positively, it would have always remained a 'special measure' and its central administrative location within the Home Office would have prevented it from providing a means for a fundamental rethinking of mainstream policy within local education authorities, social services and other departments.

(iii) Local bureaucratic control of policy-making and administration

It is not only political representatives who are resistant to pressure from below which seeks to challenge prevalent ideologies, policies and practices. Senior officers, administrators and public practitioners (e.g. teachers) have all developed strategies which can be used to inhibit initiatives aimed at promoting racial equality (cf. Young and Connelly 1981). In Wolverhampton for instance a long-waged struggle to combat the complex forms of institutionalised racism within education has been consistently resisted by senior education officers and a clear majority of teachers who prefer to work within a universalistic, 'treat them the same' ideology rather than with the ideas found among a minority of the service committed to positive change. *Ad hoc* consultative machinery has been used to exert pressure on senior education officials to provide information and to reform detailed aspects of policy and practice. But the sporadic nature of consultation, the resources available to the community, the continuity of professional involvement, its control over information and its capacity to maintain traditional bureaucratic traits of perceived self-interest, inertia and defensiveness can pose a formidable array of obstacles in the way of effective intervention from below.

(iv) Financial constraints inhibiting redistribution

Cut-backs in central government's financial support to local authorities, alongside increased controls on how local government allocates its resources, can provide strong additional arguments for resisting positive change. What is perhaps more revealing is the consistency with which positive action has been resisted over the past twenty years irrespective of changes in the levels and form of financial control by central and local government. In our view economic austerity and growing central control over local budgeting are not as significant in themselves as they are in terms of the pretexts they have provided for further inaction.

In our experience many local organisational proposals aimed at eliminating institutional racism have at best entailed no additional cost and at worst required the redistribution of current expenditure. The expansion of the black work-force within the local public sector, the attachment of equal opportunity conditions to public contracts with the private sector, the creation of participatory structures within local government involving black organisations and parents in the running of public services, the expansion of a youth counselling service at the expense of traditional youth club provision, the allocation of black applicants to council properties on an equal basis to whites, are all possible within both the limits imposed by central government and local pressure to minimise rate increases.

In conclusion to this section we would therefore argue that there exist strong forces within local government which can serve and, in our experience, have served to militate against the use of the local public sector as an instrument of positive social change in the pursuit of racial equality. Deep-seated cultural traditions within the Town Hall foster political styles of rhetoric, posturing and megalomania among politicians which not only serve to alienate the vast majority of apolitical constituents but also have a wearing effect on those committed to positive social change. These traditions can thus serve to reinforce the strength of bureaucratic tradition which has little to challenge it from above. Such effective control is thus exercised both defensively and self-interestedly and is invariably justified in the name of administrative neutrality. What is perhaps most disturbing of all, in our experience, is the extent to which both politicians and officers have joined forces in the face of pressure from anti-racist forces from outside the Town Hall. In the course of their active conscious collusion, which we have witnessed directly in the context of consultation, they have employed with considerable sophistication the clichéd practices of gerrymandering and filibustering in order to withstand the pressure from representatives of the community.

(3) Forms of anti-racist struggle

The marginalisation of anti-racist forces and the conditions which make marginalisation possible have been the focus of the first part of our analysis. The purpose so far has been to establish the context in which racism is challenged and racial equality pursued. In what remains of this paper we examine three different forms of struggle, each of which offers its own particular challenge to racial inequalities.

The three forms of struggle, i.e. spontaneous protest, pressure for community resources and planned political struggle, reflect a variety of responses to the problem of racial inequality. Although all three are committed to challenging racism, some are more explicit and specific than others in defining their objectives. Strategies correspondingly vary, according to stated (or unstated) objectives, since each form of struggle has its own priorities and its own understanding of how best these might be achieved (cf. Ben-Tovim *et al.* 1982b).

The effects or consequences of struggle may be quite concrete, e.g. a positive redistribution of resources, or more abstract and less tangible, e.g. an acknowledgement of the role of institutionalised forms of racism in creating and maintaining racial inequality. Race-related reforms can thus be seen to represent the more tangible effects of struggle. In common with other effects these reforms help to redefine the conditions of future struggle and hence should in our view play an integral role in the development of anti-racist strategy. The significance which we attach to calculation of this kind is responsible for the emphasis we place on planned political struggle. Overall our assessment of change *vis à vis* racial inequality, which we take to be the focus of our analysis, is thus based on, and will vary according to, those conditions analysed in the previous section and the particular forms of anti-racist struggle which we discuss below.

(i) 'Riots' as an issue in local politics

Spontaneous street protests are significant not only because they have proved important catalysts for reform but also for the way in which they have become issues in local politics. Contrary to much press reporting and some political interpretations, the 1981 disturbances were probably not part of an orchestrated strategy on the part of those involved. Nor can they be dismissed as hooliganism or criminality and hence as non-political. In our view spontaneous protest has through history and up to now represented a significant form of political intervention which, although distinct from other forms to be considered below, nevertheless remains a legitimate object of political analysis.

Our concern is not so much with disentangling the causes of the 1981 conflicts but rather with identifying the *effects* of the riots, particularly in terms of policy-making and mainstream political practice at a local level. Our experience here reveals that whatever the insurrectionary nature of street conflict, its major impact (ironically, probably, for many of its advocates and participants) can only be described as reformist. In many respects disturbances or the threat of them have been a more effective lever and instrument in local reform, notably resource allocation (e.g. in terms of funding for an Afro-Caribbean Cultural Centre in Wolverhampton or the Liverpool 8 Law Centre in Liverpool), than those political forces for whom such change constitutes an integral part of their political practice.

The form of response on the part of local statutory bodies to periodic street conflicts or the threat of them has however remained consistently *ad hoc* and gestural. That responses are invariably made *in the wake of* these 'crises' and not as a matter of principle or for that matter in response to formal and informal pressure through conventional political channels must encourage a cynical view of local policy development (cf. Edwards and Batley 1978). Whether these 'panic' responses take the form of one-off projects or of impromptu meetings of national or local politicians with community leaders, they are rarely followed up. Furthermore, such responses have consistently marked an absence of political will on the part of statutory agencies to tackle in any kind of sustained way the problems of racism and racial disadvantage.

(ii) Pressure for community resources

Community and project work, which incorporates explicit commitment to racial equality, varies considerably in the range of its activities. Supplementary schools, projects for young offenders, and the provision of welfare rights counselling are examples of the various forms it can take. Across this broad spectrum of activities, community and project work seeks to meet the perceived needs of the community through the making of provision which either supplements or represents an alternative to mainstream provision. In principle this kind of activity brings organisations into direct daily contact with members of the community who seek help on an individual basis or through group activity. Hence casework and project development have become important features of community work organisations.

The pursuit of these objectives has brought some organisations into conflict with the local authority (e.g. Wolverhampton Rastafarian Progressive Association's use of direct action, including a sit-in protest, in order to secure funding). In the main, however, contact with the local authority takes place in the context of making grant applications for additional resources, i.e. through channels which are both legitimate and pose no direct threat to the local authority.

The outcome of any community work initiative will appear piecemeal and minimal given the potency and prevalence of racial inequality. The establishment of a supplementary school may benefit its own pupils but will not necessarily affect the vast majority of black children in mainstream education. Welfare rights counselling may benefit a minority of individual claimants, in contrast to a change in policy and/or the law which may affect claimants as a whole. The significance of community work organisations therefore may lie in their identification of community needs and their highlighting of deficiencies in mainstream provision. Unless these needs are pursued, however, in the context of struggles for institutional change, their impact will be correspondingly limited. In so far as institutional deficiencies are tackled in this broader context, community work activity gives way to planned political struggle.

(iii) Planned political struggle: challenging local policy and the policy-making framework

Our third form of intervention may be distinguished from spontaneous protest because of its planned characteristics and from resource-bidding because of the breadth and scope of its target: i.e. it seeks to challenge policy and the existing policy-making framework.

Although the organisations we have supported have been involved in campaign activity we would not for the most part describe their involvement in political struggle in this way. Campaign activity in our experience stands for organised political struggle around a series of specific, finite and agreed-upon objectives. Liverpool City Council's decision to introduce an equal opportunity policy in 1981, for instance, resulted directly from one such grassroots campaign. In the main, however, our political involvement is less tangible, less co-ordinated, and more uneven and sporadic.

Below we identify some of the characteristic features of political activities with which we have been directly associated. These characteristics, it should be noted, reflect a series of challenges to those conditions described above which serve to marginalise anti-racist political forces. Throughout this paper we have stressed the contingency of those conditions, i.e. with respect to the possibility of predicting their realisation with any certainty. This contingency results precisely from political struggle, which in turn depends on the nature and characteristics of anti-racist forces. Overall, our experience once again makes us cautious in our appraisal of these struggles. Apparent breakthroughs often turn out to be momentary and fleeting, victories somewhat hollow, concessions gestural and reforms less consequential than they at first appear, with advance subsequently turning into retreat. What follows then are some of the characteristics of anti-racist struggle, each of which seeks to redress racial inequality by challenging those conditions which serve to reinforce it.

(a) Redefining the problem

A major undertaking of anti-racist organisations has been to argue the case for positive action, supported by evidence of institutionalised racism and resulting inequalities (cf. Prashar 1984). We have already noted the strength of colour-blind ideologies in local politics and the ways in which they act as a strong force of resistance to positive programmes for racial equality. Anti-racist forces have thus sought to provide evidence of inequalities on the one hand and of the compatibility of positive action with the broader political objectives of socialism on the other.

In Liverpool the production of a profile of opportunities in the city included evidence of the disproportionately low number of black workers in the City Council (Ben-Tovim *et al.* 1980, Ben-Tovim, ed. 1983), while a survey of council housing proved the discrepancies in the quality and location of housing allocated to black and white tenants (Commission for Racial Equality 1984). Similarly, In Wolverhampton the inadequacy of youth facilities for groups of young people of Afro-Caribbean and Asian descent, cases of alleged police harassment, evidence of disproportionate numbers of expulsions from school, the disproportionately low numbers of black school governors are just some examples from a flow of evidence of racism and inequality (Gabriel and Stredder 1981, 1982).

At the heart of these debates is the question of where responsibility lies. The argument underlying positive action places that responsibility unequivocally on the institution. The absence of black people from employment in the Town Hall, of Asian girls from youth facilities in Wolverhampton, of black people from desirable council property in Liverpool or of Asian languages from schools in Wolverhampton must be considered in terms of institutional failure to redefine job responsibilities, to develop appropriate criteria for selection and to devise recruitment procedures which ensure greater proportions of black employees and to develop provision which is attractive to young Asian women. Redefining the problem thus becomes challenging assumptions which attribute the above problems to the lack of qualified applicants, to cultural conflict within the Asian community, to community housing preferences or to the black failure to integrate with or assimilate to Western culture.

The implications of relocating the problem in these terms point unambiguously towards some kind of positive action, which may have been argued for in consultative meetings, in the local press, in Labour Party meetings and in *ad hoc* deputations to civic leaders and others. The ever-present danger is that a concession to positive action might mask a cynical lack of commitment to act on its implications. Moreover, politicians and officers by virtue of their political position and their control over administration are able to ignore sporadic pressure from consultative procedures etc.

(b) Building alliances

Those engaged in political struggle have sought in varying degrees to embrace as wide a spectrum as possible of concerned groups and organisations from within the community in order to pre-empt attempts to dismiss anti-racism as unrepresentative of community demands (Ohri and Donnelly 1982, Ouseley 1982a). In Liverpool the equal opportunity campaign included a broad range of community representation, coordinated through the Merseyside Community Relations Council, which enabled a variety of forms of pressure to be exerted at different points and in a united manner within the apparatus of local government (Ben-Tovim *et al.* 1981b, 1982a).

Nevertheless, our organisational experience has repeatedly confirmed to us the fragility of alliances. They invariably rely on a base of active support which is in reality quite narrow, however representative the views of the community spokespeople. The breadth of organisational support often masks a core of individuals working simultaneously in a number of organisations. The departure or withdrawal of a key individual, therefore, can often threaten the survival of a seemingly broad-based alliance. Collaboration between organisations, if it succeeds at all, may only do so for the lifetime of a particular issue. Invariably struggles crystallise around a set of concrete demands; in the unlikely event of their acceptance, the disbanding of the alliance structure may follow. Despite the crucial significance of the next stage of policy implementation, this political reality combines with the disproportionate responsibilities which fall to a few under-resourced organisations and over-committed activists (together with effective manoeuvring, delaying and dividing on the part of politicians and officers alike) to weaken the long-term thrust of collective community pressures.

(c) Breaking down resistance
A priority in anti-racist struggle is the identification of crucial points of potential institutional resistance and the attempt to neutralise these, if not to win them over. The significance of gaining trade union support for the principle of an equal opportunity policy in Liverpool became clear at the campaign's earliest stages. Trade unions not only represented one source of official opposition, which had to be negotiated. They were, perhaps more significantly, regarded as crucial in terms of the policy's implementation. The campaign therefore undertook various activities to persuade the Liverpool Trades Council and later local trade unions to join the call for an equal opportunity policy within the authority. This ultimately proved decisive in the campaign's success, given the marked tendency on the part of local governments to respect the views of local trade unions in so far as the latter appear resistant to the principle of positive action. In Liverpool's case, trade union support thus effectively challenged institutional recalcitrance, a condition which was only realised through the development of links between trade unions, anti-racist groups and other community organisations.

(d) Using central initiatives in support of anti-racist struggles
The relative ease with which local authorities have been able to resist pressure for positive action is in part made possible by the failure of central government to take a strong and effective positive lead on racism and racial equality. On the contrary, local authorities have invariably used central policies for legitimating inaction. Overall the onus remains heavily on local organisations to maximise the scope and use of central policy initiatives. The context provided by central government, however, is one of remoteness from local struggle. It rarely provides sustained and

co-ordinated support for local struggle, and in some situations it works as much against as for local struggle.

For example, during the equal opportunity campaign in Liverpool the Commission for Racial Equality made a general promotional visit to the city in order to gain local Council support for a positive policy in line with the 1976 Race Relations Act. Unfortunately, poor organisation on the part of the Commission for Racial Equality on this occasion, including a lack of co-ordination with the local Community Relations Council, seemed to do little to alter local official attitudes. Similarly, in Wolverhampton, local organisations planned to take advantage of a visitation from the Home Office to press the case against the local authority's misuse of Section 11 funds, but effective stage-management on the part of the authority combined with selective listening and adept manoeuvring on the part of the Home Office team to silence would-be opposition.

Our overriding experience of central initiatives should not however lead us to ignore the way in which local struggles have effectively appealed to and utilised the centre both in specific instances and in a more general sense. In Liverpool, campaign activists made use of the 1976 Race Relations Act, and in particular of Section 71's general exhortations to local authorities to promote equal opportunities. Similarly, in Wolverhampton, Home Office revisions to the administrative guidelines governing Section 11 funding were used to encourage the local authority to provide more information and to involve communities in submissions for funding.

(e) Lobbying local politicians and officials

Because political struggles against racism invariably take place at the margins of local government, the struggles often never reach the formal agendas of local decision-making machinery. In so far as they do, a successful outcome clearly depends on the support of local politicians and officers for specific demands. Hence in the case of Liverpool's equal opportunity campaign much lobbying and canvassing was carried out in the build-up to the committee meeting at which the issue was ultimately debated and accepted. This included meetings with the leaders of all parties, discussions with key officers, submission of written material to all Councillors, co-ordination with trade unions and ensuring a substantial and visible minority presence at the meeting itself.

The eventual adoption by the City Council of an equal opportunity policy statement was, then, the culmination of nearly two years' sustained and co-ordinated campaigning by an alliance of local organisations. This resulted in a complete about-turn in the way the politicians and officials had traditionally regarded issues of race in the city. But, as the Home Office was quick to acknowledge, this grassroots achievement in Liverpool was unique. Elsewhere, in our experience, continuity of effort is often broken down by institutional forces of resistance. Conditions which make for the marginalisation of anti-racist forces realise themselves despite pressure from below. Even in Liverpool, the successful conclusion to the campaign must be set against subsequent events. In other words, even a policy decision as significant as that promoting equal opportunity can only ever be regarded as a stage in a process of struggle which is ongoing and within which there may be setbacks. In the case of Liverpool, the Labour leadership has since fought and won back its control over the appointment of the Principal Race Relations Adviser. There has also been, of course, the subsequent suspension of the Race Relations Liaison Committee which was set up to oversee the equal opportunity policy.

III Conclusions

Our analysis of political struggles for racial equality in local government has confirmed the integral role of organisations and of policies in those struggles, both of which are frequently overlooked in social science literature including Marxism. Political struggle, in our experience, is marked by movements of advance and retreat which are invariably slow, sometimes imperceptible, but never predictable. Of course we can say that the forces of resistance to racial equality within local government can be formidable, particularly the prevalence of racial ideologies. The most common of these 'attitudes' in our experience is characterised by a refusal to acknowledge racism and relatedly to pursue any of the steps necessary to redress it. The continuing prevalence of colour-blind ideologies within local government is made possible through the realisation of other conditions: the ambiguity and permissiveness of central policy initiatives, the control exercised at the local officer level over information as well as policy implementation and administration, and the compatibility of colour-blindness with a broad range of mainstream political ideologies.

We have argued that the above conditions are not fixed. Their realisation depends in part on the strength of the challenge from anti-racist forces, which have challenged institutional resistance through spontaneous protest, bidding for resources and planned political struggle. The last of these, of which we have most direct experience, has sought to challenge those conditions referred to above in the most specific and direct ways. That is to say, it has engaged in struggle over conflicting definitions of the problem, it has attempted to pre-empt charges of extremism through the building of alliances, to break down resistance through negotiation and representation and to turn central resources from negative obstacles into positive initiatives in support of anti-racist struggles.

Reforms and policy initiatives which result in part from these struggles over conditions help define future conditions of struggle. For this reason alone planned struggle cannot afford to ignore or to dismiss as divisive or gestural reforms, such as equal opportunity policies, specialist race staff, new committees and units, and monitoring; instead it must acknowledge them as integral parts of the conditions of struggle. To argue this is not to deny the fragility of advances secured through struggle; nor is it to underestimate the attack on a reform's potential through the reassertion of those forces of resistance described above. The weaknesses of anti-racist forces cannot, regrettably, be ignored in this analysis. They invariably operate within a narrow conception of what is regarded as politically legitimate, so that the task facing local organisations in the struggle against marginalisation, pseudo-forms of consultation and charges of extremism is indeed immense.

In this situation, research has an indispensable role to play in helping to politicise the issue of racism by documenting and publicising forms of inequality, unravelling the structures and processes which shape them, developing strategies for intervention and change, and linking this research to the ongoing process of political struggle by anti-racist organisations.

This is clearly a radically different approach to research from the case study methodology that looks necessarily superficially at a sample of a number of local authorities, or from the more intensive but equally non-participant investigation of an externally pre-defined area of interest. We would argue that, both as a source of valid knowledge of the processes and conditions of successful/unsuccessful race relations interventions and as a responsible and purposeful use of research resources, our approach is quite as legitimate and useful as those more conventional methods. We would also insist that this is far closer to the spirit of Marxism, the 'unity of theory and practice' or 'praxis', than much of the Marxist sociology of race referred to in the Introduction that has in recent years institutionalised Marxism within mainstream social science.

NOTES

1 *The authors*
   Gideon Ben-Tovim is Lecturer in Sociology, University of Liverpool, and is also Chairperson, Merseyside Community Relations Council.

John Gabriel is Lecturer in Sociology, University of Birmingham, and is also Vice-Chairperson, Wolverhampton Council for Community Relations.

Ian Law was Public Education Officer, Merseyside Community Relations Council and is now Race Relations Officer (Housing), Leeds City Council.

Kathleen Stredder is Lecturer in Applied Social Studies, Birmingham Polytechnic, and is a member of the Executive Committee, Wolverhampton Council for Community Relations.

2 The original paper has been revised in the light of comments and discussion at the Oxford conference and subsequent editorial suggestions and draws on material from our forthcoming book *The Local Politics of Race* (Macmillan), particularly Chapter 5.

7

Ethnicity and Third World development: political and academic contexts

MARSHALL W. MURPHREE

'International' and 'Third World' politico-academic contexts

Current analytic directions in the study of race and ethnicity provide useful grist for the contemporary mills of the sociology of knowledge. Not only do they demonstrate the historical evolution of different epistemological stances, as Michael Banton has shown in chapter 2; they also reflect the ongoing synthesis that we create between these academic traditions and the specific politico-academic contexts in which we operate. These contexts to a large extent determine our perspectives, focus our interest and through criteria of relevance set our priorities and provide funding for our scholarship. In discussing the analytic salience of these contexts this paper generalises to the extent of distinguishing between 'international' and 'Third World'[1] arenas of scholarship, suggesting that in the Third World the contemporary analytic emphasis is on ethnicity rather than race, on national rather than international dimensions and on socio-political rather than socio-economic structures.

To illustrate the contrasts drawn in the generalisations made above, it is instructive to contrast two statements indicating agendas for race and ethnic relations research, one from a scholar representative of the international perspective and the other from a Third World research organisation. The first statement is by John Rex, who in his state-of-the-art paper of 1982 (Rex 1982a: 173–4) commented: 'Racial discrimination, racial oppression, the propagation of racist ideas and genocide have all been topics of international concern and sociologists have been called upon to delineate their field and indicate the major causal factors responsible for these phenomena.' The international concern mentioned is often articulated through such organisations as the United Nations and its various agencies, which provide the funding necessary for its concomitant research and analysis. Rex goes on to comment on UNESCO's sponsorship of some of the activities of the International Sociological Association's Research Committee on Ethnic, Race and Minority Relations, saying: 'The work of the research committee has therefore been dominated by practical political concerns and the theoretical problem which it has faced is how to define its field in such a way as to contribute to the understanding of those problems.' One consequence, says Rex, has been 'the underplaying of certain themes thought to be part of the sociology of race relations', such as the 'phenomenology of microsociological associations'. Another is an emphasis on 'cross-national comparative work, looking at the comparative socioeconomic systems and the effect which these have on major forms of group inter-action'. With these considerations in mind Rex offers his own formula for further developments in the comparative sociology of race relations which seeks to synthesise elements of neo-Marxist analysis on the global functions and structures of capitalism as a world system with a study of the relation of 'the position of the various ethnic and racial and minority groups to their position in the system of colonial production and exploitation' (1982a: 189). Rex's arguments are cogent; however, they are mentioned here not to debate them but as supporting evidence concerning the importance of environing politico-academic climates. Propelled by the momentum of what is today one of the most central conceptual debates in sociology, and fuelled by the geo-political concerns of bodies which have the resources to support the debate, Rex's agenda is as contextually predictable as it is theoretically seminal.

In contrast to the agenda proposed by Rex, the proposed research programme of the International Centre for Ethnic Studies (ICES) recently formed in Sri Lanka reflects a significantly different focus in context and content. A circular from the Centre (ICES 1982) sets out the following list of subjects, quoted here verbatim:

1 assessment of experience under various structural–constitutional approaches to the easing of ethnic tensions, such as Nigeria's new constitution and electoral law;
2 moves towards decentralisation and higher degrees of regional autonomy;
3 the opportunities for ethnic pluralism under federal systems of government, with extensive authority on state and local levels, etc;
4 studies of various rationales for preference policies;
5 analyses of the processes of accommodation between different interest groups;
6 impact studies to assess the effectiveness of legislation in altering social behaviour and discriminatory practices;

7 monitoring of affirmative action and other compensatory programs;
8 criteria and processes for terminating preference policies once their objectives have been fulfilled;
9 the impact of economic development on the human rights of indigenous populations (e.g. in the United States, Malaysia, India and several Latin American settings);
10 the link between ethnic conflict and international migration (e.g. in Bangladesh, Uganda and Vietnam)[2].

Of the ten items listed above, only the last two show a close congruence with Rex's concerns regarding macro-economic structures and class relationships articulated within a global system. The rest are implicitly framed within national contexts and emphasise socio-political rather than socio-economic issues and ethnic rather than racial relationships.

The generalised distinctions made above must of course be handled with some caution. For one thing, neither the statement by Rex nor the ICES research agenda can be considered to be detailed and comprehensive statements of the analytic foci of either the international or the Third World arena of our scholarship. For another, the distinctions made are matters of emphasis and are neither categorical nor mutually exclusive. They should not be allowed to conceal the common interests which many scholars in the two categories share. Many academics operating in the international arena have as their central interest the structural accommodation of ethnic minorities, the impact of legislation on discrimination, redressive policies and other issues characteristic of the ICES agenda. Conversely, many Third World scholars take as the focus of their work such issues as the impact of racism and its implications for human rights and the structures of international politico-economic relations. Particularly in the independent states of Southern Africa this work centres on attention to both the colonial experiences of the past and the present policies of South Africa, and as elsewhere there has been a shift in focus to macro-structural issues and an interest in class relationships.

These caveats having been made, the fact remains that the total configuration of emphasis is significantly different in the two contexts of scholarship. First, whereas in the international arena of debate the interest in macro-structural concerns and class relationships focuses on articulations within a global system, the focus in the Third World is on national contexts. Second, while in the international arena macro-structural issues are analysed primarily in their economic dimensions, in the Third World the central focus is on their political content and context. These differences are not simply the result of historic patterns of dissemination in respect of different analytic perspectives; rather they are largely attributable to the responses of scholars to the pragmatic imperative which demands that for their scholarship to thrive it must be seen as being relevant to environing societal concerns. In our scholarship in the prevailing international academic scene this relevance is defined largely in terms of moral and geo-political pressures on the developed societies of the West to eradicate the racism which remains within their own structures and which continues to influence their international economic and political relations. In the Third World this relevance is defined largely in terms of concern for the continued viability and growth of the post-colonial state. In the current idiom of the Third World these issues are generally subsumed under the rubric of 'development'; hence any studies on race and ethnicity are required to demonstrate their development relevance within state contexts.

Development and the state in the Third World

In the post-colonial world it is the state system which has become the authoritative arena for the definition of structures, identity, goals and obstacles, a 'contemporary paradigm of political organisation so pervasive in its impact that conscious political thought is shaped and moulded by a model so thoroughly assimilated as to be largely unconscious' (Young 1976: 73). It is the state, therefore, which provides the context of relevance.

If the state provides the context of relevance, its survival provides the content. In order to survive, the post-colonial state must successfully confront and resolve a number of issues, including the management of its resources so as to ensure the material well-being of its peoples, the maintenance of its legitimacy both internally and externally, and the creation of a sense of national participation and identity which turns the state into a nation. Almost uniquely, in the Third World post-colonial state the responsibility for the resolution of these issues lies virtually exclusively with the state and its organs of government. Not entirely uniquely, since these states have drawn heavily from models in the Marxist-Leninist world with their emphasis on the central role of the state and, more specifically, the governing party. Thus the mode of resolution is one of state bureaucratic vanguardism carried out by the inaugural and victorious nationalist party or its successors. 'The Nationalists would make the state, and the state would make the nation' (Geertz 1975: 240).

The resolution of the issues mentioned earlier, in the mode mentioned above, constitutes the operative definition of development in the Third World. As Young points out, Third World nationalism has elevated development to its place as the central defining characteristic of the purpose of the state, 'Nationalism could not be a mere rejection of foreign rule: the positive goals of cultural regeneration and escape from poverty were an inseparable component' (1976: 74). Since the Third World state is usually an historically derived heterogeneous collectivity thrown together by the processes of colonialism and welded together by the bitter struggles of nationalist anti-colonialism, both ethnic and racial factors[3] feature prominently in any attempts to achieve these goals. In the period immediately surrounding the attainment of political independence racial factors have tended to predominate, and they subsequently retain a residual salience in respect to the international political and economic dimensions of the new state's location. Internally however it is the ethnic factor which gains particular salience since the heterogeneity mentioned tends to be ethnic in character. The territorial dimensions of these states, derived from colonial partition and tenaciously maintained in the post-colonial period, embrace ethnically diverse populations which have in the process undergone a mode of forced 'in-migration', and when the unifying impulse of a common opposition to the (usually racially defined) colonial regime is gone the dynamics of ethnic sentiment and manipulation gain new momentum. Within the state development context of relevance Third World scholarship has therefore shifted the central focus of its concerns to ethnic rather than racial issues.

Ethnicity, the state and development: some current debates

It is in the specifics of the development agenda that we find the analytic nexus between ethnicity and development. Any perusal of the issues which form this agenda will indicate the potential impingement of ethnic factors on state objectives and processes, and in several dimensions. One of these dimensions relates to the colonial history of these states, their location in an exploitative system of international capitalism and the way in which racial and ethnic identities have been manipulated to serve the interests of the exploitative process. A second dimension relates to the genesis and durability of ethnically determined group consciousness and cohesion and the contexts of its salience and operationalisation. A third dimension is prescriptive and relates to the political engineering required to contain, control and possibly utilise the dynamics present in the ethnic factor.

Much of our recent scholarship has been directed, in one form or another, to the first two of these dimensions. The resultant debates have provided considerable intellectual stimulation but run the risk of sterility when measured by the criterion of relevance in the Third World context. One is the debate on the locus of responsibility for the contemporary strength of ethnic or 'tribal' sentiment in most of the Third World. One side has it that 'tribal nationalism was the end product of socio-economic differentiations originated by the process of colonialism itself' (Williame 1970: 130). The other argues that it is the imperatives of the independent state's developmental role and structures which provide the impulse: 'The unitarian impulse sires policies aimed at producing greater homogeneity; these measures are a threat to subnational solidarities and mobilise pluralism' (Young 1976: 72). The truth encompasses both positions, but the argument is in itself sterile until we move beyond the debate to the recognition that the psycho-social elements which make up the sense of ethnic identity are perdurably present, sometimes latent and sometimes operationalised, as Sithole remarks, as 'a resource, which like any other political resource, is resorted to by rational politicians because they perceive it appropriate at particular times for particular objectives' (Sithole 1983: 14). Sithole goes on to argue that we cannot regard ethnic sentiment simply as a resource of 'false consciousness' utilised by manipulative political elites; nor can we casually 'celebrate the tribal innocence of the masses'. The masses, he asserts, when acting on ethnic lines are rational actors, engaging in an 'intriguing cost-benefit analysis on many issues that affect them'. It is at this point, says Sithole, that the 'tribe-in itself' becomes the 'tribe-for-itself' (1983: 6, 13–14). Sithole's comments are congruent with those of Michael Hechter in Chapter 12 on differential preference formation and rational choice theory. Whether we choose to follow this formulation or not, the important thing for this debate in terms of Third World relevance is for it to address both the structural and the subjective components of ethnicity in any of its utilitarian manifestations, a point to which we shall return in the last section of this paper.

Another debate which risks pragmatic sterility in the Third World context is that over the relative salience of class and ethnic/racial principles of organisation. One side of the argument has it, briefly, that ethnic consciousness is a manifestation of the 'proletariat's semi-peasant psychology' which 'hampers the development of its class consciousness, the growth of its organisations and the dissemination of its ideology' (Zakine 1968: 49). What is required is an analysis which seeks 'to resolve the contradiction between the general law of class formation and the concrete forms in which it manifests itself ... by seeking to find the mediating elements' which are to be found in the structures and mode of production (Magubane 1976: 172). The other side has it that class and ethnicity coexist as organising principles, and that their relative saliences rise or fall according to specific contexts. The resultant argument is intellectually stimulating, as suggested before, and indeed highly relevant to the development of the Third World states. The danger of sterility lies in two tendencies which have emerged in the debate. One, to which scholars of the second persuasion are prone, is to project unilinear evolutionary trajectories for the relative saliences of either class or ethnicity, projections for which we have no firm empirical evidence at present.[4] The other, characteristic of those holding the first view, is a tendency to an abstract scholasticism which demonstrates little relation to the policy imperatives which currently confront Third World political leadership.

As an example of this latter tendency I quote from a seminal passage by Wallerstein in which he deals with perceived ethnic ('status group') tensions:

> These status-group tensions are the inefficacious and self defeating expression of class frustration. They are the daily stuff of contemporary African politics and social life. The journalists, who are usually closer to popular perceptions than the social scientists, tend to call this phenomenon 'tribalism' when they write of Black Africa. Tribal, or ethnic, conflicts are very real things, as the civil wars in the Sudan and Nigeria attest most eloquently. They are ethnic conflicts in the sense that persons involved in these conflicts are commonly motivated by analyses which use ethnic (or comparable status-group) categories; furthermore, they usually exhibit strong ethnic loyalties. Nonetheless, behind the ethnic 'reality' lies a class conflict, not very far from the surface. By this I mean the following straightforward and empirically testable proposition (not one, however, that has been definitively so tested): were the class differences that correlate (or coincide) with the status-group differences to disappear, as a result of changing social circumstances, the status-group conflicts would eventually disappear (no doubt to be replaced by others). The status-group loyalties are binding and effective, in a way that it seems difficult for class loyalties to be other than in moments of crisis, but they are also more transient from the perspective of the analyst. If the society were to become ethnically 'integrated', class antagonisms would not abate; the opposite in fact is true. One of the functions of the network of status-group affiliations is to conceal the realities of class differentials. To the extent, however, that particular class antagonisms or differentials abate or disappear, status-group antagonisms (if not differentials, but even differentials) also abate and disappear. (Wallerstein 1977: 280–1)

Re-phrased, this statement reads for me: 'The situations that evoke ethnically defined conflicts are really class conflict situations. But not all situations of class conflict are ethnically defined, therefore ethnicity is a particular subspecies manifestation of class conflict and can only be properly understood when its class-rooted derivation is clearly perceived.' Begging the issue for the moment of what is meant by 'class', if this proposition is taken to mean that ethnicity is only socially significant when ethnic identity is used ascriptively to assign another status which is sanction-conveying, I find it unexceptionable. There still remains the issue of why ethnic antagonism should so often be the subspecies manifestation of class conflict; if I understand some of my colleagues, they are arguing that this is the issue which should now command our attention and that scholars interested in race and ethnicity should now become a subspecies manifestation of the academic cadre concerned with class. For me this is unacceptably restrictive, but the core of my charge of potential sterility for this formulation does not lie here. It lies rather in the abstracted and hypothesised reality posited which has little immediacy for the in-place realities which demand policy initiatives in the Third World states. Re-phrased differently, Wallerstein's statement can be taken to read: 'Were social reality to be different than it is, the hypothesis could be proved correct.' As a hypothetical projection of abstract theory this is unobjectionable, but it says little to the realities of the Third World development. The reality is that ethnic consciousness is not only often pernicious; it is also persistent and pandemic. To slide over this reality into a theoretic discussion about hypothetically less 'transient' principles is to replicate the sociologically incomplete dimension of statements by biologists and geneticists who, quite properly within the context of their own disciplines, have 'declared as trivial in science what the layman sees as decisive in everyday life, namely, race' (*Columbia University Forum* 1967: 6). Such an approach is unlikely to pass the test of relevance for Third World governments struggling to contain the divisive impact of ethnicity within their polities, and unlikely to gain their approval other than for its ideologically legitimising support. For our scholarship in the Third World to be responsive to the politico-academic arena in which we find ourselves we must accept the current exigencies of ethnic salience and analyse their manifestations in policy-relevant dimensions, justifying our stance if we feel compelled to do so for pragmatic and processural reasons, in a manner reminiscent of Lenin's pragmatism in his debate with Luxemburg over the 'national question'. This is not the 'superficial empiricism' which 'substitutes for the study of the underlying nonempirical structural reality' against which Magubane warns (1976: 171). Underlying structural realities must always be at the core of our analysis, but in our situation the greater danger lies in a non-empirical theoreticism which produces nothing but contextually irrelevant abstractions. We should not allow ourselves to follow the path of William James's 'ultra-abstractionist' who prefers 'the skinny outline rather than the rich thicket of reality'; nor should we allow our neo-Marxism to become neo-Platonism. Marx's own scholarship refutes this direction, accepting that social action is based not only on the objective features of a situation but also on the meanings which the situation has for the actors concerned. These meanings are a central aspect of the social reality with which we must deal, and if journalists are 'usually closer to popular conceptions than the social scientists' this is more a critique of our own conceptualisations of reality than it is a criticism of theirs.

The analytic agenda in the Third World politico-academic context: some useful directions

Having cautioned against what I consider to be certain sterile directions in which our theoretical debates can take us, I return to the dimensions of potential ethnic impingement on the development objectives of the state mentioned earlier (pp. 157–8), with special reference to any prescriptive impact that our studies may have. In doing so I shall not belabour what should be readily apparent from these pages and an abundant literature on the subject – that ethnicity has a potentially high degree of salience across the spectrum of these objectives. Instead I shall attempt a restatement of the modalities of this salience within the context of the Third World syndrome, where socio-political issues overshadow socio-economic concerns, where 'development' defines the role of the state, and where the state is perceived in a unitary and highly centralised manner. This syndrome presents a profile significantly different from that presented by the societies of the West which have provided the material for the development of most of our theory on ethnicity, and my statement is a brief attempt to marry the common heritage of our international scholarship with the pragmatic imperatives which are characteristic of our Third World politico-academic climate. In this statement I shall focus on three topics which together subsume the core issues linking development objectives and the actual or potential impact of ethnicity.

Ethnicity and the structures of political control

At perhaps no point are the contrasting profiles thrown up by the West and the Third World more sharply delineated than in their views regarding the nature of political and state power and the definition of the nation. To illustrate these different profiles, I contrast two passages. The first is from Markovitz, who in a discussion on the new constitution introduced by the National Liberation Council in Ghana in 1966 states:

> The proposal of a system in which 'sovereign powers of the state are judiciously shared among . . . the legislature, the executive, and the judiciary' was of course inspired by the constitution of the United States; but Ghana resembles neither the US today nor the thirteen original states of 1787. In the revolutionary American colonies, the separation of powers was designed not only to ensure personal freedoms, but also to establish a 'negative' government without a social program and endowed only with limited authority. The system was intended to inhibit the formation of a tyrannous majority by deliberately pitting faction against faction; it recognised the existence of antagonistic interests, and institutionalised them in the government itself. (Markovitz 1970: 263)

The second passage is from Zimbabwe's Parliamentary Debates of 22 February 1984 and comprises a statement by the Prime Minister, Robert Mugabe, in response to a question on his Party's intentions regarding a one-party state:

> THE PRIME MINISTER: Mr Speaker, I think our position as ZANU (PF) on the question of the political system of this country is very clear. A multi-party system is what we have inherited, and we do not view that system as conducive to maximum democracy and unity under that democratic state. And, so we believe in a One Party State. I have made various utterances at various times to this effect, and I think the last statement on the subject was contained in my address to the Law Society of Zimbabwe. In that address, I stated towards the end, that ZANU (PF) will fight the next elections on a platform which will include the One Party State proposition and that if the party won those elections, then the party would not allow the will of the people to be foiled by the rigidity of our Constitution. In other words, we will have to seek ways and means of ensuring that the will of the people is given full expression by way of creation of a political order which is based on a one party system, and so our position is very clear. We accept the multi-party democracy as we have inherited it, we are operating in accordance with it, but we are also very conscious that the will of the people is paramount, and once

the will of the people has decreed that there be a One Party
State, then a One Party State shall be established.
(ZIMBABWE 1984: columns 681–2)

As Markovitz says, Ghana resembles neither the US today nor the
thirteen original states of 1787. Neither does Zimbabwe. Two aspects of
the distinction are particularly germane to our discussion here. One is the
conception of the role and nature of government. In the one instance we
have a constitution which according to Markovitz was designed to
'establish a "negative" government without a social program and
endowed with only limited authority'. Markovitz has rightly been criticised for exaggerating the limitations placed on government by the US
Constitution. The essence of American constitutionalism is not limited
authority but rather a government which is self-controlling through the
recognition of the heterogeneous nature of its constituency. This is the
antithesis of the concept of the nature and role of government defined in
the Third World development syndrome already described and implicit
in the parliamentary quote given above. This concept is given more
explicit expression in one of Prime Minister Mugabe's other statements,
drawn from the ZANU (PF) Manifesto: 'ZANU, as a People's Party,
believes that the People as a whole must come before individuals. ZANU
believes that Power must vest in the People both in respect of the Party
and in respect of the Government of the Country' (Mugabe 1982: 2–3). It
is clear from these quotes that the calculus here is that the Party
represents the People, and the Government represents the Party. More
succinctly, the Party is the People, and the Government is the Party.

The other concomitant distinction relates to the conception of the
nation and its constituent sub-divisions. The one model projects a system
recognising the existence of 'antagonistic interests', which institutiona-
lises them in the structures of government and which attempts 'to inhibit
the formation of a tyrannous majority by deliberately pitting faction
against faction'. The other model negates the concept of the 'tyrannous
majority' by conflating it with 'the people'. Once the majority of the
people, by vote, have confirmed that the Party is the People and that the
Government is the Party, the majority implicitly becomes the People
whose interests and perspectives are embodied in the One Party State.
Factional interests are then absorbed and dissolved in a unified nation:
'ZANU believes that the principle of the paramountcy of the People
demands that the national concept and the sense of national belonging
be made a dogma that should submerge and destroy tribal, regionalistic
and racial animosities' (Mugabe 1982: 3).

The American model discussed above was not, of course, specifically designed to contain ethnic and racial antagonisms. Its inaugural form did however provide an evolved framework for subsequent attempts to achieve greater structural incorporation for ethnically defined minorities, paralleled by a greater awareness of and status for the cultural configurations which they represent, in an oppositional mode. The Third World approach, dominated by the development syndrome, has tended to be different. There have been some experiments in ethno-regionalism and federalism, but more commonly one finds political structures designed to contain ethnicity either through the older assimilationist model or sometimes through simple dominance. But perhaps the most frequent approach is the attempt to satisfy ethnic sentiment through a covert ethnic arithmetic in political representation while at the same time striving to render ethnicity structurally insignificant by divorcing it from any status differentials. This is of course consistent with the Marxist-Leninist ideological stance of many of these states. Unfortunately, as Rex points out (1982a: 184), we currently have a paucity of informing scholarship on the experiences of those states in the Marxist world which have adopted this approach. The covert nature of certain dimensions of this type of policy tends to be a liability to scholarship in this area. Any state, whether Marxist or not, exhibiting the mode of 'state bureaucratic vanguardism' mentioned earlier in this paper will wish to project the image of having abolished invidious ethnic distinctions by legislative fiat, and any attempt to analyse ethnicity within its borders is likely to be equated with its advocacy. It is not the ideological posture of the state *per se* which tends to place this limitation on our scholarship; thus in certain Marxist states which have chosen to give formal recognition to ethnically defined interests we now have considerable scholarship on the issue, notably in Yugoslavia and to a lesser extent in the People's Republic of China. But for many other Marxist societies which have chosen to manipulate and control the dynamics of ethnic identity under the covering umbrella of intra-party and intra-government manoeuvres we have insufficient information and analysis. The same holds true for many of the societies of the Third World, where studies on ethnicity receive little local support and are often the target of bureaucratic suspicion. Clearly the relationship between state structures and ethnic dynamics is an analytically central and considerably neglected aspect of our studies on the nexus between ethnicity and development, as writings by Enloe (1978, 1981) and others show. Equally clearly such studies require a corpus of relevant data for comparative analysis which is currently inadequate. The augmentation of this set of data, particularly in respect of societies where information has not been readily available for the reasons mentioned, must therefore rank as a high priority in our research agenda.

The legitimacy of ethnic identity

Another issue which confronts Third World leadership is that of the determination of the limits of appropriate ethnic consciousness. When is it legitimate identity and when is it manipulative sentiment? Third World politicians, generally, recognise a legitimate place for ethnic sentiment. The ZANU Manifesto referred to above also comments; 'The People as a Nation cannot necessarily be homogeneous in respect of their cultural or racial backgrounds, but this diversity of background should become more a source of cultural wealth than a cause of division and mistaken notions of groupist superiority philosophy' (Mugabe 1982: 3). But how is the effect of this distinction achieved in practice? The easy answer is that ethnic consciousness should be stripped of all sanction-conveying correlates. The fact however is that the 'cultural wealth' referred to almost always contains elements of identity, and identity always has its inclusionary and exclusionary dimensions. It carries with it therefore a danger, the danger of being a resource for sectional interest, as mentioned earlier. The issue is in part one of value judgement; it is also one of a pragmatic assessment of the cultural and psycho-social dynamics which must be harnessed and kept in balance for the development objectives of the state. Nationalist politicians recognise the potential of these dynamics – indeed the 'national concept' contains the elements of a new, synthetic, ethnicity. Thus Third World governments readily engage, sometimes obliquely, in socio-psychological engineering through education, 'public awareness' campaigns and the like. In so doing they are giving credence to the tactic of social engineering through revised structures of socialisation, the stock-in-trade of an earlier era of race relations scholarship which we have now largely erased from our agenda (Blumer 1966: 105–15). They are also thereby according considerable importance to the 'status-group loyalties' which Wallerstein accepts as being 'binding and effective, in a way that it seems difficult for class loyalties to be other than in moments of crisis', but which he also considers to be 'more transient from the perspective of the analyst'. For political leadership in developing country contexts these 'status-group loyalties', these ethnic identities, have exhibited little transience. The fact that there is little encouragement for the analysis of their dynamics does not indicate that they are considered unimportant; on the contrary, this frequently implies that they are seen as so sensitively critical as to require removal from public debate and as such an essential component of the development equation as to necessitate direct and delicate treatment in the confines of the party caucus. Whether they are perceived as being ultimately transient depends of course on the societal model specifically adopted; whether any model which posits their transience is ultimately viable remains to be seen.

Our scholarship, and particularly the Marxist tradition within it, will be seriously delinquent unless it gives appropriate consideration to this politically generated preoccupation with the dynamics of ethnic identity and its implications for the status of ethnicity as a perdurable principle of human organisation in reciprocal relationship with the class and power structures which contextualise its salience. Such consideration does not require any form of cultural reductionism; nor is it incompatible with Marxist class analysis, as Chapter 5 in this volume by Harold Wolpe demonstrates. What it does require is the abandonment of economic essentialism, as Wolpe also argues. It also requires that far more attention than is currently provided be paid to such issues as the consideration of ethnic identity as social capital and the mode of its production. Finally, these issues require revived attention to the social psychology of ethnicity. There is a healthy vein of scholarship in this tradition pertaining to the Third World running through Memmi and Fanon which we should not allow to expire.

The contextualisation of ethnic saliences

The third topic of analytic focus requiring research priority in the Third World relates to the identification of the specific contexts of ethnic salience, particularly within the order-level hierarchies of the development process. The development syndrome produces a set of cross-cutting, superimposed interest-group networks, with a variety of economic, bureaucratic, ethnic and locational dimensions. There is a state bureaucratic apparatus, with its hierarchy of linkages from top to bottom, from centre to periphery. There are local and regional antagonisms in a competitive contest for state resources. There are conflicts between interest groups economically defined and there are ethnic divisions which draw their strength from historical and cultural particularisms. All these exhibit competitive characteristics, both within and between themselves.

Let me illustrate with an example drawn from my activities as a development anthropologist involved in a study of the sociological aspects of the agro-economic development of the Sebungwe Region in Zimbabwe, the vast hinterland lying to the southeast of Lake Kariba. My example is Simuchembu, a communal land in the Gokwe District. The people of Simuchembu are ethnically divided; there are the Shangwe, part of the autochthonous Shona-speaking group in the region. There are also the Tonga, involuntary immigrants moved here from the Zambesi Valley at the time of the building of the Kariba Dam. Relationships are generally harmonious, although Shangwe claims to a certain spiritual and temporal jurisdiction over the land and its resources sometimes create friction. But whatever internal differences may exist, the people of Simuchembu are united in contexts where they deal collectively with the Gokwe District Council, which they perceive as being an interfering group of 'southerners', unhelpful in their problems of crop depredation by wild game and interested only in siphoning off the proceeds of the culling of 'their' elephants. They are united also in their dealings with representatives of government bureaucracies, and will link on occasion with the Gokwe District Council in competition with other districts for a larger share of state resources. An antiphonal chorus sometimes heard at farmers' meetings in the area illustrates the hierarchical fusion of opposed elements involved: 'Simuchembu is the centre of Gokwe, Gokwe is the centre of Midlands (the administrative region), Midlands is the centre of Zimbabwe, Zimbabwe is the centre of Africa, Africa is the centre of the world.' The scheme involved is a modern African variant of what Evans-Pritchard identified as the 'principle of contradiction' in the Nuer political system:

> Any segment sees itself as an independent unit in relation to another segment of the same section, but sees both segments as a unity in relation to another section; and a section which from the point of view of its members comprises opposed segments is seen by members of other sections as an unsegmented unit. Thus there is . . . always contradiction in the definition of a political group, for it is a group only in relation to other groups . . . The political system is an equilibrium between opposed tendencies towards fission and fusion, between the tendency of all groups to segment, and the tendency of all groups to combine with segments of the same order . . . Hence fission and fusion in political groups are two aspects of the same segmentary principle. (1940: 147–8)

Evans-Pritchard's analysis has relevance for our interests at a number of points, and his comments on fission and fusion, and on the definitional importance of out-group relationships, are themes which we can usefully pursue. We cannot however uncritically embrace his scheme as an informing paradigm of the way ethnicity interacts with other collectivising principles to form a rank-ordered hierarchy of the saliences concerned. It would be convenient if it was, but the ethnic factor does not always emerge as an order-level category in which different segments either fuse or split. Sometimes it does, but often ethnic linkages are invoked across the order-level categories of the Evans-Pritchard model.

In Simuchembu, for instance, Shangwe will sometimes use their ethnic linkages with their Shangwe cousins on the Gokwe District Council to enhance their own position in intra-Simuchembu disputes. The Tonga in Simuchembu utilise their ethnic networks to gain privileged access to fishing grounds along the lakeshore in the neighbouring, Tonga-dominated, Binga District. Thus the reality is not as neatly nested and hierarchical as the Evans-Pritchard model, or their own choral enthusiasms, would imply. Different specific contexts evoke different principles of alliance, and in my field notes the ethnic factor either emerges or is suppressed across a broad spectrum of situations in a manner which is sometimes predictable and sometimes not. The fact that the predictability quotient is as low as it is indicates for me the need for further specification in our contextualisation of ethnic salience. In a seminal article on this issue Cross (1978) has given us some useful guidelines, but his propositions stand at a generalised level which for Third World purposes we need to particularise to levels enabling us to specify the micro-habitats of ethnic salience in the development process.

The developmental relevance of this specification should be clear. To be effective the developmental process requires a smooth flow of communicational, initiatory and supportive components throughout the linkages of the implementational hierarchy, in both directions. Indeed, in my view the centre/periphery relationship, in all its administrative, economic, political and cultural dimensions, is the core issue for successful development. As ethnicity can intrude at various points in the articulated chain of relationships involved, the specification of its micro-habitats within the implementational hierarchy becomes a valuable analytic tool in the planning process. Where its operations are dysfunctional its impact may be neutralised by modifying the structures of the hierarchy. On the other hand, it may be found that in certain contexts ethnicity plays a functional and constructive role, providing the cohesion, group initiative and integration necessary at certain order-levels in the centre/periphery chain of relationships for the success of the developmental scheme. What I am suggesting, in effect, is that a study of the ecology of ethnicity within specific bureaucratic and administrative environments is developmentally far more important than is currently recognised.

The proposals for analytic foci set out above are not made in an attempt to pre-empt or displace those which currently engage the central attention of the world of international scholarship working in the area of race and ethnicity. In this paper I have however attempted to show why the latter cannot be the exclusive objects of our analytic attention in the Third World, given the concerns and constraints of our politico-academic milieu. These concerns and constraints, pervaded by a Third World definition of development, create the imperatives for a direction in our analysis which is somewhat different from that pertaining in the arena of international scholarship; more micro-contextual than macro-contextual, more socio-political than socio-economic. The modalities of ethnic salience within the Third World development perspective thus call for a set of analytic directions creating a new synthesis between the momentums of our common theoretic concerns and the pragmatic imperatives of Third World development, a challenge to both the vigour and the relevance of our analyses.

NOTES

1 Comments on the 'Third World' context in this paper are drawn largely from materials on the post-colonial independent states of Africa, and particularly Zimbabwe. What is referred to in the text as the 'international arena' of scholarship relates largely to the literature produced in Western Europe and North America; thus these terms are used more as generalised labels than as precise categories.

2 The text goes on at this point to raise a series of questions on how ethnic policies affect the status of women. An appendix proposes a further list of twenty-five topics for research, none of which contains the word 'race' and only three of which make explicit reference to the international or economic dimensions of ethnic conflict. Most of the rest relate to ethnic or gender issues within state structures.

3 The distinction drawn in this paper between racial and ethnic factors corresponds closely to that made by van den Berghe (1967: 9–10).

4 This is not to suggest, however, that it is not possible within particular contexts and specific time-frames to make out a strong case for the shifting significance, in a relationship of inverse proportionality, between race, ethnicity and class. Wilson's thesis on race in the United States (1978) is an example, and indeed this paper argues that the saliences of race and ethnicity have varied significantly at specific points in the decolonisation and development process.

8

Social anthropological models of inter-ethnic relations

RICHARD JENKINS

In a collection such as the present volume, one expects to find both detailed expositions of particular theoretical models or analytical frameworks – typically identified with individual authors or definite schools of thought – and more general surveys of a disciplinary field or area of academic discourse. In this context the papers by M. G. Smith and Sandra Wallman represent the first category of contribution; this paper falls into the second. As such, it is my intention to provide a broad discussion of currently influential social anthropological approaches to the study of ethnicity and racism, in order that those authors' exegeses of their own positions might be understood within their wider setting. This paper is not, however, intended merely to serve as a prolegomenon to Smith and Wallman. In the closing section I shall sketch in some of the alternative approaches which social anthropologists might – and, indeed, should – explore in their attempts to understand ethnicity and 'race relations'.[1]

Social anthropology and boundary maintenance[2]

Before proceeding to the main body of the discussion, it is necessary to engage in some ground-clearing; in particular, it is important to define as precisely as possible, on the one hand, what is being included within the category of 'social anthropological approaches', and, on the other, what is being excluded and is not to be discussed in detail here. In other words, what are the boundaries of social anthropology and where do they lie?

The question of what it is that characterises the social anthropological approach can be asked in general and with respect to the analysis of ethnic and 'race' relations. Looking at social anthropology as a broad tradition, the definitional task is by no means straightforward or unproblematic. At the time of writing, the discipline appears to be experiencing

170

something of a crisis, in particular with respect to the manner of its engagement with policy-oriented research and research 'at home', as opposed to the mythical, if ubiquitous, 'Bongo-Bongoland'. As a consequence, its core content or identity can no longer be taken for granted, not least by its practitioners. It follows from this that it is less easy than it would have been, say, twenty or thirty years ago to propose a definition of the social anthropological approach which would either satisfy or encompass the majority of social anthropologists.

Bearing this caveat in mind, there are, however, four criteria which seem adequately – if necessarily somewhat approximately – to map out the boundaries of the discipline. The first of these is a *comparative perspective* on the analysis of social life, a quest for homology and equivalence in the midst of the cultural and social diversity of mankind. Second, there is an emphasis upon ethnography and *long-term fieldwork*, preferably in a culturally strange setting, to the extent that going into the field is effectively both apprenticeship and rite of passage for the social anthropology postgraduate. Third, there is a tendency to look for *corporate groups and systematic interrelationships* in the analysis of data, as a consequence no doubt of the attempt to understand unfamiliar social settings, leading to much social anthropology being characterised by stronger or weaker forms of methodological holism. Finally, many social anthropologists, either explicitly or implicitly, remain committed, at the expense of the analysis of conflict, to that emphasis upon processes of *social integration* for which they have so often been criticised (e.g. Boissevain, 1974, 9–23). With respect to the last two points in particular, the legacy and continuing influence of structural functionalism and Radcliffe-Brown is apparent, as is, by comparison with sociology, for example, a pervasive ideological conservatism.

There are, of course, a number of qualifications to be entered with respect to the above. It would not be either fair or true to caricature all social anthropologists as conservatives; nor should the influence of, for example, transactional approaches, Marxism or structuralism be ignored. However, these reservations notwithstanding, the above four criteria do accurately epitomise something of the nature of modern social anthropology: the boundary of the discipline, although situational and shifting, is none the less to be reckoned with.

Coming to the particular object of our attention in this paper, these disciplinary preoccupations and predilections have led social anthropologists, in the study of inter-group relations, typically to concentrate upon either ethnic identity as a social phenomenon or social and cultural pluralism as a distinctive form of social organisation. Both of these topics have emerged, each in its own distinct way, from the combination of an interest in social groups and systematic interrelationships with a concern with social integration. It is with these, largely complementary, approaches to our area of interest that I shall primarily be concerned here.

There are, however, a number of other bodies of work which, although more or less anthropological and therefore germane to this discussion, I shall not deal with here for reasons of space and intellectual coherence. First, there is the long-standing debate on caste as a principle of social stratification (e.g. Dumont, 1970; Leach, 1960), a notion which has on occasion been brought to bear on the analysis of 'racial' inequality (e.g. Cox, 1948; Warner, 1936). Second, there is a lively tradition of ethnographic studies of urban black communities in the United States of America, for example the studies carried out by Anderson (1976), Aschenbrenner (1975), Hannerz (1969), Liebow (1967) and Stack (1974). Third, and most recent, there is the controversy over the socio-biological explanatory paradigm, both in its general applications and as applied to inter-ethnic relations. Since this is a topic dealt with elsewhere in this volume, suffice it to recommend the contributions of Sahlins (1977) and van den Berghe (1981; below, ch. 11) as representing opposite sides of the argument.

All of the above are topics which would have to be included in any discussion, along the lines of the excellent survey provided by R. Cohen (1978), which aspired to comprehensive coverage of the field. In addition, there are other interesting foci of academic interest, such as the use of the concept of ethnicity within sociology, the developing interest in ethnicity as a facet of personal and social identity, the notions of 'ethnogenesis' and the 'ethnos', particularly as developed by Soviet anthropologists, and the analysis of nationalism. I shall discuss these in the final section of this paper.

From tribe to ethnic group

As was mentioned in the previous section, one of social anthropology's traditional theoretical preoccupations has been a concern with corporate groups and social systems. During the colonial and immediately post-colonial periods this manifested itself as an orthodox assumption that the subject matter of the discipline – 'primitive' peoples (Firth, 1958, 6) – was most commonly organised into tribal groups. Indeed, as in the following quotation from one of the founding fathers of ethnography, the notion of 'the tribe', as a real, perduring social entity, was central to both the theoretical and the methodological development of social anthropology:

> [The modern ethnographer] with his tables of kinship terms,
> genealogies, maps, plans and diagrams, proves the existence of
> an extensive and big organisation, shows the constitution of
> the tribe, of the clan, of the family ... The Ethnographer has
> in the field, according to what has just been said, the duty
> before him of drawing up all the rules and regularities of tribal
> life; all that is permanent and fixed; of giving an anatomy of
> their culture, of depicting the constitution of their society.
> (Malinowski, 1922, 10, 11)

Thus, in one move the concept of the tribe accomplished two important
things: in the first place, it served to distance *tribal* society from *civilised*
society, in both common-sensical and analytical discourse; in the second,
it provided the anthropologist with a theoretical model of the nature of
'non-civilised' social organisation which could both serve to organise his
or her ethnographic data and function as a framework for the cross-
cultural comparison of 'primitive social organisation'. Thus, while on the
one hand the distinction between 'them' and 'us' was being established,
on the other the basic similarity between different sorts of 'them' was
being proclaimed.

Following Barth (1969b, 10–11), it is possible to identify four theoretical features of the traditional anthropological model of the tribe. First,
such a group is biologically self-perpetuating; second, members of the
group (tribesmen and, of course, women) share basic cultural values,
manifest in overt cultural forms; third, the group is a bounded social field
of communication and interaction; and, fourth, its members identify
themselves, and are identified by others, as belonging to that tribe. In
addition, and in contrast to the more contemporary usages of the terms
'ethnicity' and 'ethnic group' which we will discuss below, the anthropological notion of the tribe typically implied that such groups were
isolated, primitive-atavistic, or non-Western (R. Cohen, 1978, 384).

It would be wrong to suggest, however, that this was an explicitly
formulated analytical framework; it was not, remaining instead implicitly
embedded in most ethnographic studies, never being examined or
seriously called into question. The kind of problem which this taken-for-
granted understanding of tribal identity has bequeathed to latter-day
interpreters of the classic ethnographies is well illustrated by the controversy surrounding the question of whether the Nuer – as documented
by Evans-Pritchard (1940) – are, in fact, really the Dinka (Newcomer,
1972) or whether they are both distinct components of a single plural
society (Glickman, 1972).[3]

The event which most clearly marked the paradigm shift within social anthropology from 'tribal society' to 'ethnic groups' was the publication of *Ethnic Groups and Boundaries*, a collection of essays edited by Fredrik Barth (1969a). The major thrust of the arguments presented therein is that ethnicity, the boundaries of ethnic groups, and hence their ontological status as social groups, should not be treated as 'hard', or be uncritically accepted as a fixed aspect of the social reality in question. In fact, Barth insists, ethnic identity, and its production and reproduction in routine social interaction, are to be treated as problematic features of that reality; the ethnographer must examine the practices and processes whereby ethnicity and ethnic boundaries are socially constructed. The starting point for such an examination must be a recognition that 'ethnic groups are categories of ascription and identification by the actors themselves' (Barth, 1969b, 10).

To make use of a distinction first developed by Firth (1961, 28), it appears that the theoretical emphasis has shifted, from the evocation of tribal identity as a defining feature of social *structure*, to a celebration of ethnic identity as an aspect of social *organisation*. R. Cohen has further argued (1978, 384) that the change involved 'fundamental changes in anthropological perspectives', from a Western concern with the uncivilised peoples of the colonies, to a more equitable interest in the heterogeneity of all societies.

Coming back to Barth's critique of the traditional model, there are several features of the emergent alternative analytical framework which are worth highlighting. In the first place, the analysis of ethnicity starts from the definition of the situation held by social actors. Second, the focus of attention then becomes the maintenance of ethnic boundaries: the structured interaction between 'us' and 'them' which takes place across the boundary. Third, ethnic identity depends on ascription, both by members of the ethnic group in question and by outsiders. Fourth, ethnicity is not fixed; it is situationally defined. Fifth, ecological issues are particularly influential in determining ethnic identity, inasmuch as competition for economic niches plays an important role in the generation of ethnicity.

In setting forth this model – the origins of which can of course be traced as far back as Max Weber – it is true to say that Barth and his collaborators sketched out all the essentials of the paradigm of ethnicity that has come to dominate discussion of the topic within social anthropology and, to a lesser degree, North American cultural anthropology. This remains the case despite the attempts of authors such as R. Cohen (1978, 386–7) to reformulate the concept in the light of the perceived inadequacies of Barth's formulation. Specifically, Cohen has drawn attention to the fact that, in stressing concepts such as 'group', 'category' and 'boundary' and processes of 'maintenance', Barth, despite his intentions, tends to further reify the ethnic group as a perduring corporate entity.

In British anthropology the influence of the 'ethnicity model' is exemplified by the work of Sandra Wallman and Michael Banton. In his original formulations (1967), Banton argued that 'race' is used as a role sign: social groups are unities which appear in response to various stimuli to alignment, and 'race' is a visible marker of status and role as functions of group membership. The notion of ethnicity is thus combined with a status-attainment model of stratification. The emphasis remains, however, upon inter-ethnic behaviour as transactional, albeit within a social context of stratification and/or coercion.

More recently, Banton has developed a 'rational choice' model of inter-ethnic relations (1983), which seeks to integrate the study of ethnicity and nationalism with the study of 'race relations'. This analytical framework is founded on four premises: one, men act so as to maximise their net advantage; two, action has a cumulative effect, inasmuch as present actions limit or constrain subsequent actions; three, actors utilise physical *or* cultural differences to generate groups and categories; and, four, when relationships between groups which are held to be physically distinctive are determined by an imbalance of power, 'racial' categories are created.

It should be obvious that Banton's ideas rest on many of the same underlying assumptions as Barth's. The relation between the analyses of Barth and Wallman is, however, a good deal more intimate (Wallman, 1978b; 1979; below, ch. 10). Basing her arguments very directly upon the Barthian framework, Wallman argues that:

> ethnicity is the process by which 'their' difference is used to
> enhance the sense of 'us' for purposes of organisation or
> identification . . . Because it takes two, ethnicity can only
> happen at the boundary of 'us', in contact or confrontation or
> by contrast with 'them'. And as the sense of 'us' changes, so
> the boundary between 'us' and 'them' shifts. Not only does the
> boundary shift, but the criteria which mark it change.
> (Wallman, 1979, 3)

By this definition, therefore, ethnicity is transactional, shifting and essentially impermanent. Ethnic boundaries are always two-sided, and one of the key issues becomes the manipulation of perceived significant differences in their generation. Furthermore, Wallman considers it 'useful to set the ethnic/racial quibble aside and to consider simply how social boundaries are marked' (1978b, 205); having once done so, there is an effective concentration in her work upon the mobilisation of social (ethnic) identity as a resource.

In reviewing the 'ethnicity paradigm' as used in social anthropology, it is clear that there are several positive aspects of this analytical framework which require emphasis. The approach has, for example, inasmuch as it stresses social processes and the practices of actors, encouraged a move away from any of the numerous strands of determinism which remain influential in contemporary social science. Similarly, because of the emphasis which is placed upon the social construction of ethnic or 'racial' categories, the intrusion of biologically based conceptions of 'race' into social analysis is discouraged. Finally, the importance which is attached to the views and self-perceptions of social actors – the folk view of ethnic identity – leads the analysis away from the routine ethnocentrism of much sociology. These are all important, and they illustrate the degree to which an emphasis on ethnicity marks a useful departure from previous approaches to the study of inter-group relations. However, it should also be recognised that this approach – as it is presently utilised – does also have several major shortcomings; Cohen's criticism of the continued tendency to reify the ethnic 'group' is, for example, well taken. In addition there are four other criticisms which are worth briefly mentioning here.

First, there is the apparent difficulty experienced by authors such as Wallman in distinguishing the ethnic from the 'racial'; it is not sufficient simply to dismiss the distinction as 'a quibble'. As Rex has argued, it is necessary to pay attention to the importance and significance of folk 'racial' categorisations, because:

> a far wider set of situations are based upon cultural differentiation of groups than those which are commonly called racial and . . . few of them have anything like the same conflictual consequences that racial situations do. (Rex, 1973, 184)

This is not simply a problem concerning the categories with which anthropologists – possibly as a result of their ex-colonial collective guilt complex – feel comfortable. It is related to a second criticism of the 'ethnicity school': their manifest unease when forced to broach the question of power imbalances. This appears to be the basis for their emphasis upon ethnicity as a social resource, although it deserves to be emphasised here that this is not an inherent theoretical weakness of the general approach: one of the papers in *Ethnic Groups and Boundaries* was, for example, concerned with ethnic identity as a social stigma (Eidheim, 1969). This criticism is also related to the first point, inasmuch as, to take Banton's point, 'racial' categories and racism are character-istic of situations of domination. A third criticism is similarly bound up with the previous two, namely the lack of theoretical attention which is given to the points of difference and similarity between ethnicity and class. Finally, it is worth pointing out the danger in stressing the cultural dimension of inter-group relations: an emphasis upon the orientations, values and goals of actors – particularly members of ethnic minorities – can appear to be blaming the victims for their own disadvantage. There is a paradox here, in so far as the very stance which can be a powerful counterbalance to ethnocentrism may, at the same time, let prejudice in by the back door.[4]

It is no part of the argument of this paper, however, to imply that these are *inherent* flaws in the ethnicity paradigm about which nothing can be done. If indeed weaknesses they be – and this must very largely be a matter of opinion – they are rooted in two of the defining features of social anthropology discussed earlier: a preoccupation with social inte-gration and consensus, and a theoretical bent characterised by a con-centration upon the identification of social groups. A solution to both problems may be available through a more rigorous theorisation of the distinction between *groups* and *categories* in the context of inter-ethnic relations, a distinction which is elided in the rather bald assertions by Barth and Wallman that ethnicity depends on ascription from *both* sides of the group boundary. It is important to distinguish between the process of *group identification* and the process of *categorisation*: the first takes place inside the ethnic boundary, the second outside or across it.

Categorisation, in particular, is intimately bound up with power relations and relates to the ability of one group successfully to impose its categories of ascription upon another set of people and to the resources which the categorised collectivity can draw upon to resist, if need be, that imposition. To acknowledge the significance of the distinction between the two is, therefore, to place relationships of domination and subordination on the theoretical centre-stage. By so doing, it seems likely that the problem of 'blaming the victim' can be more easily avoided.

Similarly, the contrast between ethnicity and 'race' can also be clarified by reference to the distinction between groups and categories. As Banton has pointed out, ethnicity is generally more concerned with the identification of 'us', while racism is more oriented to the categorisation of 'them' (1983, 106). Thus ethnicity is largely a matter of group identification, and 'race' or racism one of categorisation, although the possibility of categorisation on the basis of putative ethnic or cultural criteria should not be overlooked. Nor should it be forgotten that groups may choose to identify themselves in positively evaluated racial terms, as in the ideology of the *Herrenvolk*. The distinction between groups and categories can, of course, also be brought to bear upon the issue of class, Marx's distinction between a 'class-in-itself' and a 'class-for-itself' being approximately equivalent to an opposition between the categorisation of individuals as members of a class, and group identification founded upon a basis of class consciousness.

To close this section, however, it must also be recognised that although group identification and categorisation are distinct processes, each – and this is to make a partial return to the conventional wisdom of the ethnicity paradigm – may be implicated in the other. Thus ethnicity may, for example, be strengthened or generated as a response to categorisation; similarly, an aspect of one group's ethnicity may be, indeed is likely to be, the categories with which it labels other groups or collectivities. However, in both of these abstract examples, the absolute centrality of power relationships – a centrality which many ethnicity theorists have been reluctant to include in their analyses – must be emphasised. It is likely to frequently be the case that there is a significant power imbalance across the ethnic boundary.

To return briefly to the quotation from John Rex (above, p. 176), it appears that ethnicity is a more general social phenomenon than racism or 'racial' categorisation; it is equally clear – and this has already been alluded to – that ethnicity, although more commonly to do with group identification, may be implicated, through the signification of cultural or ethnic markers, in processes of categorisation. Bearing such considerations in mind, therefore, racism may be viewed as a historically specific facet of the general social phenomenon of ethnicity. As such, it characterises situations in which an ethnic group dominates, or attempts to dominate, another set of people and, in the course of so doing, seeks to impose upon those people a categorical identity which is primarily defined by reference to their purported inherent and immutable differences from, and/or inferiority to, the dominating group. Viewed from this perspective, the distinction between ethnicity and 'race' is indeed something more than a quibble; as such it is deserving of the most serious attention (cf. Miles, 1982, 44–71).

From colony to plural society

Just as the conceptual replacement of the tribe by the ethnic group may be attributed to a post-colonial movement in the moral and philosophical centre of gravity of social anthropology, so the development of the notion of the plural society appears to be another response to the loss of empire. Once again the new model emerged out of the discipline's linked concerns with social groups as the basic unit of analysis and with processes of social integration.

The notion of pluralism arose as a response to two separate, if not dissimilar, problems. The first concerned those colonial territories which, like many British possessions in Africa and elsewhere, were governed by means of a system of indirect rule, through native courts and chiefs, for example. In situations such as this, different groups of people were integrated into the administrative framework through different sets of institutions and conflicting bodies of custom and law. How was one to conceptualise the convergence of these distinct institutional systems – one (or more than one) for the tribespeople, another (or others) for the Europeans and the urbanised intermediate groups – into one integrated social system? The second problem had to do with those colonial states which were, by contrast, basically unitary institutional systems for the purposes of politics and government. In such systems the native peoples, although contained within and controlled by the state, were rarely, if at all, considered to be jurally adult members of the polity. As the twentieth century drew towards its mid-point there were signs that this situation was about to change: black people, in short, were increasingly moving from subjection to citizenship. The meek, it appeared, were about to (re)inherit their earth. What would be the political structure of the resultant new nation-states?

Both of these problems, in fact, were products of the same historical trend: the creation, by the European powers, of poly-ethnic colonies – and later emergent new states – whose boundaries bore little or no resemblance to the 'real' or 'natural' social and geographical boundaries of ethnic identity or cultural continuity and discontinuity. As such, they lacked the clear-cut national identities which seemed to characterise the older states of the Old World. As the effective monopolists during this period of the sociological study of the 'developing' states of the Third World, social anthropologists had to develop a new analytical model in order to understand the changing situation.

They did not, in fact, develop a new model; instead they turned to political science. The notion of 'pluralism' and the concept of the 'plural society' have their origins in Furnivall's analysis of colonial policy in South East Asia in the 1940s (Furnivall, 1948). The social anthropologists who are most closely associated with the elaboration of his ideas are M. G. Smith, in the context of West Africa and the Caribbean (Smith, 1965; 1974), and Leo Kuper, in his studies of South Africa and other African states (Kuper, 1971; Kuper and Smith, 1969). A number of sociologists have also found the plural society model both attractive and useful; Schermerhorn (1978, 122–63) and van den Berghe (1967, 1981) are perhaps deserving of particular mention in this respect.

When these writers talk about pluralism, they are talking about the incorporation of different ethnic groups or collectivities into one societal or state system. In other words, as opposed to the homogeneous *nation-state*, there is the heterogeneous *plural society*. Even though the model's initial formulation predated the seminal contribution of *Ethnic Groups and Boundaries*, the concept of pluralism, as both Barth (1969a, 16) and R. Cohen (1978, 398) have pointed out, sits very comfortably with the ethnicity paradigm. Logically and theoretically, in fact, the progression from an awareness of the importance of ethnicity to the identification of a pluralist social system is an obvious, although not a necessary, step to take. As such, even though not many social scientists are these days concerned with the theoretical elaboration of contrasting models of pluralism, it is probably true to say that the notion of pluralism has carelessly passed into the anthropologist's *lingua franca* (or pidgin?) as a loose and apparently useful descriptive term for labelling all multi-ethnic societies.

There are, however, those who are concerned with precision in the concept's usage. Following Smith (1974, 108–10, 205–39, 341–2), it is possible to distinguish between three types of pluralism. The first of these is *cultural pluralism*, in which, although a society is composed of different ethnic groups, these are not relevant in the political sphere or as a criterion of citizenship. Examples of such a situation are Brazil or, arguably, the United Kingdom. Second, there is *social pluralism*; in this situation, although ethnicity is relevant in terms of political organisation, it does not affect citizenship, the incorporation of individual members of ethnic groups into the state. Here one can point to the West Indies, the USSR or Belgium as examples. Finally, Smith talks about *structural pluralism*, in which ethnic identity directly affects citizenship and the incorporation of collectivities into full membership of the state, as in South Africa, Israel, the USA (with respect to native Americans) and Burundi. These different kinds of pluralism appear to correspond in an approximate fashion to what Smith describes as different modes of incorporation, the principles through which individuals or collectivities are incorporated into membership of the society: uniform or universalistic, equivalent or segmental, and differential (1974, 333–7). To make the situation even more complicated, Smith also talks about 'the' plural society as a generic type, in which cultural diversity is associated with the rule of a dominant minority through the medium of a state system (e.g. 1974, 214).

Schermerhorn too has attempted to introduce a degree of rigour into our thinking about pluralism, distinguishing (1978, 122–5) between *normative pluralism*, which is a political ideology in its own right, *political pluralism*, which describes a society with a multiplicity of political interest groups, *cultural pluralism*, which relates to a multi-ethnic society, and *structural pluralism*, a society which is institutionally internally differentiated in a manner which reflects the differentiation of its population. While cultural and structural pluralism are analytically distinct, 'they have a dialectical relation of mutual implication in the empirical world' (1978, 127). Inasmuch as Schermerhorn understands ethnic relations as being intimately bound up with relationships of integration and conflict and with processes of group identification and categorisation, cultural and structural pluralism are, in his scheme of things, necessarily interconnected. In adopting such a view his debt to social anthropology becomes plain; his attempt to analyse conflict in a framework which also explicitly emphasises an integrative dimension owes something to Max Gluckman's analyses of 'custom and conflict' (Gluckman, 1956, 1965).[5] It remains important, however, to distinguish between the model of pluralism put forward by Schermerhorn and Smith's model, in which there is no necessary association 'in the real world' between structural pluralism and cultural pluralism.

Such differences notwithstanding, the two authors are clearly working within a framework of shared understandings, a social scientific field concerned with the study of 'plural societies'. As such there are a number of broad criticisms to which they, and others such as Kuper and van den Berghe, are equally vulnerable. The most basic of these, following R. Cohen (1978, 399), is that the notion of pluralism implies a culturally or politically homogeneous norm: 'monoism', to coin an unlikely neologism. This, of course, harks back to the anthropological atom of comparative analysis, the bounded tribal society, which we have already discussed. In fact, it is poly-ethnic collectivities, with fluid and permeable boundaries, which are likely to be the norm. Neither the isolated tribal group nor the ethnically homogeneous nation-state, to take the extreme 'monoist' theoretical alternatives, are much in evidence in either the historical or the contemporary sociological record.

A second criticism is that, at the end of the day, the notion of pluralism is theoretically vapid. The best which can be said is that it is merely profoundly descriptive, going no further than the extensive cataloguing of concrete situations by reference to a classificatory scheme of ideal-typical plural societies, an approach exemplified by van den Berghe (1967, 113–15, 132–48). A more serious criticism is that the model resolutely resists the incorporation of other principles of stratification, such as class, or of international relations.

Finally, there are the trenchant criticisms of the pluralist model made by Heribert Adam, a sociologist who has written extensively about South Africa (Adam, 1972, Adam and Giliomee, 1979, 42–50). Although not all of these need detain us here, there are three of particular moment. First, Adam argues that the pluralism approach overestimates the autonomy of the segments of a supposedly plural society, and neglects to examine the necessary degree to which they are all reciprocally implicated in a societal framework of common political, social and economic institutions. This is an implied criticism of the pluralism model which can also emerge from a reading of Gluckman's analysis of inter-ethnic relationships in South Africa (1956, 137–65). Second, the emphasis on cultural and political diversity as the main sources of heterogeneity ignores the role and importance of economic disparities and inequalities in the production of social cleavages. Finally, with respect to Smith's general notion of 'the' plural society, Adam denies that there is a necessary association between cultural diversity within the political boundaries of one state and domination by a cultural minority; he argues that such a condition could, in theory, lead just as easily to a system which granted each cultural segment equality of representation.

The above set of criticisms amounts to a major challenge to the pluralist perspective. So much so, in fact, that there seem to be no compelling reasons for insisting upon its continued usefulness in the analysis of ethnicity and 'race relations'. This is particularly the case with respect to the 'strong' version of the pluralist model, as associated with Smith or Kuper, for example. Even with respect to the 'weak' version of the notion, however, the everyday, almost casual, usage which equates plural societies with multi-ethnicity, there are – if the above criticisms are admissible – strong grounds for removing it from the social science vocabulary altogether. After all, if, in this sense, *all* societies are effectively plural societies, from what is pluralism being differentiated?

Finally there is another reason, not yet discussed, for dismissing the plural society model. Schermerhorn, as we have already noted, recognises the ideological or normative uses of the notion; similarly, Adam has pointed to the use to which the South African government has put the notion of pluralism in legitimating its apartheid and 'homeland' policies (Adam and Giliomee, 1979, 45). This is all the more reason for treating the concept with caution in academic discussions of inter-ethnic relations; if we cannot talk about pluralism without potentially importing into our discourse ideological baggage of this kind, then perhaps we are better not talking about it at all. At the very least, the word perhaps deserves to live out its days in the inverted commas which, as with 'race', may be used to denote a degree of dissension or contestation.

Redrawing the boundaries

To summarise the discussion so far, I have argued that, although there are undoubtedly criticisms which can be made of the specific uses to which the concept of ethnicity has been put, the basic notion remains useful and worthy of further development. By contrast, however, the pluralism model has been more stringently criticised as something of an analytical cul-de-sac. In this closing section, I shall briefly discuss a few of the theoretical and research directions which might be open to development within a broadly social anthropological framework which is concerned with the analysis of ethnicity.

It must be acknowledged, however, that in putting these suggestions forward, I am also proposing that social anthropologists move away from those disciplinary preoccupations which are the root of the problems to which I have referred. In particular, the related concerns with processes of social integration, on the one hand, and corporate groups and systematic interrelationship, on the other, must be undermined, if not totally abandoned. There is already a movement within the discipline which is concerned to do precisely this,[6] so taking such a line need not involve the repudiation of social anthropology. Nor, however, is there any sense in which the approaches which I shall consider below can be considered to be exclusively anthropological; they all inhabit that usefully imprecise academic no man's land which is the meeting place of a number of subject areas and the site of so much of the best contemporary social science.

In the first place, it is high time that anthropology turned more of its attention towards racism and processes of ethnic categorisation. Doing so is more a matter of a shift in emphasis than the performance of a total volte-face. In making such a move, anthropologists would also be forced to confront the tricky question of power, its sources and uses, and, inevitably perhaps, the issue of class differences. In attempting these tasks some critical attention might be given to the theoretical work of those sociologists – such as, for example, Bonacich (1980), Miles (1982) and Rex (1983c) – who have already begun to engage with these topics. Similarly, there is a body of work in social geography which might be usefully plundered as a source of new insights and perspectives on ethnic conflict; for example, the collections edited by Boal and Douglas (1982) and Peach, Robinson and Smith (1981).

A second avenue which would seem to be appropriate for anthropological exploration leads eventually into social psychology: the question of the nature and content of ethnic identity at both the personal and social levels. Although at least one eminent anthropologist has already made an excursion into the field (Epstein, 1978), seeking to enlarge our understanding of the affective dimensions of ethnicity, it has, by and large, been left to the psychologists to open up the area for discussion.[7] In addition to the work of writers such as Lange and Westin (1981) and Weinreich (1980, below, ch. 14), a useful starting point for the consideration of the psychology of ethnic identity is the work of the late Henri Tajfel (1978; 1981; 1982a). Despite the undoubted conceptual and terminological distance which separates the two academic communities, there seems to be little doubt that anthropologists have both a lot to offer – by way of their long-standing interest in the interpretation and analysis of culture and symbolism – *and* a lot to learn in the broad area of social and personal identity. In this respect, an encouraging pointer to the future may be Sherwood's ethnographic field study of the psychodynamics of 'racial' identity in Britain (Sherwood, 1980).

Staying within the boundaries of anthropology, broadly defined, there is an interesting body of work on ethnicity developed by Soviet anthropologists.[8] Theoretically speaking, these authors are centrally concerned with the linked concepts of the *ethnos*, 'stable human communities, tied together by unity of territory and history of their formation, and by a common language and culture' (Arutiunov and Bromley, 1978, 11), and *ethnogenesis*, the social processes which, over time, produce, reproduce and modify the ethnos. With their roots in a common, if distant, intellectual heritage, particularly the early work of Shirokogoroff and other Russian scholars, Afrikaans-speaking 'cultural anthropology' in South Africa and Soviet anthropology appear, in their concerns with the ethnos/ethnie and ethnogenesis, to have much in common. There are, however, grounds for believing that the similarities are no more than superficial, each having developed the basic ideas in very different directions.[9]

Looking at the concepts of the ethnos and ethnogenesis, as used by Soviet scholars, it is fairly clear that the former, in particular, can be criticised along many of the same lines as the formulations of Barth and Wallman; in fact, it is arguably the case that the notion of the 'ethnos' reifies ethnicity even more than the concept of the 'ethnic group' does. However, inasmuch as Soviet writers are explicit in their view that models of ethnic entities, and the concept of ethnicity, are hierarchic, extending in their applicability to the level of the nation, this school of thought does direct our attention to the similarity which exists between processes of ethnicity and processes of nationalism.

Similarly, the stress in this model upon the historical processes whereby ethnicity is constituted (ethnogenesis), may serve to point social anthropologists towards the study of nationalism and the processes which result in the (often violent or conflictual) establishment of nation-states, whether ethnically homogeneous or heterogeneous.

It is precisely the processes which transform (or not) ethnic heterogeneity into some kind of national unity that are of the greatest importance. It is concepts such as ethnogenesis which may allow one to engage with the issues raised – although unsatisfactorily resolved – by the plural society model. Much that is of interest has been written recently on nationalism, some of it by anthropologists (e.g. Anderson, 1983; Breuilly, 1982; Gellner, 1983; Lewis, 1983), but there is little doubt that more remains to be done, particularly with respect to the emergent nation-states of the ex-colonial Third World. As a corollary, of course, there is the equally interesting question of the resurgence of ethnicity, regional ethnicity one might almost want to call it, within apparently securely established nation-states, particularly, although not exclusively, in Europe (e.g. Nairn, 1981; A. D. Smith, 1981; TeSelle, 1974). This, once again, is an area which is ripe for further research and theorisation by social anthropologists.

In closing, it should perhaps be emphasised that although I have been highly critical of some of the traditional planks in the social anthropological platform, in particular the emphasis upon groups and processes of social integration, my intention in so doing has simply been to sketch out some of the potential areas of development for the discipline. Other commentators would doubtless, and quite rightly, have offered other suggestions: the proposals contained in the closing section of this paper are not, therefore, intended to be final or exclusive. That having been said, however, some movement towards new or alternative theoretical frameworks and substantive areas of research is long overdue, if social anthropology is not to be increasingly marginalised in its contribution to the academic field of ethnic and 'race' relations.

NOTES

1 Throughout this paper I have placed the word 'race' in inverted commas; this is to signify that it is a contested concept, whose meaning may not be taken for granted. In my own usage it refers simply to folk 'racial' categorisation, and no other meaning should be presumed for it.
2 I gratefully acknowledge the helpful advice of my colleagues, John Hutson, Margaret Kenna and Hilary Stanworth, in writing this paper. I have not, however, always paid attention to that advice, and the argument's shortcomings are my own responsibility.

3 For further argument on whether the Nuer are really the Dinka (and vice versa), see the correspondence pages of *Man*, (N.S.) 8 (1973).
4 The point being made here is similar to Bourne and Sivanandan's comments on the ethnicity approach (1980, 345).
5 It must, of course, be acknowledged that Gluckman derived much of his theoretical position from the earlier sociological work of Coser and Simmel.
6 See, for example, Boissevain (1974), Holy and Stuchlik (1983).
7 For a comprehensive overview of the psychological literature on inter-group relations, see Tajfel (1982b).
8 For an introduction to this literature, see the relevant chapters in the collections edited by Bromley (1974), Gellner (1980) and Holloman and Arutiunov (1978).
9 The intellectual resemblance between South African *volkekunde* and Soviet anthropology is too complicated a matter to discuss here: see, however, the controversy in the pages of *RAIN* (Royal Anthropological Institute News), numbers 35, 36, 37 and 38 (1979–80).

9

Pluralism, race and ethnicity in selected African countries

M. G. SMITH

Introduction

For the most part, in formulating and evaluating 'theories' of race and ethnic relations, Western scholars rely disproportionately on descriptive analyses of relevant situations in Western societies provided by other Western scholars, thereby entrenching the myopia and ethnocentric bias from which scholarly studies of these questions have perennially suffered. In an effort to open a small window on the wider world and to persuade colleagues to devote more time to the systematic study of foreign situations, I present here a comparative analysis of data from twenty-seven contemporary African states in an attempt to determine the relative significance of pluralism, race and ethnicity for social order and political stability in these societies. I do so in the belief that better understanding of the ways in which these three sets of variables affect conditions of social order and political stability in the emergent 'nation-states' of post-colonial Africa may provide a sound base for general theories of race and ethnicity in modern societies. To that end I shall outline the social bases and developments of these twenty-seven countries up to the end of 1982, as that was the latest date for which such information was readily available at the time of writing.

In this paper I use data drawn from the following states: Algeria, Benin, Cameroon, Cape Verde Islands, Central African Republic, Chad, Equatorial Guinea, Ethiopia, Gabon, Gambia, Ghana, Guinea, Guinea-Bissau, the Ivory Coast, Lesotho, Liberia, Malawi, Mali, Mauritania, Mozambique, Niger, Nigeria, São Tomé and Príncipe, Senegal, Sierra Leone, Togo and Upper Volta.[1] Two-thirds of these states lie in West Africa, four in Central Africa, one each in East and North Africa, and the remainder in the southern part of the continent. Although these states do not form a statistical sample of African, Third World or indeed any other category of state, they do represent approximately half the states in Africa, and display patterns that cannot be dismissed as entirely unrepresentative of social conditions and developments in contemporary African societies.

The inclusion of Algeria in this set is deliberate, given its long colonial experience, Islamic culture, racial homogeneity, relative prosperity, northerly location, and other conditions which may be casually expected to differentiate its post-colonial political and social development from those of sub-Saharan African societies. The inclusion of Ethiopia and Liberia is also deliberate, since recent developments in these long-independent black African states illustrate conditions and processes that operate in the younger states created by white rivalries and imperialism.

As this paper addresses the implications of race, ethnicity and pluralism in these contemporary states, I shall review certain salient indicators of their internal order and political stability since independence, and, for Liberia and Ethiopia, in the fifty years from 1932 to the end of 1982, since these are the most relevant decades for our enquiry and together illustrate the difference between their traditional and recent experience. It is also appropriate to include Ethiopia and Liberia in this review in order that its conclusion may not be summarily dismissed as relevant only to the recently decolonised countries of Africa or other tropical zones.

Data cited below on these twenty-seven states were taken from various Year Books and other comparative compilations.[2] These differing accounts were collated and supplemented as necessary by data from other sources on particular topics and countries. Though influenced by discussions with Ms Rebecca French of Yale University, and by the texts from which the data were drawn, responsibility for the criteria, categories and concepts that structure the argument of this paper is mine. Particular care has been taken in sorting and tabulating these data to minimise errors and misclassifications. Before proceeding to the data it is best to define and distinguish the variables under study, namely race, ethnicity and pluralism.

Race and ethnicity

By 'race and ethnic relations' I understand all relations which are either based on or influenced by racial and/or ethnic factors, interests and considerations, and which take place within and between racial blocs and/or ethnic units in multi-racial and/or poly-ethnic populations. Normally, multi-racial populations are also poly-ethnic; but the reverse does not always hold, since all ethnic units are sub-divisions of some single racial stock, differentiated in the beliefs of those who do and those who do not belong to them by real or putative community of descent and cultural practice. In contrast, races are biological divisions of mankind differentiated by gross phenotypical features which are hereditary, polygenic, highly resistant to environmental influences, distinctive and of doubtful adaptive value. When persons of different race mate, their offspring differ modally in phenotype from either parent in various ways. By their physical appearance such hybrids demonstrate the objective nature and biological differences of the parental races to which they are affiliated.

In my view, race is an essentially biological concept based on those distinctive sets of hereditary phenotypical features that distinguish varieties of mankind. There have never been any 'pure' races since raciation – the process by which races evolve, change and come into being – is an essential aspect of human evolution and proceeds within isolated populations as well as by miscegenation. Most biologists today reject this concept of race for reasons I do not find persuasive or convincing. They generally deny the biological validity of race and race differences on the familiar ground that genetic variation within populations often exceeds that between them, and sometimes assimilate notions of racial phenotype to Platonic ideal types whose earthly manifestations are erratic rather than normal (King 1981; Klass and Hellman 1971).

Neither the argument nor the data adduced to support it convince me that those gross hereditary physical differences that all men remark between Negroes, Asiatic Mongols, Whites (or Caucasians), Australian Aborigines, Amerindians, Pygmies, Bushmen and certain other populations are neither objective nor genetic in their base. Instead, it seems clear that contemporary biologists have committed an elementary *non sequitur* in deducing the 'non-existence of human races' from the prevalence of genetic clines. For, if 'there are no races, only clines' (Livingstone 1962), can the biologists cite reliable cases in which White (Caucasian) couples have begotten and borne offspring having Negro, Pygmy, Australoid, Amerindian, Mongol or other racial phenotypes, or vice versa? If so, why are not such marvels so frequent that they lose their novelty? If not, can the biologists explain why not, given their much-repeated assertion concerning the variable distribution of genetic factors within and across human populations? As it is patently ridiculous to treat blood groups as racial diacritica, I wonder how and why it happened that the results of research on blood groups and other monogenic characters were misinterpreted thus, and why such a patent misinterpretation has not long since been repudiated.

When couples of the same race, whatever that may be, produce children who are randomly black, white, Mongol, pygmoid, Australoid, Amerindian, etc. I shall gladly acknowledge my error in disputing current biological ideology on the 'non-existence of human races'; but not until then. As it is with animals, so should it be with humans in this matter. German Shepherd dogs, Jersey cattle, Siamese cats and Berkshire pigs differ among themselves phenotypically, in colours, marking, stature, etc., and therefore genotypically as well. None the less, mated with others of their own stock, German Shepherds reproduce their like and neither spaniels, dachshunds nor retrievers. Likewise, mated with one another, Jersey cattle do not bring forth Angus or Friesian calves, Siamese cats do not bear Persian or common kittens, and neither do Berkshire pigs bear litters of the native Chinese or Melanesian varieties. Must we none the less deny the objective differences between these differing breeds, varieties or races of animals because each contains some genetic variation? If so, then presumably only a population of perfect clones would satisfy the current biological criteria of race, however ludicrous that is to logic and common sense, since it defines races as separate species that reproduce asexually.

To demonstrate how irrelevant for the differentiation of biological stocks are variations in the distribution of genes that account for blood groups and other monogenic characters, we may note that similar variations in the frequency distributions of blood groups occur among horses, zebras and donkeys. For that reason must we therefore deny that they are distinct species? Yet, if we admit that, on what basis can we consistently deny that mankind, as a single species, also contains several races that exhibit modally different phenotypes which require parallel differences of genotype, for all the pervasively clinal distribution of monogenic characters between and among them?

For these and other reasons, I recognise as races those varieties of mankind characterised by distinctive sets of gross hereditary phenotypical features. I therefore distinguish sharply between 'race relations' and 'ethnic relations', reserving the first term for relations between peoples of differing racial stock and the second for relations between people of the same racial stock who feel themselves, and are felt by others, to differ ethnically by virtue of their differing descent and culture. The interactions of ethnic populations that differ also in race, as, for example, the Portuguese and BaVenda in Angola, the Afrikaner and Zulu, are thus examples of *race relations*, and must be distinguished sharply from the interactions of ethnic units of the same racial stock, such as, for example, Boers and Britons in South Africa, Zulu and Xhosa, Portuguese and Spaniards, etc., which are strictly *inter-ethnic relations*.

Of many reasons why it is essential to maintain this distinction clearly and to separate such cases for study, I can here only mention the following. First, unlike ethnic identity, racial identity and/or difference is immutable, manifest and *normally* unambiguous in multi-racial societies and contexts. By comparison, as the literature indicates, ethnicity is generally latent and situational in its assertion. The manifest and immutable nature of racial identity and difference, as compared with the optional anonymity of ethnic identity among people of the same racial stock, ensures that racial differences and communities have far greater prominence, visibility and collective appeal than ethnicity in multi-racial societies which are also poly-ethnic, such as the USA, South Africa and Britain. For individuals and in interpersonal relations, differences between racial and ethnic identity are equally pervasive, immutable and salient. Accordingly, to understand relations of either kind, it is essential to distinguish them clearly as subjects of study, and not to conflate them, as is now the dominant fashion among white 'experts' on race and ethnic relations, who treat inter-racial and inter-ethnic relations as one and the same for purposes of documentation, analysis and comparison. (Glazer and Moynihan, 1975; Thernstrom *et al.*, 1980; Banton & Harwood, 1975; Banton 1983). Such procedures commit the study of these topics to a crippling confusion at its very foundation (M. G. Smith 1982), and do so on ideological grounds that preclude our understanding of either complex and of both, since that may only be gained by their careful distinction, study, analysis and comparison. Moreover, by treating as one and the same what men in practice distinguish and invest with strong values and sanctions, human biologists and social scientists commit their studies of race and ethnicity to irrelevance in advance, by categorically rejecting as error the daily experience of mankind, in order to preserve as dogma the fallacy cited above, which they hold so dear on ideological grounds.

Most sociologists nowadays set aside biological race in favour of a looser 'sociological' concept. In such usage, 'races' are whatever divisions or aggregates the members of a given society or set of societies traditionally distinguish and identify as such. In this view, races are whatever the people say they are. That approach precludes study of the correspondence between folk ideas of race or ethnicity and the manifest biological differences or apparent homogeneity of populations, though the study of such correspondences of folk beliefs and objective conditions is indispensable for any full understanding of collective thought and social process. For example, despite the evidence, Hitler and his Nazi followers chose to distinguish Jews as a race separate from Germans and elaborated a racist ideology to 'legitimate' their elimination. We cannot fully understand Nazi racism if we ignore the invalidity of the racial distinctions and concepts on which this most elaborate ideology and programme were based. Any thorough analyses of ideologies require their confrontation with objective evidence of the conditions to which they refer; and this is especially necessary with regard to folk beliefs about race, which is itself so significant but plastic a basis for human identity and difference that almost all versions of the concept can be made to serve various sectional interests and functions. In treating as real what men believe to be real, sociologists pursue direct knowledge of folk beliefs in specific social contexts; yet since cultural schemes are arbitrary historical by-products whose hidden foundations and significance can never be fully known until the precise nature of their differences from and correspondences with objective phenomena are fully understood, it is surely inadequate to restrict their study to the social contexts and processes in which they occur. The simple fact that a people, or some of them, assert or deny racial differences among themselves or others, and act accordingly, says nothing about relations within and between objectively different racial stocks if, as often happens, such folk distinctions are misconceived or inappropriately applied, as, for example, by de Gobineau in opposing 'Franks' and 'Gauls'.

As used below, the term 'race' refers to aggregates whose members are objectively distinguished from others by certain gross hereditary phenotypical features. Altogether, in the African states discussed here, there are five racial categories, namely, Blacks, Whites, Indians, Pygmies, and a rather variable residual category of hybrids. For example, in Mauritania and Senegal that category includes the 'Black Moors' who, though dark, are rarely black and have non-negroid features that distinguish them from the true *harratin*, or negroid slaves, settled along the southern border with Senegal; in Chad and Niger, the Tubu are hybrids of similar complexion and features; but in São Tomé and Príncipe, the Cape Verde Islands and Guinea-Bissau, the *mesticios* are mulatto hybrids descended from white and black ancestors, as are the Amhara who dominate Ethiopia. Objectively, in each of these cases, the hybrid population is readily distinguished from and by others in its society by certain characteristic phenotypical features.

As mentioned above, in my view an ethnic unit is a population whose members believe that in some sense they share common descent and a common cultural heritage or tradition, and who are so regarded by others. The notion accordingly requires concordance between the views of outsiders and those of members of such collectivities concerning their distinctive ethnic status and identity. It is not necessary that ethnic beliefs should correspond closely to historical or other facts, though to some extent they do. For the identification of ethnic groups, what matters is the belief, held by their members and by others, in a shared distinctive culture or tradition and community of descent.

In Western societies ethnic dispersal often reflects historical migrations that link citizens of differing ethnic stocks to other nation-states, thus adding to differences of ethnic status and identity the problems of dual or alternative national allegiance. During periodic Western conflicts in this century and the last, such ethnic linkages among warring states have confronted them with difficult questions of foreign relations as well as internal security.

In contemporary Africa, partly as a function of the arbitrary boundaries inherited from colonial rule, partly as a function of the more recent movements of people from overseas as well as within the continent, members of some ethnic units now reside in two or more nation-states, while all or almost all members of many others live in one only. Such differences in the political implications of ethnic identity are always important and sometimes critical for those concerned, as, for example, in Gabon's expulsion of Cameroon immigrants, or in the deposition of President Luis Cabral by natives of Guinea-Bissau, who thus sought to free themselves from rule by the hybrid Cape Verde elite on whom Cabral and the Partido Africano de Independencia da Guiné e Cabo Verde had relied from the period of anti-colonial struggle.

Likewise, citizens of non-African states resident in these African countries differ in ethnic identity, as well as in nationality, from those around them. The differing national affiliations of ethnic units may also vary in their political and social significance. Thus, in Africa, while residents from many overseas countries lack political significance, the nationals of others retain it, as, for example, the French in former French colonies such as Senegal, Ivory Coast and Gabon; the Cubans and Russians in Ethiopia, São Tomé and Príncipe; and the Libyans in Chad. Given such differences, it is necessary to distinguish those ethnic entities in any society that have nationality ties to other states, and to ask if such ties are or are not exclusive. For example, in West Africa such peoples as the Mandinka, Fulani, Kanuri, Tuareg and Hausa have spread widely from pre-colonial days and are currently found in two or more contemporary nation-states. It is therefore necessary to recognise the wide but variable transnational affiliations of such dispersed ethnic units, and to record their links with at least one other 'nation-state' insofar as those links are, or are likely to be, politically relevant to either country.

Intra-ethnic relations differ from inter-ethnic relations primarily because their principals share a common set of understandings, values and attitudes that reflect their common culture and community. Fellow ethnics laugh at the same jokes, enjoy the same food and drink, treasure the same collective memories, myths, heroes, dances and songs, dress, patterns of bodily decoration, house style, and so much more that identifies their common distinctive culture, including folk beliefs, fears, assumptions, and those axioms that provide the common foundations of collective thought and morals. With such common background, they usually marry one another and so reproduce the ethnic community by perpetuating its shared, distinctive culture within a relatively closed reproductive group.

Language, religion, homeland and mode of subsistence figure prominently in the creation and perpetuation of these ethnic cultures and collectivities. In Africa indigenous peoples characterised by differences of language, religion, social organisation, subsistence practices and location have high rates of endogamy, and are generally referred to as tribes or ethnic groups. Of course, many of these are not groups, since they lack the inclusive or representative organisation that is essential for the common collective action by which groups pursue and regulate their distinctive common affairs. Thus such peoples as the Nuer, Tallensi, Tiv, Gusii and many others are ethnic units of another kind. Moreover, many African peoples lacked the features generally used to differentiate 'tribes'. Such peoples as the Djola, Fulani, Yoruba and Kru were widely scattered by migrations across West Africa in pre-colonial days. In short, not all indigenous ethnic units in West Africa conform to the simple tribal model cited above. It is essential none the less to include within the ethnic inventory of any African country all those collectivities, indigenous and other, that are locally recognised as ethnically distinct.

Pluralism

There is an obvious and profound difference between societies whose members all share a common culture and language, common forms of social and political organisation, modes of subsistence, ways of life, and generally a common religion, and those that contain two or more aggregates that differ in these respects, and perpetuate their differences without substantial attrition by the familiar processes of social reproduction. Societies of the latter type are culturally plural, and display their cultural pluralism in their social composition. All twenty-seven African countries discussed below are of this kind. However, while many populations within them differ in every institutional dimension of culture, as, for example, do the Kadara and Hausa of Nigeria, in other cases their cultural differences are limited to certain institutional spheres of activity, such as kinship and marriage, cult, social control and subsistence modes, or, perhaps, to certain forms of social organisation. Though language generally differs among peoples of differing cultures, this is not always the case; and in many areas lingua francas facilitate intercourse across cultural frontiers. For example, in the USA and other modern societies, ethnic aggregates participate freely in the common public domain and use identical institutions, including the national language, currency, law and patterns of economic and political organisation, while cherishing and developing their distinct traditions, including language, cult, cuisine, family patterns and the like, among themselves. Such ethnic patterns flourish in the private domains reserved by law for individual and collective activities of equal indifference to the rights and status of their participants as citizens in the common public domain in which the collective affairs of the inclusive population are conducted. By comparison with the differences among tribal peoples in societies of colonial and contemporary Africa, various kinds of hyphenated Americans – Greek-, Swedish-, Italian-, Irish-, Jewish-, etc. – neatly illustrate how variable institutional and other cultural differences between collectivities in a common society may be, in their nature and extent.

To indicate the nature of pluralism and illustrate its main varieties and structural conditions, the USA is a most rewarding subject of study. Its constitution provides that all hyphenated white Americans of the same sex enjoy the same formal rights at law, in the state, and in all activities and structures directly related to it, such as public education, the armed forces, the market, transport, communications, etc. This situation illustrates the universalistic incorporation of white persons as citizens in the American polity under its constitution. That mode of incorporation simultaneously confers equal citizenship and identical legal rights and obligations on individuals. In these circumstances differing ethnic cultures do not entail any difference of formal status in the public domain of political, legal, economic and ancillary activities between ethnic units. Thus ethnic differences cannot involve formal differences of political and legal status if everyone is directly incorporated on uniform conditions in the state and the public domain.

However, until recently American blacks have not enjoyed the same status and rights as American whites, hyphenated or other, in government and law, even where, as in certain states, the laws did not formally differentiate them from whites. In other words, besides the *de jure* conditions of incorporation of citizens, following Max Weber's advice (1947: 37) we need to look closely at the prevailing *de facto* conditions, at the actual conditions in which men live. For American blacks until the late 1960s, the political reality consisted in their differential incorporation and virtual exclusion from free and equal participation in the fundamental institutions of American society. Though flagrantly inconsistent with the proclaimed ideals and rules of the American constitution and polity, this differential incorporation of black Americans was none the less asserted and upheld by powerful segments of the white population, primarily on grounds of race. Yet in different spheres black and white Americans had more in common than did either, for example, with resident Chinese, Japanese and Mexican Americans, or with the earliest immigrants from Central and Eastern Europe. None the less, on racial grounds blacks were denied equal status with whites in the USA, and therefore could neither enjoy the same life chances and situations as whites nor participate freely in white society. This was equally true for the Amerindians, for the vast majority of Orientals until 1946, for Chicanos, and for certain other immigrant populations such as Polynesians and West Indians.

Behind the prevailing social barriers, these differentially incorporated aggregates practised, adapted and developed further their distinctive ethnic culture, life styles, and forms of organisation as best they could to protect and advance their interests in their respective situations. In consequence, American society throughout this period had two radically different bases on which peoples of differing race – whites and non-whites – were incorporated within it and within the state, namely the universalistic or uniform mode of incorporation reserved for whites, and the differential mode of incorporation of blacks and other non-whites. As an effect of such differential incorporation, US society was structurally plural, its white and non-white sections being distinguished by two sets of radically different rights, obligations and relations with the common public domain. Along with this structural pluralism also went the segmental incorporation of Amerindian, Oriental and certain other subordinate non-white populations under differing juridical provisions and agencies which ascribed individuals on grounds of descent to some natal collectivity as the decisive condition of their membership and status in the state. Ideally such segmental incorporations assume equivalence of the incorporated segments that thus mediate individual citizenship in the inclusive unit; but, as with the structural disjunctions laid down by differential incorporation, such segmental incorporation defines social units which inevitably develop distinctive traditions, cultures and social forms as adjustments to their peculiar situations, even if formerly alike, although of course in the USA and generally elsewhere cultural differences antedate the segmental incorporation of discrete collectivities.

In consequence, despite its universalistic constitution, the USA is a highly complex plural society in which all three modes of incorporation – the universalistic, the equivalent or segmental and the differential – have their place, each being associated with a particular type and level of pluralism (Smith 1969: 436–46; 1984). Thus, as we have seen, the legal equivalence of culturally different ethnics in white American society indicates its cultural pluralism and simultaneous exclusion of social and structural pluralism from the public domain of white America. Conversely, the critical differences that have historically distinguished whites and non-whites and led to their differential incorporation entailed the structural pluralism that positively fosters cultural differences between the unequal sections, whatever their original condition. Finally, the *de jure* and *de facto* segmental incorporation that still regulates certain non-white populations in the country preserves and intensifies their cultural and social difference, from other groups. Ethnic differences among whites, while formally excluded from the public domain as irrelevant, figure prominently in the private domain as bases for the formal and informal organisations of ethnic communities that may then act to protect and foster their distinct collective interests within limits allowed by government and law. Thus white America likewise illustrates *de facto* segmental organisation on ethnic lines within the private domain.

It is evident from this discussion that pluralism is a variable in several senses simultaneously. First, there are variations in the number and nature of cultural and other differences that are institutionalised as bases for collective disjunction whether *de jure* or *de facto*, and whether in the public or only in the private domain. Second, there are significant differences between the cultural pluralism that prevails, as among white Americans, without corresponding social and political disparities between culturally distinct collectivities and their members, and differences of the same kind accompanied by the social exclusions that institute social pluralism through the consociational incorporation of social segments as, for example, in the cantons of Switzerland. Finally, there are the cultural differences that accompany or emerge from the structural pluralism instituted by differential incorporation of collectivities that normally differed culturally in the first place, whatever the historical grounds for their structural disjunctions. It is thus appropriate to describe societies based on differential incorporation as *hierarchic pluralities*, those based on equivalent or segmental incorporation as *segmental pluralities*, and those that combine both these modes of incorporation as *complex pluralities*.

When culturally distinct peoples are incorporated together segmentally and differentially, two distinct and highly significant kinds of social exclusion constitute and pervade the societal order. The segmental and differential modes of incorporation generate quite distinct social and cultural tensions, problems and developments, none of which are associated with cultural pluralism incorporated under a universalistic liberal regime. For example, during the 1960s the USA experienced prolonged national upheavals, as blacks campaigned, at first peacefully and then by violent means, for abrogation of the *de facto* differential incorporation that had hitherto regulated their lives and flagrantly violated the most fundamental and dearly held principles of American democracy and society. The stresses intrinsic to consociational structures differ in their nature and source from those intrinsic to differential incorporation, *de jure* as in South Africa, or *de facto* as still prevalent in the USA.

The argument

It is the argument of this paper that, like certain other social conditions, such as differences of language, religion and provenience, race and ethnicity both depend for their significance in each society on their relations to the prevailing structures of incorporation, *de facto* as well as *de jure*, and on the composition and alignments of the collectivities that such structures constitute and regulate. This generalisation is implicit in the preceding discussion, and virtually explicit in the sketch of American society given above; but its validity for other societies needs to be demonstrated, given its implications not only for academic studies of race and ethnicity but also for projects and policies to diagnose and deal with the problems they often present.

There is in recent American discussions of the subject an unfortunate tendency to regard 'ethnicity' as some kind of substance like one of Clifford Geertz's 'primordial givens' (1963a: 109). Whether ethnicity, gender, age or any other aspect of the human condition is better conceived as a quality, relation, or substance for literary and philosophical discussion is not in question; but whatever its 'real nature', the phenomenon of ethnicity depends for its social significance on its place in and under the prevailing structures of incorporation, directly or otherwise. It is easy to cite examples of structures that have fostered or created ethnic divisions where these were formerly absent, and ignored or eliminated them where formerly important. Though familiar, the implications of such data are commonly ignored by writers determined to present ethnicity as some kind of irreducible socio-cultural substance that, although universal, has only recently appeared in the USA (Glazer and Moynihan, 1975).

With the reservations expressed above, sociological studies of race have fared somewhat better by focusing on 'race relations' rather than race itself as the significant phenomena, and as a nexus of social problems that require social action. However, much confusion obtains among sociologists concerning those contexts and kinds of relations that are most important for sociological studies of race, and the reasons therefor. One set of scholars advocates the psychological or socio-psychological study of situations and relations that have racial relevance. Commonly such studies rely heavily on concepts of prejudice and discrimination, and focus on attitudes and opinions that the groups involved may have about one another and/or some others and their activities. Such work evidently presumes that whatever their nature, race relations reflect and are governed by the mental states of individuals, and gives variable attention to other social conditions and prevailing arrangements. Other writers interpret race and ethnic relations as effects of the economic order and dominant economic motivations in any society. For such scholars race relations are primarily relations of inequality and exploitation that emerge with the rise of capitalism and European expansion overseas (UNESCO 1980). On this line of argument, the Soviet Union should be a racial and ethnic paradise, free of the hostilities and abuses that inherently accompany capitalism and other monetised non-Marxist economies. Unfortunately for that thesis, neither the USSR nor any of its satellite states fulfils this dream. Nor does China under Mao and his successors, despite its much-vaunted programme for the liberation and incorporation of its national minorities, which total about fifty million people in 'autonomous republics' or districts under local control. Events in Tibet in 1983 as in 1950 and subsequent years demonstrate otherwise. Finally there are those who try to subsume the diverse historical patterns of race relations in any country and the differing patterns in diverse countries under some universal principle or determinant, such as the 'inclusive fitness' of sociobiology (van den Berghe 1981), rational choice theory (Banton 1980; Hechter *et al.*, 1982), or some grand evolutionary scheme such as Park's 'race relations cycle' (Park, 1957). However, on closer study these paradigms rarely satisfy the claims made for them (as, for example, Smith 1983).

Without listing other approaches to the formulation of a general 'theory' or set of 'theories' of 'race relations', it is my argument in this paper that race and ethnic relations alike are equally subject to and shaped by the place and sphere assigned to them by the structure of incorporation that prevails in each society. Thus identical ethnic or racial compositions may be regulated by different structures in different societies, while societies with differing compositions may have very similar structures. As usual, what happens in society and matters critically for sociological study is normally at variance with objective phenomena. To substantiate these observations for the societies listed above, I shall briefly indicate their racial, ethnic and cultural compositions, and then review the recent political experiences that indicate their levels of internal order and political stability. In conclusion I shall try to show how the structures of incorporation rather than the particular racial or ethnic compositions of these states best accounts for their recent experiences of social order as independent states.

The political record

The African countries under review include such mini-states as the Cape Verde Islands, São Tomé and Príncipe, and Equatorial Guinea and such large, important countries as Algeria, Nigeria and Ethiopia. Seven of these states are entirely land-locked, namely Mali, Niger, Upper Volta, Chad, the Central African Republic (CAR), Malawi and Lesotho, the latter being also geographically hostage to South Africa. While some states, such as Nigeria, Guinea and the Gambia have relatively dense populations, several, notably the Saharan countries, have relatively sparse and low populations. Of the twenty-seven countries only Algeria, the Ivory Coast, Gabon and Nigeria do not fall clearly into the category of Lesser Developed Countries (LDCs) with very low national and per capita average incomes. Nigeria, once rich, is now engulfed in wasteful debts it wants to reschedule. While poverty is the norm throughout these territories, their national elites as a rule have expensive tastes and lifestyles. Of the twenty-seven countries, Senegal and the Gambia established a confederation in 1982, following a violent attempt to seize power in the Gambia prevented only by Senegalese troops with considerable bloodshed. The uneven regional distribution and West African bias of this set of states have already been noted.

As of December 1982 four of these states, namely Mozambique, São Tomé and Príncipe, Cape Verde Islands and Guinea-Bissau, all former Portuguese colonies, had been independent for less than ten years; another four, namely Equatorial Guinea, Lesotho, the Gambia and Malawi, for less than twenty; Algeria for twenty, Sierra Leone for twenty-one years, Guinea for twenty-four and Ghana, the first West African state to achieve independence in 1957, for twenty five. Two countries, Liberia and Ethiopia, have long been independent, though from 1936 till 1941 Ethiopia was colonised by Mussolini's Italy. Accordingly, to put recent developments in Liberia and Ethiopia into proper perspective, I shall take account of their political experience from 1932 to 1982. Of these twenty-seven states thirteen – Niger, Ivory Coast, Mali,

Senegal, Benin, Cameroon, Upper Volta, the Central African Republic (CAR), Mauritania, Togo, Chad, Gabon and Nigeria – became independent in 1960, twelve of these being former French possessions, while Nigeria, the thirteenth, had then known sixty years of British rule. Excluding Liberia and Ethiopia, in December 1982, the other twenty-five states averaged 18.8 years of independence each. With Liberia and Ethiopia given a nominal fifty years each as the period of greatest relevance for this enquiry, the twenty-seven averaged 21.1 years each as independent states.

Though variable, the short independent lives of most of these states, set beside their generally hectic recent experiences, direct attention to the levels of instability and disorder within them, and to their sources. A few indices will give an idea of their social and political fragility. For example, all twenty-seven countries have experienced changes of regime or institutional structure since independence; four, each once only; four, twice apiece; four, three times each; two, four times and five, five times each; four, six times each; and four, seven or more times.

If governments are ruling groups under particular leaders, then some governments perdure through or by means of changes of their regimes, as for example, those of Sekou Touré, Senghor and Ahmadou Ahidjo in Guinea, Senegal and Cameroon. As of December 1982, three governments in these twenty-seven states had held power for twenty years or more, namely those of Guinea, Ivory Coast and Cameroon; five others, of Togo, Gabon, Lesotho, Malawi and the Gambia, had held power for between fifteen and twenty years, the last thanks largely to its restoration by Senegalese troops after an armed revolt in July 1981; and two, of Sierra Leone and Mali, for ten to fifteen years. On the other hand, of these twenty-seven countries one, Chad, had no effective government in 1981 or 1982, while of five – Upper Volta, Ghana, Guinea-Bissau, Central African Republic and Senegal – whose governments were less than two years old, only the last-named had come to power by peaceful succession to its predecessor. As of December 1982, five governments had held power for two to five years, and six for six to ten. During the brief months of this paper's gestation, one of the few 'democratically elected' governments in the set, Nigeria's, was swept aside by military coup. On my information, since independence, and for Liberia and Ethiopia, during the past fifty – or, really, the last ten – years, there have been eighty-four attempted coups in twenty-four of these states and forty-two successful ones in all twenty-seven. On average, half of the attempted coups achieved their aim; and only two or three successful coups, as in Lesotho and the Central African Republic, were not initiated by military personnel. Such a record leads one to ask why the rulers of these African countries recruit or maintain any armies at all, since they are clearly difficult to control and are inclined to remove their paymasters. I shall return to this question later on.

Of these twenty-seven states, in December 1982 three were under military men, fifteen had purely civilian rulers and nine were ruled jointly by military and civilian personnel, with the military normally holding decisive power. Of the twenty-seven governments, one espoused an Islamic ideology, another identified itself as 'democratic socialist', three were authoritarian socialist of a non-Marxist African variety, three were ideologically nationalistic and populist and five claimed to be Marxist, though of differing kinds, including Saõ Tomé and Ethiopia. Eight proclaimed some variety of capitalist development as their goal. I cannot say whether the other six held any particular ideology, or if so what that was.

As of December 1982 the political regimes that prevailed in these states had on average existed for 5.2 years. Of these one, Chad, being then involved in a civil war with various external interventions, had no agreed political regime; seventeen had regimes that were less than five years old, nine of these being two years old or less, six three and two four years old; six had regimes aged five to ten years; and only three regimes were older than that, Guinea's being formally seventeen years old, since its government, while upholding the regime, interpreted and supplemented its rules freely without changing its structure. Altogether by December 1982 the regimes of these twenty-seven countries had lasted for a total of 140 years, or 5.2 on average, while the twenty-seven states had experienced 114 changes of regime since independence, or, for Ethiopia and Liberia, during the past 50 years, averaging 4.22 regime changes each.

As of December 1982, seven states were governed by military dictatorships, five by joint military and civil personnel exercising authoritarian control, ten by civil dictatorships in one-party states, three by elected civil governments, including the ill-fated government of Nigeria, one, Chad, then at civil war, had no nationally accepted government, and one, Mozambique, following its revolutionary and anti-colonial war against Portugal, was Marxist in method as well as claim. Evidently few of these African states allowed free choice of their rulers by citizens through those free electoral processes by which democracy is identified in Western countries. It is therefore no surprise that few of these current governments have achieved power by 'democratic means'; and that holds as well for processes of succession to power in one-party states as in any others.

Social composition

With such evidence of the political instability of these African states, it is appropriate to seek its source in the composition of the societies for whose co-ordination and regulation they were first established. Of these twenty-seven countries, only one, Algeria, consists essentially of people of the same racial stock, whites or Caucasians. Thirteen contain only blacks and whites, such whites as Tuareg or Arab being indigenous, while others were alien. Eleven include, besides black and white, people of another race, whether Pygmies as in Gabon and the Central African Republic or various hybrid stocks such as Moors in Guinea-Bissau and Senegal, Tubu or Tebu in Niger and Chad, Mestizos in Guinea-Bissau and Equatorial Guinea, São Tomé and Príncipe and the Cape Verde Islands, or Amhara and Tigre in Ethiopia, all in their different ways being clearly distinct from Negroes and Whites, though of diverse origin and appearance. Of these twenty-seven societies two, namely São Tomé and Príncipe and Ethiopia, have elements of four distinct racial stocks, the former having a sizeable Mongol population of Chinese and North Koreans as well as whites, blacks and Mestizos, while Ethiopia had Indian immigrants as well as Amhara, blacks and whites. Of the twenty-seven countries, eight have ten or fewer ethnically distinct collectivities; six have between eleven and twenty; nine between twenty-one and fifty; three between fifty-one and 100; and one, Nigeria, has well over 100 such units, indeed more than 300.

This paper seeks to determine how significant such differences of racial or ethnic composition may be for the internal order and political stability of these twenty-seven countries; but before proceeding to those questions, I should present other data on the group as a whole. For example, of these twenty-seven countries ten – Algeria, Guinea, Mali, the Gambia, Chad, Niger, Senegal, Nigeria, Mauritania and Ethiopia – have Muslim majorities within their populations; five – Lesotho, Gabon, Equatorial Guinea, São Tomé and the Cape Verde Islands – have Christian majorities; and in the rest most people remain animists, although devotees of as many different cults as the state has tribes, with the result that their fragmentation precludes power and weakens their resistance to Islam and Christianity.

Of these twenty-seven societies, eight contain people speaking ten or fewer distinct first languages, while ten have between eleven and twenty-five distinct language groups; six have from twenty-six to fifty different first languages, and two, Ethiopia and the CAR, have between fifty-one and 100 first languages, while Nigeria has over 100 – indeed, over 300 first languages are spoken among its people. Given the central role of language in human society and social reproduction, such extreme degrees of linguistic fragmentation imply and presume equivalent degrees of social and cultural fragmentation in the populations of these African states. Of course, not all locally spoken first languages are indigenous, although even in the most fragmented units the majority are of that kind. Such resident aliens as Frenchmen, Britons, Cubans, Portuguese and the like must be included, since their first languages are also distinct; yet it is obvious that in overwhelming majority the differing languages to be found in any African state are of local origin.

Of the twenty-seven countries, six contain between two and four ethnic units having other national identities and/or ties; three have five such units, four have six, seven have seven, and seven have nine or more, two of these each having thirteen groups with such foreign nationality, one fourteen and one sixteen. None of these African states lacks people of differing nationality; and of course such extra-state national ties are not all of equal significance. For example, in former French colonies, the political, economic and cultural significance of French nationality exceeds in importance all identities except those inflated by such irresistible ideological currents as Islam or Marxism.

Race

In all but one of these twenty-seven countries (Algeria), blacks are the great majority of the population, including Ethiopia, where Amhara and Tigre together approximate one-third of the total. Algerians are a nation of Arabs and Berbers, most of whom have been substantially Arabised, and all of whom are now Muslim, if one classes as Muslim the heretical Kharadjites of the Mzab. Nearly half of the twenty-five sub-Saharan states contain two races, while the remainder have three or more, if resident aliens are included. If differences of racial composition possess intrinsic importance, then presumably societies with one, two three or more races in this set should differ significantly in their levels of stability, internal violence, and the like. However, as just mentioned, in almost all cases the overwhelming majority of the population in these societies belongs to a single race – whites in Algeria, hybrids in Mauritania, and blacks everywhere else. In São Tomé and Ethiopia, as in the Guinea-Bissau of Luis Cabral until 1980, a racial minority dominates and rules the majority. In Algeria the Arabs, estimated at forty-five per cent of the population, dominate the state with the support of Arabised Berbers and with resistance from others.

Setting aside Algeria as the only racially homogeneous state in the set, there does not appear to be any significant difference of internal order

Table 9.1 *Some social and political conditions of twenty-seven African countries (Dec. 1982) classified by number of racial stocks in each*

| | Number of racial stocks per country | | | | |
	1	2	3	4	Total
Number of countries	1	13	11	2	27
(1) SOME SOCIAL CONDITIONS					
(a) *Number of ethnic divisions*					
−10	1	1	5	1	8
11–20	–	4	2	–	6
21–50	–	7	2	–	9
51–100	–	1	1	1	3
101+	–	–	1	–	1
(b) *Ethno-linguistic index*					
Total score	0.43	9.85	4.87	0.69	15.84
Number of states	1	13	8	1	23
Average	0.43	0.76	0.61	0.69	0.69
(c) *Other nationalities present*					
Number	7	97	76	20	200
Cases	1	12	12	2	27
Average	7	8	6.3	10	7.4
(d) *Number of first languages*					
−10	1	1	5	1	8
11–25	–	7	3	–	10
26–50	–	5	1	–	6
51–100	–	–	1	1	2
101+	–	–	1	–	1
(e) *Religious majority*					
Muslim	1	4	4	1	10
Christian	–	–	4	1	5
Animist	–	9	3	–	12
(f) *Societal type*					
Complex plurality	1	7	4	2	14
Segmental plurality	–	6	5	–	11
Hierarchic plurality	–	–	2	–	2
(g) *Largest ethnic unit*					
as % of total population	45	48	84	67	–
% range	45	20–48	24–84	40–67	20–84
% average	45	32.8	46	53.5	41.3
(h) *Dominant ethnic units*					
NK	–	4	2	–	6
None	–	3	1	–	4
Largest	1	3	6	–	10
Minority	–	3	2	2	7

Table 9.1 (*cont.*)

| | Number of racial stocks per country | | | | |
	1	2	3	4	Total
Number of countries	1	13	11	2	27

(2) SOME POLITICAL CONDITIONS

(a) *Years independent*

	1	2	3	4	Total
Total	20	298	195	57	570/470
Number of countries	1	13	11	2	27/25
Average	20	22.9	17.7	28.5	21.1/18.8

(b) *Change of regime*

	1	2	3	4	Total
	3	67	35	9	114
Cases	1	13	11	2	27
Average	3	5.1	3.2	4.5	4.22

(c) *Duration of regime*

	1	2	3	4	Total
at Dec. 1982 (years)	6	66	56	12	140
Cases	1	13	11	2	27
Average	6	5.1	5.1	6	5.2

(d) *Duration of government*

	1	2	3	4	Total
at Dec. 1982 (years)	3	153	81	12	249
Cases	1	13	11	2	27
Average	3	11.8	7.4	6	9.3

(e) *Number of attempted coups*

	1	2	3	4	Total
	2	51	23	8	84
Cases	1	13	9	1	24
Average	2	4.0	2.6	8	3.5

(f) *Number of successful coups*

	1	2	3	4	Total
	1	23	14	4	42
Cases	1	13	11	2	27
Average	1	1.8	1.3	2	1.55

(g) *Internal violence*

	1	2	3	4	Total
None	–	2	3	–	5
Little	1	2	2	1	6
Violence without war	–	5	5	–	10
Internal war	–	4	1	1	6
Total	1	13	11	2	27

(h) *Ethnic units involved in violence*

	1	2	3	4	Total
Total	3	32	17/117	13	65/165
Cases	1	12	9/10	2	23/24
Average	3	2.7	1.9/11.7	6.5	2.8/6.9

(i) *De jure mode of incorporation, Dec. 1982*

	1	2	3	4	Total
NK	–	2	1	1	4
Differential	–	1	–	–	1
Differential and universalistic	–	1	–	–	1
Universalistic	1	9	10	1	21
Total	1	13	11	2	27

(j) *De facto mode of incorporation, Dec. 1982*

	1	2	3	4	Total
NK	–	3	3	–	6
Differential	–	6	4	–	10
Differential and segmental	1	2	–	2	5

Table 9.1 (*cont.*)

	Number of racial stocks per country				
	1	2	3	4	Total
Number of countries	1	13	11	2	27
Segmental only	–	–	1	–	1
Universalistic	–	2	3	–	5
(k) *Type of government, Dec. 1982*					
Military and civilian dictatorship	1	3	1	–	5
Civilian dictatorship	–	4	5	1	10
Military dictatorship	–	3	3	1	7
Civilian democracy	–	1	2	–	3
Marxist-Leninist	–	1	–	–	1
None	–	1	–	–	1
(l) *Type of party organisation, Dec. 1982*					
None	–	4	4	1	9
One only	1	8	4	1	14
Two or more	–	1	3	–	4
(m) *Ruling units, Dec. 1982*					
Army	–	6	4	1	11
Sole legal party	–	5	–	–	5
NK	–	–	2	–	2
Largest ethnic unit	1	1	2	–	4
Ethnic minority	–	–	–	1	1
None	–	1	3	–	4

and political stability between states with two or more racial stocks. Minority races have exercised, directly or otherwise, disproportionate influence in the development of several countries in the last twenty-five years. In several of these countries the French still exercise undue influence, while in others such as Saõ Tomé, Mozambique or Ethiopia, Soviet Russians, Cubans, Angolans, East Germans, Chinese or Koreans do so. Chad at the time of writing is torn apart by civil war in which French and Libyan forces participate. Countries with two and three resident racial stocks are the only category in this set having sufficient representatives to permit careful comparison, and they will therefore receive most attention here, but there is evidently no simple correspondence between the numbers of racial stocks and ethnic units of these two categories as shown in Table 9.1, despite their different distributions.

The higher average incidence of nationalities in states with two as against three races cannot be attributed to differences in their numbers of racial stocks; and this is equally true for differences in the average incidence of attempted and successful coups in countries with these differing compositions. Of the thirteen biracial states, four have Muslim and nine have animist majorities; of the eleven triracial states, four have Muslim and three have animist majorities, the remainder being predominantly Christian; but it is obvious that these differing racial compositions neither account for nor follow from such differences in the dominant religious persuasion of these societies. Likewise, while states with two racial stocks, including Liberia, average *c.* twenty-three years of independence each, and without Liberia, 20.5, those with three races average 17.7 years' independence each. Again, it would be difficult to argue that such differences in the length of independent rule can be attributed to the number of racial stocks in states of either category, or vice versa. This holds true also for variations in the average duration of the governments and/or regimes of these states, as well as for the average number of regime changes in either category. It would be difficult to establish causal connections between the differing incidence of such events and the differing number of racial stocks in these societies. And so too for those differences in the kinds of government, ruling units and party political organisations of these two sets of states, as well as the demographic positions of the dominant and largest ethnic units within them, set out in Table 9.1.

Of greater relevance and interest is the relation between differences in racial heterogeneity and the incidence of internal violence in these two categories of state. As regards internal order and violence, the distinctions I shall make are between those states with no internal collective violence, those with little, those with significant outbreaks of violence at intervals, and those that have had internal wars such, for example, as that now underway in Chad. By internal war I mean organised collective violence that proceeds continuously over a sufficient period and area to indicate the operation of two or more centrally co-ordinated armies.

Of the thirteen states with two racial stocks in this set, till December 1982 two have had no internal violence since independence, two have had little, five have known such violence without war, and four have had internal wars, one of which, in Chad, has proceeded intermittently for nearly ten years. Excluding Nigeria, most of whose people had some part in the civil war against Biafran independence, in the triracial states, on average 1.9 ethnic units had been involved in collective violence since independence, as against 2.7 of those with two racial stocks. On such evidence one can scarcely argue that simple difference in the number of racial stocks has had any direct bearing on the levels of internal stability and social order in these states since they became independent or, in the case of Liberia and Ethiopia, during the past fifty years. As ethnic units are the most significant divisions of racial stocks, it is thus perhaps to those that we should turn in search of clues to the social and political dynamics of these African states.

Ethnicity

As noted above, eight of these countries contain ten or fewer ethnic units, six have eleven to twenty, nine have twenty-one to fifty, three have between fifty-one and 100, and Nigeria, with the largest and densest population, has well over 100. To compare these levels of ethnic heterogeneity with those of other independent states, I refer to the work of Charles L. Taylor and Michael Hudson (1976). Using global data from the Soviet *Atlas Narodov Mira* (1964) on the 'ethnolinguistic' composition of independent countries, Taylor and Hudson developed a measure of ethnolinguistic fractionalisation in those societies based on the 'probability that two randomly selected persons from one country will not speak the same language' (216), partly on the assumption, adopted from the *Atlas Narodov Mira*, that language differences are decisive indicators of ethnic differences (215), but modified to reflect the differing demographic structure of national societies. Of the 136 countries for which the data needed to calculate the index were secured, North and South Korea were most homogeneous as regards the identities of their people, with ethnolinguistic fractionalisation measures of 0.00, while Tanzania at the opposite pole was the most fragmented, with an index of 0.93 (271–4).

Of the twenty-seven countries in our set, Taylor and Hudson calculate such measures for 23. Of these, sixteen rank among the thirty-one most heavily fragmented national societies in their list as regards ethnicity and language. Altogether the twenty-three countries of our set for which these measures are available average 0.69 – which is also the index for Gabon, Ethiopia and the CAR – as regards ethnolinguistic fractionalisation, compared with 0.68 for Bolivia and the USSR. Since this index of ethnolinguistic fractionalisation refers to the probability that two randomly chosen individuals will be able to speak the same language, it integrates demographic data on the population of each country with the number of these ethnolinguistic groups which it contains. Thus societies like Ethiopia, with relatively large numbers of languages, may have lower fractionalisation rates than certain others if most of their people speak one or other of a few major tongues, such as Amharic, Gallinya or Tigrinya. These demographic factors ensure that the ethnolinguistic fractionalisation index of Taylor and Hudson is not a simple measure of language differences within nation-states. None the less, as an accurate measure of ethnic diversity, the fractionalisation index suffers from its basic assumption that language indicates ethnicity.

Predictably, despite this bias, units in our selection with relatively few ethnic groups have lower average fractionalisation indices than those with more. Thus states with ten or fewer ethnic units average an index of 0.48 as against 0.68 for those with eleven to twenty such units. States with twenty-one to fifty ethnic units have an average of 0.77 as against 0.76 for those with fifty-one to 100 ethnic divisions, and 0.87 for Nigeria, with over 300. Mainly as a result of demographic factors, the fractionalisation means of countries with twenty-one to fifty ethnic units and of those with between fifty-one and 100 hardly differ.

As regards extra-state national affiliations, the average incidence increases steadily with the number of ethnic units in these states, from 5.25 for states with ten or fewer units to thirteen for Nigeria with over 100. However, as some of these ties relate to resident aliens, their increase may not be due primarily to increases in the number of indigenous ethnic units.

As regards attempted and successful coups, there is no discernible trend associated with increasing ethnic heterogeneity among these states. Similarly, neither as regards the average length of their independent existence, nor the frequency of their changes of regime, nor the average duration of their December 1982 political regimes and governments, is there any indication that the differing numbers of ethnic units in these states were salient or decisive.

However, there is a predictably close correlation between the numbers of ethnic units and first languages in these twenty-seven states. All countries with ten or fewer ethnic units have ten or fewer first languages, and likewise all six countries with eleven to twenty ethnic units have fewer than twenty-five first languages. However, of nine states with twenty-one to fifty ethnic units, four have fewer than twenty-five and five have twenty-six to fifty languages. Likewise, of three states with fifty-one to 100 ethnic units, one has fewer than fifty first languages, two have more. In short, while close and general, these ethnolinguistic correspondences are far from perfect.

As regards their experiences of internal violence since independence, and in Liberia and Ethiopia since 1932, three of the five countries that have had none, and three others that have had little, have ten or fewer ethnic units. On these and other such distributions it seems that internal violence may be less common and severe in states with fewer ethnic groups, but those are also the units with the shortest average independent life. However, while none of the fourteen states with twenty or fewer ethnic groups have had internal wars, one-third of those with

Table 9.2 *Some social and political conditions of twenty-seven African countries (Dec. 1982) classified by number of ethnic divisions in each*

		Number of ethnic units per country					
		−10	11–20	21–50	51–100	100+	Total
	Number of countries	8	6	9	3	1	27
(1)	**SOME SOCIAL CONDITIONS**						
	(a) *Number of racial stocks*						
	One	1	–	–	–	–	1
	Two	1	4	7	1	–	13
	Three	5	2	2	1	1	11
	Four	1	–	–	1	–	2
	(b) *Ethno-linguistic index*						
	Total score	2.39	3.39	6.92	2.27	0.87	15.84
	Cases	5	5	9	3	1	23
	Average	0.48	0.68	0.77	0.76	0.87	0.69
	Range	0.22–	0.62–	0.69–	0.69–	–	0.22–
		0.73	0.73	0.86	0.89	–	0.89
	(c) *Other nationalities present*						
	Number	42	41	70	34	13	200
	Average	5.25	6.7	7.8	11.3	13	7.4
	(d) *Number of first languages*						
	−10	8	–	–	–	–	8
	11–25	–	6	4	–	–	10
	26–50	–	–	5	1	–	6
	51–100	–	–	–	2	–	2
	101+	–	–	–	–	1	1
	(e) *Religious majority*						
	Muslim	3	1	4	1	1	10
	Christian	3	1	1	–	–	5
	Animist	2	4	4	2	–	12
	(f) *Societal type*						
	Complex plurality	5	1	5	2	1	14
	Segmental plurality	1	5	4	1	–	11
	Hierarchical plurality	2	–	–	–	–	2
	(g) *Largest ethnic unit*						
	as % of total population	84	80	40	40	30	84(2)
		(2 cases)					
	% range	30–84	24–80	21–40	20–40	–	20–84
	% average	70.5	44.1	28.3	30.7	30	41.3
	(h) *Dominant ethnic unit*						
	NK	1	1	4	–	–	6
	None	–	1	1	1	1	4
	Largest	6	2	2	–	–	10
	Minority	1	2	2	2	–	7
(2)	**SOME POLITICAL CONDITIONS**						
	(a) *Years independent*						
	Total	124	118	212	94	22	570/470
	Average	15.5	19.7	23.4	23.4	22	21.1/18.8
	(b) *Changes of regime*						
	Total	20	40	32	17	5	114
	Average	2.5	6.7	3.55	5.7	5.0	4.22

Table 9.2 (*cont.*)

		Number of ethnic units per country				
		−10	11–20	21–50	51–100	100+	Total
Number of countries		8	6	9	3	1	27
(c)	*Duration of regime at Dec. 1982 (years)*						
	Total	39	37	35	14	4	129
	Average	4.9	6.1	3.9	4.7	4	4.77
(d)	*Duration of government at Dec. 1982 (years)*						
	Total	48	65	100	29	4	246
	Average	6	10.8	11.1	9.7	4	9.1
(e)	*Number of attempted coups*						
	Cases	14	29	25	11	5	84
	Average	2.3	5.8	2.8	3.7	5	3.5
(f)	*Number of successful coups*	9	14	9	6	4	42
	Cases	8	6	9	3	1	27
	Average	1.1	2.3	1	2	4	1.55
(g)	*Internal violence*						
	None	3	1	1	–	–	5
	Little	3	1	2	–	–	6
	Violence without war	2	4	3	1	–	10
	Internal war	–	–	3	2	1	6
(h)	*Ethnic units involved in violence*						
	Totals	13	8	28	16	100+	65/165+
	Cases	8	4	8	3	1	23/24
	Average	1.6	2	3.5	5.3	100+	2.8/6.9
(i)	*De jure mode of incorporation, Dec. 1982*						
	NK	–	1	2	1	–	4
	Differential	1	–	–	–	–	1
	Differential and universalistic	–	–	1	–	–	1
	Universalistic	7	5	6	2	1	21
(j)	*De facto incorporation, Dec. 1982*						
	NK	2	1	3	–	–	6
	Differential	3	3	4	–	–	10
	Differential and segmental	2	–	1	2	–	5
	Segmental only	–	–	–	1	–	1
	Universalistic	1	2	1	–	1	5
(k)	*Type of government, Dec. 1982*						
	Military and civilian dictatorship	2	1	2	–	–	5
	Civilian dictatorship	4	1	4	1	–	10
	Military dictatorship	2	3	–	2	–	7
	Civilian democracy	–	1	1	–	1	3
	Marxist-Leninist	–	–	1	–	–	1
	None	–	–	1	–	–	1
(l)	*Type of party organisation*						
	None	3	2	2	2	–	9
	One only	4	3	6	1	–	14
	Two or more	1	1	1	–	1	4

Table 9.2 (*cont.*)

	Number of ethnic units per country					
	−10	11–20	21–50	51–100	100+	Total
Number of countries	8	6	9	3	1	27
(m) *Ruling units, Dec. 1982*						
Army	3	4	2	2	–	11
Sole legal party	–	–	4	1	–	5
NK	1	–	1	–	–	2
Largest ethnic unit	3	–	–	–	–	3
Ethnic minority	1	1	–	–	–	2
None	–	1	2	–	1	4

twenty-one to fifty ethnic divisions, two-thirds of those with fifty-one to 100, and the only state in the set with more than 100 ethnic units have all suffered internal wars, two of which were proceeding in Mozambique and Chad when this was written. On these data the probabilities are that internal violence will increase in scale and incidence in these African countries as ethnic heterogeneity increases. Yet obviously the mere increase or decrease of ethnic heterogeneity cannot of themselves account for such phenomena. Nonetheless, as Table 9.2 shows, on average the number of ethnic units involved in incidents of internal violence increases steadily as the numbers of such groups increase, perhaps, because any severe national conflict, such as the Nigerian civil war, will involve people drawn from a correspondingly broad range of ethnic units.

Given data already reported on the political organisation and governments of these states, it is appropriate to enquire whether their regimes may or may not differ as a function of their differing levels and degrees of ethnic fragmentation. As noted above, if we may rely on these category means, there is no obvious correlation between increasing ethnic heterogeneity and changes of regime; and the same is true for duration of governments, seen as teams of ruling personnel under specific leaders, to go by these ratios as of December 1982. Nor can I discern any linkage between the differing degrees of ethnic heterogeneity and types of government in these twenty-seven states, on the data summarised in Table 9.2. While nine states permitted no political party organisation, fourteen were one-party states, *de jure* or *de facto*, and four – Senegal, the Gambia, Nigeria and Lesotho – had two or more parties each. On these data, there is no obvious association between type of party organisation and degree of ethnic heterogeneity in these units. The same point applies as regards their ruling groups. In eleven states the army rules on its own or as the dominant partner in association with civilians, while in five the sole political party under its president and leader was the effective ruling group, without itself being subordinate to any ethnic division. In Chad, as of December 1982, there was no effective ruling unit, the country then being torn apart instead by an inconclusive civil war which had thus far brought profit only to Libya. In three other countries there was no single 'ruling unit'; and for two we lack sufficient data. In three the rulers represented the largest ethnic group and sometimes ruled through the sole legal political party; but in two countries, São Tomé and Ethiopia, both containing four racial stocks, the ruling units were ethnic minorities, namely Amhara who dominate the Dergue and Ethiopian army, and the *criollos* or *mesticios* who approximate 5 per cent of the population of São Tomé.

It is useful to distinguish between ruling and dominant units, since dominant ethnic units may not always engage directly in ruling, while ruling units, such as the Front de la Libération Nationale in Algeria, may themselves sometimes be simply organs for pursuit of the interests of dominant ethnic groups. Of these twenty-seven states, to my knowledge four had no dominant ethnic units in December 1982, and for another six I lack the necessary information. In the remaining seventeen, the dominant ethnic units were numerical majorities in ten and demographic minorities in seven. Of the ten states effectively under the domination of their ethnic majorities, six had ten or fewer ethnic units, two had eleven to twenty, and another two had twenty-one to fifty. In half of the countries dominated by ethnic minorities, the army had the government firmly under control; but only one of these had ten or fewer ethnic units, as against two each with eleven to twenty, twenty-one to fifty, and fifty-one to 100. On these inconclusive data the chances that the largest ethnic group will be the dominant one seem highest in societies with ten or fewer units of this kind and decrease steadily as ethnic heterogeneity increases, all of which perhaps is no great surprise.

Collective relations

Our problem is to account for the differing levels of internal disorder and political instability as reflected by changes of regime and government, coups and collective violence during the independent lifetimes of these states, and, for Ethiopia and Liberia, during the past 50 years, paying special attention to the relations of their differing racial and ethnic composition to these developments.[3] As we have already seen, while not irrelevant, biological races are rarely mobilised as such in these contexts;

and even when that happens, populations generally identify and group themselves as ethnic rather than racial groups, however forcefully they may state their aims in racial terms. As each of the major racial stocks of mankind contains a large number of ethnic units distinguished by language, culture, homeland, social organisation and history, these ethnic divisions are especially relevant to the order and stability of the societies and states of which they are part; and as ethnic units are both the basic components of national societies and often their chief rivals for the loyalties of citizens, we should perhaps concentrate on inter-ethnic relations and factors in our search for a key to the political instabilities and collective orders of these African societies. However, since evidence reviewed above indicates that their differing degrees of ethnic and/or racial heterogeneity cannot account for the differing social and political experiences of these states, where shall we seek the key?

If simple differences in the numbers of racial stocks and/or ethnic units cannot account for the recent socio-political upheavals and experience of these twenty-seven states, separately or together, clearly neither race nor ethnicity by itself operates as an independent variable to promote or subvert their social order and/or political stability. None the less, since all but two of the states have recently achieved their independence from white foreign rule, sometimes through bloody and protracted wars, the potential significance of racial differences for their political and social orders cannot be denied. The secessionist movements that have shaken Ethiopia following the deposition of Haile Selassie also have prominent racial overtones, since the Cushitic Somali and Oromo (Galla) and the ruling Amhara differentiate and contrast themselves in those terms. In Guinea-Bissau the coup of 1980 that removed Luis Cabral from power simultaneously swept away the ruling *mesticio* elite in the Cape Verde Islands, on whom Cabral relied. In Mauritania the horizontal cleavages between 'white Moors', 'black Moors' and the black slaves (*harratin*) are also racial at base, as is the division in São Tomé and Príncipe between the *filhas de terra* or *criollos* of mixed descent, who are a very small ruling minority, and the black Forros, Angolares and others who are obliged to obey the ruling minority by the large, well-equipped Angolan force at their disposal, backed by Cuban technicians and advisers and strong Soviet support for the 'Marxist' regime. Such situations all display the use of racial differences to structure relations between collectivities of differing stocks. When that occurs, race differences provide the sole base or part of the base for the differential incorporation of collectivities in hierarchic or complex plural societies, *de facto* or *de jure*.

However, relatively few of the hierarchic and complex pluralities in this set, all of which depend for their structures on differential incorporation *de facto* or *de jure*, make such prominent use of racial criteria for the hierarchic ordering of groups within them. In Guinea under the government of Sekou Touré, the Malinke have dominated the state since 1958, although they are not the largest ethnic unit within it. As Guinea's population is of one race, racial differences play no part in their *de facto* conditions of incorporation. Likewise, in the Ivory Coast, where the Baoule under Houphouet-Boigny have controlled the state since 1960, racial differences cannot be invoked to justify or explain Baoule domination. The same point holds for Sierra Leone where Temne, though not the largest ethnic group, have exercised dominion under President Siaka Stevens over the more numerous Mende and others. In Togo and the Central African Republic, where the governments and peoples are controlled by members of the small Kabre and Mbaka minorities respectively, differential incorporation prevails *de facto* without reference to race; and in other countries, such as Niger, Nigeria, Liberia and Benin, as of December 1982, although there were no single dominant groups, differential incorporation none the less prevailed, *de facto* if not *de jure*, as the basis for radical differences of political status and opportunities among the population. In short, as Liberia before Sergeant Doe's coup illustrates, differential incorporation is frequently instituted and maintained on grounds quite indifferent to race, and among populations of the same racial stock. On the other hand, where present, as in Chad, Senegal or Niger, race differences are often unaccompanied by any structures of differential incorporation that involve race. On this evidence it seems clear that the social significance of racial variables reflects their relationships to the prevailing modes of incorporation that provide the basic framework of societal structure. While freely available as a basis for the differential or segmental incorporation and articulation of collectivities, race, like culture, ethnicity and other variables, depends for its expression and social and political significance on the prevailing *de facto* and *de jure* modes of incorporation, and the place in the social order that those structures assign to it.

   This conclusion holds also with respect to the social expression and significance of ethnic variables in the public domain or national life of each of these countries. Thus far, since independence, none of these states has experienced internal violence as an expression of conflict between economically distinct and contraposed groups, however strenuously such interpretations are advocated by certain scholars, politicians and news commentators. The reasons for this are, as Sekou Touré long ago indicated, that, including Mauritania, Liberia and Ethiopia in their colonial and independent phases, these African societies all lacked the necessary conditions for class organisation defined as a hierarchy of social strata distinguished by relations to the means of production. Even where such formations have recently begun to develop in the urban sectors of such states as Senegal, Ghana, Ivory Coast, Nigeria and Gabon, their nature and articulations are confused and overlaid by a variety of cross-cutting structures such as ethnicity, cult, regional and national allegiances. Class differences and relations are further obscured by the role of corruption in the monetised sectors of these economies; by the basic differences of status between new and traditional elites and others, whatever their political background; and, finally, by the control of these elites over the productive processes and means as a function of their bureaucratic power in the army, the sole or dominant political party and the civil service. Coupled with the absence of an economic base adequate for the development of class organisations coextensive with their populations, these societal conditions operate to frustrate, restrain and diffuse those forces and tendencies that would perhaps in other conditions generate the kinds of class organisation that many Western scholars have come to expect in contemporary societies. However, while contemporary, these African states incorporate societies that are still sorely underdeveloped, economically and otherwise. It would indeed be extraordinary if these nations none the less exhibited the kinds of class formation that are found in developed industrial societies.

As mentioned above, of the twenty-seven states in this set, twenty-two have known internal violence of differing degree, extent and duration since independence or, in the case of Ethiopia and Liberia, during the past fifty years. Of these, six have had little violence, while ten have had considerably more, but without internal war, and six have been torn by internal wars of differing scale and duration. In several cases these incidents have attracted foreign interventions, sometimes directly, as recently in Chad by Libyan and French field forces, in Ethiopia by Cuba, Soviet Russia and Somalia, in the CAR by France, in the Gambia by Senegal and in Mozambique, though covertly, by South Africa.

As shown in Table 9.2, of eight states with ten or fewer ethnic units, three have had little and two considerable violence without internal war, while three have so far had none. Of six countries with eleven to twenty ethnic units, four have experienced internal violence without war, one little violence, and one none at all. Of nine countries with twenty-one to fifty ethnic divisions each, one has had no and two have had little violence since independence, while three have had internal wars and three have had violence without civil war. Of the four countries with more than fifty ethnic units each, three have suffered internal wars, while one has had internal violence without war. On these data, ethnic units have been involved as aggressors or victims in these episodes in twenty-two states; but as so many units were implicated in the Nigerian civil war, and as that country has such an exceedingly large number of ethnic divisions, it is useful to reckon the incidence of violent ethnic involvements in these countries without Nigeria, in which case the average is 2.8 rather than *c*. 6.9. Their incidence increases steadily from 1.6 for those with ten or fewer ethnic units to 5.3 for those with fifty to a hundred.

On this evidence it is abundantly clear that within these African states collective violence often has ethnic bases and orientations even when, as periodically in the Ivory Coast and Gabon, it takes the form of indiscriminate xenophobic attacks on immigrant workers of foreign nationality, having previously identified them in ethnic terms. Even so, our data also show that despite their polyethnicity, nearly one-fifth of these states have as yet had no internal violence, and six have had little, as many as have had internal wars. It seems clear, despite the correlated increases in the incidence and levels of internal violence as ethnic fragmentation increases in these states, that of itself ethnicity cannot 'explain' these patterns, since several states with identical levels of ethnic fragmentation differ in this respect, while others with differing levels of ethnic fragmentation have very similar records, both as regards the kind and frequency of their internal violence and as regards the number of ethnic units that violence involved. We are thus once more obliged to reject the idea that ethnicity or ethnic divisions, by their presence or number, may in some curious way explain or account for the historical experiences of these African states, and must look elsewhere for light on this question.

Modes of incorporation

It seems self-evident that if some ethnic units are engaged in internal violence as aggressors or targets while others are not, whether or not the other party is a unit of the same kind, by itself ethnic status cannot explain the differing experience of these ethnic units; and the same conclusion holds for race differences as 'explanations' of violence between racial stocks. These data on violence and collective involvement provide the clue to a better understanding of the dynamics involved, since violence like conflict, is a social relation between two or more parties; and collective violence characteristically incorporates the aggregates it articulates *de facto*, if they have not before been so aligned, whether as superior and subordinate, as formally equivalent though in practice otherwise, or as complementary in some symbiosis as allies or rivals. It is by virtue of such differences in their articulations with one another or with the rulers and their regime that ethnic collectivities become or do not become involved as aggressors or targets in episodes of collective violence that differ in scale, duration and intensity, as reported above. Therefore, since such collective articulations must pre-exist, by definition, the conflict situations in which they find violent expression, and since on our data the latter are so very widespread and frequent in these African states, both those recently created and the two older ones, it behoves us to see whether the modes of incorporation that furnish the basic frameworks for these societies and states may not themselves generate the forces and issues that promote internal violence, by selecting ethnic divisions on specific grounds as aggressors or as targets of the government or of one another.

Those xenophobic riots that periodically express the hostilities of citizens to immigrants among them – generally Africans, but recently in Abidjan during the economic recession, against French and other white expatriates – illustrate the ways in which the structure of incorporation that prevails identifies in advance the parties to the conflict by defining their respective statuses. For in all such cases, while the citizens as members of the polity hold rights and duties in it, the immigrants as non-members and excorporated persons depend for the rights and facilities they enjoy on the effective support of the host state and its representatives; but rarely has any African state moved to redress their wrongs, following xenophobic attacks upon them by its nationals, preferring instead to arrest these demonstrations by displays of force and to expel the immigrants as soon as possible.

Setting aside the Senegambian confederation which was established in 1982 without any changes in the internal organisation of either country, none of the twenty-seven states currently prescribes the incorporation of its citizens in primary units of equivalent or complementary status, as is now true of Senegal and the Gambia. From 1960 to 1966 that was *de facto* the situation in the first Nigerian federation, but under the constitution of 1978 Nigerians were incorporated universalistically on formally identical conditions in the new federal republic, while exercising political rights in the states they lived in. In December 1982, of these twenty-seven states, twenty-one proclaimed in their constitutions the universalistic incorporation of their citizens on identical grounds within the polity, as do most other contemporary states, under the influence of the American constitution. Of the remaining six, I do not know the precise conditions on which citizens were then incorporated in four – namely Liberia, Chad, Equatorial Guinea and Ethiopia – primarily because of the general obscurity in which recent events had shrouded their regimes. In Mali, while the constitution of 1974 proclaimed universalistic incorporation of all citizens, it excluded from political office all who had held senior offices during the presidency of Modibo Keita (1960–8), whom the present ruler, Moussa Traore, then a lieutenant, overthrew in a coup. The prevailing version of the Mali constitution therefore combines differential incorporation of Modibo Keita's office-holders with the universalistic incorporation of everyone else, at least formally. Substantive conditions, of course, differ widely. Apart from that anomaly, only in Mauritania was differential incorporation prescribed *de jure* by the constitution, which, as befits an Islamic republic, restricts citizenship to Muslims; but when that constitution was suspended in 1978 following a military coup, the preceding differential incorporation of Negro slaves (*harattin*) and Moors, who form the vast majority of the population, prevailed *de facto* and probably in law as well, despite several ineffectual attempts to abolish slavery by Mauritanian rulers over the past hundred years. Thus, of the twenty-three states for which our information is adequate, twenty-one profess to incorporate their citizens universalistically and on formally identical terms. However, professions and performance often differ, and this is especially true and significant as regards the *de jure* and *de facto* conditions on which citizens are incorporated in these African states.

Of the twenty-one states that proclaim the universalistic incorporation of their citizens as equal in law and government, and assure all of those rights and freedoms necessary for their free and full participation as individuals in the state, in December 1982 only four, namely Senegal, Nigeria, Gambia and the Cape Verde Islands, did in fact implement these provisions and maintain such regimes. So, despite its lack of a constitution at that date, did Ghana under the military rule of Flight-Lieutenant Jerry Rawlings and his colleagues. All other seventeen countries whose constitutions proclaimed their universalism in fact incorporated their citizens on very different grounds. Thus in Gabon, Niger, Benin, Togo, Sierra Leone, Ivory Coast and Upper Volta citizens were differentially incorporated, the primary differences of status in most of these states being those between the military or ruling party and their civilian dependents on the one hand, and all other citizens en masse. In Algeria, Cameroon and São Tomé, which also proclaimed universalistic incorporation, citizens were incorporated *de facto* both differentially and segmentally, as, for example, the Forros and Angolares of São Tomé, the Kabyles, Mozabites and other non-Arabised Berbers in Algeria, the Bamileke, Gbaya, Bamenda, Bamun, Fulani and other ethnic divisions of Cameroon. In the Central African Republic, which also proclaimed its universalistic commitment, citizens are in fact incorporated as members of one or other of the ethnic units that furnish the primary components of that society. For Guinea, Mozambique, Guinea-Bissau, Malawi and Lesotho, although the information suggests that differing combinations of differential and segmental incorporation prevail despite the universalistic proclamations of their constitutions, we lack decisive evidence on the actual status of the mass of their citizens. This is also true of Liberia under the government of Commander Doe.

Of the remaining states in this set, Mauritania incorporates its people differentially, as do Mali and Equatorial Guinea. Chad and Ethiopia each combine differential and segmental incorporation for differing sections of their populations. There is no evident association between the differing numbers of ethnic units in these societies and their *de jure* or *de facto* structures of incorporation, or between such numbers and any divergence between *de jure* and *de facto* structures. For example, of the eight countries having ten or fewer ethnic units, seven proclaimed the universalistic incorporation of their citizens, but only one, the Cape Verde Islands, fulfilled that promise. We lack appropriate data on the *de facto* status of the citizens of Guinea-Bissau and Lesotho; but the other countries, namely Algeria, Niger, Mauritania, São Tomé and Upper Volta, all maintain regimes of differential incorporation in fact, with or without supplementary segmental incorporation of some citizens.

Similar patterns appear when we examine the constitutionally proclaimed and actual conditions of incorporation in states with differing numbers of ethnic units. Of six countries having between eleven and twenty such components, five claimed to incorporate their citizens equally and freely on universalistic conditions; but of these only the Gambia in fact does so. For Malawi we lack decisive data, but for Togo, Benin and Equatorial Guinea the evidence indicates that *de facto* differential incorporation prevails.

Of the nine states in this set that have between twenty-one and fifty ethnic components, six have committed themselves constitutionally to the universalistic incorporation of their citizens, information is lacking on two, and the last, Mali, as noted above, combined universalistic and differential incorporation in its laws. Of the six countries that proclaim their universalistic commitments, only one, Senegal, in fact fulfils them. The *de facto* situation in two others, Guinea and Mozambique, is not clear enough to permit classification, as also in Liberia, which had no constitution in December 1982. Of other states in this group committed to universalistic incorporation, three, namely Sierra Leone, the Ivory Coast, and Gabon, incorporated their citizens differentially in fact. Of the three states that have fifty-one to a hundred ethnic units, though Cameroon and the CAR proclaimed the universalistic incorporation of their peoples, both display structures of segmental incorporation; and

Cameroon, like Ethiopia, combines that with *de facto* structures of differential incorporation. On the other hand, in December 1982, Nigeria fulfilled its constitutional commitments to the free and equal incorporation of all its citizens on formally identical terms. This is no longer the case following the military coup of December 1983 which swept away both the regime and its constitutional base.

In fact, of the twenty-one states for which our information is adequate, ten differentially incorporate their citizens *de facto* and another five do so with simultaneous segmental incorporation of at least some collectivities. Five, namely Ghana, Gambia, Senegal, Nigeria and the Cape Verde Islands, in December 1982 incorporated their citizens universalistically, and one, the Central African Republic, relied solely on segmental provisions for the *de facto* incorporation of its people. In effect, most of these states in practice incorporate their populations differentially, and sometimes combine this with their *de facto* segmental organisation. Such gaps between the constitutionally proclaimed conditions and rights of citizens and the realities of their condition and organisation clearly provide fertile grounds for collective concern and protests within these states, and simultaneously oblige their civilian rulers to maintain sufficient forces to assure their security and ability to control and suppress internal protests or outbreaks of violence.

Most of the violent incidents cited above involve action by the government against opposition, or protests against and challenges to the government, its regime, policies, personnel or actual conduct of affairs. This is equally true of attempted and successful coups aimed at replacing rulers, of internal wars and of most internal violence without war, whether limited or considerable. However, while coups normally involve the planned action of small groups of military personnel, civilian violence and protests against government, its programmes and the like either involve the co-ordinated action of political parties or industrial groups such as trade unions or the spontaneous action of unco-ordinated collectivities. Only in response to heavy government reaction do such initially unplanned communal movements acquire the organisation, leadership, techniques and resources necessary to extend the protests in time and space. For this reason among others, however unrepresentative they may be, given the support of their armed forces, African governments can generally contain, disperse or suppress those collective protests that do not have sufficiently large and extensive populations behind them. In differing situations the alternatives in such major confrontations either involve internal war between the government and its opponents, or replacement or control of the government by some other force, whether internal or external, as sometimes happens in the former French territories, Chad, Gabon and the CAR.

The striking difference noted above between the *de jure* and *de facto* modes by which the people are incorporated into these states simply reflects the difference between these states and their constitutions, and the societies on which they are based. Of eight states in the set with ten or fewer ethnic units each, two were hierarchic pluralities, one was purely segmental and five were complex pluralities that combined differential and segmental pluralism. Of six societies having from eleven to twenty ethnic units each, five were segmental pluralities and one complex, since it also incorporated its population differentially. Moreover, of these five segmental pluralities, three were manifestly anomalous, since one or more of the segments enjoyed superior status, power and opportunities. Of nine nations that have twenty-one to fifty ethnic units, five were complex pluralities and four segmental, three of the latter displaying similar anomalies in the unequal resources and articulations of the segments. Of the remaining four countries, one was segmental without anomaly, and the others were complex pluralities that combined segmental and differential incorporation.

Conclusion

Given the poly-ethnic composition of these African states (some of which – São Tomé, Guinea-Bissau, the Cape Verde Islands, Mauritania, Niger, Mali, Chad and Ethiopia – are also characterised by racial differences of considerable significance among their native peoples, and all of which exhibit ecological, economic and demographic differences between their ethnic and regional populations), however deep the universalistic commitment of their rulers to the freedom and equality of their citizens, those ideals are very difficult to establish and maintain as routine conditions of life in these societies. The fundamental difficulties derive from the plural structures of these national societies, which reflect their historical origins and composition.

Without exception these units include peoples of different language, culture, religion, social organisation, wealth, power and numbers, most of whom still live in their ancestral homelands, despite increasing migratory trends. In consequence, neither are all these collectivities truly equal in resources, needs, societal position, population, territory, wealth and power; nor, given membership in a common state, will they readily accept perceived inequalities of status and treatment, if they have the resources and leadership necessary to challenge them. For much the same reason, a people that feels, on economic, demographic, historical or other grounds, that it represents the core of the nation is likely to expect and demand differential treatment in recognition of its claims to superior status. In these African nations such ethnic, religious, linguistic, regional and racial interests operate within the army, the sole or dominant political party, the ruling elite, government bureaucracy, public and private firms, and other industrial groupings, as well as among the people in the towns and villages. If such differences of language, race and/or ethnicity, culture, religion, social institutions, homeland and collective interests coincide, as they commonly do, then, even within the new educated national elites, intense loyalties to one's natal group normally take precedence over all others except self-interest, and are so powerful and pervasive that almost everyone automatically gives priority to the claims and interests of his group over those of other units and the state. Thus, whether or not some African countries institutionalise conditions to fulfil their constitutional declarations of freedom and equality for all citizens before the law, given the tensions inherent in their plural compositions and in the actual conditions of collective life, unless some centrally co-ordinated unit has such preponderant power as to discourage challenge, they are unlikely to escape the disruptive effects of the contradiction between the structures of their societies and the conditions of universalism intrinsic to the state. It is this fundamental contradiction between the societal and political structures of these African countries that generates the social unrest and internal violence from which they suffer, and the political instability that commonly involves military coups, changes of constitution, government and regime.

The internal disorder and instability of these states reflects the basic contradiction between the plurality of their societies and the political requisite of equality before the law for all citizens, as the necessary condition of social order and stability. This contradiction derives from the fact that the national society incorporates its members in various plural divisions, segmentally or differentially, and sometimes together, by descent and socialisation, language, birthplace, culture and other means. Whether old or new, African states can neither deny, eliminate nor dissolve these societal divisions and structures of *de facto* incorporation by proclaiming universalism and the equality of their citizens; but neither can these states formally sanction the *de facto* inequalities and divisions among their peoples without thereby inviting their own disruption, whether through revolt, sucessionist movements, internal conquest, civil war, foreign interference, or by subordinating themselves to some foreign power willing to guarantee their political order. In effect, the *de facto* structures and units of societal incorporation that pre-existed and resisted the creation of these states still persist and disrupt their universalistic political orders by permeating the public domain, its organs and processes. In consequence, their proclamations of the freedom and equality of citizens are either suspended, ignored or violated so frequently as to lose credibility. The *de facto* segmental and/or differential incorporation of individuals in the basic societal divisions thus orders their articulation in the public domain as well as the private. The integrity, autonomy and stability of the government, the regime and the state are increasingly compromised until, intending to 'save the state and protect the people', some set of soldiers seizes power, or public protests initiate the familiar cycle of official repression and further protests, whose outcome depends substantially on the resources, organisation and leadership of the conflicting parties. It is ultimately the failure of these African states to maintain the separation of their public and private domains against these communal ties and interests that destroys their integrity and ruins their regimes.

These conclusions show that the solidarities and estrangements associated with differences of race and ethnicity depend for their form and content, their significance and intensity, on the prevailing structures of incorporation, *de facto* and *de jure*, through which individuals and collectivities hold their places as members of the national society and citizens of its state.

NOTES

1 The research summarised here is part of a much broader study of the social and political background of collective violence in contemporary states undertaken in association with Ms Rebecca French at Yale University.
2 To avoid unnecessary repetition I list the works I have found most relevant and helpful for this essay in the bibliography. By author, they were as follows:

Amnesty International 1983	Kurian 1982
Banks 1978	Legum 1981, 1982
Banks and Overstreet 1982	Paxton 1981
Davidson 1983	Taylor and Hudson 1976
Decalo 1976	Taylor and Jodice 1983
Europa Publications 1983	United Nations 1979, 1983
International Bank of	USA State Department 1983
Reconstruction and Development	
1981	

3 The discussion of 'Democratic Stability and Ethnic Parties' by van Amersfoort and van der Wusten (1981) deals with a different set of issues and conditions.

10

Ethnicity and the boundary process in context

SANDRA WALLMAN

Ethnic categories are organisational vessels that may be given varying amounts and forms of content in different sociocultural systems. They may be of great relevance to behaviour but they need not be; they may provide all social life, or they may be relevant only in limited sectors of activity.

(Barth 1969b: 14)

Introduction

Various kinds of context are relevant to an anthropological discussion of ethnic boundary processes: the analytic context of custom and practice in the discipline; the practical context of popular and official discourse on population difference; and the social context in which ethnicity is expressed. This paper refers to all of them but treats only the last at length. It identifies a logic which extends the explanatory value of the approach illustrated by the quotation at the top of this page and reports the dimensions of context affecting ethnic relations in two inner London areas.[1] The result is summarised in four linked propositions which suggest a general theory of boundary process and have important implications for practical policy.

For the purposes of this multi-disciplinary volume three background points may be useful. The first is that relative to other social scientists, anthropologists are seldom professionally concerned with vertical relations between ethnic groups and macro-state structures, and they rarely undertake studies of social stratification and minority status as such. The second is that, under a common rubric of interest in lateral relations at the micro-level, anthropological studies can be distinguished according to whether they concentrate on relations within an ethnic 'community', on relations between one ethnic group and another, or on the possibility of some kind of dynamic relation between inside and outside in a particular circumstance. The third is that differences of this sort do not indicate that the various studies are built on different theoretical premises. They demonstrate rather that a single analytic perspective may be adapted to different research settings and objectives. Some of these variations on the basic anthropological theme are spelt out in the following sections.

The view from anthropology

Some anthropologists doubt that ethnic relations can be separated out from the general range of social interactions. 'Us'/'them' distinctions, after all, are essential to social grouping of any sort. If there are definitively *ethnic* social relations, they must occur between members of different ethnic groups as such – i.e. there must be a specifically ethnic dimension to social life.

In one way or another of course, every analytic approach to the topic leans heavily on this assumption. They diverge because they build on it in different directions, and in the extent to which each takes the ethnic dimension for granted. Along this scale, the anthropological approach to be demonstrated here is among the more sceptical: because anthropologists pay attention to a 'whole' context and to the logic of connections between its constituent parts, we are bound to ask 'what else is happening?' and to consider what other dimensions count when seeking to understand so-called ethnic matters.

Two other items in the anthropologist's conceptual repertoire are as germane. One is the comparative perspective: it is to us axiomatic that not everyone classifies the same event in the same way; and that 'our' view of it is no less exotic/contingent/problematic than 'theirs'. The other is a model of the social system which identifies separate domains of activity or exchange or meaning within it, which recognises that different resources or kinds of resources pertain to each of them and which notices that each of those resources is regularly 'converted' into others, and may be transposed from one domain to another when conditions are right. With these perspectives the anthropologist can take serious note of ordinary contradictions and anomalies in what people say and do and want, and may occasionally even be able to account for them.

This characteristic combination is peculiarly appropriate to the study of ethnic relations when they are distinguished from the general social scene. Only a comparative and cross-cultural perspective will make sense of conflicts between two populations relating to the same environment in different ways (Barth 1969b), or of people who behave like Englishmen in public but have private lives based in other-than-English culture

(Saifullah Khan 1981). Only attention paid to a 'whole' context of other things happening will account for the fact that the same opportunity or encounter will not be experienced as the same event by all the parties involved (Wallman 1979). Add to that the notion of separate resource domains, and we can even understand how it is that some (migrant/minority group) workers manage to bring extra resources into the market place when they are neither economically better off nor technically better qualified than the rest (Barth 1963). And because this many-layered model exposes the possibility that gain in one domain may be experienced as loss in another (as Marris 1974), it explains why no public policy or private strategy can ever be entirely 'successful'.

For all these reasons, the total satisfaction of a set of people who have origins in common is no more likely than the equal satisfaction of competing interest groups. The assurance of a minority's right to follow its own practices may work to the disadvantage of its separate members (C. Cohen 1983); its separate members may disagree fiercely over the content of the ethnic culture (Talai 1983); and the affirmation of the culture may end up provoking exactly the discrimination and danger it was intended to avoid (Freedman 1955). There is nothing to be done about these realities. Certainly no analytic model will of itself increase the general sum of consensus and toleration. This approach only provides a logical limit to our expectations of either.

Ethnicity and race

The anthropological perspectives noted all have some bearing on social classification. In fact it is arguable that boundary definition is the central concern of anthropology – whether the limits of nation and culture, of structure and context, of resources and their value, of exchange systems and networks, or of a particular 'us' are in question. But other things happening in and around the discipline have affected the cogency of ethnic boundary issues. Despite the concern with social taxonomy that is implicit in the foundations of British social anthropology and probably defines the purview of the discipline (as Leach 1976), problematising the boundaries of social systems as such is rather new.

Throughout the early decades of anthropology the significant context of people's actions seemed always to be within a designated group, or between members of that group and designated 'others' defined by/necessary to institutionalised enmity or exchange relations (as, classically, Malinowski 1922; Evans-Pritchard 1940). But when anthropologists began to follow their subjects into towns they had to come to analytic terms with the fact that migrants must deal with new kinds of relationship (Mitchell 1966; Hannerz 1980), must learn to accept that urban contacts are more likely to be single-stranded than multiplex (Gluckman 1963), and must occasionally struggle with divisions of loyalty in industrial settings that could not have occurred in their traditional homes (as e.g. Kapferer 1969; Brooks and Singh 1979). Since some kind of 'us'-consciousness arises as soon as the actor encounters difference, and since in cities he encounters different kinds of difference, ethnic boundaries soon came to be recognised as a problematic feature of the migrant's experience of poly-ethnic urban life.

In the same historic period, the wider scientific community began openly to debate the validity of racial typology – both because it went against modern knowledge of genetics and because the assumption of evolutionary hierarchy on which it rested became politically more objectionable and scientifically less credible as time went on. But to say that race has lost its scientific credibility is not to say that the concept is no longer current. On the contrary: ordinary discourse reveals a gap between scientific and folk models that has implications for policy as well as for social analysis (Banton 1977). The word 'race' is still used when the speaker wishes to indicate objective and immutable differences between human groups or individuals, i.e. it continues to denote difference that *seems to be* immutable (Lowenthal 1972). In the same popular language, 'ethnicity' is apparently of a different order. Usage changes over time and varies from one country to another (see e.g. Bromley 1979; Wallman 1978a); but in Britain it signifies allegiance to the culture of origin and implies a degree of choice and a possibility for change which 'race' precludes. Epistemologically, however, the two terms are alike: in both cases it is the classifier's *perception* of choice or immutability which is decisive; the differences observed and the way they are interpreted say as much about the classifier as about the classified. Given a prior interest in meaning systems, all these anomalies are significant to anthropological analysis. Once it is clear that ethnic relations follow on the *social* construction of difference, phenotype falls into place as one element in the repertoire of ethnic boundary markers.

Boundary processes

The facts of migration and the faults of racial typology combined to sharpen the general interest in ethnic boundaries, but each discipline responded to the challenge in some characteristic way. Given the special perspectives of anthropology, its practitioners were drawn to one aspect of the problem over others. Whatever else concerns them, anthropologists studying ethnic relations take account of the effect of context on the marking and meaning of ethnic difference. And since it is impossible to understand contextual factors without noticing change, it is the variability of ethnic boundaries which catches the anthropologist's eye, and the logic of ethnic boundary processes which holds the profession's attention.

There are numerous process issues involved, and all of them have been dealt with by more writers than the few cited here. All the issues can be summarised under three headings: the nature of the boundary; the dynamics of the relation between its two sides; and the context or 'structural ecology' of the boundary process.

The debate begins with the premise stated in Fredrick Barth's 1969 essay: all kinds of items are sometimes used to mark ethnic difference, but they are not used consistently. The bases of boundedness can be visible or invisible, symbolic or real. Those most often converted into ethnicity are territoriality, history, language, economic considerations, and symbolic identifications of one kind or another (Y. Cohen 1969), but there is no logical limit to their number: the editors of a recent encyclopaedia of American ethnic groups listed fourteen (Thernstrom *et al.* 1980). But even having itemised the range, the problem of predicting whether the actors will 'use' them, or which they will choose at any one time remains.

Barth is prepared to predict whether but not which. Boundary variation for him comes in the content given to the ethnic category as a boundary 'vessel'. That content affects or reflects the firmness of the boundary and the significance of any of the diacritica which differentiate 'us' from 'them'. The more signs of difference available, the greater the boundary potential, but even where diacritica abound, there will be times when the 'vessel' is left empty. The metaphor implies that ethnicity is always there, sometimes cool in the belly (like Azande witchcraft perhaps), but even then primordial.

Other writers doubt that ethnicity has value in 'empty' or 'cool' versions. When people are not acting ethnic, not actually beating the boundary, how can we assume they are identifying ethnically? And if they are not themselves involved in the boundary process, who is the observer to say that ethnicity is there at all?

Worried by these questions, anthropologists have come to recognise that it is the identity element in ethnic boundaries which moves the boundary process. Differences between groups of people turn into ethnic boundaries only when heated into significance by the identity investments of either side (Wallman 1978b), irrespective of their purpose (as Paine 1974) or the actors' consciousness of it (Schwimmer 1979). Sometimes these investments can readily be shown to match the economic or political interest of the actor(s) quite explicitly (Abner Cohen 1974b). Alternatively the match may be inferred from the way in which information and other resources are distributed (A. P. Cohen 1978; Paine 1974b; Wallman *et al.* 1982). When no such correspondence can be demonstrated, identity has no visible purpose or expression; it is only affect. At one time this would have put it outside the proper limits of anthropology. Now there is a suggestion that affect is the discipline's new frontier (Epstein 1978) and efforts are made to map it explicitly (as Wallman 1984).

When the 'other' side of any boundary enters the picture, the boundary process is more than doubly complex. Not only do all the elements of shift and change pertaining to the first side pertain also to the second, but each side is affected by the dynamic of the relationship between them. In the topographical metaphor, a social boundary of any sort is a limit or demarcation between two sets of pressures, inward and outward (Y. Cohen 1969). An alteration of one shifts the boundary and impinges on its other side – like the change of air pressure in a balloon. Certainly in the case of an ethnic minority, alteration of the external (majority) system puts more or less 'pressure' on the internal system of the group itself (Saifullah Khan 1982).

Equally, the transparency and permeability of the boundary affect the whole system, although of course they do not always affect both sides equally. Opacity can go one way only; more often it is the majority's view of the minority which is obscured. The more opaque the boundary, the more chance an ethnic group has to manipulate others' perception of it (Okely 1979; 1983), or to stay invisible when it chooses (Talai 1983). Permeability certainly governs the kinds of items, influences or people that can cross from one side of the boundary to the other, and may possibly also affect its resilience. There is evidence that weak ties are stronger (Granovetter 1974), perhaps because they reach further, perhaps because the more tightly bounded a system, the less resilience it has against impact. Whether it is besieged by outsiders trying to get in or by insiders trying to get out, it is as though a boundary which will not bend can only break (Graburn 1971). But there is also evidence that ethnic groups and networks of any sort persist only to the extent that incomers can be excluded or at least controlled by rites of passage to membership. The contradiction implies the ethnic double bind: more integration makes for less pressure on the ethnic system, but for loss of integrity as well (Freedman 1955). Similarly, it would seem, for local systems – whether they are rural isolates (A. P. Cohen 1982) or inner city areas (below): tightly bounded local networks preserve the integrity of the local system and they also limit its ability to adapt to change.

Process and structure

While anthropology's interest in these first two aspects of boundary is peculiar to it, interest in the context/ecology/structure of ethnic relations is more general. For present purposes, the significant difference between theories of structure is not whether macro- or micro-issues are in focus, but whether other-than-anthropological models allow for the facts of process. Thus the psychologist's model of identity structure (Erikson 1968; Weinreich 1979b), the economist's of market forces (Sowell 1975) and the sociologist's of a cultural division of labour (Hechter 1978) are ready grist to the anthropologist's mill, and the analysis reported later in this paper gains from insights implicit in all three. It is built, however, around a strand of anthropological theory that deals explicitly with the relation between structure and process.

The strand begins with Raymond Firth's (1964) distinction between social structure and social organisation. Structure in this sense is the shape of the social system. It constrains the people who make up that system because it constitutes the framework of behavioural/institutional/ symbolic options available to them. Social organisation in the same model is a product of the choices people make from among those options – i.e. from among the possibilities that the structure allows. In sum, structure is the form and organisation the process. Barth (1966) carries the same reasoning a step further. He too conceives of social organi- sation in terms of choices made among options available, but he goes on to describe how the choices accumulate to generate new kinds of structure. A 'generative' model of structure can deal with change in a way that 'typological' models cannot; and it can deal with the process by which individual choices are converted into (new) group structures.

When he proceeds to explain *why* ethnic (or other) choices are made, however, Barth's argument is dismally circular: because individuals and groups act (by nature?) in their own best interests, they always choose to 'maximise value'. Whatever they choose is therefore what they value most.

This 'transactionalist' assumption is echoed in the rational choice theory expounded by Hechter in Chapter 12 of this volume (see also Banton 1983). The circularity of the reasoning is not the most interesting flaw in either case. The obvious negative instance (What of people who 'choose' bankruptcy or persecution by exaggerating ethnic difference or revealing ethnic stigma that could have remained invisible?) can be logically accommodated by reference to imperfect knowledge: a 'rational' choice or decision is the best the actor could do *given the information available and the consequences intended*, so rationality has nothing to do with outcome. Or behaviour that is 'irrational' by conventional economic or political measures is made 'rational' by reference to affective increments: any kind of opposition from 'them' identifies 'us' more sharply, and group identity is so vital that we may go so far as to set 'them' up in symbolic competition to ourselves if the realities of the boundary are too remote or too 'soft' to mark the necessary sense of difference (Schwimmer 1979).

Both *information* and *affect* rationales are achieved by switching the domain of discourse and focusing on a different element in the system – in the former case on what people *know* rather than on what they value, and in the latter on identity or existential benefit rather than on power or money gains. The real weakness of these models is not logical but explanatory. In real life the various elements are interdependent and real people must operate them as a single system. Thus, in general terms, an explanation of behaviour which rests on any element *out of context* underrates the ordinariness of contradictions of value and conflicts of priority which are a proper focus of the anthropological endeavour (see *inter alia* Gellner 1973; Paine 1974b). And, specifically, the pure forms of transactionalist and rational choice models ignore contextual shifts in the limits and objectives of choice.

These caveats stated, the perspective is vital to the extent that it draws attention to the combined realities of choice and constraint. Whatever you choose, your self-interest is limited by other people's interests and by environment, climate, opportunity structure and the like. If you 'choose' ethnic organisation or ethnic identity in circumstances which give it no scope, the choice will not advance any of your interests. The ultimate constraint must lie in the fact that no one can take up an option which is not there.

Practical limitations

Much has been written about the potential range of meaning attaching to ethnic resources and about the different uses made of ethnicity for individual or group benefit. Here it is enough to say that because the value of ethnic origin is dependent on context, ethnic boundaries are matters of process in every case.

The practical limitations of a process view are clarified when it is compared with models in which ethnicity is ascribed by a categorical marker of some sort – colour, religion, immigrant status, birthplace or the like. It is important both that any once-for-all typology of people is necessarily tidier than life and that it can take no account of whether, when and how far the actor identifies with those who share the same categorical status. It is also important that official purposes demand fixed classifications. Whether a government intends to make a demographic census, to legislate for 'multi-cultural' development or to correct economic disadvantage, it needs to be able to assign each person or group to one population category and to know that each category is distinct from every other. In the face of this bureaucratic need, anthropological models of boundary process tend to look untidy and rather vague. Even bureaucrats 'know' that social boundaries are fluid because they too have experienced the fact that the same difference can have a different meaning in another context, but in the official domain process models are not helpful. Consequently they have little general application and only limited relevance to public policy. Consequently too, anthropological perspectives have less impact on the realities of ethnic or race relations than some of the discipline's practitioners might have wished.

Short of giving up either the convictions of anthropology or its claim to relevance, the only course is for us to make explicit the perspectives of the discipline which are implicit among its members. As a first step, the limits of context, the procedure' of comparison and the connection between the separate domains of the social system have to be brought into the open. The second step is a critical test of the assumptions underlying the perspectives. Not all research problems or agendas lend themselves to a test procedure. The appropriate conditions are most closely approximated where there is both a commitment to practical policy issues and sufficient time and personnel for academic enquiry.

Take for example, the case in point. On observation of inner London it is plain that similarly low-income, multi-ethnic areas of the same inner city have different styles of livelihood. They operate within the same metropolitan system and are part of the same (dominant) national culture, but socially speaking they are known by the population to be different kinds of places, and economically speaking some are plainly more adaptable, more flexible than others – even in periods of rapid change or recession. At the same time, according to popular wisdom expressed in the news media and by the proverbial person on the Clapham omnibus, only particular areas of the city suffer racial tension or racial conflict as such. But when anthropologists are asked to explain this kind of variation, we say it is a matter of context: the significance of ethnic origin/recession/innovation varies with context. These are correct anthropological statements, but the policy-makers and the residents of blighted inner city areas have good reason not to be satisfied with them. What do we mean by 'context'? *How* does it affect ethnic relations? What *dimensions* of context account for the fact that two parts of the same inner city can be specifically different in terms of race relations, and are generally very different kinds of places to live?

Building on the distinction between *structure* as the framework of social or economic or conceptual options available and *organisation* as the pattern of choices made from among those options, it should be possible to understand the scope for and constraints on ethnicity as a principle of economic organisation and group identity in two similar but different London areas. The practical and theoretical question is: What differences of context account for marked contrasts in ethnic relations within the same inner city?

Context and comparison

The following sections summarise the content of a systematic comparison between Battersea, an area of South London, and Bow in the East End. Battersea is here the control case. It was the setting of a previous study designed to monitor the salience of ethnicity in the sphere of work. On the basis of historic, economic and ethnographic survey that study found that ethnicity counts for rather little in Battersea. On the whole it is not possible to predict on the basis of colour or ethnic origin how people will organise their lives, what kinds of networks they will build, or what access to local resources they will have (Wallman *et al.* 1980; 1982). Bow was selected for the comparison as an area similar to Battersea in superficial ways but different from it in two specific respects: it is popularly considered 'racist', and its industrial and demographic history is known to be very different from Battersea's. In short, the two areas have very different local styles.

The word 'local', like the notion of 'context' in anthropology as a whole, is very elastic. Here it is applied equally to the largest and smallest areas of each local system. The striking feature of the Battersea material is the extent to which the same style shows in the large new South London Borough of Wandsworth, in the old Metropolitan Borough of Battersea within Wandsworth and in the Louvaine Area Residents' Association area, known as LARA, in which we did the ethnographic survey (Figure 10.1). Just as there is a consistently a-ethnic style in the South London/Battersea case, so we hypothesised that the opposite East London/Bow case would be consistently ethnic throughout.

The ethnographic neighbourhoods in both cases are ethnically mixed (Figure 10.2), and both provide the opportunity for ethnic exclusion or ethnic nicheing. There are three things to be said about this. One is that it is clearly impossible to look at the significance of ethnic difference in a mono-ethnic area, and to compare a mixed with an unmixed area would have defeated the point of the comparison (Wallman 1983a). Despite the problems of selection, it was important that the second area be similar to the first in this respect. The second point is that the demographic profiles shown are based on birthplace – i.e. on a categorical statement about the population – which masks socially significant distinctions between birthplace, ethnic origin and ethnicity. None of these is the same as colour, but all tend to be inferred from colour in Britain. Anyone who is New Commonwealth born is assumed to be black, and anyone who is black is assumed not to be English (Wallman 1978b). But the black population born and raised in inner London is numerically quite significant and analytically crucial to a proper understanding of racism. Given a batch of people who have little or no experience of anything other than the local London scene and are likely to include Englishness among their identity options (Wallman 1983b), it is possible to discover how far residents are excluded from local resources on the basis of their colour *as such*. The third point to note is that, as Figure 10.2 recognises, even members of the white majority have birthplace, ethnic origin and ethnicity characteristics. At the bottom of each of the UK born columns, the categories SLEO and ELEO (South London Ethnic Origin and East London Ethnic Origin) are indicated. They refer to people who were born in the area of parents born in the area. These 'local ethnics' are decisive in each case because they tend to be the people setting the style to which newcomers must adapt.

The overall contrast is between a relatively closed and homogeneous system in the Bow version and a relatively open and heterogeneous system in the Battersea case. The points of contrast are itemised in Figure 10.3. It is important that the list is *not* a causal chain: all we can say is that the structural items vary together in each case.

The first and most objective point of contrast between the two areas is *industrial structure*. In Battersea this is made up of small industries. There are small factories, each with a relatively small work-force, small engineering firms, small garages, small laundries etc. The industrial structure of Bow on the other hand is dominated by the three big industries of industrial London: the docklands, the rag trade and the furniture trade. Although these industries are now very much reduced in economic importance, the local patterns set by them continue. Going along with these structures are differences in *industrial type*: in the Battersea area service industries are numerically dominant; in the Bow area manufacturing industries prevail (Hall 1964).

Different *employment opportunities* follow. If there are only three dominant industries, as in Bow, there is a relatively limited range of jobs available. If there are, on the contrary, lots of small employers/

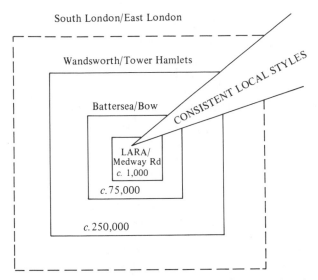

Figure 10.1 Levels of 'LOCAL' AREA – showing approximate population size at each level

workshops/factories, as in Battersea, then employment opportunities are more varied. There are also more of them: when a workshop or laundry service closes in Battersea, it is likely that some of the people thrown out of work will be able to find jobs in other similar firms that have not folded. This possibility of course refers to the availability of jobs; it says nothing about the quality of work or the conditions of employment the jobs may entail (see Jahoda 1982).

The contrast in *labour movement* shows in our ethnographic data and is confirmed by the statistical material collected by the labour market economists. Both kinds of data show a different day/night population balance. Battersea, the more open version, is something like a dormitory area in the sense that there are more people there at night than in the daytime. Local residents tend to move out to work and few outsiders commute to jobs in the area. Bow is part of Tower Hamlets, which now covers the old industrial heartland of London. Because it is a manufacturing centre, the population of the area is bigger in the daytime than it is at night. 'Area' here again applies to some degree throughout the local system shown in Figure 10.1.

Travel to work patterns show a similar contrast. Looking at the smaller areas where the figures are more persuasive, the same thing applies as in the larger labour market: people living in the East End/Bow/Medway Road area are significantly more likely to walk to work, significantly

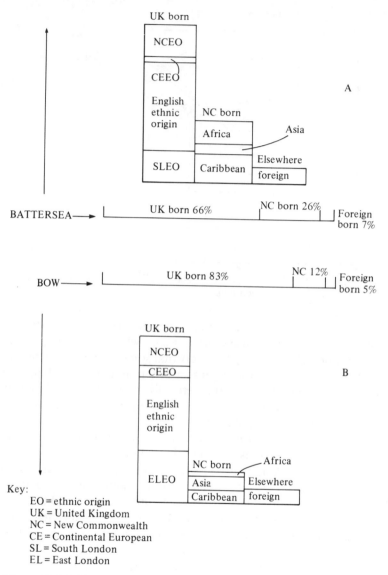

Figure 10.2 POPULATION of the two neighbourhoods – showing percentage born in UK, NC and foreign countries, and ethnic origin

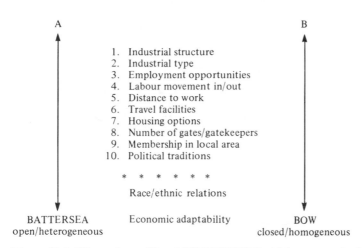

A   B

1. Industrial structure
2. Industrial type
3. Employment opportunities
4. Labour movement in/out
5. Distance to work
6. Travel facilities
7. Housing options
8. Number of gates/gatekeepers
9. Membership in local area
10. Political traditions

*   *   *   *   *   *

Race/ethnic relations

BATTERSEA   Economic adaptability   BOW
open/heterogeneous   closed/homogeneous

Figure 10.3 Dimensions of local STRUCTURE which contrast in the two areas – the contrast being consistently open/heterogeneous in Battersea and closed/homogeneous in Bow

more likely to work in the area in which they live. In South London/ Battersea/LARA, the pattern is quite the reverse: more than 65% of the male work-force travels out to work from Battersea, just as 65% in the Bow case remain where they live (Morrey 1976, cited in Wallman 1983a). *Travel facilities* match this. Making no assumption about whether bus routes or work patterns came first, travel facilities for getting in and out of the East End are notoriously bad. Battersea by contrast is the home of what is still the biggest railway junction in the world: if you live near to Clapham Junction you can get anywhere in or around London quite readily.

Housing options in the two areas sustain the heterogeneous/ homogeneous contrast. On the Battersea side, housing options are mixed. There are all kinds of buildings and all types of tenure. In the small LARA area there are people who own their own houses, people who rent privately and people who rent from the local government authority, and the housing stock is visibly varied. But Bow is a part of Tower Hamlets, in which 94% of housing is publicly owned, so residents do not have the same range of choice concerning how they will live, where they will live, whether to buy or sell, whether and when to move. And in the Medway Road area, where the Victorian terraces remain intact, the houses are structurally identical. At both borough and neighbourhood level, there is much less fluidity, much less flexibility, because the system is much more homogeneous.

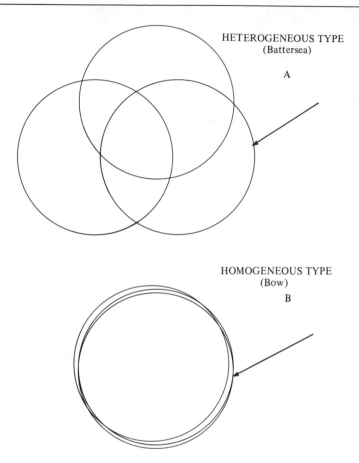

Figure 10.4 Local systems: BOUNDARY OVERLAP – showing implications for entry by arrow

On both counts, i.e. in the matter of jobs and in that of housing, the number of *gatekeepers* is quite sharply contrasted again. Where there are lots of industries and lots of housing options there is structural scope for lots of gatekeepers. Thus in the Battersea case there are many gates and many routes of access to local resources and it is difficult for one person or for one ethnic group to monopolise any of them. In the Bow case there are correspondingly fewer gates and the possibility of controlling them and making them exclusive to the use of one group or the other is enhanced.

Criteria for membership in each local area also differ in predictable ways. Membership in the Battersea area seems to be possible as long as

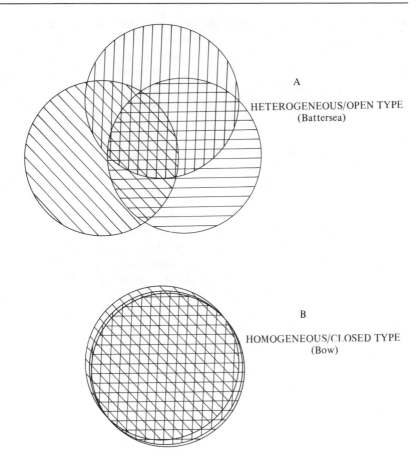

A

HETEROGENEOUS/OPEN TYPE
(Battersea)

B

HOMOGENEOUS/CLOSED TYPE
(Bow)

Figure 10.5 Local systems: NETWORK EFFECT – showing more or less density and reach of local connections

you behave like a local: an incomer can become a local person just by moving in, behaving appropriately and staying around. Membership in the Bow area, in line with East End tradition, is not so readily achieved. It is ascribed by birth, or perhaps by marriage, but generally it is much more difficult to become 'local' in the East End than in South London – much more difficult in Bow than in Battersea.

Finally the *political traditions* of the two areas are very different. Here the evidence for gatekeeping and membership patterns begins to focus itself more sharply. Battersea has a reputation which matches the open, heterogeneous ideal; its working-class ethos has always been internationalist and it has been relatively little interested in people's origins.

For a brief period at the turn of the century Battersea refused to fly the Union Jack over the Town Hall because it opposed national policy in South Africa. It could boast the first popularly elected black mayor in the English-speaking world in 1913. He was elected as a local man committed to local interests and concerned with local issues. The fact that he was also a Pan-Africanist and active on the international scene did not put Battersea residents off at all. It was a point of pride. That's the way we are in Battersea ... The same electorate sent an Indian Communist to Parliament in the 1920s, when either of those characteristics would have disqualified a man from being elected virtually anywhere else in the country. This a-ethnic style in Battersea's political traditions does not show Battersea people to be pro-ethnic or pro-black or pro-foreign, but it underlines the fact that the ethnic dimension plays little part in the public domain (see further Kosmin 1979; 1982).

Bow/East End political patterns are quite the reverse. The East End is the part of London where the famous British fascist, Sir Oswald Mosley, began an effective racist campaign, and it is also the part of London which stopped him. It is the part of London where some street conflicts are unambiguously race conflicts. Brick Lane, which was once entirely Jewish and is now almost entirely Bengali, is the one place where the National Front and the non-white population can be expected to clash. Like Battersea people, Bow people are predominantly working-class and are usually Labour supporters. But where Battersea's style is internationalist, East End politics are nationalist. It is English issues, British issues, the 'condition of Britain' debate that catch the political imagination.

Local boundary systems

It would seem overall that the more closed and homogeneous the local structure, the sharper the recognition of ethnic difference on the one hand, and the less flexibility and resilience of the local economy on the other. We are not talking about different absolute amounts of resources: it is not that one area has no shortages and the other many. We are talking about differences in the way resources are distributed, differences in the way resources are managed, differences in the way the system is bounded – i.e. about different styles of organisation throughout the two local systems.

When these two areas are visualised as different kinds of boundary system (Figure 10.4), the contrast between them begins to make ethnographic sense. Because the Battersea/South London structure is relatively open in terms of the dimensions of Figure 10.3, there is no neat overlap of the domains of people's lives or of the local resource systems.

In the idealised figure, let us suppose that one ring represents housing resources, another represents jobs and the third represents, say, leisure activities.

In the Battersea case (Figure 10.4: type A) the people you live with are not likely to be the same as the people you work with or the people you drink with. In practical terms, in order to get into this kind of system, a newcomer has only to breach one boundary. By achieving access to one resource domain (housing, for example), anyone can begin to behave like, and to be treated like, a local. The longer you are there, the more 'local' you become, whatever your colour or ethnic origin, and the more access you have to local resources of all sorts – including information about jobs which, in LARA, tends to be held locally (Wallman *et al.* 1982: 182–3).

By contrast, in the homogeneous East London type (Figure 10.4: type B) the boundaries of the various systems overlap much more tightly. The people you live with tend to be the same as the people you work with. You are likely to grow up with them, drink with them, marry their daughters, depend on them in everything. At the same time, the people that control information about jobs tend to be the same as the gate-keepers for housing, leisure opportunities, etc. If as a newcomer you want to be granted local status you actually have to breach all the boundaries together. Becoming a member of this type-B local system is extremely difficult, because it cannot be achieved just by entering into one domain.

Network effect

The network effect of these boundary patterns brings the contrast down to the ethnographic level (Figure 10.5). In the more open and hetero-geneous Battersea case (Figure 10.5: type A), there is a core of multiplex relationships in the middle which constitute the local community, the heart of the local system, but most people have connections of different sorts outside it. And because their ties spread more widely, the friends of their friends reach further, and they are more able to adapt, more able to pull in resources from other areas, less dependent on the local core. The Bow version on the contrary shows a more cosy and much more tightly bounded local community (Figure 10.5: type B). When all your resources are in one overlapping local system, the possibilities for adaptation are much more limited, and your social relationships tend to be multiplex, – i.e. the person you work with is also your neighbour etc. – local relations are not linked with domains or systems outside in the same way, and ethnic groups are more likely to remain distinct (cf. Gluckman 1963).

And because incomers can only take up the options that are there, members of minority ethnic groups who do move into the East End tend to live in ethnic enclaves. The tendency is confirmed by different sorts of data. First, when we asked people how they found out about the jobs they now have, how come they moved into this area, who did they go to for housing, many Medway Road residents reported using ethnic resources and LARA residents showed themselves more dependent on local contacts as such. Second, it is officially recognised in Tower Hamlets that members of ethnic minority groups like to or at least ask to live next to each other, and official resources are allocated accordingly. The residents of each (public) housing block, for example, will be almost entirely Irish, or Bengali, or of East London ethnic origin. Third, members of minority ethnic groups in the East End are said to feel safer when living close together. Some Asian groups have lately claimed that they must have vigilante or citizens' watch groups in order to protect themselves against racist attack. Neither the sense of ethnic collective danger nor the ethnic collective response are reported for South London areas.

Conclusion

The systematic comparison of structure and organisation illustrates the relation between option and choice and begins to explain styles of living in inner London. The theory which underpins this comparison then turns out to have as much predictive clout as any other – indeed it does better than some by taking extra layers of context, more 'other things happening' into account. The scope of its relevance to race and/or ethnic relations is both practical and theoretical.

On the practical side we may confidently predict that the same input of government or other outside resources will have different effects in the two kinds of area because these resources will be distributed in different ways, and because the local systems are not equally adaptable or receptive of change and will react differently. We may even go so far as to rank inner city areas in terms of the likelihood, under a common set of circumstances, of strictly racial or ethnic conflicts.

On the theoretical side the value of this approach is shown when the contrast between Battersea and Bow is translated into four general statements about boundary process. None of them is startling by itself: it is the cogency of the whole set which shows promise.

(i) The significance of ethnicity and so the expression of 'racist' sentiment varies from one inner city area to another because different local resource systems, different systems of organisation and identity give it different scope.

(ii) The character of a local resource system is governed in some part by the local industrial structure: as the heterogeneity of Battersea's industrial structure is echoed at all levels in the local social system, so homogeneity resonates throughout Bow.

(iii) The homogeneous/heterogeneous dimension also affects boundary principles and processes. In a heterogeneous area (like Battersea) localist principles are stronger: insider status can be achieved by residence and recognition. In the homogeneous case (like Bow) ethnic principles will tend to prevail: insider status will be ascribed by birth, perhaps by in-marriage, perhaps through offspring. Boundaries of the first (heterogeneous) type are by this token more permeable, more flexible than in the second (homogeneous) case.

(iv) As the resilience of any system varies with the flexibility of its boundaries, so areas of the first (Battersea) type are relatively more resilient in the face of economic change or population movement; they are economically more adaptable because a heterogeneous and open local structure offers more scope for generative and regenerative organisation. There is a correspondence between economic and identity resource systems in this respect. Diverse options in one domain imply flexibility also in the other.

NOTE

1 This research was funded by an SSRC (now ESRC) programme grant in two phases – the first based in the Research Unit on Ethnic Relations at the University of Bristol, the second in the London School of Economics.

11

Ethnicity and the sociobiology debate

PIERRE L. VAN DEN BERGHE

In convening the conference at which the original version of this paper was presented, John Rex mandated intellectual combat, and I was happy to comply. He wrote me: 'What I want to do on this occasion is to have a real confrontation between theoretical positions. I would therefore like you if possible to speak about your move towards sociobiology in the light of the criticisms which that move has encountered from your colleagues' (Rex, 1983b).

Let me, therefore, indulge in an analysis of fourteen recent reviews of *The Ethnic Phenomenon* (van den Berghe, 1981), a reasonable sample of the range of both ideological and theoretical criticisms levelled at my approach. The sample is biased in the direction of intellectual competence and honesty as it includes several distinguished contributors to the field of ethnic relations. So, I have no complaints. I knew my book was touching on practically every raw nerve in the social sciences, since I had the audacity not only to espouse the label of sociobiology but also to apply it to the most burning ideological issues of our times: race, ethnicity and, in another book, sex (van den Berghe, 1979).

I face two formidable barriers in communicating with most of my social science colleagues. The first is ideological and, therefore, impervious to rationality, but none the less fascinating to analyse. The second is substantive and, in principle, open to rational discourse, but nevertheless difficult to overcome because of methodological biases, discrepant 'domain assumptions', and misconceptions of modern evolutionary biology. Interestingly, the only reviews which demonstrate a total understanding of (though not necessarily agreement with) my approach (Maxwell, 1983; Lange and Westin, 1981) are also ones that do not raise ideological red herrings or imagine discontinuities between biological and cultural explanations. Maxwell, for instance, clearly sees the compatibility of the Marxist and the sociobiological strands of my arguments.

By contrast, Rex (1983a) is only willing to grant me 'a quite simple form of Marxism', and Banton (1982) thinks that the only similarity between sociobiology and Marxism is that both are unfalsifiable 'philosophies of history'.

Any attempt to summarise my position immediately opens a Pandora's box of pseudo-problems. The mere mention, for instance, of biology and evolution as basic to understanding human behaviour evokes in the minds of many social scientists a simplistic, mechanistic model of 'genetic determinism' and 'reductionism'. Social scientists who reject the relevance of biology to human behaviour, and who proclaim the irreducible uniqueness of human culture, assume that a sociobiological approach implies the polar opposite of their position. All these assumptions are false. Biology is not 'genetically determinist'. The evolutionary model is one of *interaction* between genotype and environment to produce phenotype. Evolution is not deterministic; in fact, it is so indeterministic that evolutionary theory has been denied theoretical status and has been characterised as an *ex post facto* description, or worse still, a tautology (Ruse, 1979).

To say that human behaviour has a genetic basis is not to deny its flexibility or to minimise the importance of learning and culture. To analyse human behaviour in a comparative, cross-species perspective is not to dismiss human uniqueness. It is merely a statement that not everything about us is unique, and that we share uniqueness with all other species. Diversity and uniqueness are as much features of the natural world as of the cultural world. If there is any distinctiveness at all to sociobiology, it is an insistence that human culture is an integral, though differentiated, part of the natural world and that its development can only be understood in adaptive co-evolution with reproducing, biological organisms. Sociobiology refuses to conceptualise nature and nurture, or heredity and environment, as binary oppositions. It insists on looking at culture *in* nature. Sociobiology *complements* the social sciences; it does not threaten them.

Any summary of *The Ethnic Phenomenon* will inevitably activate even more erroneous preconceptions than the full treatment, but I should like to quote the shortest, unfortunately anonymous, review of my book (*Choice*, 1981):

> Human beings are thought to behave in ways designed to maximize their individual fitness. Since members of one's kinship group share more of one's genes than do outsiders, nepotism is a means of ensuring individual fitness ... Favoring others of one's own race or ethnic group is seen as an extension of the sentiments of kinship.

In short, ethnicity is made up of the outer layers of an onion of nepotism, with ego at the core. Ego is predicted to behave as a selfish maximiser.[1] Thus, my model makes much the same assumptions as a number of established social science models such as utilitarianism, classical economic, Marxian class analysis of capitalist societies, behaviourism, exchange theory, game theory and, as represented here by Michael Banton and Michael Hechter, rational choice theory. Like these it is individually reductionist and materialist; and it states that the best predictive model of behaviour is one that assumes that people behave co-operatively with others to the extent that:

(1) they share interests, or

(2) they believe they do, or

(3) they are coerced into behaving in ways contrary to their interests (in which case they are forced to play the game of minimising loss rather than maximising gain).

I should add parenthetically that, while my model does not *assume* rationality, free will, or even consciousness, it certainly does not *preclude* any of these either. It simply states that behaviour is channelled into 'options' or 'choices' (whether consciously or not), and that the outcome of behaviour tends to be maximising for ego.

All these utilitarian models, whether rooted in evolutionary biology or not, have been resisted in social science on a variety of grounds, the principal ones being the following:

(1) They are *reductionist*, that is they treat social structure and culture as strictly derivative of interaction between individuals. They do not necessarily deny that social organisation possesses some emergent properties not easily deduced from individual behaviour. However, they insist that social structures are always in the last analysis people interacting. Furthermore, they favour a strategy of analysis which *starts* at the individual level, instead of postulating the existence of a culture and social structure as disembodied realities *sui generis*.

(2) They tend to be *materialist*, that is to treat ideational culture as superstructural. This is not to say that ideology, religion, values, norms and so on are unimportant but that they are *derivative* and, by and large, serve to promote, disguise or undermine material interests.

Those first two lines of attack lead to virtually irreconcilable differences, because they are based on radically different premises concerning both epistemological strategies and the nature of human social reality. There is no way an anti-reductionist, anti-materialist will ever concede more than trivial relevance to any of these approaches. Reductionism is the fundamental epistemological strategy, and materialism the fundamental 'domain assumption', of *all* the sciences. Within the scientific enterprise, there simply is no competing framework. A social *science* that rejects these is a misnomer: it becomes a cosmology.

(3) They are too *rationalist*. This is, I believe, a false issue, for despite the rationalist idiom of many of these theories, it has been repeatedly stated by classical economists and others that actors need not be rational; they only need to appear so. That is, the models work to the extent that behaviour produces maximising (or optimising) consequence, irrespective of whether these consequences were consciously sought.

(4) They are too *teleological*. This is perhaps the most common misunderstanding of evolutionary theory. Suffice it to say that in a partially self-conscious animal such as man, the teleology is in the eye of the beholder, not in the theory. However, there are clearly teleonomic elements in many aspects of human action. These are relevant to, but not *necessarily* present in, all human action.

(5) They are too *simplistic*. *As parsimony is a key criterion of scientific theory construction, to object to simplicity of formulation per se* is, in fact, to object to social science.

(6) They are too *deterministic*. This criticism typically confuses the research strategy of developing manageable models which make simplifying *ceteris paribus* type assumptions with attempts to arrive at rich contextual accounts of reality. The deterministic model is only a heuristic first approach to a highly indeterministic reality. Explanation and understanding are complementary, not mutually exclusive, approaches.

(7) They are too *indeterministic*. The opposite of the previous criticism is frequently made, not uncommonly by the same people, and it takes several forms:

(a) These 'theories' are not really logico-deductive theories of the 'if . . . then' type. They are merely *ex post facto* descriptions. To this, the answer is that, at some level of abstraction, any theory that has an empirical referent becomes a description.

(b) These 'theories' are tautologies. It is easy to demonstrate that they are not if predictable differences in dependent variables can be linked to manipulation of independent variables. The fashionable misrepresentation of evolutionary theory as explaining survival through adaptation and adaptation through survival is a typical example of this type of criticism. Neither adaptation nor survival is the *explanandum* of evolutionary theory. Evolutionary theory explains *change* and specifically the *directionality* of change in the *absence* of teleology. Differential reproduction is merely the mechanism whereby random change (mutations) becomes directional.

(c) These 'theories' are unfalsifiable, because contradictory evidence can always be accommodated, defined away, or reconciled through modification. Insistence on a test of instantaneous falsifiability is based on a naïve perception of the development of scientific theory. Theories seldom if ever arise full-blown; nor are they suddenly invalidated. They grow and evolve, wax and wane in gradual response to an accumulating mass of evidence (Kuhn, 1962). If the theory is any good, discrepant evidence typically leads to refinement or to a narrowing of the scope of the theory rather than to its rejection. Rejection, when it occurs, is typically a gradual process of supplantation under the weight of evidence by a 'better' theory, that is one of greater scope, or parsimony, or both. And the discredited theories of yesteryear frequently reappear later as special cases and in more sophisticated garb.

Strictly speaking, of course, theories do not 'do' anything. Theories are nothing but the by-product of interacting individuals who adapt to their environment through better understanding. A main reason why social scientists do such a rotten job of theory construction is probably that they apply their biologically evolved brain to problems which the brain has not evolved to understand. The human brain has evolved to track environmental change *around* itself, not to understand *itself* (Lumsden and Wilson, 1981). In fact, it has developed a vast adaptive potential for self-delusion.

Getting back to *The Ethnic Phenomenon*, my framework of analysis is specifically biological on only two major points:

(1) It makes individual inclusive fitness (as measured by reproductive success) the ultimate currency of maximisation.

(2) It identifies nepotism based on proportion of shared genes as the basic mechanism of ethnic solidarity, and it advances commonality of genetic interest as a type of interest distinct from others, such as class interests.

Let me now turn specifically to my critics. First, let me dispose of the ideological remarks, not because they are amenable to rational discourse, but because they are both amusing and revealing of the state of social science. I have never adopted a positivistic stance of separating the domains of science and ideology, and I have repeatedly stated that the field of race and ethnic relations is a weathercock forever shifting in the ideological cross-winds. So I am more amused than surprised at the reception I got. Even my most enthusiastic supporters attribute to me mephistophelean or bestial qualities. The anonymous reviewer quoted earlier says: 'The base argument is devilishly simple' (*Choice*, 1981). Political scientist Crawford Young warns my colleague Paul Brass to 'resist the temptation to follow van den Berghe into his sociobiological lair' (private communication). Michael Ruse, a Canadian philosopher of science, concludes a glowing review of my *Human Family Systems* with the words: 'Opinionated, biased, unfair, dirty-minded, funny, brilliant, important – van den Berghe's work is all of these. Read it' (Ruse, 1981).

My good friend and critic, Heribert Adam, privately expressed the view that a good book was marred by a gratuitous resort to sociobiology, and he seems to be in numerous company in that assessment. Thus, Hirschman in a recent review article stated: 'van den Berghe's (1981) most recent theoretical work begins with a sociobiological framework *but* then turns to an exceedingly insightful review of comparative ethnic relations' (1983; italics are mine). Lopez (1983) observes that *The Ethnic Phenomenon* can be read as a conflict-oriented, materialist approach without any reference to sociobiology (as I myself suggest in my last chapter), fears that many potential readers will be turned away by my biological approach, and rejoices that, in his view, I fail in my attempt to bridge biology and the social sciences. The first paragraph of his favourable review is worth quoting in full, because it is, I think, a fair representation of the prevailing ideological climate in the social sciences:

> This book can be approached in two ways: as the sociobiology of ethnicity, or as a contribution to our understanding of ethnicity in spite of the author's biosocial orientation. I fear that many will simply not approach it at all. The ideological associations of sociobiology are so antithetical to the beliefs of liberal and progressive social scientists that many have simply chosen to ignore work identified as sociology. [*sic*]. This is a pity and, as the author points out, hardly a scientific attitude. Pierre van den Berghe is one of our most insightful and consistently interesting students of race and ethnicity. He is also among the most persuasive exponents of sociobiology, in part because he disassociates himself from those ideological associations. As such, he is the ideal person to forge a link between these two fields. In my judgement this book fails to accomplish that task, and it is precisely in that failure that the book makes its greatest contribution.

The American sociologist William Newman writes: 'This is a sophisticated treatment of a highly controversial set of ideas. In the hands of the uninitiated this could become a very dangerous book' (1982). Newman reminds me of Bishop Wilberforce's wife on hearing of Darwin's theory of evolution. She hoped that Darwin was wrong, and she prayed that, if he was right, his views would not become generally known. Newman's alarm is shared by another notable North American student of ethnicity,

Leo Driedger (1984). In a generally positive review he states that *The Ethnic Phenomenon* 'will also be controversial, in that the biosocial theme can be dangerous if it is carried too far in promoting master race themes as some are prone to do.' In his long, perceptive, searching review, John Rex (1983a) sees me as having undergone a profound metamorphosis from my earlier liberal days, and feels obliged to defend me against the charge of racism to which he feels I open myself. He appears to come to the conclusion that I am an honest cynic posing difficult and embarrassing questions.

In his *Times Literary Supplement* review, Michael Banton (1982) does not take me to task on ideological grounds, but in his recent book, *Racial and Ethnic Competition* (1983), he squarely puts me in the 'Selectionist' school, his label for Social Darwinism. Faced with conflicting evidence, he charges me (page 49) with 'equivocating' on biological determinism, and proceeds to ignore everything else I have written, even where my contributions would have been most relevant (as in his treatment of the pluralism school or in his South African chapter). By implication, he seems to think that I have undergone such a total metamorphosis as to have obliterated my old self.

Joe Feagin (1981), an American sociologist, makes a more openly ideological attack on my position on 'affirmative action'. He is, of course, correct that, on this point, I took an explicitly ideological stance, and he knows exactly what my stance is because we shared a debate platform in a plenary session of the American Sociological Association meeting in New York in 1980. Yet, he misrepresents it as 'neo-conservative'. In fact, I attacked affirmative action (and indeed all policies that invoke race as a criterion) long before the neo-conservative wave, and for reasons which only partially overlapped with those of the neo-conservatives (Glazer, 1975; Sowell, 1984). My principal reasons for opposing race-based policies is that, whatever their purported intent, such policies heighten racial consciousness, divide minority groups against each other, exacerbate class divisions within minority groups, and are a fundamentally reactionary ploy to prevent the emergence of class-based solidarity. Affirmative action co-opted a small black middle class and left most members of minority groups worse off, relative to whites, than they were ten or fifteen years ago.

I suppose that before we turn to substantive issues, a personal statement on ideology is in order here. As a rough approximation, I was a communist at the age of twelve, a liberal at twenty-one, a social democrat at thirty-five, and have been an anarchist since my forties. I never could warm up, incidentally, to the intellectual mush of the 'New Left'. That evolution was accompanied by those creeping symptoms of age and experience which are often mistaken for conservatism, namely pessimism about the future and a cynical view of ideology as a smokescreen for interests. Applying my materialist analysis to the entire political spectrum, I developed a generalised distaste for politics, tempered only by an attraction for unpopular, hopeless, and quixotic positions. I therefore refrained from activism, except on issues where I felt I had some expertise, or which directly affected my professional integrity. On issues such as racial discrimination in universities, or racial representation in professional associations, I fought with equal vigour in South Africa and in the United States, being labelled a communist in the former and a racist in the latter.

We academics are the court jesters of advanced capitalist societies. It is our *raison d'être* to be irreverent, iconoclastic, challenging, infuriating. Our role is not to play politics, but to question our society and make people uneasy. We should be grateful that we are not taken seriously, for, if we were, we would be thrown in jail or in mental asylums, as many of our colleagues are in 'people's democracies'. We have, I think, only one social responsibility: to be intellectually honest and not to shift our ground to suit the fashion or the expediency of the moment. We must have the courage to be unpopular, not only with the high and the mighty but also, if necessary, with the downtrodden, whose apparent virtue is, alas, but a manifestation of their impotence.

Now, to the substance of the criticisms. There is a common theme to many of the reviews, namely: Do we really *need* sociobiology to explain human behaviour in general, or ethnicity in particular? Or, put differently: What does sociobiology explain *better* than a competing explanation such as rational choice or utility theory? Underlying the question in the minds of all those who pose it, especially Banton, Rex, Feagin, Newman and M. G. Smith (1983), is the belief and the hope that sociobiology is irrelevant and quite possibly deleterious to an understanding of human behaviour. They all subscribe to a dichotomous view of nature and nurture: animals behave, humans act, and never shall the twain meet. All these critics, implicitly or explicitly, suggest that I myself demonstrated the limitations of sociobiology by 'equivocating' on the importance of culture, by devoting most of the space to the demonstration of ecological variation, by presenting a voluntaristic, manipulative view of ethnicity, by allegedly failing to relate the last two-thirds of my book to the first third, or by trying to have it both ways on the issue of whether common descent is real or fictive. Rex and Smith, in particular, seem to conclude that it is a great pity I brought sociobiology into an otherwise interesting and stimulating book. As to Banton, he astonishingly fails to see the striking congruence and convergence of my book with his *Racial and*

Ethnic Competition, based on a loose framework of rational choice theory.

In *The Ethnic Phenomenon*, I did not waste space developing the case for sociobiology in general or indeed for kin selection in particular. There are already at least a dozen books that give lucid, non-technical introductions to the subject, and I did not want to cover the same ground (see especially Barash, 1982; Dawkins, 1976, 1982; Ruse, 1979). Nor did I want to rehash my previous book *Human Family Systems*, which presents the case for the application of the sociobiological model to the analysis of human systems of kinship and marriage. Since I argue throughout *The Ethnic Phenomenon* that ethnicity is an extension of kinship, the later book is conceptually grounded in the earlier one. Here, I cannot even begin to give a précis of the range of current ideas on gene-culture co-evolution (Alexander, 1979; Lumsden and Wilson, 1981), or even to summarise both of my books. Yet, I am frustrated by my conviction that many of our apparent differences could be easily resolved through a better understanding of evolutionary theory. I say that on the basis of intimate familiarity with, and profound respect for, the work of several of my critics reviewed here, and of my personal assessment that their work is eminently compatible, indeed, convergent, with mine.

Let me try to clarify at least a few of the issues. At the outset, let me gladly concede that alternative analytical frameworks, notably 'rational choice theory' or some other variety of utilitarianism, also give one considerable mileage in the analysis of human sociality. Like my colleague, Michael Hechter, I see no discontinuity between 'micro-' and 'macro-sociology', and I subscribe to a reductionist methodology of *starting* at the micro-level. As many of my prior writings demonstrate, my thinking has both benefited from and often meshed with that of Rex, Smith and Banton, and Newman's 1973 book, *American Pluralism*, is peppered with references to my previous work, so we too seem to have been on parallel tracks. I suppose it is incumbent on me to show that I have not been derailed from my earlier concerns.

Why do I irritate my colleagues with my insistence on a genetic basis for human behaviour? Because that conclusion is *inescapable* to anyone who surveys with an open mind the available evidence from linguistics, human palaeontology, developmental psychology, endocrinology, biochemistry, brain physiology, human genetics, clinical psychology, psychiatry, population ecology, primate ethology, ethnography, and half a dozen other sub-disciplines which all converge on an interactive model of gene-culture co-evolution. There is unfortunately no way to convey the excitement generated by the emergent synthesis to those unfamiliar with these many hitherto disparate sources of evidence.

How is sociobiology superior to the suggested alternatives? On at least two grounds I think. First, sociobiology is a theory of much broader *scope* than the proposed alternatives. It subsumes our species under an account of the evolution of all life-forms on this planet. Second, sociobiology reintroduces the lost *historicity* of so much of social science, and especially negates the absurd dichotomy between history and science. Evolutionary theory is both scientific and historical. Why social scientists should still man the last anti-Darwinian barricade, that erected to protect the human mind, is baffling. Perhaps the human mind is programmed to resist demystification. The more general theory is commonly accepted as the better one. Why the resistance here?

Why do I insist on reproductive success as the ultimate currency of evolutionary success? There is a tough preconception to overcome here, because fitness maximisation seems so counter-intuitive to social scientists living in advanced industrial societies. Perhaps, if we all spent a few years in the more prolific tropics, we would become more aware of how unusual our reproductive behaviour is. Theoretically, the question is easy to answer: because differential reproduction is the principal mechanism of natural selection. Since human culture is necessarily 'carried' by biological organisms who reproduce, it is absurd to try to dissociate human behaviour and culture from reproduction. It is true, of course, that culture itself is non-genetically transmitted, but it cannot be transmitted except through flesh-and-blood individuals who, if they fail to reproduce, generally stop passing on their culture. Even inanimate places of cultural storage, like libraries, must have live humans in order to continue as cultural artefacts.

This is the minimum and, many would say, trivial, reason why culture cannot be divorced from reproduction. The more interesting and, as yet, still largely unexplored reason for linking culture to reproduction is that culture itself evolved genetically. That the mental capability for culture is the product of biological evolution is widely accepted. That culture is genetically channelled, however flexibly, remains a controversial proposition, but such evidence as we have makes alternative views extremely improbable. The issue is no longer *whether* culture has a genetic basis, but how we can begin to map the incredibly complex linkages and pin-point the mechanisms.

Why do I regard nepotism as the genetic basis of ethnicity? The case for nepotism as an important mechanism of animal sociality is now solidly established up and down the phylogenetic scale, from colonial invertebrates, to social insects, to birds and mammals, to primates, to humans (Barash, 1982; Wilson, 1975). The case for humans is presented in my *Human Family Systems* (1979), along with a rapidly growing bibliography now running into hundreds of titles (see Alexander, 1979; Chagnon and Irons, 1979). In *The Ethnic Phenomenon* I merely *extended* the argument from kin groups to ethnic groups. The evidence for this extension is that, practically everywhere, ethnicity is based on descent. M. G. Smith was quick to point out that the idiom of descent in humans is frequently fictional or putative (as I too recognise), and that, for my argument to hold, the descent must be genetic. I quite agree. His criticism that I want to have it both ways is based on a misunderstanding. Few, if any, cultures have a *perfect* correspondence between cultural and biological kinship, but in all cultures there is a *close* correlation between the two. The same is true of ethnicity over time. It is impossible to constitute an ethnie on a basis other than a *credible* concept of common descent, and the concept is only credible if it corresponds at least partly to reality. It is a credible myth, for example, that the Japanese emperor or the Swazi king is the father of his people, but it was a transparent fiction that Queen Victoria was the imperial mother of her Indian subjects. In the former case, the myth legitimates ethnicity; not so in the latter.

The overlap between the cultural idiom and the biological reality of kinship and descent is an empirical question, but ethnicity can only come into being when the overlap is considerable. It takes several generations of intermarriage for hitherto separate and unrelated groups to fuse into a new ethnie. Everyone knows that Nigeria, for example, is not yet a nation; the United States, on the other hand, is clearly in the process of becoming one; Japan and Korea have long been nations. Ethnicity is not a static concept. In addition, the dynamics of ethnogenesis are not disembodied cultural events; they are cultural events *linked* (like the rest of culture) to a genetic process through the flesh-and-blood humans who undergo them. Ethnicity always involves the cultural *and* genetic boundaries of a *breeding population*, that is, a population bounded by the rule or practice of *endogamy*.

This brings me to the important issues raised by Rex at the end of his review, namely the relationship between ethnie, class and estate (in the Weberian sense of *Stand*). Ethnie and class, I have argued, are fundamentally distinct bases of sociality, the former rooted in commonality of genetic interest, the latter in commonality of material interest. An estate is an intermediate or transitional group: a class is the process of becoming an ethnie. Again, the overlap between class and ethnicity is an empirical question. A caste is yet one step closer to being an ethnie; in fact, it may be looked at as a rigidly bounded ethnie with a narrow niche specialisation in an occupational or ecological niche.

Why, having annoyingly insisted on the genetic roots of nepotism, do I then proceed for two-thirds of the book to deal with ecological and cultural variables that look much like conventional social science and seem, to some of my critics, to bear no relationship to the genetic arguments early in the book? The illusion that cultural and ecological explanations are unrelated to genetic explanations can only be sustained if one adheres to the obsolete notion that genes and environment are discrete realities. The biological view of the world is not the polar opposite of cultural determinism. It is an interaction model in which genes, biotic and physical environments and, in the human case, culture *always* interact to produce behaviour.

Let me illustrate from two reviews how the insistence on the separation of genetics from environment and culture creates a trained incapacity to understand evolutionary theory, and especially its application to humans. Jenkins (1983) represents the most glaring example. He writes that I am 'confusing two distinct types of explanation, unconscious evolutionary selection and conscious purpose', and he also states that I 'combine a biological argument focusing on the unintended consequences of behaviour for the gene pool of the species and a cultural argument depending on the sentiments and goal-maximising behaviour of individuals'. Banton (1982) makes a basically similar assessment: 'So on to his sociobiology van den Berghe adds an individual choice model which is intended to explain the way people consciously manipulate ethnic boundaries ... This does not sound reductionist, yet on the next page we are told that in the last analysis competition over resources is ultimately converted into reproductive success.'

First, my position is not that resources are *always* converted into reproduction. I recognise that, as modern technology created surplus production, we have increasingly diverted resources from reproduction to the satisfaction of hedonism, sometimes to the actual detriment of reproduction (as with smoking, alcoholism, gluttony and other maladies of affluence). The argument is simply that over the long evolutionary haul, we have converted garnered resources into survival and reproduction, and that the cultural arrangements which enhanced the reproductive success of their 'carriers' have, by and large, been 'selected for'. Thus, cultural change cannot be divorced from biological reproduction, and cultural and genetic evolution are intertwined in multiple causal loops.

Jenkins makes two gross errors, Banton only one. Jenkins dissociates group selection from individual selection, and consciousness from unconsciousness.[2] He accuses me of juxtaposing and 'confusing' two models: a biological model of unconscious group selection, and a cultural model of conscious individual choice. In fact, I advance a single model of *individual* selection which can be both unconscious and conscious depending on species, time and place, and which, in the human case, is *both* biological and cultural. The consensual thinking of sociobiologists is in fact almost the precise opposite of the position Jenkins falsely attributes to me. Most human sociobiologists share a predominantly *individual* selectionist view of genetic evolution (and, notwithstanding Banton's suggestion that kin selection is group selection, this is a fundamental misreading), but are prepared to concede that, if group selection is to be found anywhere, it is likely to operate in the cultural superstructure.[3]

Banton is also confused on the great biological debate of levels of selection, but at least he is not as blatantly wrong on this issue as Jenkins. Both Jenkins and Banton, however, seem to share an opposition to a biologically reductionist view of consciousness, implicitly adhering to the obsolete view that self-awareness, conscious choice and free will are human monopolies. By now, even social scientists should know better. Consciousness is not an all or none phenomenon. Like everything else it gradually evolved in the vertebrate brain, becoming increasingly salient in the birds and mammals, even more so in the more intelligent orders of mammals such as canids, felids, cetaceans and primates, and ever increasingly so in the line of hominid evolution. How is it possible to conceive of consciousness as anything apart from a genetically evolved kit of adaptive tools?

All this is not to deny that culture has some emergent properties and therefore *partial autonomy* at the level of proximate mechanisms from genetic evolution. But culture grew out of the natural, material world and necessarily remains in it. The challenge for the social sciences is to specify and uncover the multiple and complex mechanisms of gene-culture co-evolution, mediated through the human brain. This is obviously no easy task, as the human mind is probably the ultimate scientific black box: it evolved to adapt by tracking change in its environment, not to understand itself.

The reason why, in *The Ethnic Phenomenon*, I devote more space to analysing environmental and cultural variability is that it takes longer to describe change and variability than to deal with the commonalities of human experience. I can also readily understand that most of my colleagues find the variability more interesting, and I share that bias. But I insist that the variability only becomes meaningful when anchored in the commonality of human biology.

The boundaries of what is human, in turn, can only be understood if we compare ourselves to other species. How else can we discover what is human except by reference to what is not? How else can we understand the evolution of human specificity except by comparison with other evolutionary trajectories? What more logical step to take for someone like myself whose concern for cross-cultural comparison marked all his work, than to open the forbidden door of cross-species comparison?

Rex remarks: 'For a sociologist who had [note the past tense] taken the notion of culture and structure ... seriously an explanation in terms of genetically determined behaviour would, on the face of it, seem to have little value.' It is precisely because I took (and continue to take) culture and social structure seriously that it became impossible to keep explaining culture purely in terms of culture. Ultimately, this type of explanation is reducible to that of the proverbial native who, on being asked why he behaves as he does, answers: 'Because it is our custom.' The social sciences have been giving that kind of 'explanation' for a century. I like to try to push the search for final causes a step further back. And that step necessarily takes us from *Homo sapiens*, to *Homo erectus*, to *Homo habilis*, to *Australopithecus afarensis*, etc ... to the origin of life. It is the supreme folly of human hubris to postulate a gaping discontinuity between ourselves and the rest of the universe. *The Ethnic Phenomenon* is merely an invitation to rejoin the organic world.

Indeed, my undertaking is not as distant from that of some colleagues as it may appear to be at first sight. Three of the authors in this volume – Hechter, Banton and myself – have converged on much the same reductionist and utilitarian model of ethnic relations. All three of us have, with remarkable parallelism and simultaneity, moved increasingly toward a model that sees macro-level structures as derivative of individual-level choices by maximising actors (Banton, 1983; Hechter, 1983; van den Berghe, 1981). In the case of Hechter and myself this might be discounted in view of the fact that we have been colleagues for some thirteen years, but the convergence with Banton is even more striking, all the more so for being unacknowledged by Banton.[4]

The only major argument I have with rational choice theory is the gratuity of the rationality assumption. The model of individual choice tending to maximise or optimise ego's benefit/cost ratios works equally well with or without rationality. As economists have long known and stated, actors do not have to be consciously rational for classical economics to 'work': they only have to behave as if they were. This proposition seems like a cute intellectual game until one sees that this very same model is being successfully applied by evolutionary ecologists to countless species whose benighted brains presumably do not even possess glimmerings of consciousness and rationality, e.g. social insects. Seen in cross-species perspective, economics is a human application of 'optimum foraging strategy'.

This is not to say, of course, that the measure of consciousness and rationality with which our millions of years of cerebral evolution have endowed us is unimportant for humans. Choice can and frequently is conscious and rational for humans, and this ability enables us to adapt much more rapidly to environmental changes than would be possible without consciousness. However, consciousness is not a *necessary* basis of human action, and nothing is gained by postulating its universality. The utilitarian choice model works with or without consciousness. Behaviour can be maximising without being rational. Choice can be unconscious.

The very presence of non-rational elements in human behaviour, and most especially in ethnic sentiments, is left unexplained by the Hechter–Banton brand of rational choice theory. Both set out to 'explain' ethnicity, yet both are reduced, through their rationality assumption, either to treat ethnicity as a black box or to regard it as merely one basis of interest group formation among many. They may reluctantly concede that ethnicity is 'different', but they fail to explain *why*.

The one major attempt in social science to make room for the non-rational in human action has, of course, been psychoanalysis, and it is little wonder that the field of ethnicity, fraught as it is by seeming irrationality, has turned so assiduously to psychoanalysis for answers. Indeed, it was the psychoanalytic rampage of the 1940s and 1950s in the field of race and ethnic relations which turned so many scholars, myself included, resolutely against it. Psychoanalysis has always struck me as the extremely implausible and totally unprovable figment of Freud's imaginative but unhinged mind, the preaching of a charismatic guru. The proof of its unscientific nature is that, in its century of existence, it has become a non-cumulative scholastic tradition led by a priesthood in medical garb.

To be sure, psychoanalysis was grounded in biology, but much as astrology is based on astronomy. In the field of ethnic and race relations we also had to live down the pseudo-biology of Social Darwinism (perhaps the most mischievous misnomer in the intellectual history of the social sciences). For over a century, we made a virtue of throwing out the biological baby with the Freudian and Spencerian bathwater.

It is high time that we re-ask the fundamental questions. What is ethnicity? A form of sociality, of course, but a very special form. So, *what* is so special about it? The answer lies ultimately in our mammalian tradition. Why do mothers feed their babies instead of feeding *on* them, as a strict rational choice model might lead us to predict? Because unfed babies die, and babies are the only way that mothers have of replicating themselves. To put it less teleologically, genes that predispose mammalian mothers to lavish tender, loving care on their infants do better than genes that predispose their carriers to devour their offspring when hungry. Ruthless selfishness will not be evolutionarily successful in competition with nepotistic selfishness.

Starting from the most irreducible forms of mammalian sociality, the mother–infant tie, many (but not all) species develop much more complex forms of co-operative behaviour between larger numbers of individuals. What the record does not show is any abrupt discontinuity or saltation, either between or within species. At most, one sees quickenings in the pace of evolutionary change, as, in the human case, with the development of the hominid brain, agriculture, the state and industrial technology. Even then, new developments incorporate rather than overturn previous conditions of the system.

From that perspective, ethnicity is clearly an extension of kinship, the addition of outer skins to the onion of nepotism. This is very clear in many pre-industrial societies where the web of nepotism is seamless, rippling out from ego to the confines of his ethie. Many contemporary African societies, despite their size and complexity, still project a clear image of ethnicity as a *nested* concept which shades into the clan, the lineage, the extended family, the nuclear family, and ego. In geographically mobile, industrial societies, the continuity of kinship and ethnicity is less marked, as well as sporadically disrupted by migration, intermarriage, and the interplay of many other forces and interest groups. The simple model of sociality based on nepotism becomes complicated by reciprocity and coercion. But, at the core, you still have maximising individuals.

My model easily accommodates everything that Banton or Hechter try to incorporate into their 'rational choice' model, and more. Theirs is a special case of mine. Mine has two additional merits besides scope:

(1) It sidesteps the thorny issues of rationality, not to dismiss it, but merely to see it as one adaptive mechanism among many, one of particular significance in our species, but *not* a prerequisite of choice.

(2) It both explains and gives evolutionary anchorage to ethnicity as a *special* form of sociality, categorically distinct from class, prior to class, but certainly not *a priori* any more or less important than class in industrial societies.

Why the vision of the unity of nature and the continuity of evolution should be so threatening to so many social scientists never ceases to puzzle me. Perhaps looking at mothers suckling infants does not tell one everything one wants to know about ethnicity, but it is a remarkably powerful starting point.

NOTES

1 The editor invited me to expand on this brief and perhaps cryptic summary statement of *The Ethnic Phenomenon*. To do so adequately would take ten or twelve pages and unduly burden this paper with a précis of behavioural ecology as it has developed over the last twenty years or so in the works of Richard Alexander, Richard Dawkins, W. D. Hamilton, John Maynard Smith, R. L. Trivers, G. C. Williams, K. O. Wilson and many others. Among the best treatments of the theoretical issue in book-length but non-technical form are Barash (1982), Dawkins (1976, 1982) and Ruse (1979). The literature on *human* sociobiology is increasing exponentially. The following books give a fair sample of recent thinking: Alexander (1979); Chagnon and Irons (1979); Lumsden and Wilson (1981, 1983); Shepherd (1983); Symons (1979). Numerous articles can be found in journals such as *Ethnology and Sociobiology*, *The Behavioral and Brain Sciences*, *American Anthropologist*, *American Ethnologist*, and *Current Anthroplogy*.

As for my own thinking on ethnicity, the basic argument is that ethnicity is an extension of kinship, and, thus, that biological principles of maximisation of inclusive fitness through nepotism, reciprocity and coercion are applicable both to human systems of kinship and marriage and to systems of ethnic relations. The case for kinship was developed in my 1979 book, *Human Family Systems*, and has also been supported by much empirical research in anthropology (e.g. in the 1979 Chagnon and Irons collection already cited). The application of the argument to ethnicity was first formulated in my 1978 *Ethnic and Racial Studies* article which thus constitutes both a prelude to and a précis of *The Ethnic Phenomenon*. The reader interested in exploring those ideas further, but loath to read the book, is thus referred to the shorter article treatment, which, incidentally, gave rise to a debate between Reynolds (1980a, 1980b) and myself (1980) in the pages of the same journal.

The view of ethnicity as extended kinship is also developed by some 'mainstream' social scientists who do not claim allegiance to a biological evolutionary perspective (Francis, 1976; Keyes, 1976). Most recently, the biological version of the theme was picked up (curiously without acknowledgement to *The Ethnic Phenomenon*) by Joseph Lopreato (1984).

2 In a vigorous verbal exchange in Oxford, Jenkins disclaimed any misunderstanding of evolutionary theory, and stated that his remarks applied only to me, not to sociobiology in general. When he uses such phrases as 'consequences of behaviour for the gene pool of the species', however, I conclude that he attributes group selectionism to sociobiologists in general, since I defy him to find any such phrase or even suggestion in my own writings.

3 In fact, there is a growing tendency in modern evolutionary theory to reduce the level of selection even further from the individual organism to the gene. This view has been most lucidly popularised by Dawkins (1976, 1982) but is widely shared by leading theorists such as W. D. Hamilton, John Maynard Smith and E. L. Charnov.

4 Amusingly, both Hechter and Banton expressed considerable discomfort at my suggestion of convergence of 'rational choice' and evolutionary theory, as they well might, since I regard the former as a special case of the latter. Banton also felt that my remark about the convergence being unacknowledged on his part was uncalled for, and that, perhaps, *I* should have

acknowledged *his* contribution to a seminar on Ethnicity and Nationalism held at the University of Washington in October 1976. I certainly did not mean to suggest a deliberate slight on his part. Rather, I regarded his lack of acknowledgement as symptomatic of the general reluctance of social scientists to link their thinking with evolutionary theory, even when there seems to be a *prima facie* case for it.

12

Rational choice theory and the study of race and ethnic relations

MICHAEL HECHTER

Rational choice theory is the closest thing to a paradigm in current social science. Found in disciplines as disparate as economics and anthropology, this doctrine assumes the theoretical primacy of individual actors rather than of pre-existent social groups. These actors are conceived to have particular goals that cannot all be equally realised, for people live in a world of scarcity and uncertainty and, as a result, must select between alternative courses of action. The hallmark of this approach is the view that their selection of a course of action is rational and will be the most effective means of realising their preferred goal (Heath 1976 offers a good introduction).

Although rational choice has a very long pedigree in social science – its parentage derives from Thomas Hobbes's writings in the seventeenth century – only recently has the approach been applied to the study of ethnic and race relations (some examples include Rabushka and Shepsle 1972; Sowell 1975; Landa 1981; Hechter, Friedman and Appelbaum 1982; and Banton 1983). Rather than generating new evidence or testing specific hypotheses, applications such as these tend to synthesise evidence about intergroup relations and interpret it in the light of a particular explanatory scheme. Even a sympathetic observer would have to concede that it is far too early to predict the success of this kind of enterprise.

Why has such an untested and frankly reductionist point of view piqued so much interest? The answer has much to do with the current state of research in the field of race and ethnic relations. Like its elder sibling macro-sociology, this field resembles a congeries of distinct substantive areas in which the centre does not hold.

There are disputes aplenty, but even after decades of diligent labour the new disputes seem little different from the old ones. Scholars often have no compelling intellectual rationale for selecting their research problems, and other criteria – the availability of grants and the political considerations of the day chief among them – become popular justifications. There is a growing sense that many of these difficulties stem from a lack of theoretical consensus.

For two reasons I am persuaded that rational choice offers the best hope of arriving at a higher degree of theoretical consensus in the field.

In the first place, there is nothing about ethnic and race relations *per se* that warrants the development of a special theory. Indeed, the subject concerns phenomena – like group formation, solidarity, assimilation and collective action – that also occur among many other kinds of groups, be they based on class, religion, or territory. Ethnic and race relations therefore constitute instances of more general kinds of inter-group processes. And it is a good thing that this is so, for if we had to erect an entirely new theoretical edifice to guide our research, the prospects for intellectual development in this field would be dismal.[1]

In the second place, given this premise, it is worthwhile to determine how much we can learn about ethnic and race relations by systematically applying some general theory to a broad range of empirical problems. But which theory should be applied? My own candidate is rational choice. This is not because rational choice is the be-all and end-all of social theory, but merely because it seems to be the best of the theories that social science has been able to place at our disposal. Some reasons for this judgement are offered below.

Nevertheless, as it stands, rational choice theory appears to leave some fundamental questions begging. I shall conclude by arguing that the relationship between rational choice and the field of ethnic and race relations should have a good deal to learn from the theory of rational choice, rational choice theory itself might well be strengthened by attending to some of the insights to be found in the ethnic and race relations literature. Therefore, this paper may be read either as yet another encomium on behalf of better inter-group relations, or as yet another repetition of the famous Smithian proposition that there are gains to be made from trade.

1

To some, the claim that scholars of racial and ethnic relations ought to take rational choice theory seriously is controversial. Sociologists, in particular, have long waged a strident campaign against rational choice in all of its emanations. Since the inception of the discipline, sociologists have tried to explain the basic mechanisms of social order and social change. Few contemporary sociologists see it as their task to speak to these problems *tout court*. Yet another they seek to explain why certain people act to attain collective ends and respect the law, while others engage in crime and act opportunistically, they implicitly raise the question of social order. Similarly, whenever sociologists discuss the transition from feudalism to capitalism, the causes of ethnic stratification, or the reasons why institutions like the family take different forms in different places and historical eras, they implicitly raise the question of social change.

Traditionally, sociologists have believed that groups – and not individuals – are responsible for both social order and social change. This belief is founded on the premise that the behaviour of any group is not reducible to the actions of its individual members. Instead, groups are 'emergent' phenomena that deserve to be studied in their own right. To understand social order and change, they aver, it is necessary to renounce 'methodological individualism', and to replace this unsavoury doctrine with a distinctively sociological alternative. Normativism and structuralism have been the two leading candidates thus far.

Normative theorists hold that the maintenance of social order depends on the existence of a set of overarching rules of the game, rules that are to some degree internalised, or considered to be legitimate, by most actors. Among other things, these rules – or institutional arrangements – serve to set appropriate goals for each member of society, and to specify the appropriate means by which these ends are to be pursued. Without such rules, social order would be precluded, for everyone would be compelled to participate in an unceasing war of all against all. Yet it is not the content of these rules that is important: this can vary widely from one society to another and from one historical era to another.

When I entered graduate school in the mid 1960s normativism was still the dominant perspective in the field. Soon after, however, its popularity began to falter in the face of withering criticism.[2] My own reservations were both conceptual and empirical. Since the effect of norms is to promote consociation at the expense of anti-social behaviour, the problem of order rather neatly disappears in this formation. As for social change, normativists tend to explain this by positing breakdowns in an already extant normative order. But the 'solutions' thereby provided are only satisfactory if they shed light on the origins of norms, and on the processes by which they are transformed. When it comes to these critical issues of social causation, normativists have conspicuously little to offer.

Normative explanations also have serious empirical failings. It is impossible to measure the salience of a norm to an individual apart from observing that person's behaviour (*pace* legions of survey researchers). Yet normativists are among the first to admit that individual behaviour is *not* solely determined by internalised controls: sanctions, habits and individual preferences are all recognised as having their due. However, disentangling the effects of norms from those of sanctions, habits and preferences is a herculean task that normativists have too frequently chosen to ignore.

Partly for reasons of this kind, along with many others of my generation I began to explore the utility of structural explanations in sociology. In these, individuals are seen as subject to particular sets of social relations (such as a historically specific stratification system) or environmental conditions (such as fluctuations in the business cycle). Both social relations and environmental conditions have the effect of narrowing the individual's choice set. In extreme versions of this argument, these elements narrow the individual's choice set all the way to one. In less extreme versions, they limit the scope for choice to such an extent that the individual is left with merely trivial decisions to make. When all the members of a given group are in the same boat, their individual differences cannot significantly affect their behaviour.

Social order is really no more problematic for structuralists than for normativists: it is imposed by the set of structural and environmental constraints currently in force. Naturally, when these constraints change, so do the resulting behaviours.

Some historical and contemporary situations are undoubtedly amenable to analyses couched in these terms. Because patterns of social relations and environmental conditions – the causal factors in such arguments – can often be objectively measured, structural explanations also tend to be falsifiable. This affords them a great advantage over normative explanations. Indeed, my own first book *Internal Colonialism* (1975), which attempted to explain the causes of nationalism in modern British history, was heavily influenced by structuralist reasoning.

Subsequently, however, I have become increasingly aware of the limitations of the approach. Structural explanations are not appropriate for every kind of analytical problem. At best they reveal why specific groups come to share common circumstances and interests. But they are less helpful in explaining just how these groups will *react* to their circumstances.

Individuals typically have some choice-making discretion in all groups and societies. To the extent that they have such discretion, their behaviour will confound expectations derived from theories that only countenance aggregate-level causal factors. By ignoring the individual level entirely, structuralists are left with two serious problems.

On the one hand, the causal factors in their explanations are contextual, like those of the normativists, and must always be treated as exogenous in their models. Hence, structuralists have no way to explain changing environmental conditions or the rise and fall of social structures from their own theoretical premises. This leads to a demand for historical studies, which – though informative – ultimately produce new data to be explained rather than any satisfactory explanations themselves. It is difficult to imagine how history can ever serve as the Rosetta Stone for a truly theoretical social science.

On the other hand, the claim that structurally imposed commonalities are sufficient to account for group behaviour is rather easily challenged. If collective action is facilitated when the individual members of a group share common interests, then why does it occur so rarely? How can we explain why some people in the same structural position are free riders (Olson 1965), whereas other similarly situated actors are not? Marxists, for instance, have long faced the uncomfortable fact that the proletariat does not always (or even very often) change from a *Klasse an sich* to a *Klasse für sich*. Although structuralists profess no need to countenance individual behaviour, on reflection it is hard to see how the issue can be avoided.

This is the chief merit of the rational choice approach. Rational choice considers individual behaviour to be a function of the interaction of structural constraints and the sovereign preferences of individuals. The structure first determines, to a greater or lesser extent, the constraints under which individuals act. Within these constraints, individuals face various feasible courses of action. The course of action ultimately chosen is selected rationally: in Parsons's (1937: 19) words, 'individuals adapt means to their ends in such a way as to approach the most efficient manner of achieving them'. When individual preferences are assumed to be known, transitive and temporally stable, behaviour can be predicted in the face of any combination of structural constraints.

How can these assumptions be justified in macro-sociological research, especially when rational choice theorists also assume that each individual may have a set of preferences that is unique?

Whereas a certain (but unknown) proportion of every individual's preferences are idiosyncratic, the rest (such as preferences for wealth, honour and power) are commonly held by many others. These common preferences impel everyone in the group to act similarly. Some of the idiosyncratic preferences may result in singular action, but so long as the common preferences are known (a significant caveat, and one to which I will return below), then the idiosyncratic ones will cancel one another out and their average will be zero.

This may be true enough, but how can these common preferences ever be known? They can't be assumed *a priori*, for there is no practical limit upon them: as the adage has it, *chacun à son goût*. But it can be expected that everyone will prefer more wealth, power and honour to less, because attaining these goods often makes it easier for individuals to attain other (perhaps more idiosyncratic) goals. Although it would be foolish to predict the behaviour of any given individual, the law of large numbers allows predictions for the aggregate to be rather precise (Hechter and Friedman 1984).

According to such reasoning, individuals will only fulfil their corporate obligations when they receive a net benefit by doing so. As a result, both collective action and social order depend on the belief of most people that free riding and crime do not pay.[3] The rational actor will commit crime to attain his or her goals, unless deterred by the fear of incarceration (or some other punishment). Similarly, in large groups, where informal social controls lose their efficacy because individual networks rarely overlap, collective action is problematic because free riding is hard to detect.

Now unlike the other theories – both of which are curiously static – this one is eminently capable of explaining *changes* in behaviour. The mechanism it proposes in this respect is refreshingly simple. Changing relative prices leads to corresponding changes in behaviour: the more costly it is for people to choose a traditional course of action to achieve a given benefit, the more likely it is that they will consider an innovative alternative to reach the same end. Further, the causes of these price changes are endogenous to the explanation, since they are at least partly the result of a myriad of independent individual decisions which together comprise aggregate demand. Aggregate demand, in turn, pushes supply.

In contrast to both normative and structural theories, then, rational choice offers the prospect of arriving at predictive statements, rather than at the *post hoc* descriptions for which sociologists have had to settle too frequently in the past. This is a cherished goal for those who are committed to the development of a more scientific discipline. Three examples should suffice to illustrate something of the range of applications of rational choice theory in the field of ethnic and race relations.

Sowell (1975: 165–7) uses rational choice principles to explain patterns of racial discrimination in the job market. Consider a society having a low-status racial group whose members command a relatively low price in the labour market. Distancing typically occurs as a result of this kind of racial hierarchy: thus, members of the high-status group prefer to limit their social interaction with low-status individuals. If it is assumed that employers are profit-maximisers, and if they cannot effectively collude against the members of a particular group, then racial discrimination in hiring should be greater in non-profit-making organisations and regulated industries than in unregulated and profit-making enterprises.

Why should this be so? Even if all employers prefer to exclude low-status workers from their firms, whenever their pay is lower than their productivity there is an economic incentive to hire them. However, if employers are prevented from maximising profits by government regulatory agencies, or are legally non-profit-making, then they have no opportunity to earn more profit by hiring relatively inexpensive (and racially low-status) labour. Regulated industries are usually controlled by political bodies, so their hiring policies are less subject to economic constraints and more subject to political ones. This fact suggests an additional implication: should public objections to racial discrimination arise, the racial hiring policies of regulated industries will undergo a more rapid turn-around than those of unregulated industries.

Landa (1981) seeks to explain why ethnically homogeneous middlemen are so much more common in Third World societies than in developed ones. Her argument begins with the problematic nature of exchange in rational choice theory. If two parties to a contract are both wealth-maximisers, what keeps either of them from abrogating the contract whenever this becomes profitable? In societies where contract law is both well-developed and easily enforced, the judicial system is often sufficient to deter traders from breach of contract. But this remedy is unavailable in countries with poorly developed or non-existent judicial systems. In such settings, ethnically homogeneous networks provide traders with the best alternative means of insuring against breach of contract.

Rational traders will choose to participate in the least costly type of trading network. They are likely to choose ethnically homogeneous trading networks because these economise on co-ordination and enforcement costs. On the one hand, traditional codes of conduct (think of the Confucian or Talmudic codes) can have many of the same effects as systems of contract law. On the other hand, confining trade to members of one's own ethnic group permits one to take advantage of an informationally efficient screening device. This allows the merchant to predict the contractual behaviour of a potential trading partner with a high degree of accuracy. For these reasons, then, the prevalence of ethnically specialised middlemen should be greatest (*ceteris paribus*) in societies having the least developed judicial systems.

Finally, Hechter, Friedman and Appelbaum (1982) seek to predict the conditions under which ethnic collective action will arise. In their view, the likelihood of collective action does not rest on factors – like the degree of inter-ethnic inequality, or changing levels of relative deprivation – that affect members' desires for structural change in the society at large. Instead, the members of any ethnic group will engage in collective action only when they estimate that by doing so they will receive a net individual benefit.

In this regard, ethnic organisations are critical for two basic reasons. First, they are the major source of the private rewards and punishments that motivate the individual's decision to participate in collective action. Second, because the individual's benefit/cost calculation depends in part upon his estimate of the probability of success of any collective action, organisations can play a key role by controlling the information available to their members. When members have few alternative sources of information, organisations can easily convince them that the success of a contemplated collective action is a real possibility, perhaps even a foregone conclusion. On this basis, the likelihood of ethnic collective action varies positively with organisational resources, monitoring capacity, solidarity, control over information, history of equitable distribution of collective benefits, and adoption of non-violent tactics, while it varies negatively with organisational size, and the capacity of antagonists – including the state – to punish prospective participants.

Structural factors alone cannot account for such phenomena. In each instance adequate explanation requires the establishment of a link between the structural constraints on the one hand and the preferences that motivate individual behaviour on the other. Rational choice theory offers the best current hope of wedding micro- and macro-levels of analysis into a logically consistent whole that is also empirically falsifiable (Hechter 1983 and forthcoming).

2

However, it also raises two basic questions which, as yet, have no convincing answers. To be fully satisfactory, a theory that accounts for behaviour as the result of an interaction between individual preferences and structural constraints must be able to explain the determinants of both these parameters.

The question about preferences arises in the context of social order problems (including the problem of collective action). Whereas normative and structural theorists are overly optimistic about the realisation of social order, rational choice theorists instead tend to be overly pessimistic.

In their view, a rational person will only comply with group norms – and thereby contribute to the maintenance of social order – when there is a positive or negative sanction, or selective incentive, for so doing. This is as true for the economist's analysis of the provision of public goods as it is for the game theorist's analysis of co-operation in the Prisoner's Dilemma (see Hardin 1982 for a recent review). Since it is costly to provide such sanctions, the key prediction of rational choice theory is that the realisation of social order is highly problematic.

Sociologists traditionally part company with rational choice theorists in their assessment of the sufficiency of sanctions or selective incentives as causes of social order. Rational choice theorists argue that sanctions are necessary *and* sufficient for the attainment of social order in large groups. On the other hand, many sociologists feel that there is more social order than can be explained on the basis of sanctions alone.

This question, I submit, is one of the core issues separating sociological from rational choice analysis. Whereas rational choice theorists attend only to external constraints on individual action, in addition to these sociologists return again and again to admittedly fuzzy notions like 'charisma', 'legitimacy', and 'internalised norms' in their explanations of human behaviour. This is because they are often more aware of the monitoring costs that are necessary to control deviants or free riders than are rational choice theorists.

Careful rational choice analysis reveals that selective incentives represent only one of three types of monitoring cost that must be incurred if deviance or free riding is to be curtailed in large groups (Hechter 1984). Selective incentives are necessary but insufficient causes of an individual's decision to comply with the obligations imposed in any social order. In addition, there are two other costly requirements that many rational choice theorists tend to ignore.

On the one hand, groups must be able to detect whether or not an individual actually does comply. Call the attendant costs the costs of monitoring. On the other, groups must ensure that each member receives the particular sanction or selective incentive which is appropriate to his or her past behaviour: that is, rewards for compliance, and punishment for non-compliance. This activity entails the costs of properly allocating the sanctions.

Now when monitoring and allocation costs are added to the costs of providing the sanctions themselves, it is evident that free riding and deviance are likely to be even *more* pervasive in large groups than many rational choice theorists appreciate. Hence there is probably more ethnic collective action than can be explained solely by the provision of selective incentives. Likewise, there is probably far more obedience to the law than can be explained solely by police deterrence.

Can this problem be resolved within current rational choice theory? At this point the best that can be said is maybe. Several familiar means of economising on control costs in large groups seem to be consistent with rational choice principles. I shall mention only three of them here. First, groups can adopt specific institutional arrangements – such as profit-sharing, group rewards or communal distribution rules more generally – that give members incentives to monitor each other. Second, they can provide public sanctions that make a spectacle of apprehended deviants, thereby convincing many others to walk the straight and narrow path. Third, sanctions need not be imposed every time someone deviates; decades of research in experimental psychology have shown that intermittent sanctioning is even more effective than the constant variety.

However, there may be another kind of solution as well. Perhaps under certain conditions individuals can be induced to maximise some collective rather than individual utility schedule. Were this the case, then people would want to act in the interests of their ethnic or racial group and would not even be tempted to take a free ride. What might account for the development of such a preference?

3

Many people feel that rational choice has an Achilles' heel, and that this is the problem of preference-formation. 'Preference' is the generic term used in rational choice analysis to designate internal states. Together with environmental constraints that impose costs, preferences help determine individual action. Yet since they cannot be measured, their independent role is accorded too little importance. Claims for their insignificance can only really be justified by making very stringent assumptions – that preferences are temporally stable, transitively ordered, and not endogenously determined. Even some of the most ardent proponents of rational choice sheepishly admit that these assumptions are questionable (Michael and Becker 1973; Hirshleifer 1977; Sen and Williams 1982). In consequence, rational choice sometimes seems as if it is a hollow shell that has too little relevance for the study of non-economic phenomena (Sen 1977; Hirschman 1982).

There can be no doubt that the problem of preference-formation is a most difficult one. *De gustibus non est disputandum* can be read as a warning to all those who believe this question is tractable. Because of its difficulty, the economists – with their customary generosity – have smirkingly bequeathed it to the sociologists. Not for nothing do they believe in rational choice! We should certainly look this gift horse carefully in the mouth. Even so, we are not totally ignorant of processes of preference-formation, and, as a matter of fact, there is much material in the literature on ethnic and race relations that bears on the issue.

Where do preferences come from? It appears that they can be formed through both selection and learning mechanisms (Hechter 1986). Selection mechanisms favour individuals with adaptive preferences – to take a trivial example, inhabitants of the tropics who like cold drinks – as against maladaptive ones – inhabitants of the tropics who like hot drinks. People with maladaptive preferences are likely to be less wealthy, healthy, happy and ultimately long-lived than people with adaptive preferences. As such, they are less likely to transmit their preferences to others on account of their reduced life-expectancy as well as their disproportionate lack of 'success', however relativistically this is defined – unsuccessful people are not likely to be viewed as worthy of emulation. Thus, in whatever ways preferences are transmitted, adaptive ones will tend to be selected over maladaptive ones.

But many preferences, probably the majority of them, are intrinsically neither adaptive nor maladaptive: consider preferences for eating scones as against croissants, or for doing sociology as against anthropology. Many such preferences result from learning processes, and particularly from modelling. A major determinant of the distribution of these preferences is differential association, because this is the factor that limits the feasible set of models, or persons whose behaviour is available for observation. Further, there is wide agreement that childhood experiences have a privileged status during the rest of a person's life. For these reasons, families are often capable of transmitting preferences across the generations.

From this it follows that critical loci for the study of preference-formation include the family as well as other institutions that encourage differential association. Many kinds of minority groups fill this bill.

Consider groups that successfully resist assimilation into their host society. Whether they are in relatively newly established Utopian communities or in ancient ethnic ones, the members of such groups appear to be acting on the basis of preferences, or values, widely discrepant from those held in the surrounding community. Here, then, is a rich body of evidence about differential preference-formation.

Rural 'intentional communities' have been established in many parts of the world, but especially in the United States (see Nordhoff 1875 (1965); Hostetler 1963; Kanter 1972; Zablocki 1971). Typically, these communities attempt to be economically autarkic – that is, to approach the ideal of an *oikos* economy. Since in virtually every instance membership provides a lower standard of living and less freedom of dress, sexual behaviour and inter-personal relations generally than is available in the host society, how are such groups able initially to attract members, to mould the preferences of succeeding generations, and to retain the allegiance of their adult members?

Initial recruitment is not terribly problematic because it is guided by self-selection. The benefits which such communities can provide for their members need not be universally attractive. At a minimum, membership in an intentional community offers relief from loneliness (which is attractive to the lonely); a heavy dose of directedness (which is attractive to those with low self-esteem (Zablocki 1971)); and, often, economic security (which is attractive to the economically insecure). Such benefits can have an extremely narrow appeal: the Shakers, for example, gave physically unattractive women with reduced marital prospects a chance to lead stable, respectable and celibate lives in nineteenth-century America.

Retaining members in succeeding generations is a different task because, unlike their parents, the children do not voluntarily choose to become members. A community's success in influencing their preferences – so that they come to value community membership more than the lures of the host society – has much to do with its chances of survival. But how can this bit of preference-formation be managed? Perhaps the most common mechanism of preference-formation in such communities is the systematic limitation and distortion of information about alternatives existing beyond the group's boundaries. Here the guiding maxim seems to be that it is hard to prefer something if you do not know it exists.

But limiting information in the intentional community is no simple task: it is far easier to do in small and geographically isolated communities (as in many 'tribal' societies) than in the midst of vast national societies like the contemporary United States, where information is aggressively trumpeted through the air waves and other mass media. Even among the Amish – a prototypically successful intentional community – the adults cannot be naïve about conditions in surrounding Pennsylvania towns. What keeps them from passing this knowledge on to their children, and thereby piquing their interest in defection?

Amish parents are likely to present information about the surrounding society to their children in an unfavourable light in order to warn them away from temptation, because they believe that their own salvation depends upon keeping their children in the faith. But parental incentives to colour and limit information about the outside world do not have to rest on such fundamentalist religious beliefs. The status[4] and style of life of parents in all such groups depend on the continued existence of their communities. Should these groups fail to survive, then the parents' livelihoods cannot be sustained, and their remaining prospects tend to be unremittingly bleak.

If parents are motivated selectively to inform their children about life in the wider society, this limitation of knowledge typically continues in secondary socialisation. Most critically, such groups prevent their children from attending state-supported schools.[5] Often ownership of radios and televisions is forbidden; in the case of one Seattle commune that I studied, programmes deemed suitable for watching were carefully screened by elders.

By controlling education, intentional communities not only maximise their chances of moulding children's preferences – giving them a taste for community-provided benefits and an aversion to those provided in the outside world – but also raise their exit costs by denying their children access to the kind of training that would enable them to compete successfully in the external labour market.[6]

Most urban ethnic and racial groups do not persist for these reasons. Few parents in such groups are as strongly motivated to keep their children by their side as are the parents in the intentional community. The persistence of urban ethnic and racial minorities is most often due to limitations of opportunity emanating from outside group boundaries, that is to a panoply of forces that channel group members into distinctive positions in a cultural division of labour (Hechter 1978).

The case of the Gypsies, however, is an interesting exception (Banton 1983: 158–64). Far from attempting the kind of economic autarchy that permits substantial limitation of information, the Gypsy economy is highly dependent on the *gaje* world. As is well-known, Gypsies tend to cluster in extremely narrow occupational niches – serving as coppersmiths, fortune-tellers, musicians, horse-traders, and so forth.

Although the barrier separating the Rom from the *gaje* is to a degree permeable, the Gypsies probably manage to retain a large majority of their young within the group. Due to their economic interdependence, it is much harder to do this by limiting their children's knowledge of outside opportunities, as each family's welfare depends almost entirely on the exploitation of such opportunities. How, then, are Gypsies so successful in retaining their young?

A common explanation is that Gypsy survival is due to strongly held Gypsy beliefs that the *gaje* world is polluted, and only the Rom are clean. Here again, parents have a strong personal incentive to inculcate such beliefs in their children. Since Gypsy children contribute to household income, their defection would diminish it. Further, the Gypsies have developed ample means of warding off assimilationist pressures. They have an ability to remain anonymous in urban society by avoiding registration at birth, for school, for the census, for the draft and with the local tax authorities. By denying their children the training necessary to enable them to compete successfully in the labour market, the Rom ensure their continued economic dependence on the Gypsy community.

Altogether this suggests that preferences tend to be formed and moulded in solidary communities. Community solidarity, in turn, is sustained by dependence and monitoring mechanisms (see Hechter forthcoming) that operate in a fashion wholly consistent with rational choice principles. Hence, I suspect that a close reading of the evidence about religious, ethnic and racial assimilation would reveal that rational choice theory does a reasonably good job of accounting for gross differences in inter-group preferences.

This would be significant, for it would do away with a persistent criticism of rational choice analyses: namely that to be falsifiable such explanations have to specify individual preferences *ex ante*, but that in practice they are always specified *ex post*. There seems to be no intrinsic reason why group preferences cannot be inferred from detailed case-studies, and then employed for the purposes of prediction.

4

The last question is even more trenchant. We have seen that all the competing theories in sociology – including most current versions of rational choice – take institutional and environmental constraints (such as ethnic stratification systems) as givens, rather than explaining them. Population ecologists also do this, but they can be forgiven for it because few, if any, of the environmental conditions that drive natural selection are themselves the creations of mankind. But even sociobiologists recognise that the principal forces in history have been the results of human action. Does it not follow that the ultimate task of social science is to account for the establishment of these institutional constraints, and for the conditions under which they become transformed?

There is little doubt that this task lies far ahead of us. As always, it pays to stand on the shoulders of giants. Of all the social theorists, Marx set it as his special task to construct such a theory. That its final version is inadequate should not dissuade others from taking up where he left off.

At the end of his blisteringly critical evaluation of Marx's general theory of institutional change in *Capitalism, Socialism and Democracy*, Joseph Schumpeter could not repress his immense admiration for the attempt. I cite his praise of Marx's project as a challenge to new generations of scholars. Schumpeter wrote:

> Through all that is faulty or even unscientific in his analysis
> runs a fundamental idea that is neither – the idea of a theory,
> not merely of an indefinite number of disjointed individual
> patterns or of the logic of economic quantities in general, but

of the actual sequence of those patterns or of the economic process as it goes on, under its own steam, in historic time, producing at every instance that state which will of itself determine the next one. Thus, the author of so many misconceptions was also the first to visualize what even at the present time is still the economic theory of the future for which we are slowly and laboriously accumulating stone and mortar, statistical facts and functional equations.

And he not only conceived that idea but he tried to carry it out. All the shortcomings that disfigure his work must, because of the great purpose his argument attempted to serve, be judged differently even when they are not, as they are in some cases, fully redeemed thereby. (Schumpeter 1950: 43–4)

The building of a more adequate theory of endogenous institutional change will require the co-operation of scholars in many different branches of social science (for a useful review, see Elster 1983). In spite of its evident incompleteness, there is a final reason for the appeal of rational choice theory. It alone commands a wide enough consensus among social scientists to make the prospect of such a concerted research effort seem not entirely unrealistic at the present time.

NOTES

1   While this may appear to be an uncontroversial assessment, it turns out that few general statements in this field are uncontroversial, and this one is no exception. Let me merely cite two examples. At a recent conference in Berlin attended by many of the participants in the Oxford conference, Patterson (1983: 26) took offence at the statement that 'there is nothing to distinguish the causes of ethnic collective action from the causes of any other kind' (Hechter, Friedman and Appelbaum 1982: 413). He felt that this conclusion was self-evidently off the mark, but did not bother to enumerate the reasons why. And in a paper presented at the Oxford conference, van den Berghe (this volume) not only states that there is something 'different' about ethnicity but also manages to imply (quite misleadingly) that I agree with this notion! I suspect it would be very difficult to make a convincing case for the distinctiveness of ethnic and race relations as opposed to other kinds of inter-group relations, but before such a claim should be taken seriously, the case first must be made. To my knowledge, it has not been.

2   Not that this criticism caused normativism to die. One of the ineluctable signs of sociology's dilemma is the fact that none of its ideas ever die. As Marx (1970: 145) pointed out in quite a different context, history has a way of (nearly) repeating itself. If the first time was Parsons (1937), then the second was Alexander (1981).

3   It is seldom recognised that the problems of collective action and social order are analytically similar. This similarity rests on the fact that each involves a collective-good situation (Olson 1965; Taylor 1982). Social order is a collective good that no rational egoist has an interest in upholding. Similarly, the rational member of a minority group may well profit from affirmative action legislation on the group's behalf, but will free ride on other people's efforts to attain this collective good. The danger in each case is that the collective good will not be provided at all because of free riding, or deviance, as it is known in the sociological lexicon.

4   Since most such groups are highly stratified with respect to authority and consumption, if not ownership of property, and elders often occupy the position of an aristocracy, status considerations are by no means irrelevant in the intentional community.

5   The fact that the United States has so many intentional communities is partially explained by constitutional guarantees of religious freedom, as well as by generous tax incentives that are available to groups that manage to become identified as religions.

6   Abandoning the community also imposes significant social costs – most such groups deny members any contact with apostates – including contact of parents with children. Needless to say, successful intentional communities also rely on efficient control systems whose task is aided by norms against individual privacy. Here too there are significant parallels with primitive communities.

13

The 'Chicago School' of American sociology, symbolic interactionism, and race relations theory

BARBARA BALLIS LAL

Introduction

The contributions of the 'Chicago School' to the study of race and ethnic relations have been, undeservedly, neglected by sociologists. In this paper, I set out what I take to be the most important and fruitful ideas that this group of scholars contributed to the study of race relations. I argue that the dominant perspective and method used by the Chicago sociologists to investigate race relations was that of symbolic interactionism. In particular, I refer to the work of Robert E. Park, the major force within the Chicago School, to suggest the effectiveness of the symbolic interactionist approach and how it influenced the thinking of later generations of scholars, and most notably the work of Herbert Blumer.[1] My purpose, then, is to present an overview of the contributions of the Chicago School to the study of race relations and to suggest the usefulness of the approach generated by Park and those sociologists influenced by him. I also point out some of the striking similarities between this approach and current work in urban anthropology and social geography.

In the first section of the paper I discuss the concerns of the Chicago sociologists and the concepts and methods developed to pursue these concerns. I argue that the focus of the theoretical inquiry complemented a general doubt among American intellectuals, confronted by evidence of the disorder in cities, about the possibilities of maintaining a cohesive, orderly urban society capable of reforming itself through the democratic participation of its citizens. Their concerns and their concepts were translated into a programme of social investigation in Chicago which resulted in the establishment of urban ethnography as an important sociological research strategy.

280

In the second section I go on to discuss some of the Chicago sociologists' insights into urban race and ethnicity. I include what I have described elsewhere as the discovery of the 'ethnicity paradox' and the importance of 'culture-building'. These concepts draw attention to interdependence of the process of adjustment to urban life with the development of strategies for social mobility. I use the work of Herbert Blumer and Troy Duster to suggest developments in the ideas that originated with Robert E. Park, W. I. Thomas and other members of an earlier generation of sociologists at Chicago. I then go on to point out in the third section, some of the problems which sociologists who identify themselves as symbolic interactionists raise with regard to this body of theory and research.

In the final section of the paper I suggest that there are significant similarities between the perspective and methods of research which originated at Chicago during the 1920s and 1930s and some of the recent work of urban anthropologists and social geographers investigating race and ethnic relations. Consideration of these affinities indicates the deficiencies of other types of sociological perspectives, and in particular of structuralist and holist perspectives, whether functionalist or Marxist, which substitute simplified and rigid patterns of association between groups for the complexity and fluidity of ongoing group life. I conclude by urging that efforts be made to combine what is most fruitful in the Chicago tradition with the recent work of these urban anthropologists and social geographers.

The perspective and method of symbolic interactionism

The group of sociologists working at the University of Chicago in the 1920s and 1930s was concerned with the absence of effective communication between heterogeneous groups in cities, which, they believed, impaired their capacity for collective action. Louis Wirth expressed such apprehension when he observed that:

> If a society is a set of common understandings, a system of reciprocally acknowledged claims and expectations expressed in action, it follows that a human aggregate cannot be regarded as a society until it achieves this capacity for collective action ... the degree to which the members of the society lose their common understandings, i.e., the extent to which consensus is undermined, is the measure of that society's state of disorganization. (Wirth, 1964b: 46)

Cities represented a threat to democratic institutions precisely because these institutions, as Robert E. Park and W. I. Thomas suggested, depended upon 'participation by all, both practically and imaginatively, in the common life of the community' (Park and Miller, 1921: 261).[2]

In 1900, immigrants and their children constituted almost 80% of Chicago's population of 1,698,575. By 1930, the foreign-born were about 35% (886,861) of a population of 3,376,438. Chicago's foreign-born consisted of both the 'older' immigrants from North-Western Europe, such as Scots, many of whom shared both the English language and Protestantism with old-stock Americans, and the 'newer' immigrants from South-Eastern and Eastern Europe, who spoke Greek, Italian, Polish, Russian or Yiddish (among other languages) and who were by-and-large Catholics or Jews (Philpot, 1978: 6–41).

In 1900, Afro-Americans in Chicago numbered 30,150, which was 1.8% of the city's population. By 1930, they numbered 223,803, which was 6.9% (Philpot, 1978: 116). Like the foreign-born with whom they competed for jobs and living space, these Southern blacks were mainly 'rural folk' who came to the city in pursuit of education and economic opportunity. In addition, they came to escape from the burdens of Southern racism.

Southern blacks were old-stock Americans in terms of language, religion and shared history. Yet it soon became apparent to prescient onlookers, such as Park and Thomas, that the stigma of colour was to render the lot of Chicago's black native sons even more onerous than that of the immigrant.

The 'sociological problem' was thus dictated: to investigate and to resolve the paradox of 'physical propinquity' and 'social isolation' that the city as a 'spatial pattern' and a 'moral order' presented. (Park, 1926, 1916, 1922). Sociological research, and especially fieldwork, contributed to efforts to bridge social distances because sociologists communicated to 'men of diverse experiences and interests' the varying realities of their lives (Wirth, 1964a: 25). Other more far-reaching methods of communication, such as the mass media and especially the press, complemented social contacts in informal and formal settings.

As I have already suggested, the major theoretical interests of the Chicago sociologists were communication and collective action. Such action was itself a euphemism for what Park and Ernest W. Burgess called 'the processes of social interaction', namely conflict, accommodation and assimilation, and what Blumer calls 'symbolic interaction' (Park and Burgess, 1921; Blumer, 1969). Communication, collective action, social interaction and symbolic interaction all emphasise the subjective aspects of group activity as opposed to merely outlining what are seen to be objective 'structures'. These concepts assume that meaning emerges from interaction, which includes a process of interpretation by participants and the mutual adjustment of their 'gestures'. Meanings which both underlie and emerge from interaction may be reinforced, modified or radically changed. Interactions between individuals and groups are located in situations. The meanings, attitudes, outlooks and other predispositions that people bring to bear on the situations they encounter, as well as the situations themselves, have a history, that is to say, they are the outcome of a 'historical run of experience' (Mead, 1934a; Blumer and Duster, 1980).

Socialisation consists of the transmission of a relevant world of 'objects' and their meanings and is an ongoing process in the life of the individual who is required to fit into new groups and learn the meanings appropriate to each of these. Socialisation depends upon the ability of the individual to make an object of himself, that is to say, to act towards himself on the basis of being able to get out of himself and 'take the role of the other'. The object a person makes of himself, his self-conception, is largely determined by the roles that he adopts in approaching himself. These, in turn, depend upon the way in which 'significant others' have approached him. A person's actions are in large part based upon his conception of the kind of object that he takes himself to be (Mead, 1934a).

These basic elements of what is now called 'symbolic interactionism' have been overlooked or distorted by many of those sociologists who have chosen to write, mostly critically, about this perspective and style of social research. Reviewing this literature in the field of race and ethnic relations, a literature mostly of censure, it appears to me that one serious source of misunderstanding stems from the tendency to see Park's idea of a 'race relations cycle' as his major contribution to the sociology of race and ethnicity (Myrdal, 1944: 1025–64; Cox, 1948; Lyman, 1972: 27–70). The race relations cycle is of minor significance when compared with Park's ideas about the social-psychological dimensions of race relations, race as an aspect of social stratification, the ecological dimension of intergroup relations, the role of the mass media in influencing race relations, and race in the urban environment (Lipset, 1950; Matthews, 1978). Moreover, Park did not intend the race relations cycle to justify substituting speculation about race relations in general for the detailed empirical study of specific cases of race relations.

A second and more serious source of confusion stems from the view that symbolic interactionism, particularly as this outlook is presented by Herbert Blumer, is a social-psychological perspective which cannot be used to describe and explain large-scale historical events, such as race riots and revolutions, or those persistent patterns of behaviour which are identified by sociological holists as social structure (Berger and Luckmann, 1967:193–4; Martindale, 1960; Skidmore 1975: 245).

Since 1930, with characteristic cogency, Blumer has insisted that sociologists take a critical look at increasingly fashionable social systems theories and structural functional theories in the light of the style of sociological work generated within the symbolic interactionist tradition. Ironically, the very success and popularity of Blumer's elucidation of Mead's social psychology appears to have eclipsed both his writings about the appropriate way to go about studying group life and his own research inquiries into race relations, mass communications and collective behaviour (Blumer, 1933, 1948, 1951, 1958, 1959, 1965a, 1965b, 1968, 1969, 1978; Blumer and Duster, 1980). The failure, on the part of others, to integrate these aspects of his work with his writings about social theory *per se*, in which he emerged as the major exponent of symbolic interactionism, has resulted in the distorted view of symbolic interactionism as social psychology.

There are significant differences between the imagery and the concepts that symbolic interactionists have developed to reflect the patterns of association that exist between individuals and groups and the imagery and concepts used in other types of sociological theory. For example, their observations that patterns of association are always in a state of potential flux, that they vary with respect to the situations in which interaction occurs and that they often change because they are a condition as well as an outcome of the process of interpretation, mean that abstract or static conceptions of social structure are not congenial to the perspective or method of interactionism. Similarly, the claim that patterns of association enjoy a degree of generality that renders them useful in the description of all societies, or all societies of a certain type, or social systems *per se*, contradicts the interactionist understanding that the situations in which interaction takes place, as well as the meanings which people bring to these situations, is the outcome of a particular 'historical run of events'.

Of equal importance are differences regarding method. Blumer notes that 'there is a persistent tendency among human beings in their collective life to build up separate worlds, marked by an operating milieu of different life situations and by the possession of different beliefs and conceptions for handling these situations'. He goes on to ask us to think of the 'different empirical worlds' of groups as socially distant from one another as a peasant revolutionary body, the directing management of a large industrial corporation, a gambling syndicate and a university faculty. He concludes that 'No theorizing, however ingenious, and no observation of scientific protocol, however meticulous, are substitutes for developing a familiarity with what is actually going on in the sphere of life under study' (Blumer, 1969: 38–9). For this reason, fieldwork and especially participant observation, and the analysis of human documents, are the preferred research strategies of interactionism.

The type of methodology that Blumer is advocating is in keeping with the monographs which were written by sociologists at Chicago during the 1920s, 1930s and 1940s. Consider, for example, the report *The Negro in Chicago*, which was the outcome of research into the Chicago race riot of 1919 and was undertaken by the Chicago Commission on Race Relations. The Commission's research team was effectively headed by one of Park's students, Charles Spurgeon Johnson, and was very much influenced by Park himself. The report is a massive, detailed social history of race relations in Chicago. It covers topics such as 'the Negro population', 'the migration of Negroes from the South', housing, education and employment opportunities for Afro-Americans. It also includes interviews, excerpts from casual conversations and extensive coverage of the way in which the city newspapers, including the black press, portrayed racial groups and race relations. The report's description of the race riot suggested how members of the black community and the white community responded to and created anew a stream of situations, not least as a result of the outpourings of the daily press (Chicago Commission on Race Relations, 1922). Two decades later, Horace Cayton and St Clair Drake published *Black Metropolis*, which further investigated the 'different empirical world' of Afro-Americans (Cayton and Drake, 1946).

These studies, as well as the large number of monographs published by the Chicago scholars and their students, offer ample evidence that their approach combined a concern with the subjective aspects of group life with an appreciation of its objective features. In particular, the Chicago sociologists were in no sense indifferent to the historical context in which experience takes place and in which attitudes arise, flourish or disappear.

Contributions to the sociology of race relations

1. 'Race prejudice as a sense of group position' and 'the process of collective definitions'

Park suggested that race prejudice is not an attribute of individuals but a property of the shifting relationship between racial groups. He argued that race prejudice is aroused, and racial conflict occurs, when there is a real or imaginary threat to an existing pattern of 'social accommodation'. By 'social accommodation' Park meant 'a process of adjustment, that is, an organisation of elements more or less antagonistic to each other but united for the moment'. 'Social accommodation' describes a relationship in which there is consensus, however short-lived, about matters of obligation, duty, appropriate attitudes of deference, and 'respective spheres of action' (Park and Burgess, 1921). Social distances are preserved through the monopolisation of particular kinds of experience and the restriction of access to the lifestyles enjoyed by a dominant group. Conventions and etiquette are internalised and reinforce social distances, as Bertram Doyle's monograph, *The Etiquette of Race Relations in the South*, suggests (Doyle, 1937). It is only in the process of 'social assimilation' that social distances give way to social solidarity based upon participation in a common cultural life in which there is unrestricted access to the range of experience previously monopolised by a dominant group (Park and Burgess, 1921; Park, 1913, 1928).

Park and Burgess insisted upon differentiating between the objectives of 'competition', which they believed to be economic or material advantage, and the objectives of conflict, which they took to be status and the enlargement of spheres of privilege in a pattern of social accommodation. Park argued that status, which has to do with self-conception, social control and how one sees one's group in relation to other groups, is usually of greater importance in influencing collective action than the distribution of material rewards (although he acknowledged that the two were interrelated). 'In general we may say that competition determines the position of the individual in the community; conflict fixes his place in society ... Status, subordination and superordination, control – these are the distinctive marks of a society' (Park, 1921).[3]

Park thought that cities are most often the context in which 'race problems' emerge because it is here that racial groups which were either previously isolated, or which enjoyed (or suffered) a fixed 'place' in an existing mode of social accommodation, meet as competitors for jobs and housing and become antagonists in a process of social conflict aimed at preserving or changing their group's status (Lipset, 1950; Killian, 1970). In cities new situations require that groups fit their lines of action together in new ways. Moreover, Park, like Simmel, believed that a money economy offered new possibilities for a subordinate group to improve its status and widen its sphere of influence (Simmel, 1969).

In cities, both formal organisations and informal institutions, such as boarding houses, contribute to the development of a type of conflict group that Park referred to as 'publics'. Publics are groups that are differentiated from one another in terms of membership and often of goals but which are agreed about the procedures for gaining goals and negotiating about the division of scarce resources. 'Crowds' and 'social movements' are also features of urban life, but unlike publics have no traditions and no permanent organisations; they exert control over their participants but generally do not achieve their goals on the basis of negotiation with other groups (Park, 1972).

Finally, Park was very definite about the role of historical evidence in social research generally, and in race relations research in particular. He observed that 'opinions, creeds and doctrines become intelligible when we know their history; when we know, in other words, the experiences out of which they have sprung . . . Not merely events, but institutions as well become intelligible when we know their histories, and particularly when we know the individual experiences of men and women in which they have their origin and on which they finally rest' (Park, 1927).

The ideas of 'race prejudice as a sense of group position' and the 'process of collective definitions', which are introduced into the race relations literature by Herbert Blumer and Troy Duster, build upon Park's perspective on race prejudice and race conflict. In his essay 'Race Prejudice as a Sense of Group Position', first published in 1958, Herbert Blumer agrees with Park's view that race prejudice is 'fundamentally a matter of the relationship between racial groups' rather than between individuals, and he reiterates the conditions that Park suggested give rise to or intensify race prejudice (Blumer 1958). In a later essay, 'The Future of the Color line', published in 1965, Blumer includes alongside what he calls a 'domination–subordination' axis of the relationship between racial groups an 'inclusion–exclusion' axis (Blumer, 1965a).

However, in these and also in later essays, Blumer modifies and extends Park's ideas in several ways. First, Park tended to emphasise personal experience and 'equal status contacts' within a 'bi-racially organized society' as a likely mechanism of social change between racial groups, despite his theoretical interest in the role of publics and collective behaviour in the process of change. Blumer, on the other hand, locates change in the public and in the intervention of politically powerful leaders, especially those of the dominant group. Political leaders may initiate social change by altering the objective conditions under which racial groups co-exist, or by changing the imagery of these groups and hence the 'collective definitions' which he and Troy Duster claim to be the fulcrum of race relations (Blumer and Duster, 1980). For example, in his essay 'Industrialisation and Race Relations', Blumer insists that 'political pressures' rather than 'inner considerations of industrial efficiency' are likely to lead to changes in a prevailing pattern of race relations. Thus, he notes of the American South that changes 'have not sprouted indigenously in Southern industry or for that matter Southern society' but have instead emanated from the Federal Government (Blumer, 1965b: 247).

A second way in which Blumer and his colleague Troy Duster develop the previous work of Park is by focusing upon the process of 'collective definition' (Blumer and Duster, 1980). What Blumer and Duster mean by 'collective definition' is the

> basic process by which racial groups come to see each other and themselves and poise themselves to act towards each other; the process is one in which the racial groups are defining or interpreting their experiences and the events that bring these experiences about. The outcome of this process of definition is the aligning and realigning of relations and the development and reformulation of prospective lines of action towards one another. (Blumer and Duster, 1980: 222)

They go on to note that the process is collective 'in that judgements and interpretations are presented to others and are subject to their evaluation; and, in turn, the views of these others enter back into the circle of consideration' (220). Moreover, they also point out that 'one cannot gainsay the presence and occurrence of an ongoing process of "experiencing" among racial groups in association with one another ... A scholar who is removed from this body of experience or who ignores it is cut off from the elementary ingredients of race relations' (230).

In addition to noting that racial groups interact in a variety of situations, all of which must be studied by students of race relations, Blumer and Duster contend that there are 'variable interpretations' of human experience and that 'It is the variable interpretation of these human experiences that is the starting point of social theory' (218). In addition, they suggest that the relationship between the mass media and the process of collective definitions be looked at.

The third contribution which Blumer and Duster make to the study of race relations, and which is an inherent part of their theory of collective definition, has to do with what they term 'dualisms'. The problem of dualisms refers to subordinate groups vacillating between an insistence upon their own 'specialness' and thus reinforcing solidarity among group members, or emulating the behaviour of a dominant group in an effort to improve the rank order of the group as a whole. 'The conflict for groups (and individuals inside these groups) at the base of the social, economic and political structure, most simply put, is whether to celebrate and retain their "likeness" (which some may come to feel consigns them to the base), or whether to emulate and assimilate' (225). These two contradictory attitudes may be held by different members of the group at the same time.

Blumer and Duster suggest that a trend towards emulation usually occurs under favourable economic conditions, when members of the subordinate group might reasonably hope to improve their lives and their status by economic activity which results in increased rewards. On the other hand, an insistence upon 'specialness' usually occurs when economic mobility is not likely and the group members instead opt for an improvement of their lives through political action. Blumer and Duster later talk about this dualism as 'two major divergent directions of effort' which they call the 'assimilationist' orientation and the 'separatist' orientation.

Blumer and Duster see the duality of emulation/assimilation and specialness/separateness as a useful way of describing the internal discussions within the subordinate group which contribute to the stability of, or to shifts in, collective definitions. As such, duality is an important part of their theory of collective definition. For example, they use this conception of dualism to explain changes in the outlook of American blacks between 1920 and 1980 (226–38).

I would like to suggest that the opposing orientations that Blumer and Duster depict as dualisms have also been commented upon by the historians August Meier and Allan Spear. In his study, *Negro Thought in America, 1880–1915*, Meier documents the vacillation among black leaders between ideologies of 'accommodation' and those of 'integration' between 1880 and 1915. Meier contends that ideologies of accommodation and the growth of separate black institutions (which through the passage of time took on their own characteristics and therefore emerged as specifically 'black' institutions) were a response to the antagonism of white Americans to black aspirations – aspirations which did not differ much from those of the prevailing 'white' culture. However, Afro-Americans discovered the benefits of a separatist ideology and organisational life, once articulated and established, in advancing group interests (Meier, 1964: 13).

Similarly, Spear's work suggests that the growth of Chicago's physical black ghetto hastened the growth of the institutional ghetto, that is to say, the development of black churches, hospitals, newspapers and self-help organisations. Spear agrees with Meier that only after the exclusion of black people from jobs, housing, educational facilities and other aspects of white institutional life did black leaders opt for separatist policies, which represented a strategy for survival (Spear, 1967).

Moreover, as I have pointed out in my discussion of what I call 'the ethnicity paradox' and 'culture-building', a duality similar to that noted by Blumer and Duster had already been discussed by Park and Thomas in their work on immigrants and blacks (Lal, 1983: 159–65). What I mean by an 'ethnicity paradox' is the finding that in American society participation in ethnic institutions and the celebration of separate groups identities, while valued in and of themselves, are at the same time strategic devices for facilitating participation in all areas of social life and a fair share of scarce resources in the wider community.

The idea that immigrant institutions and, in particular, the immigrant neighbourhood, served to ease the immigrant's transition to American urban life, although not without its critics, has since become a familiar interpretation in the study of immigrant history (Warner and Burke, 1969; Philpott, 1978; Conzen, 1979; Yancey and Ericksen, 1979). However, Park also anticipated the relationship between this finding and subsequent analyses which see the self-conscious creation of a genuine black culture, separatist ideologies and separate institutions as a prerequisite for the political mobilisation of blacks in pursuit of their shared interests (Cruse, 1967; Carmichael and Hamilton, 1967; Blauner, 1972).

To sum up: rather than being a response to a specific state of the economy, as Blumer and Duster suggest, dualisms, and in particular an insistence upon specialness/separateness, are strategic devices to facilitate an improvement in the collective status of the group as a whole and to secure a larger share of scarce resources.

2. Group status and self esteem

Park and Thomas suggested that social conflict between immigrant groups and between these groups and America's native sons was largely concerned with the distribution of status. As Park noted: 'Status means position in society. The individual inevitably has some status in every social group of which he is a member . . . Every smaller group, likewise, has a status in some larger group of which it is a part.' He went on to point out: 'It follows from what is said that an individual may have many "selves" according to the groups to which he belongs and the extent to which each of these groups is isolated from the others' (Park, 1921: 181). Thus Park chose to emphasise the judgemental aspects of the self which shape and are shaped by social interaction. The intellectual antecedents of this view are to be found in the concepts of the 'social self', the 'looking-glass self' and the 'generalised other' (James, 1892; Cooley, 1909; Mead, 1934a).

With this in mind, Park and Thomas observed that foreigners

> who begin by deserting their groups end by attempting to improve the status of these groups – seeking to make them something with which a man may be proud to identify himself. The fact that the individual will not be respected unless his group is respected becomes, thus, perhaps the most sincere source of nationalist movements in America. *To this extent the*

> *nationalist movements represent an effort to increase*
> *participation in American life.* (Park and Miller, 1921: 143–4,
> my emphasis)

In this remarkable passage, as well as elsewhere, Park and Thomas conclude that while the celebration of Old World heritages and the assertion of a separate group identity may be valued in and of themselves, they are also strategies for improving the status of the immigrant group and the self-esteem of its members.

In American society, membership in a racial group is of greatest importance in conferring or denying status and self-esteem. The Chicago sociologists took note of the importance of group status and self-esteem. However, race relations research has yet adequately to explore the relationship between a group's status and self-esteem on the one hand and its achievement and mobility on the other. Studies by Lee Rainwater and Geoffrey Driver, neither of them interactionists, are examples of what might fruitfully be done in this area of research (Rainwater, 1970; Driver, 1979).

3. 'The urban community as a spatial pattern and a moral order': physical spaces, social distances and culture-building

Park believed that human 'society' as opposed to plant and animal 'communities' is organised on two levels, 'the biotic' and 'the cultural', and can be presented analytically as 'a spatial pattern' and 'a moral order'. Human ecology deals with the biotic dimension of group life. It charts the spatial distribution of groups, institutions and activities. The focus of inquiry is upon patterns of population movement and settlement and of land use. It also includes the description of groups' positions in an occupational order. Sociology investigates the 'cultural' nature of group life (Park, 1926, 1927).

Park summarised his view of the relationship between human ecology and sociology in the essay, 'The Urban Community as a Spatial Pattern and a Moral Order', first published in 1926, in which he noted that:

> It is because communication is fundamental to the existence of
> society that geography and all the other factors that limit or
> facilitate communication may be said to enter into its structure
> and organization at all ... Mobility is important as a
> sociological concept only in so far as it insures new social
> contact, and physical distance is significant for social relations
> only when it is possible to interpret it in terms of social
> distance. (Park, 1926)

The Chicago studies in human ecology anticipated such recent efforts of social geographers as that of understanding the 'roles of choice and constraint' underlying patterns of segregation and dispersal and explaining 'the ethnic component of segregation in terms of its meaning for the groups involved' (Peach and Smith, 1981: 9).

Park believed that for Afro-Americans isolation had been of two kinds (Lal, 1982b). The first of these was physical isolation, which resulted in ghettos in cities such as Chicago and New York, in which blacks who were differentiated by occupation, class, education and place of birth were forced to live together and to recognise their shared status. The second kind of isolation was cultural, that is exclusion from education and 'the techniques of communication and organisation of the white man' (Park, 1913). In the rural South, cultural isolation inhibited the development of race-consciousness, race solidarity and race pride as well as a sense of shared destiny (Park, 1934; 1937). Southern blacks constituted a 'folk' whose 'habitat' was 'fixed', whose culture was 'local' and whose intellectual horizons were circumscribed by 'the shadow of the plantation'. (Park, 1934). Urban ghettos in the North, which brought Afro-Americans into close contact with each other, presented opportunities for education and participation in intellectual and political activities (Park, 1935).

Park also thought that opportunities for blacks to enter into occupations from which they were excluded in the South would contribute to the growth of a black middle class and of 'bi-racial organizations' (Park, 1943). He pointed out that:

> The most profound changes in race relations, if not in racial ideology, have come about with the rise of a hierarchy of occupational classes within the limits of the Negro race ... at present, at least in the Northern cities, to which Negroes in recent years have migrated in such large numbers, the status of the Negro population is no longer that of a caste. It is rather that of a racial and a cultural minority. (Park, 1943: 311)

As early as 1923, Park had begun to celebrate the emergence in Northern cities of an Afro-American leadership composed of politicians and intellectuals who saw themselves and their racial group in new ways. He pointed out that blacks were less interested in emulating the dominant white world and 'more concerned ... in defining their own conception of their mission and destiny as a race' (Park, 1923: 290–3). His work thus foreshadowed Robert Blauner's conclusion that 'in American life, ethnic culture is identity, there is no clear individual or group progress without a clear sense of who one is, where one came from and where one is going' (Blauner, 1972: 421–3).

Discussion of dissension

The following brief discussion of three of the differences within symbolic interactionist thinking about race relations provides a convenient way of also exploring some of the more frequent criticisms of this perspective and method by non-interactionists (Shils, 1970; Gouldner, 1970; Schwendinger and Schwendinger, 1974; Lal, 1982a).

One major source of disagreement has to do with the nature of sociological explanation and, in particular, with the level of generality to which findings in sociological inquiry should aspire. This difference is explored by Bernard Meltzer and James Petras in their essay 'The Chicago and Iowa Schools of Symbolic Interactionism', in which they argue that Manfred Kuhn developed his variant of symbolic interactionism in order to re-cast Mead's social psychology so that it would fulfil a 'nomothetic (or generalizing) function' rather than an 'idiographic (or nongeneralizing) function' (Meltzer and Petras, 1970: 6). Arthur Brittan, another sociologist sympathetic to symbolic interactionism, warns against an 'over-emphasis on the situation', and on meanings, such that 'we allow ourselves to be taken in by a completely relativistic account of social interaction, in which episodes are elevated to the status of the prime unit of methodological and theoretical interest' (Brittan, 1973: 200–2).

In the area of race relations, Blumer and Duster's insistence that sociologists pay attention to the variety and complexity of racial groups' experience of each other reveals the tension inherent in a perspective and method which seeks to discover general, 'collective' orientations and patterns of association and, at the same time, to respect the particular instances in which social interaction between racial groups occurs. Blumer and Duster resolve the tension between the 'collective', or the general, and the 'particular' by arguing that 'Race relations, certainly in their problematic form, do operate inside of an essentially common and constant framework. Thus while the variability that is suggested by the process of definition may, and indeed does, take place, it is held within the framework and takes place along the line that is set by the framework'; and, later, 'the defining process is relentlessly brought inside a common framework, a framework which forces the definitions to deal with the basic orientations of racial groups' (Blumer and Duster, 1980: 232, 236). What their outlook implies in terms of fieldwork, the analysis of human documents and the sociological interpretation of ongoing group life is suggested by monographs, such as *Black Metropolis, The Negro Family in Chicago, Negro Politicians, In the Shadow of the Plantation* and *The Etiquette of Race Relations in the South*, in which a variety of racial 'experiencing' is analysed in terms of the fundamental hierarchy of colour, or what Blumer has also referred to as 'the color line' and its accompanying 'sense of group position' (Cayton and Drake, 1946; Frazier, 1932; Gosnell, 1935; Johnson, 1934; Doyle, 1937; Blumer, 1958, 1965a).

What these monographs further suggest is that although symbolic interactionists do not generally aspire to explain race relations (or any other aspect of social life) through the discovery of general laws of behaviour or by generating universal hypotheses on which to base predictions about the future, their construction of 'sensitising' concepts has enabled their analyses of group life to uncover some interesting patterns of association between racial groups (Blumer, 1969). 'Collective definitions', 'dualisms', 'the ethnicity paradox', 'race prejudice as a sense of group position', 'the city as a spatial pattern and a moral order', all make sense of empirical data in the study of race and ethnic relations. I would argue that these sensitising concepts are good examples of what John Lofland calls 'mini-concepts' and that these are amenable, by and large, to the types of research procedures outlined by Barney Glaser and Anselm Strauss (Lofland, 1970: 37; Glaser and Strauss, 1967; Strauss, 1970). Moreover, it is precisely because these sensitising or mini-concepts are tied to actual instances of racial experiencing that they are sometimes used by, and might be useful to, social geographers, social historians and anthropologists as well as sociologists (Peach, 1975; Jackson and Peach, 1981; Peach and Smith, 1981).

A second problematic area which divides symbolic interactionists from one another, as well as dividing them from many of their critics, has to do with assessing the importance of social class as a determinant both of the situations in which racial groups experience each other and of the meanings which racial groups bring into play in resolving these situations through joint action. The conclusion that symbolic interactionism overlooks the significance of social class in the determination of 'objective' historical conditions and 'subjective' consciousness is one expression of a more widespread criticism based upon symbolic interactionism's purported 'avoidance of macrostructural emphasis in favor of its microscopic interactional one' (Fisher and Strauss, 1978: 457).

Park preferred the category of occupation to that of class. More importantly, as I have already suggested, he saw 'status' based upon colour as the most significant feature of the interaction between racial groups. This outlook is generally shared by Blumer and Everett Hughes (Blumer, 1958, 1965a, 1965b; Blumer and Duster, 1980; Hughes, 1971). Among Park's students, however, colour coupled with class became of increasing importance (Cayton and Drake, 1945; Cox, 1948; Cayton,

1965). Elsewhere, following a suggestion made to me by the historian Stanley Engermann, I explore the view that the Great Depression played a significant part in this theoretical development (Lal, forthcoming).

A third and related division within the ranks of symbolic interactionists has to do with the extent to which the actor and his interpretation of the situation, as opposed to disembodied variables such as social class, social role or social institution, are kept at the centre, rather than at the periphery, of sociological analysis (Blumer, 1954). Such a difference in emphasis is noticeable in a comparison of Blumer's outlook with *some* (but by no means all) of the essays of Hughes.

Thus, for example, in an early monograph Hughes observed that 'institutions are just those social forms which grow up where men collectively face problems which are never completely settled ... It seems likely that when they do so, and continue to do so for long enough, they produce relationships and ideas which succeeding generations accept somewhat involuntarily' (Hughes, 1931: Preface). Ironically, in some of his later writings on social institutions, Hughes adopts a functionalist approach which contradicts his earlier preference for keeping the actor at the centre of the analysis and which influenced some members of a later generation of Chicago scholars (Hughes, 1971: 14–20; Janowitz, 1952, 1966; Fisher and Strauss, 1978: 475, 478 9).

New inputs, new directions

The contributions of Park and the Chicago sociologists, and more recently those of Blumer and Duster, suggest that in addition to a commitment to ethnography as a method of social research, and to the use of material such as human documents, there are a number of areas of special theoretical importance to sociologists in the symbolic interactionist tradition (Park, 1929). Clearly Blumer and Duster's idea of the process of collective definition argues for consideration of the role of political leadership in the ongoing process of redefining the nature of dominant and subordinate racial groups. These authors also emphasise the importance of observation of the process of collective definition as this occurs within each racial group and, in particular, of 'the differences in interpretation that may be in play within each racial group', and of how these interpretations shift over time. Finally, they argue that sociological study must take into account unfolding events and the 'objective changes in the position of racial groups' (Blumer and Duster, 1980: 221–2). One fairly recent study that represents a start in these directions is Lewis Killian and Charles Grigg's monograph, *Racial Crisis in America* (1967).

In addition to these areas of research, I believe that attention must be paid to several problems which the concepts of an 'ethnicity paradox' and 'culture-building' raise. In my forthcoming book about Park and the Chicago School of American sociology, I argue that much more needs to be known about why a strongly adhered-to culture and a sense of identity are assets for members of minority groups. How does participation in separate racial and ethnic institutions contribute to greater participation in the dominant institutions of a society? In what ways do the status of a group and the self-esteem of individuals work towards individual and collective mobility? Recently these questions, which were first raised by the Chicago sociologists, have been taken up by scholars as diverse in their approaches as Harold Cruse, Nathan Glazer, Thomas Sowell, Robert Blauner and Stanley Lieberson (Cruse, 1967; Glazer, 1983; Glazer and Moynihan, 1963, 1975; Sowell, 1981; Blauner, 1972; Lieberson, 1980). Empirical studies of 'ethnic enterprise' and race politics provide us with some useful insights into these problems (Light, 1972; Frye, 1980). Geoffrey Driver's article, 'Classroom Stress and School Achievement: West Indian Adolescents and their Teachers', is suggestive of how collective definitions and communication failures lessen self-esteem and the possibilities for academic success on the part of students and teachers in a multi-cultural classroom (Driver, 1979: 131–44). However, what are needed are additional 'Chicago-oriented ethnographies' to capture the day-to-day workings and sentiments of entrepreneurs and their families, as well as of political leaders, teachers and school-children.

Also of importance is the analysis of how ideas about a shared identity and a shared fate held by minority group members not only influence their own activities but also, because these ideas are taken into account by others, affect the attitudes and behaviour of culturally dominant groups.

The contributions of the Chicago sociologists to human ecology have been taken up by social geographers interested in 'spatial sociology'. Recent collections of essays such as *Social Interaction and Ethnic Segregation* suggest how patterns of settlement are related to patterns of communication and social relations between heterogeneous groups in cities (Jackson and Smith, 1981; Peach and Smith, 1981, see also Rex and Moore, 1967). Here it is worth noting that the recent concern of anthropologists with 'ethnic boundaries' has been picked up by those social geographers exploring the physical boundaries between ethnic areas (Jackson and Smith, 1981: 9).

I would like to conclude this paper by arguing that we are witnessing a fundamental shift in the approach to race relations which, while not directly attributable to the Chicago School or to symbolic interactionism, is based upon concerns, concepts and directives for social research which reiterate much of the wisdom that comes from the Chicago School. This new approach has the following features. First, a preference for talking about race and ethnic relations in terms of the 'transformation of traditional cultures' rather than in terms of categories such as integration and assimilation. Second, a suggestion that race and ethnicity are variables rather than a constant feature of ongoing group life and that ethnic and racial 'boundaries' are constantly in the process of being negotiated and renegotiated. Third, an emphasis upon meanings and the subjective and symbolic aspects of race and ethnic relations. Finally, a concern with historical events, such as migration, and the human experiences which spring from these events.

The affinities of this new approach, which owes much to the work of Fredrik Barth and those whom he has influenced, with the Chicago School seem apparent to me (Barth, 1981; Wallman, 1978b, 1979). The idea of 'the transformation of traditional cultures' was discussed by Park and Thomas, who agreed with the anthropologist Franz Boas and the philosophical pragmatists George Herbert Mead and John Dewey that cultures are constantly transformed and re-created by groups in their attempts better to adapt themselves to their environment (Lal, 1983: 163–4). The suggestion that 'ethnic boundaries' are important both as a mode of adjustment to an 'encompassing society' and as a mechanism for preserving the autonomy of minority groups bears some resemblance to what Park thought to be the functions of bi-racial organisations (Park, 1928; Barth, 1981).

During the early part of this century Thomas and Znaniecki investigated the transformation of rural Polish culture in cities in the United States at the level of the individual and of the group (Thomas and Znaniecki, 1918–20). Their study, *The Polish Peasant in Europe and America*, was based upon the currently fashionable insight that 'it is impossible to gain a true picture of immigration as a process without investigating the people and their families on both sides' (Watson, 1977: 2; Saifullah Khan, 1979: 1–11)

The logic of symbolic interactionism is to argue that the meanings of objects, including categories of people such as racial groups, are influenced by the nature of the specific situation in which interaction occurs. In this sense, while not disputing the importance of history and tradition, the Chicago scholar might well agree with Sandra Wallman's observation that 'ethnicity is not always relevant to social relationships in which people of different "race" or culture interact; and when it does count it does not always count in the same way' (Wallman, 1979: 6).

Anthropological studies pay attention to the complexity of social life, including its subjective aspects. Anthropological studies which explicitly seek to anchor activity and its *interpretation* in specific contexts face the dilemma of finding patterns or constructing generalisations about race and ethnic relations while at the same time respecting the complex nature of any instance of empirical life, a dilemma which, as I have already noted, has often been attributed to symbolic interactionism as well.

Finally, the new studies in urban race and ethnicity locate social groups in a present which has a historical past to it and, like the Chicago sociologists, seek to understand human experience in terms of the play of historical events.

We would do well to consider the ways in which recent work of these urban anthropologists might be usefully incorporated into the ethnographic tradition associated with the Chicago School and symbolic interactionism.

NOTES

* I would like to thank Martin Bulmer, Steven Dobson, Sarah Gregory, Mike Levin, Paul Rich, John Stone and James Wood for their helpful comments on an earlier draft of this paper. I would also like to thank my neighbours, Maureen and Stuart Shields, for giving me a place to work when my children decided that home was a place to play. In Washington DC, the Library of Congress Resident Scholar facilities served this same purpose. Finally, I must thank Robert Frailey, Director of Athletics, the American University, Washington, DC, for letting me keep my head above water in the American University pool and my feet on the ground on its tennis courts.

1 As I have already argued elsewhere, the dominant outlook of the Chicago School was that of symbolic interactionism (Lal, 1982a). Also see Shibutani, 1961; Rucker, 1969; Rose, 1971; Fisher and Strauss, 1978; Lofland, 1980.

2 It is generally acknowledged that W. I. Thomas was primarily responsible for the text of *Old World Traits Transplanted* and that Park worked in collaboration with him. However, due to Thomas's involvement in a scandal at about the time the study was to be published, his name was deleted from it and Herbert Miller was asked to step in as co-author with Park (Janowitz, 1966: xvi; Matthews, 1978: 118).

3 Park argued that what differentiates plant and animal 'communities' from human 'society' is communication and corporate action, which is present only in human society. Sociology must concern itself primarily with society, that is to say, with the cultural order. Competition, which is non-social interaction, refers to community.

14

The operationalisation of identity theory in racial and ethnic relations

PETER WEINREICH

Identity structure analysis

The main task of this paper is to introduce a conceptual framework for the operationalisation of identity theory in the arena of racial and ethnic relations. This conceptual framework, known as Identity Structure Analysis (ISA) (Weinreich, 1969, 1977, 1979a, 1979b, 1980, 1983a, 1983b), consists of a synthesis of concepts in part derived from aspects of psychodynamic (Erikson, 1959, 1968; Hauser, 1971, 1972; Marcia, 1966, 1980), personal construct (Kelly, 1955; Bannister and Mair, 1968; Fransella and Bannister, 1977) and symbolic interactionist (Mead, 1934b; Goffman, 1959; Harré, 1979) perspectives on the socio-psychological processes of identity development. It is informed by the social anthropologists' clarification of differences in shared cultural value systems according to actors' membership of specific ethnic and sub-cultural groups (LeVine and Campbell, 1972). It is able to incorporate the distinction made by some sociologists between, on the one hand, internally recognised categorisations of self as being a member of an ethnic group, with an emphasis on 'ethnic identity', and, on the other, externally ascribed definitions by others of self as being a member of a general category, with an emphasis on an imposed 'racial identity'. In part, the conceptual framework of ISA is able to integrate these disparate concerns by being aware of the conceptual distinction between personal and social identity (Tajfel, 1974, 1978; Harré, 1979; Weinreich, 1983b), without divorcing these aspects in an artificial way. It is therefore also able to delineate individual vulnerabilities in identity development at the same time as it locates commonalities in identification patterns in people sharing a common niche in society. It is expressly concerned with the pragmatics of establishing people's complex amalgamations of partial identifications with significant others within and across social boundaries, within and across groups, within and beyond the family. In any person such complex amalgamations of one's partial identifications cannot occur without some degree of conflict in one's identifications with specific significant others. In the case of the migration of whole groups of people, some conflicts in identification will invariably be related to the ethnicities of the groups that become situated in proximity to one another.

'Identity conflicts', or, more specifically, patterns of actors' conflicts in identification with particular others, are the fundamental conditions that give rise to processes of identity development and redefinition (Weinreich, 1979a, 1983a, 1983b). ISA operationalises a definition of a person's conflicted identification with another, so that the relative magnitudes of self's various identification conflicts may be estimated. Common patterns of identification conflicts within a group of people may therefore be ascertained; from this it may be established whether such conflicts are greater with respect to own group or other group members.

Conflicts in identification may, on occasion, denote vulnerable identities, but more usually they will provide the impetus for processes of redefinition of identity and they may, in many instances, be regarded as 'resources' for successful and flexible identity negotiations in the prevailing social context (Weinreich, 1979a, 1983a). Vulnerable identities are something other: they may be 'foreclosed', 'negative', or 'diffused', among other states (Erikson, 1968; Marcia, 1966, 1980; Weinreich, 1982, 1983b). However, beyond the fact that some people's identities may be vulnerable, there is the possibility that any person's identity may be 'threatened' by fundamental discrepancies between that which a person defines self to be and that which others define that self as being. A person with a vulnerable identity is unlikely to withstand such a threat, but will become 'broken' as a consequence, whereas someone else with no such vulnerability is likely to fight back and remain 'unbroken'.

It will clarify certain issues of identity theory and its operationalisation to sketch in some features of complex societies where a generally 'superordinate' ethnic community contains within it different 'subordinate' ethnic communities. First, attention will be given to aspects of social change and their ramifications for people's identities within the superordinate community, in which vulnerabilities in identity and reactive salience of ethnic identity will be considered. Then, attention will be directed to the subordinate groups, especially ones that have become established as the result of past, and perhaps continuing, migrations, in which redefinition of ethnic identity may be an ongoing process.

Identity concerns of the superordinate community

While institutionalisation and legitimation of social structures within society provide inertial mechanisms inhibiting social change (Berger and Luckmann, 1967), some individuals and groups of people nevertheless induce modifications to societal institutions by their adoption of differing aspirations, values and norms of behaviour compared with previous generations. In some instances, the impetus for social change may be economic, as when there is a booming economy and a rich diversity of opportunities, or when there is a slump with whole industries in certain regions closing down and unemployment soaring. In other instances, the impetus may be due to the availability of new kinds of technology which allow new options in lifestyles to become available, such as occurred with the introduction of artificial birth control, or with the implementation of rapid means of transport and communication. In adopting different aspirations, people redefine the meaning of their social identities; witness the contemporary connotations in the West of: being of the one or other gender; being waged or unwaged; being married, unmarried or divorced; and having or not having a family, or being a single-parent family.

In so far as *significant* groups of people come to redefine the meanings of their social identities, other people, who are unable to do so, may become vulnerable in theirs, especially if they are conscious of being unable to 'keep up with the times'. If they also feel that some core dimension of their already vulnerable identities is under threat, they may fight to re-establish its primacy.

Within any complex and stratified society, the meanings of social identities will invariably differ according to the place of the group within the society. A member of the elite class will have social identities which differ from those of members of various subordinate classes ranging from professional, through skilled, to unskilled worker (see Abner Cohen, 1981, for an analysis of the presentation of social identities by elite group members). Social identities will likewise vary according to gender.

However, although there are manifest differences in the social identities one person has compared with another, the vast majority of people in the typical nation-state will have one core social identity in common, namely that of a common ethnicity. If, in particular circumstances, that core ethnic identity becomes the most salient of people's social identities and if, in addition, those sharing it agree on its meaning and value, then it will dominate their behaviour. Their other social identities (such as gender, social class, marital status and work) would become subordinated. Thus, in times of war, national ethnicity tends to dominate over stratified, sub-cultural and personal social identities. In cases of polarisation within sectarian communities, sectarian ethnic identities tend likewise to dominate over other social identities across a widespread set of circumstances (e.g. in Northern Ireland, sectarian identities dominate in politics, housing, education, employment, leisure centres, pubs and, of course, places of worship, and represent two 'nations', the 'Protestant-British' and the 'Catholic-Irish', within the same territory).

Contemporary migrations of significant numbers of people, who constitute whole communities from other lands, introduce additional ethnic identities with lifestyles that differ from those of the superordinate community. Such alternative lifestyles may be perceived as threatening to those whose own identities are already the most vulnerable. The latter may be individuals, or whole sections of the population, who are vulnerable as a consequence of their location within society. They may be those who lack a sense of worthwhile identity and are confused in their aspirations, because of unemployment or non-achievement, or those who feel that, while employed and comfortably well-off, their aspirations have been overtaken by social change and become meaningless given contemporary norms. The former are likely to be more concentrated in the working class, while the latter are likely to constitute the 'restrictionist right' on 'immigration' in Britain.

Such people may come to rely increasingly on their core ethnic identity for a centre to their otherwise vulnerable identities. If they do, they are likely to feel personally threatened by alternative ethnicities that challenge the meaning that they have always accepted for their own superordinate one. Populist rhetoric appealing to their own 'undiluted' and 'untainted' ethnicity and decrying 'alien cultures' thereby arouses strongly affirmative responses from these sections of the community, despite the fact that they may have had no direct contact with migrant peoples, nor have experienced direct competition from them. They will tend to ascribe derogatory 'racial' identities to such 'immigrants'. An account of the impact of such rhetoric, concerning the Powellite theme of the number of 'immigrants' and their 'threat' to British 'culture', on the political scene in Britain is given by Ben-Tovim and his colleagues (1982b). Similar appeals are currently evident in France, made by the leader of the French National Front, M. Jean-Marie Le Pen, whose appearance on French television 'was implicit acknowledgement that his party has the biggest potential voting power of any single party in the opposition outside the Gaullists' (Webster, 1984).

On the other hand, some well-established open communities, a majority of whose members have robust identities, may witness direct competition from migrant people for jobs and housing, but not feel their identities to be threatened. Such people are likely to accommodate to the presence of alternative lifestyles alongside their own. A general robustness in their identities in other respects would be accompanied by a relative lack of 'defensive' centrality of their ethnic identity. Hence, alternative ethnic communities and lifestyles would not be perceived as threats. Such would appear to be the case of Moss Side in Manchester, where the Housing Action Group, concerned with rehousing problems, was able to emphasise the common live-and-let-live attitudes of a well-integrated community (Ward, 1979).

However, in other more closed communities, where many are vulnerable and depend more centrally on the ethnic dimensions of their identities, direct competition and alternative lifestyles in their midst are likely to be experienced as potent threats to their 'cherished' identities, against which some will retaliate with derogatory 'racial' abuse. In Britain, areas with New Commonwealth 'immigrants' which have exhibited the more overtly racist vote in supporting the National Front, primarily in local elections (15–20% support), are such places as Leicester and London's East End (Taylor, 1979).

In terms of operationalising identity theory, the following emerge as some of the key requirements for investigating the issues outlined in relation to the superordinate community: assessment of vulnerabilities in identity development; estimation of the relative centrality of ethnicity as a dimension of identity; establishment of perceived threats to identity; and ascription of derogatory 'racial' identities to subordinate communities.

Identity concerns of subordinate communities

The identity concerns of members of the subordinate communities will tend to differ from those of the superordinate one. Most of the resources within society will be in the control of the latter, so that most members of subordinate groups will tend to start off with considerable disadvantages in material wealth and, if they are recent migrants, in access to information. Problems over information will in part be due to language difficulties, but also to the impenetrability of the established institutions of the superordinate culture. Being disadvantaged, they can be readily exploited. In addition, they have a limited power base for combating the pervasive forms of the more subtle discrimination against them, let alone the more blatant racist attacks upon them.

Offspring of migrants in Britain experience a distinctive kind of dual socialisation. During primary socialisation within their homes, they form their early identifications with their parents and other members of their own ethnic community. Subsequently, during secondary socialisation at school, representing a different culture, and within the wider community, they form further identifications with significant others embodying values and aspirations of the superordinate community. Elements of the latter identifications will be incompatible with the earlier, home-based, ethnic ones, so that these earlier identifications become conflicted. Thus, by adolescence, second-generation boys and girls will tend to have conflicted identifications with people of their own ethnicity (Weinreich, 1979a).

However, this is not to say that the second-generation adolescents from different ethnic communities experience their identity concerns in the same way. The major differences between ethnic groups in their cultural values, which represent their different kin organisations, sexual mores, religious beliefs and characteristic lifestyles, will give rise to substantial differences in both the nature and the patterns of their ethnic identification conflicts, beyond the common feature of a focus in their own ethnicity. For example, whereas adolescents of 'Asian' and 'Caribbean' ancestry in Bristol both have high levels of identification conflicts with their own ethnic group people, 'Asian' adolescents exhibit high idealistic-identification with their parents and strong ego-involvement with them, compared with 'West Indian' adolescents, an orientation which carries over into their involvement with their school teachers (Weinreich, 1983a).

The person, experiencing discrimination and presented with derogatory images of self by others, may accept these as typifying self, but may, on the other hand, reject them. The social identities that others attempt to impose upon self, that is 'alter-ascribed social identities', more often than not differ from those recognised as characterising self, that is 'ego-recognised social identities' (Weinreich, 1983b). The extent to which this is the case will depend on such factors as the degree to which others within self's community, rather than those outside, act as positive reference models who give reliably favourable judgements of self (Weinreich, 1983a).

When people cross social boundaries, they are likely to experience disjunctions in the ways in which they relate to other people. As they cross from one bounded situation, say, being at work, to another, such as being at home, alternative facets of the self may be brought into play. People, when they are with their own 'crowd', feel, experience and act in ways which may be quite dissimilar from when they are with some other group. In a sense, their 'situational selves' differ (Doherty, 1982; Weinreich, 1983b). They may in this way act with alternative self-images that imply attenuated patterns of identifications with others, depending on which side of a social boundary their interactions take place. Thus, members of a subordinate group may feel confident on home territory, but alienated when crossing into the territory of the institutions of the superordinate community.

In practice, because of their part-identifications during secondary socialisation with significant others from the superordinate community, their experiences of social boundaries are likely to be complex. Some subjective blurring of boundaries is established within self at the level of such cross-identifications. However, while in some situations the social boundaries themselves may prove to be permeable (perhaps on the school sportsfield), in others they may be quite impermeable (as when one is pointedly excluded from a range of social activities and opportunities). The self's task of attempting to re-synthesise complex identifications across boundaries is further complicated by self's having to learn to negotiate the idiosyncracies in the permeability of social boundaries between the ethnic groups.

Dual linguistic-personality systems in bilinguals

While the complexities of 'dual socialisation' caution against a simplistic view of ethnic identification, there is another strand of complication in offspring who are bilingual. The 'problem' of the bilingual may be of a special kind. Which way does one *as a bilingual* face, when speaking in one or other language: towards one's own ethnic community when speaking one's mother tongue, and towards the other community when speaking the 'host' tongue? One may be a different personality when participating in interactions in the one language compared with interactions in the other. In an important sense, one may be a different person when cued into the one language, and that may have ramifications for switching of aspirations and feelings about lifestyles (Ervin-Tripp, 1964). If bilinguals have dual linguistic-personality systems, then one may be dealing with a different kind of person within the ancestral ethnic-linguistic boundary as compared with outside it.

The evidence of one case study is fascinating and unexpected in some respects. It indicates the following possibilities: (i) that individuals can indeed be somewhat different beings according to which ethnic context they cue into; (ii) that, when cued into the one ethnicity, the valued characteristics of the *alternative* ethnicity may be emphasised (i.e. the Pakistani woman in question emphasised the merits of English people and their values when she cued into Pakistani ethnicity, but contrariwise, the merits of Pakistani people and their values when cued into English ethnicity); and (iii) that, in both linguistic contexts, the identity structures of individuals are essentially the same kind of complex amalgamation of identification elements across both ethnicities (Weinreich, 1979c). Evidently, the discourse of bilinguals of subordinate ethnic groups within their own group may not coincide with that towards the superordinate group, not only because of differences in orientation but also because of attenuations in personality cued by the language of discourse.

A meta-theoretical framework for the operationalisation of identity theory

Further requirements for the operationalisation of identity theory highlighted by issues for investigation in the subordinate communities are: establishment of people's value systems and the place of their positive role models within and across ethnic boundaries; assessment of the amalgamation of their part-identifications within and across ethnic boundaries and their conflicts in identification related to ethnicity associated with dual socialisation; determination of differences between their alter-ascribed and ego-recognised social identities; delineation of their situational selves associated with own and other ethnic groups; and, in bilinguals, differentiation of their possible dual linguistic personality systems.

The task of conceptualising all these socio-psychological features of the interactions between members of different ethnic groups in a coherent fashion appears to be daunting, yet an approach to the task can in principle be clearly enunciated. This is to conceptualise a *common meta-theoretical framework within which an extensive number of specific theories may be generated.* While the meta-theoretical framework would provide a common set of theoretical concepts, specific theories would be elaborated out of these concepts, together with additional pertinent concepts, in the service of explaining particular phenomena. This strategy is one by which intercommunicating specific theories are co-ordinated within the overarching meta-theoretical framework (e.g. the theories of the development of the authoritarian personality syndrome, of cross-ethnic identification, of dual linguistic personalities, of reactions to threatened identities, etc.).

In the realm of ethnic and race relations, an appropriate meta-theoretical framework should be fundamentally sensitive to (i) the different values and aspirations of peoples from varied cultural and sub-cultural backgrounds, (ii) the cognitions, everyday ideologies and folklores held by people, (iii) the evaluations they put upon themselves, and upon their own and other groups, and how these are related to their cognitions, for example as core evaluative dimensions of their identities, (iv) the historical development of people's identities, through processes of forming new identifications and resolving identification conflicts, and (v) vulnerabilities in identity development. The theoretical framework should be capable of empirical operationalisation, so that the specific theories may be grounded in empirical data. This requires a set of explicitly defined concepts devoid of ambiguity.

ISA is a meta-theoretical framework which attempts to fulfil these criteria. As a part-synthesis of certain concepts derived from the psychodynamic approach to identity, personal construct psychology and the symbolic interactionist approach to the situated self, it is essentially open-ended without being diffuse and ambiguous in its definitions and their operationalisation. By giving a central place in its conceptualisation to the individual's own value system, it is directly sensitive to differences from person to person in their values and aspirations as they vary according to ethnicity, sub-culture and individual experience.

The core conceptual definitions of ISA are given in Appendix A, while further definitions of more elaborated concepts are given in a recent publication (Weinreich, 1983b). Basic to the conceptualisation is the definition of identity, which integrates the psychodynamic concern with continuity in self-development (Erikson, 1959, 1968) and the personal construct psychology emphasis on the person's construal of events, using self's personal constructs, or categories, for making sense of the social world (Kelly, 1955):

> One's identity is defined as the totality of one's self-construal, in which how one construes oneself in the present expresses the continuity between how one construes oneself as one was in the past and how one construes oneself as one aspires to be in the future. (Weinreich, 1983a: 151, see also 1977, 1982, 1983b)

Not that continuity, rather than the more traditional reference to sameness, is here regarded as being the defining characteristic of identity. Development of, and change in, identity become processes that can be readily encompassed within this definition.

Other definitions of the ISA theoretical framework given in Appendix A concern various component aspects of identity, so that, for example, the individual's value system is incorporated within the concept (see the definitions of 'positive values' and 'negative' or 'contra-values'). The symbolic interactionists' emphasis on the 'situated self' is featured as an integral part of the concept (see the definitions of 'positive' and 'negative' role models and reference groups). The symbolic interactionist perspective may be further accommodated by explicitly designating 'situational selves' in empirical investigations (for example, the facets of self: 'me when I am at work' and 'me when I am at leisure'). For a statement of the theoretical assumptions upon which ISA is based, the reader is directed to the same publication in which the more elaborated concepts are defined (Weinreich, 1983b). Here the distinction between 'alter-ascribed social identity' and 'ego-recognised social identity' is made explicit and consideration is given to theoretical variations in identity development derived from Erikson's observations (these variations include: 'diffuse high self-regard', 'identity crisis', 'confident identity', 'defensive negative identity', etc.).

The above-quoted definition of identity provides a useful framework for understanding component parts of one's identity, such as ethnic identity, gender identity, occupational identity, familial identity, socio-economic class identity, and so on. Thus:

One's *ethnic identity* is defined as that part of the totality of one's self-construal made up of those dimensions that express the continuity between one's construal of past ancestry and one's future aspirations in relation to ethnicity;

One's *gender identity* is defined as that part of the totality of one's self-construal made up of those dimensions that express the continuity between one's construal of one's past gender and one's future aspirations in relation to gender (consider the case of transsexuals);

One's *familial identity* is defined as that part of the totality of one's self-construal made up of those dimensions that express the continuity between one's construal of one's past position and one's future aspirations in relation to familial status (for example, son or daughter of one's parents, father or mother of one's child, etc.);

One's *socio-economic class identity* is defined as that part of the totality of one's self-construal made up of those dimensions that express the continuity between one's construal of one's past position and one's future aspirations in relation to class (for example, from a working-class background with no aspirations beyond the working class, or upwardly mobile with aspirations towards the managerial class, or downwardly mobile with aspirations away from the upper classes).

Such an approach to the concept of identity, which builds upon contributions from Erikson's psychodynamic approach and Kelly's personal construct psychology, is congruent with developments within the symbolic interactionist perspective of concepts associated with a range of identities (gender identities, role identities, institutional identities, etc.).

(See the recent review by Weigert (1983).) It does so, however, without making these 'identities' divorced from one another. They are parts of the totality.

This approach cautions against the tendency to reify a particular aspect of identity, because of the evident lack of a fixed sameness of that aspect from person to person and from one category of people to another. For example, the meaning and experience of *ethnic identity* will vary from one ethnic group to another. In addition, it is apparent that it becomes an empirical question to find out the relative importance of the various aspects of identity to the totality. Any one aspect of identity may dominate in particular circumstances.

The conceptual definitions of ISA are operationalised in such a way that both idiographic studies of individuals and nomothetic ones of groups or categories of people are possible simultaneously. The way in which this may be done is given in detail in a manual (Weinreich, 1980) which also contains in an appendix a semi-structured interview schedule that can be adapted for use with different ethnic groups. In brief, the procedures require first the elicitation from the individual of the personal bipolar constructs (for example: 'feels safe enough' – 'feels threatened and intimidated') used to construe self and others, and also the particular entities (individuals, groups, institutions, etc.) of significance to self. The entities and constructs collected together form an identity instrument, whereby the individual systematically construes each entity and component of self using centre–zero rating scales for each construct. The results of the systematic construal of self and others is analysed with the aid of the IDEX (identity exploration) computer program (Weinreich *et al.*, 1981). This computes quantitative estimates of the parameters of identity structure, as defined in the ISA conceptualisation and given in Appendix A. These are based upon the individual's own value system, the degree of consistency of which is given in terms of the 'structural pressure' estimate for each bipolar construct.

In the idiographic mode, in-depth case studies of a clinical kind may be adopted in order to investigate the detailed socio-psychological processes involved in such phenomena as cross-ethnic identification and skin-colour rejection. Paradoxically, this psychological state in a black adolescent appears to be a consequence of growing up in a society that has benevolent as well as discriminatory characteristics, in which some respected white people show concern and proffer practical help, which is, however, experienced against a backdrop of racial abuse. In resolving his conflicted identifications with certain blacks and increasing his overall self-evaluation, he increases his identification with admired whites, a process that results in him rejecting his skin-colour (Weinreich, 1979a).

The outcome resembles that of the colonial black identifying with white culture as described by Fanon in *Black Skin, White Masks* (1967).

For group investigations, when sufficient commonality of experience may be assumed, preliminary work with a pilot sample provides the basis for a standard instrument of common bipolar constructs and entities. Analysis of each respondent's ratings using the standard instrument is carried out by the IDEX computer program, after which the estimated parameters of identity structure are collated across criterion groups (based, for example, on ethnicity and gender).

In this nomothetic mode of analysis, 'normalisation' procedures, computed internally to each respondent, enable comparisons of indices of identity to be made across groups. Comparative studies in ethnicity using ISA have addressed such issues as the outcome of dual socialisation (Weinreich, 1979b), the contribution of people's identifications within and across ethnic boundaries to processes of redefinition of ethnic identity (Weinreich, 1983a), and the reciprocal nature of one ethnic group's conflicts in identification with another, when both are locked in sectarian conflict (Weinreich, 1983c). ISA, given that it anchors the value system for each person, enables comparisons to be made of indices of identity structure between people irrespective of language or dialect.

Application of ISA to Belfast sectarianism

As an example of the use of the ISA theoretical framework, the following set of theoretical propositions, grounded in empirical data from 160 Belfast adolescents, constitute a theory to explain the *ongoing* socio-psychological processes that sustain the sectarian conflict in Belfast (Weinreich, 1983c). The data were collected using a standard identity instrument constructed for use with the Belfast adolescents following preliminary work with a pilot sample. Indices of identity (those given here in Appendix A) for each individual were computed and then collated within categories designated by criteria of ethnicity, gender and school achievement. The resultant propositions are given here in brief outline only, without further explication and without the data upon which they are based.

(1) National allegiance (being *Irish* or *British*) and religious affiliation (being *Catholic* or *Protestant*) on either side of the psychological divide in Ulster generally combine as emotionally charged dimensions of identity.

Psychologically, these dimensions together represent two nations or two ethnic identities, the Catholic-Irish 'nation' and the Protestant-British 'nation' in Ulster.

(2) National allegiance and religious affiliation are considerably more dominant as core *evaluative* dimensions of identity than are other important cognitive ones such as gender.

(3) Members of the one ethnic group have salient conflicts in identification with the other group.

It is postulated that the attempted resolution of these identification conflicts with the other group provides the continuing psychological impetus to and the socio-psychological processes sustaining the sectarian conflict.

(4) The psychological dynamics related to these salient identification conflicts are generally reciprocally common to members of both ethnic groups.

This means that the two Ulster identities do not stand apart, but are interdependent. Therefore, the *Protestant-British* one is distinct from a British identity in *Britain*, and the *Catholic-Irish* one is distinct from an *Irish* identity in the Republic of Ireland.

(5) The one identity, while being interdependent with the other, is at the same time *threatening* to the existence of the other.

(6) However, the threats to the one identity by the other do not undermine its rationale, or thereby give rise to self-doubt among its adherents, but instead the pervasive certainties of the two identities are generally accompanied by high self-esteem.

(7) The societal pathology of sectarianism is generally not a result of individual psychopathology.

(8) Individuals in whom 'nationality' and 'religion' do not combine to form core evaluative dimensions of identity and who deviate from the norm are characterised by special circumstances (such as early childhood outside Ulster), or by emphatic decisions on their part to pursue doctrines contradistinctive to those prevailing in their ethnic group.

Full details of the data upon which these propositions are based and of the implications of these socio-psychological processes for constraints on possible political solutions to the constitutional crisis in Northern Ireland are given in a paper presented to the meeting of the International Society for Political Psychology held in Oxford in July 1983 (Weinreich, 1983c). An important caveat to these propositions is that they hold most strongly for adolescent Protestant boys and girls, whether they are achievers or non-achievers, and also for their achieving Catholic counterparts, but noticeably less so for Catholic non-achievers. While ethnicity is generally emphatically a dominant evaluative criterion for Catholic achievers, who are successful within the ethos set by the Catholic schools, it is not so to the same extent for Catholic non-achievers.

An important general finding which is emerging from the empirical work in which ISA is applied to a variety of settings is that people's early identifications have a powerful impact on the development of their identities. Their subsequent attempts to re-synthesise their part-identifications with significant others (Erikson, 1959, 1968) necessarily follow from their earlier identifications with people with whom they have been highly ego-involved. People's ego-involvement with such others remains high, though generally with them as symbolic reconstructions rather than as the initial identifications. In terms of ethnicity, therefore, the earlier identifications of young children in the home, at school and in the wider community have a thoroughgoing impact on the development of their identities.

If people's ethnicity is coterminous with a nation-state, then that ethnicity, when it becomes reactive to special circumstances and thereby becomes salient (Weinreich, 1983a), will be experienced as something akin to 'nationalism'. The taken-for-granted 'ethnicity' of the superordinate community will become consciously activated in people's minds in such terms as their 'way of life', a way of life grounded in their earliest identifications, attenuated as these may be later on. Processes of identification occur when there are considerable power differentials between ego and alter and when such processes afford some comfort or relief from anxiety. They involve much emotional investment. People who otherwise may not be especially articulate will speak out strongly concerning what they feel to be their way of life. Likewise, in subordinate ethnic groups, differing ways of life may be similarly asserted, even though in practice these will be undergoing active redefinition as actors attempt to resolve their conflicted identifications resulting from the special circumstances of their dual socialisation. In so far as major differences in lifestyles according to ethnic group membership remain (as between groups espousing Islam and Christianity), so will people wish to live out their different ethnic identities and assert them publicly on occasion. They will defend them if they feel that they are being threatened, though, as we have argued, the experience of threat and the reactions to it will depend on such factors as prior vulnerabilities in identity.

Theory building using ISA

Issues of the nature of theory building using the ISA operationalisation of identity theory, together with questions of its validity, will now be briefly reviewed. Within the ISA meta-theoretical framework, distinctions are drawn between three features of theorising: theoretical *assumptions*, theoretical *process postulates*, and *empirically derived* theoretical *propositions*.

Certain theoretical assumptions of ISA are given in detail elsewhere (Weinreich, 1983b). They provide the general context for the concerns of ISA, which are expressed in the definitions of the basic concepts given in Appendix A. Theoretical process postulates are statements about socio-psychological processes, such as people attempting to resolve conflicted identifications with others, or forming new identifications with others. Two such are (Weinreich, 1983a):

Postulate 1, concerning the resolution of conflicted identifications
When one's identifications with others are conflicted, one attempts to resolve the conflicts, thereby inducing re-evaluations of self in relation to the others within the limitations of one's currently existing value system.

Postulate 2, concerning the formation of new identifications
When one forms further identifications with newly encountered individuals, one broadens one's value system and establishes a new context for one's self-definition, thereby initiating a reappraisal of self and others which is dependent on fundamental changes in one's value system.

Empirically derived theoretical propositions are grounded in empirical data (which depend on the application of the theoretical assumptions upon which ISA concepts are based) to which are applied the theoretical process postulates and other considerations. Such propositions derived in the arena of ethnic relations involving adolescents of native white, 'Caribbean' and 'Asian' origins in Bristol are given in another publication (Weinreich, 1983a): they have to do with the following issues – salience of ethnicity in self-concept change, part-identification with dominant cultural values, 'dialogue' of gender roles across ethnic boundaries, variable routes towards ethnic redefinition, new ethnic coherence, and reactive ethnicity in the dominant culture. The propositions concerning these issues are statements of limited applicability to particular populations in particular situations at particular historical periods. Nevertheless, they have generality to the extent that there exist common features from population to population, from situation to situation, and from one historical period to another.

In summary, it is seen that the basic *theoretical assumptions* provide the framework for the unambiguous definitions of concepts, which enable parameters of identity to be operationalised, thereby making it possible to gain empirical estimates of such indices of identity for individuals. Common features of identity across individuals may therefore be ascertained, as can also, of course, deviations from such commonalities. *Theoretical postulates* about processes may then be applied to the resultant empirical generalisations in order to derive further empirically based *theoretical propositions* that are pertinent to the specific circumstances of interest.

The argument behind this sequence of theorising is that this is a fundamentally necessary orientation in the social sciences, given that people (as opposed to the inanimate objects of the natural sciences) have the capacity to create new circumstances, to generate novel ways of defining the world, to invent new technologies and new institutions that alter lifestyles, and radically to attenuate traditional value systems (cf. Hollis, 1977; Harré, 1979).

In other words, unless it could be demonstrated empirically that there is a basic commonality in both the historical and the societal circumstances of two situations, there would be no justification for making assumptions about the total set of socio-psychological processes in which people in these situations are engaged. Thus, the historical and societal circumstances of the Catholic and Protestant identities in Belfast are different from those of the 'Caribbean', 'Asian' and native white identities in Bristol. Hence, although the social realities of ethnic identities feature in both situations, the corresponding socio-psychological processes are quite different. The empirically based theoretical propositions for the one situation predict the general maintenance, with little redefinition, of the 'sectarian' ethnic identities in Belfast. Those for the other situation predict redefinitions of their 'migrant' ethnic identities for the 'Caribbean' and 'Asian' adolescents in Bristol, and also predict different directions between the two groups in their redefinitions.

In so far as historical events might occur that radically alter societal circumstances and radically influence people's value systems, then quite clearly the empirically derived theoretical propositions of one era would give way to a modified set. Even so, the theoretical assumptions and the theoretical process postulates, in so far as they have had useful conceptual and explanatory power, remain as before to be used in deriving the modified propositions pertinent to the new era.

The empirically derived theoretical propositions do not therefore necessarily hold for all time. They provide an explanation for the socio-psychological processes in which persons and groups of people are engaged in the particular societal context and historical era under scrutiny. By the same token, when commonalities can be demonstrated across societal contexts and historical eras, there is every reason to expect them to be represented by the same general theoretical propositions. Thus, in so far as the disturbance of identity in the clinical syndrome of anorexia nervosa is of a particular kind and is the consequence of specified socio-psychological processes in the interaction of the parents, or caretakers, and the anorexic, then the theoretical propositions, initially empirically based, would be expected to hold for anorexics whenever and wherever they might be found (Harris, 1980, 1982; Weinreich, Harris and Doherty, 1984).

The question of the validity of the explanations so given is one that can be tackled in the usual way. Criterion group validity is demonstrated when groups separated according to independent criteria are shown to be differentiated on ISA indices in comprehensible ways. For instance, on ISA indices patients suffering from anorexia and bulimia nervosa are differentiated both from other psychiatric patients and from normal 'controls', while anorexics are further more finely differentiated from bulimics (Weinreich, Harris and Doherty, 1984). Likewise, first-time mothers who suffer from maternity blues are differentiated on other ISA indices from those who do not (Needham, 1984). Such demonstrations of validity also provide support for the basic theoretical assumptions upon which ISA is founded.

Further, the empirically derived theoretical propositions are explicitly stated in such a way that they can in principle be readily refuted (allowing that no *radical* change in societal and historical circumstances has intervened) by disconfirming data, if they are of no substance. They are presented as explanations of the phenomena under scrutiny, until such time as more adequate, or more complete, explanations might be provided.

Conclusion

In conclusion, it needs to be stated why identity theory should be operationalised in the way outlined here. It is apparent that this approach to identity, which uses a meta-theoretical framework, is strategically quite different from the grand theory approach to ethnic and race relations. The purpose of formulating a grand theory is to account for all cases of race and ethnic phenomena as instances of a single universal theory, a recent example being Banton's rational choice theory,[1] which 'formulates principles that govern the development of relations between racial and ethnic groups everywhere' (Banton, 1983). By contrast, the adoption of a meta-theoretical framework would be to deny the possibility of a single universal theory that is all-encompassing. Instead, it would attempt to generate an empirically grounded particular theory within its framework, which would then intercommunicate with other such theories addressed to specific sets of phenomena and sharing common theoretical concepts.

As an example of this strategy, assume an even more extensive theoretical framework than ISA, then take Banton's 'rational choice theory', in which group competition reinforces boundary markers between communities, whereas individual competition dissolves them. This theory would not give quite the appearance of the 'rationality' of people if it were intercommunicating with another theory which, for example, explained why one person should identify primarily with aspirations of individual competition, and another with own ethnic group mores rather than those of another group. The latter theory would be one concerned with identity processes, which are far from rational and depend on early and subsequent identifications. Both theories could be considered to be generated within the extended meta-theoretical framework.

To be sure, with respect to each specific set of phenomena, the aim would be to develop a particular theory that would be universally applicable (such as one stating that individuals from subordinate ethnic communities experiencing dual socialisation tend to develop conflicts in identification with their *own* group). However, this strategy assumes that there will be no one grand theory which will be equivalent to the meta-theoretical framework, a framework that is always, *in principle* open to extension. Instead, it points to the necessity for generating particular empirically based theories for explaining specific sets of phenomena encompassed in the diversity of relationships between peoples of different ethnic groups. This necessity arises from an awareness of changing historical circumstances, such as the continual interplay of cultural and individual aspirations, the changing values and everyday ideologies of people, the development of new institutions and technologies, and the dismantling of old ones, and major historical and social upheavals. Within the realm of the operationalisation of identity theory, ISA is an attempt to provide the beginnings of a wide-ranging meta-theoretical framework.

NOTES

1   Banton's work is clearly masterly, but he would be the first to say that he could not in practice account for all race and ethnic relations phenomena.

APPENDIX A

Definitions of theoretical concepts used in determining parameters or indices of identity development using the IDEX computer program

These definitions are to be found in Weinreich (1980). Since they refer to both males and females, the convention 'one' has been adopted here in preference to that which uses the male pronoun to cover both male and female, and, in the interests of economy of expression, to that which continually uses both the male and female pronouns together. The reference numbers correspond to those used in Weinreich (1980) where, however, the male pronoun featured in the definitions.

3.1 Definition of identity
One's identity is defined as the totality of one's self-construal, in which how one construes oneself in the present expresses the continuity between how one construes oneself as one was in the past and how one construes oneself as one aspires to be in the future.

3.1.1 Ideal self-image (or ego-ideal)
One's ideal self-image is defined as one's construal of 'me as I would like to be'.

3.1.2 Positive values
One's positive values are defined as those personal characteristics and guidelines for behaviour which one aspires to implement for oneself in accordance with one's ideal self-image.

3.1.3 Negative values (or contra-values)
One's negative values are defined as the contrasts of one's positive values, that is, those characteristics and patterns of behaviour from which one would wish to dissociate.

3.1.4 Current self-image
One's current self-image is defined as one's construal of 'me as I am now'.

3.1.5 Past self-image
One's past self-image is defined as one's construal of 'me as I used to be'.

3.2 Positive and negative role models, and positive and negative reference groups
3.2.1 Positive role model (and reference group)
One's positive role model (reference group) is defined as some other person (group) construed as having many of the attributes and values to which one aspires, that is, ones associated with one's ideal self-image.

3.2.2 Negative role model (and reference group)
One's negative role model (reference group) is defined as some other person (group) construed as possessing many of the attributes and contra-values from which one wishes to dissociate, that is, ones aligned with one's contra-value system.

3.3 Identification with another or with a group

A. Empathetic identification
3.3.1 Current identification (perceived similarity)
The extent of one's current identification with another is defined as the degree of similarity between the qualities one attributes to the other, whether 'good' or 'bad', and those of one's current self-image.

3.3.2 Past identification (perceived similarity)
The extent of one's past identification with another is defined as the degree of similarity between the qualities one attributes to the other and those of one's past self-image.

B. Role model identification
3.3.3 Idealistic-identification (positive role model and reference group)
The extent of one's idealistic-identification with another is defined as the degree of similarity between the qualities one attributes to the other and those one would like to possess as part of one's ideal self-image.

3.3.4 Contra-identification (negative role model and reference group)
The extent of one's contra-identification with another is defined as the degree of similarity between the qualities one attributes to the other and those from which one would wish to dissociate.

3.4 Identification conflicts and overall identity diffusion

3.4.1 Identification conflicts with others
In terms of one's current self-image the extent of one's identification conflict with another is defined as a multiplicative function of one's *current* and contra-identification with that other.

A similar definition holds for identification conflicts in terms of one's past self-image. As one's current (past) and contra-identifications with another simultaneously increase, so will one's conflict in identification with that other become greater.

3.4.2 Overall identity diffusion
The degree of one's identity diffusion is defined as the overall dispersion of, and magnitude of, one's identification conflicts with significant others.

This may be assessed in relation both to one's current and to one's past self-images.

3.5 Evaluation of others and self-esteem

3.5.1 Evaluation of another
One's evaluation of another is defined as one's overall assessment of the other in terms of the positive and negative evaluative connotations of the attributes one construes in that other, in accordance with one's value system.

3.5.2 Evaluation of current (past) self
One's evaluation of one's current (past) self is defined as one's overall self-assess-

ment in terms of the positive and negative evaluative connotations of the attributes one construes as making up one's current (past) self-image, in accordance with one's value system.

3.5.3 Self-esteem
One's self-esteem is defined as one's overall self-assessment in evaluative terms of the continuing relationship between one's past and current self-images, in accordance with one's value system.

Used as a single indicant of one's psychological well-being, the self-esteem measure should be regarded as unreliable. For example, one may evaluate one's current self-image more highly than one's past and thereby indicate greater satisfaction with oneself currently compared with before. A lower current than past self-evaluation will reflect diminishing self-satisfaction. While representing quite different psychological states, both may generate the same self-esteem value. In addition, all kinds of different identification patterns and magnitudes of conflicts in identification can accompany a particular self-esteem value. In certain cases, a high level of self-esteem may be associated with a foreclosed identity and a defensive denial of conflicts in identification.

3.6 Ego-involvement with entities
3.6.1 Ego-involvement with another
One's ego-involvement with another is defined as one's overall responsiveness to the other in terms of the extensiveness both in quantity and in strength of the attributes one construes the other as possessing.

3.6.2 Self-involvement
One's ego-involvement in oneself as one aspires to be (or as one is now, or as one was in the past) is defined as one's overall self-responsiveness in terms of the extensiveness both in quantity and in strength of the attributes of one's ideal self-image (or current self-image, or past self-image).

3.7 Ambivalence and ego-ambivalence towards an entity
3.7.1 Ambivalence
One's ambivalence towards an entity (e.g. another person, or a facet of self-concept) when evaluated on balance in positive terms is defined as the ratio of negative to positive attributions, and, conversely, when negatively evaluated as the ratio of positive to negative attributions.

3.7.2 Ego-ambivalence
One's ego-ambivalence towards an entity is defined as the product of one's ambivalence towards it and one's ego-involvement with it (also known as entity dissonance).

3.8 Structural pressure on constructs (consistency or stability of their evaluative connotations)
The structural pressure on one's construct is defined as the overall strength of the excess of compatibilities over incompatibilities between the evaluative connotations of attributions one makes to each entity by way of the one construct and one's overall evaluation of each entity.

3.9 Splitting in construal of entities

The extent of splitting in one's construal of two entities is defined as the ratio of the deficiency in actual overlap possible between their attributed characteristics to the total possible overlap, given the set of constructs one uses to construe them both.

Bibliography

Adam, H. (1972), *Modernizing Racial Domination*, Berkeley: University of California Press.
Adam, H. and Giliomee, H. (1979), *Ethnic Power Mobilized: Can South Africa Change?*, New Haven, Ct.: Yale University Press.
Adorno, T. W., Frenkel-Brunswik, E., Levinson, D. J., Sanford, R. N. (1950), *The Authoritarian Personality*, New York: Harper and Row.
Alexander, J. C. (1980), 'Core Solidarity, Ethnic Outgroup, and Social Differentiation: A Multidimensional Model of Inclusion in Modern Societies', in Jacques Dofney and Akinsola Akiwowo (eds.), *National and Ethnic Movements*, Beverly Hills, Calif.: Sage Publications, 5–28.
 (1981), *Theoretical Logic in Sociology*, Berkeley: University of California Press.
Alexander, Richard (1979), *Darwinism and Human Affairs*, Seattle: University of Washington Press.
Allport, G. W. (1954), *The Nature of Prejudice*, Cambridge, Mass.: Addison Wesley.
Altemeyer, B. (1981), *Right-Wing Authoritarianism*, Winnipeg: University of Manitoba Press.
Amnesty International (1983), *Report, 1983*, London: Amnesty International Publications.
Anderson, B. (1983), *Imagined Communities*, London: Verso.
Anderson, E. (1976), *A Place on the Corner*, Chicago: University of Chicago Press.
Anderson, P. (1983), *In the Tracks of Historical Materialism*, London: Verso.
Aptheker, H. (1946), *The Negro People in America* (Introduction by Doxey Wilkerson), New York: International Publishers.
Arrow, K. J. (1971), *Some Models of Racial Discrimination in the Labor Market*, Santa Monica, Calif.: Rand Corporation.
Arutiunov, S. A. and Bromley, Y. V. (1978), 'Problems of Ethnicity in Soviet Ethnographic Studies' in R. E. Holloman and S. A. Arutiunov (eds.), *Perspectives on Ethnicity*, The Hague: Mouton.
Aschenbrenner, J. (1975), *Lifelines: Black Families in Chicago*, New York: Holt, Rhinehart and Winston.
Backman, C. (1981), 'Attraction in Interpersonal Relations' in Morris Rosen-

berg and Ralph H. Turner (eds.), *Social Psychology: Sociological Perspectives*, New York: Basic Books, 235–68.

Bagley, C. and Verma, G. K. (1979), *Race Prejudice, the Individual and Society*, Farnborough: Saxon House.

Bagley, C., Verma, G. K., Mallick, K., Young, L. (1979), *Personality, Self-Esteem and Prejudice*, Aldershot: Saxon House.

Banks, Arthur S. (1978), *Domestic Conflict Behavior, 1919–1966* (ICPSR 5003), Ann Arbor, Michigan: Inter-University Consortium for Political and Social Research.

Banks, Arthur S. and Overstreet, William (1982), *Political Handbook of the World, 1981*, New York: McGraw-Hill.

Bannister, D. and Mair, J. M. M. (1968), *The Evaluation of Personal Constructs*, London: Academic Press.

Banton, M. (1967), *Race Relations*, London: Tavistock.

(1977), *The Idea of Race*, London: Tavistock.

(1980), 'Ethnic Groups and the Theory of Rational Choice' in *Sociological Theories: Race and Colonialism*, Paris: UNESCO.

(1982), 'Our Own Kith and Kin', *Times Literary Supplement*, January 29: 95–6.

(1983), *Racial and Ethnic Competition*, Cambridge: Cambridge University Press.

Banton, M. and Harwood, J. (1975), *The Race Concept*, Newton Abbot, UK: David and Charles.

Barash, David (1982), *Sociobiology and Behavior*, New York: Elsevier.

Barker, M. (1981), *The New Racism*, London: Junction Books.

Barresa, M. (1979), *Race and Class in the Southwest*, South Bend, Ind.: University of Nôtre Dame Press.

Barth, F. (1963), 'Introduction' in *The Role of the Entrepreneur in Social Change in Northern Norway*, Oslo: Scandinavian University Books.

(1966), *Models of Social Organisation*, Occasional Paper No. 23, London: Royal Anthropological Institute.

(ed.), (1969a), *Ethnic Groups and Boundaries*, Bergen: Universitetsforlaget.

(1969b), 'Introduction' in F. Barth (ed.), *Ethnic Groups and Boundaries*, Bergen: Universitetsforlaget.

(1981), 'Ethnic Groups and Boundaries' in *Process and Forms in Social Life: Selected Essays*, London: Routledge and Kegan Paul.

Bates, R. (1973), *Ethnicity in Contemporary Africa*, East African Studies 14: Syracuse University Press.

Becker, G. S. (1971), *The Economics of Discrimination*, 2nd edn, Chicago: University of Chicago Press.

Ben-Tovim, G. S. (ed.) (1983), *Equal Opportunities and the Employment of Black People and Ethnic Minorities on Merseyside*, Liverpool: Merseyside Association for Racial Equality in Employment.

Ben-Tovim, G. S., Brown, V., Clay, D., Law, I., Loy, L., Torkington, P. (1980), *Racial Disadvantage in Liverpool – An Area Profile*, Liverpool: Merseyside Area Profile Group.

Ben-Tovim, G. *et al.* (1981a), 'Race, Left Strategies and the State' in *Politics and Power 3*, London: Routledge and Kegan Paul.

Ben-Tovim, G. S., Gabriel, J. G., Law, I., Stredder, K. (1981b), 'The Equal Opportunity Campaign in Liverpool' in J. Cheetham *et al.* (eds.), *Social and Community Work in a Multi-Racial Society*, New York: Harper and Row.

Ben-Tovim, G. S., Gabriel, J. G., Law, I., Stredder, K. (1982a), *'Race Politics and Campaign Activity – A Comparative Study in Liverpool and Wolverhampton'* in G. Craig *et al.* (eds.), *Community Work and the State*, London: Routledge and Kegan Paul.

Ben-Tovim, G. S., Gabriel, J. G., Law, I., Stredder, K. (1982b), 'A Political Analysis of Race in the 1980s' in C. Husband (ed.), *'Race' in Britain*, London: Hutchinson.

Berger, J., Rosenholtz, S. J. and Zelditch, M. Jnr (1980), 'Status Organizing Processes', *Annual Review of Sociology*, 6: 479–508.

Berger, P. (1979), *Facing Up to Modernity*, Harmondsworth: Penguin.

Berger, P. and Luckmann, T. (1967), *The Social Construction of Reality*, Harmondsworth: Allen Lane, The Penguin Press.

Black Linx (1984), Merseyside Community Relations Council Newsletter (December 1984).

Blauner, R. (1969), 'Internal Colonialism and Ghetto Revolt', *Social Problems* 16, Spring: 393–408.

(1972), *Racial Oppression in America*, New York: Harper and Row.

Blumer, H. (1933), *Movies and Conduct*, New York: Macmillan.

(1948), 'Sociological Theory in Industrial Relations', *American Sociological Review*, 12: 271–8.

(1951), 'Paternalism in Industry' in *Social Process in Hawaii*, 15: 26–52.

(1954), 'What is Wrong with Social Theory?', *American Sociological Review*, 19: 3–10.

(1958), 'Race Prejudice as a Sense of Group Position', *Pacific Sociological Review*, 1: 3–7.

(1959), 'Collective Behaviour' in Joseph B. Gittler (ed.), *Review of Sociology: Analysis of a Decade*, New York: John Wiley.

(1965a), 'The Future of the Color Line', in J. C. McKinney and E. Thompson (eds.), *The South in Continuity and Change*, Durham, NC: Duke University Press.

(1965b), 'Industrialisation and Race Relations' in Guy Hunter (ed.), *Industrialisation and Race Relations*, London: Oxford University Press.

(1966), 'United States of America' in *Research on Racial Relations*, Amsterdam: UNESCO, 87–133.

(1968), 'Fashion' in *International Encyclopaedia of Social Sciences* V, New York: Macmillan.

(1969), 'The Methodological Position of Symbolic Interactionism' in *Symbolic Interactionism, Perspective and Method*, Englewood Cliffs, NJ: Prentice Hall.

(1978), 'Social Unrest and Collective Protest' in N. Denzin (ed.), *Studies in Symbolic Interaction*, Greenwich, Ct.: Jai Press.

Blumer, H. and Duster, T. (1980), 'Theories of Race and Social Action' in *Sociological Theories: Race and Colonialism*, Paris: UNESCO.

Boal, F. W. and Douglas, J. N. H. (eds.) (1982), *Integration and Division: Geographical Perspectives on the Northern Ireland Problem*, London: Academic Press.

Boissevain, J. (1974), *Friends for Friends: Networks, Manipulators and Coalitions*, London: Basil Blackwell.

Bonacich, E. (1972), 'A Theory of Ethnic Antagonism: The Split Labor Market', *American Sociological Review*, 37: 547–59.

(1976), 'Advanced Capitalism and Black/White Relations in the United States:

A Split Labor Market Interpretation', *American Sociological Review*, 41: 34–51.

(1980), 'Class Approaches to Ethnicity and Race', *Insurgent Sociologist*, 10, 2: 9–23.

(1981a), 'Capitalism and Race Relations in South Africa: A Split Labour Market Analysis', *Political Power and Social Theory*, 2: 239–77.

(1981b), 'Reply to Burawoy', *Political Power and Social Theory*, 2: 337–43.

Bourne, J. with Sivanandan, A. (1980), 'Cheerleaders and Ombudsmen: The Sociology of Race Relations in Britain', *Race and Class*, 21, 4: 331–52.

Breuilly, J. (1982), *Nationalism and the State*, Manchester: Manchester University Press.

Brewer, M. B. and Campbell, D. T. (1976), *Ethnocentrism and Intergroup Attitudes: East African Evidence*, Beverly Hills, Calif.: Sage.

Brittan, A. (1973), *Meanings and Situations*, London: Routledge and Kegan Paul.

Brittan, A. and Maynard, M. (1984), *Sexism, Racism and Oppression*, Oxford: Basil Blackwell.

Bromley, Y. V. (1979), 'Towards a Typology of Ethnic Processes', *British Journal of Sociology*, 30, 3: 341–8.

Bromley, Y. V. (ed.) (1974), *Soviet Ethnology and Anthropology Today*, The Hague: Mouton.

Brooks, D. and Singh, K. (1979), 'Pivots and Presents' in S. Wallman (ed.), *Ethnicity at Work*, London: Macmillan.

Brotz, H. (1983), 'Radical Sociology and the Study of Race Relations', *New Community*, 10, 3: 508–12.

Buchanan, Susan Huelsebusch (1983), 'The Cultural Meaning of Social Class for Haitians in New York City', *Ethnic Groups*, 5, July: 7–29.

Burawoy, M. (1981), 'The Capitalist State in South Africa: Marxist and Sociological Perspectives on Race and Class', *Political Power and Social Theory*, 2; 279–335.

(1985), *The Politics of Production*, London: Verso.

Burawoy, M. and Skocpol, T. (eds.) (1983), *Marxist Enquiries: Studies of Labour, Class and States*, Chicago: University of Chicago Press.

Burbidge, M. (ed.) (1981), *Department of the Environment Priority Estates Project: Improving Problem Council Estates*, London: HMSO.

Cain, Glen G. (1976), 'The Challenges of Segmented Labour Market Theories to Orthodox Theory: A Survey', *Journal of Economic Literature*, 14, Dec.: 1215–57.

Carchedi, G. (1979), 'Authority and Foreign Labour: Some Notes on a Late Capitalist Form of Capitalist Accumulation and State Intervention', *Studies in Political Economy*, 2; 37–74.

Carmichael, S. and Hamilton, C. (1967), *Black Power*, New York: Vintage Books

Cashmore, E. E. and Troyna, B. (1983), *Introduction to Race Relations*, London: Routledge and Kegan Paul.

Castells, M. (1975), 'Immigrant Workers and Class Struggles in Advanced Capitalism: The Western European Experience', *Politics and Society*, 5, 1: 33–66.

Castles, S. and Kosack, G. (1973), *Immigrant Workers and Class Structure in Western Europe*, London: Oxford University Press.

Cayton, H. (1965), *Long, Old Road*, New York: Trident Press.

Cayton, H. and Drake, St. C. (1946), *Black Metropolis*, London: Jonathan Cape.

Centre for Contemporary Cultural Studies (1982), *The Empire Strikes Back: Race and Racism in 70s Britain*, London: Hutchinson.

Chagnon, N. and Irons, W. (eds.) (1979), *Evolutionary Biology and Human Social Behavior*, North Scituate, Mass.: Duxbury.

Chicago Commission on Race Relations (1922), *Negro in Chicago*, Chicago: University of Chicago Press.

Choice (1981), Review of *The Ethnic Phenomenon*, September.

Clark, K. B. (1965), *Dark Ghetto: Dilemmas of Social Power*, New York: Harper and Row.

Clemente, F. and Sauer, W. J. (1976), 'Racial Differences in Life Satisfaction', *Journal of Black Studies*, 7, Sept.: 3–11.

Cohen, Abner (1974a), 'Introduction' in Abner Cohen (ed.), *Urban Ethnicity*, ASA Monograph No. 12, London: Tavistock.

(1974b), 'Ethnic Groups as Interest Groups', in Abner Cohen (ed.), *Urban Ethnicity*, ASA Monograph No. 12, London: Tavistock.

(1974c), *Two-Dimensional Man*, Berkeley: University of California Press.

(1981), *The Politics of Elite Culture*, Berkeley: University of California Press.

Cohen, Anthony P. (1978), 'The Same – But Different: The Allocation of Identity in Whalsay, Shetland', *Sociological Review*, 26, 3: 449–69.

(1982), *Belonging*, Manchester: Manchester University Press.

Cohen, C. (1983) 'Affirmative Action and the Rights of the Majority' in C. Fried (ed.), *Minorities, Community and Identity* Dahlem Workshop Reports, No. 27, Berlin, Heidelberg, NY: Springer Verlag.

Cohen, E. G. and Roper, Susan S. (1972), 'Modification of Interracial Interaction Disability: An Application of Status Characteristic Theory', *American Sociological Review*, 37, Dec.: 643–57.

Cohen, P. S. (1972), 'Need There Be a Sociology of Race Relations?', *Sociology*, 6, 1: 101–8.

Cohen, R. (1978), 'Ethnicity: Problem and Focus in Anthropology', *Annual Review of Anthropology*, 7: 379–403.

Cohen, Yehudi (1969), 'Social Boundary Systems', *Current Anthropology*, 10.

Columbia University Forum (1967), 10, 1, Spring.

Commission for Racial Equality (1984), *Race and Housing in Liverpool – A Research Report*, London: CRE.

Connolly, W. E. (1981), *Appearance and Reality in Politics*, Cambridge: Cambridge University Press.

Connor, W. D. (1979), *Socialism, Politics and Equality*, New York: Columbia University Press.

Conzen, K. N. (1979), 'Immigrants, Immigrant Neighborhoods and Ethnic Identity: Historical Issues', *Journals of American History*, 66, 3: 603–15.

Cooley, C. H. (1909), *Social Organization*, New York: Scribner's.

Cottrell, A. (1984), *Social Class in Marxist Theory*, London: Routledge and Kegan Paul.

Cox, O. C. (1948), *Caste, Class and Race*, New York: Monthly Review Press.

(1976), *Race Relations: Elements and Social Dynamics*, Detroit: Wayne State University Press.

Cross, M. (1978), 'Colonialism and Ethnicity: A Theory and Comparative Case Study', *Ethnic and Racial Studies*, 1, 1: 37–59.
Cruse, H. (1967), *The Crisis of the Negro Intellectual*, New York: Morrow.
Cutler, A. *et al.* (1977–8), *Marx's Capital and Capitalism Today*, 2 vols., London: Routledge and Kegan Paul.
Davidson, B. (ed.) (1983), *Africa South of the Sahara*, London: Europa Publications.
Davies, R. (1979), *Capital, State and White Labour in South Africa 1900–1960*, Brighton: Harvester Press.
Dawkins, R. (1976), *The Selfish Gene*, Oxford: Oxford University Press.
(1982), *The Extended Phenotype*, Oxford: Oxford University Press.
Decalo, S. (1976), *Coups and Army Rule in Africa: Studies in Military Style*, New Haven, Ct.: Yale University Press.
Department of the Environment (1978), *Policy for the Inner Cities*, Cmnd. 6845, London: HMSO.
DeVos, G. and Romanucci-Ross, L. (eds.) (1975), *Ethnic Identity*, Palo Alto, Calif.: Mayfield Publishing Company.
Dhooge, Y. (1981), *Ethnic Difference and Industrial Conflicts*, Working Paper No. 13, Birmingham: SSRC Research Unit on Ethnic Relations.
Dobzhansky, T. (1962), *Mankind Evolving*, New Haven, Ct.: Yale University Press.
Doherty, J. (1982), 'A Comparison of the Self-Concept of Married Women Engaged in Sex-Role Stereotyped Occupations', Final Year Student Project: School of Psychology, Ulster Polytechnic.
Doyle, B. (1937), *The Etiquette of Race Relations in the South*, Chicago: University of Chicago Press.
Driedger, L. (1984), 'Review of *The Ethnic Phenomenon*', *The Canadian Journal of Sociology*, 9, 1: 120–2.
Driedger, L. and Clifton, R. A. (1984), 'Ethnic Stereotypes: Images of Ethnocentrism, Reciprocity or Dissimilarity?', *Canadian Review of Sociology and Anthropology*, 21, 3: 288–301.
Driver, G. (1979), 'Classroom Stress and School Achievement: West Indian Adolescents and Their Teachers' in V. Saifullah Khan (ed.), *Minority Families: Support and Stress*, London: Macmillan.
Duffield, M. (1982), 'The Theory of Underdevelopment and the Underdevelopment of Theory: The Pertinence of Recent Debates to the Question of Post-Colonial Immigration to Britain', Working Paper 15, Birmingham, RUER: SSRC Research Unit on Ethnic Relations.
Dumont, L. (1970), *Homo Hierarchicus*, London: Weidenfeld and Nicolson.
Durkheim, E. (1964), *The Division of Labour in Society*, New York: Free Press.
Edgley, R. (1983), 'Philosophy' in David McLellan (ed.), *Marx: The First Hundred Years*, London: Fontana, 239–302.
Edwards, J. and Batley, R. (1978), *The Politics of Positive Discrimination*, London: Tavistock.
Ehrlich, H. J. (1973), *The Social Psychology of Prejudice*, New York, John Wiley and Sons.
Eidheim, H. (1969), 'When Ethnic Identity is a Social Stigma' in F. Barth (ed.), *Ethnic Groups and Boundaries*, Bergen: Universitetsforlaget.
Elster, J. (1983), *Explaining Technical Change*, Cambridge: Cambridge University Press.

Endelman, Judith R. (1981), 'Review of *The Ethnic Phenomenon*', *Library Journal*, September 1: 1643.
Enloe, C. (1978), 'Ethnicity, Bureaucracy and State-Building in Africa and Latin America', *Ethnic and Racial Studies*, 1, 3, July: 336–51.
—— (1981), 'The Growth of the State and Ethnic Mobilisation: The American Experience', *Ethnic and Racial Studies*, 4, 2, April: 123–36.
Epstein, A. L. (1978), *Ethos and Identity: Three Studies in Ethnicity*, London: Tavistock.
Erikson, E. H. (1959), 'The Problem of Ego Identity', *Psychological Issues*, 1: 101–64.
—— (1968), *Identity, Youth and Crisis*, New York: Norton.
Ervin-Tripp, S. M. (1964), 'Language and TAT Content in Bilinguals', *Journal of Abnormal and Social Psychology*, 68: 500–7.
Europa Publications (1983), *Europa Yearbook of the World, 1983*, 2 vols., London: Europa Publications.
Evans-Pritchard, E. E. (1940), *The Nuer*, Oxford: Clarendon Press.
Fanon, F. (1967), *Black Skin, White Masks*, New York: Grove Press.
Feagin, J. R. (1981), 'Review of *The Ethnic Phenomenon*', *Contemporary Sociology*, 10: 835–6.
Feuchtwang, S. (1982), 'Occupational Ghettos', *Economy and Society*, 11, 3: 251–91.
Firth, R. (1958), *Human Types: An Introduction to Social Anthropology*, New York: Mentor Books.
—— (1961), *Elements of Social Organisation*, 3rd edn, London: Watts.
—— (1964), *Essays on Social Organisation and Values*, LSE Monograph in Social Anthropology, No. 28, London: Athlone.
Fisher, B. and Strauss, A. (1978), 'Interactionism' in *A History of Sociological Analysis*, London: Heinemann.
Forsythe, D. (1979), 'Race Relations from Liberal, Black and Marxist Perspectives', *Research in Race and Ethnic Relations*, 1: 65–85.
Fox-Genovese, E. and Genovese, E. D. (1983), *Fruits of Merchant Capital*, Oxford: Oxford University Press.
Francis, E. K. (1976), *Interethnic Relations*, New York: Elsevier.
Fransella, F. and Bannister, D. (1977), *A Manual for Repertory Grid Technique*, London: Academic Press.
Frazier, E. F. (1932), *The Negro Family in Chicago*, Chicago, University of Chicago Press.
Freedman, C. (1983–4), 'Overdeterminations: On Black Marxism in Britain', *Social Text*, 8: 142–50.
Freedman, M. (1955), 'Jews in the Society of Britain' in M. Freedman (ed.), *A Minority in Britain*, London: Vallentine Mitchell.
Freund, J. (1968), *The Sociology of Max Weber*, London: Allen Lane, The Penguin Press.
Frye, H. (1980), *Black Parties and Political Power: A Case Study*, Boston: G. K. Hall.
Furnivall, J. S. (1939), *Netherlands India – A Study of Plural Economy*, Cambridge: Cambridge University Press.
—— (1948), *Colonial Policy and Practice*, Cambridge: Cambridge University Press.
Gabriel, J. and Ben-Tovim, G. (1978), 'Marxism and the Concept of Racism', *Economy and Society*, 7, 2: 118–54.

(1979), 'The Conceptualisation of Race Relations in Sociological Theory', *Ethnic and Racial Studies*, 2, 2: 190–212.

Gabriel, J. G. and Stredder, K. (1981), 'Multi Racial Education in Wolverhampton – The Case for Reform', unpublished paper.

(1982), 'The Youth Service and Provision for Racial Minorities – The Case of ILEA', unpublished paper.

Galaty, J. G. (1982), 'Being "Massai"; Being "People-of-Cattle"': Ethnic Shifters in East Africa', *American Ethnologist*, 9, Feb.: 1–20.

Gambino, R. (1975), *Blood of My Blood: The Dilemma of the Italian-Americans*, New York: Doubleday.

Gans, H. J. (1979), 'Symbolic Ethnicity: The Future of Ethnic Groups and Cultures in America', *Ethnic and Racial Studies*, 2, Jan.: 1–20.

Geertz, Clifford (1963a), 'The Integrative Revolution: Primordial Sentiments and Civil Politics in the New States' in Clifford Geertz (ed.), *Old Societies and New States*, New York: Free Press.

(1973), *The Interpretation of Cultures*, New York: Basic Books.

(1975), *The Interpretation of Cultures*, London: Hutchinson.

Geertz, Clifford (ed.) (1963b), *Old Societies and New States*, New York: Free Press.

Gellner, Ernest (1977), 'Positivism Against Hegelianism', unpublished lecture, University of Bristol; now published in E. Gellner, *Relativism and the Social Sciences*, Cambridge: Cambridge University Press (1985), 4–67.

(1973), 'Concepts and Society' in I.C. Jarvie and J. Agassi (eds.), *Cause and Meaning in the Social Sciences*, London: Routledge and Kegan Paul.

(1983), *Nations and Nationalism*, Oxford: Basil Blackwell.

Gellner, E. (ed.) (1980), *Soviet and Western Anthropology*, London: Duckworth.

Genovese, E. (1971), *In Red and Black*, New York: Vintage.

(1975), *Roll Jordan Roll*, London: André Deutsch.

Gilroy, P. (1982), 'Steppin' Out of Babylon – Race, Class and Autonomy' in Centre for Contemporary Cultural Studies, *The Empire Strikes Back: Race and Racism in 70s Britain*, London: Hutchinson.

Ginsberg, Morris (1963), 'Facts and Values', *Advancement of Science*, 19, 81: 407–20.

Gintis, H. and Bowles, S. (1981), 'Structure and Practice in the Labour Theory of Value', *Review of Radical Political Economics*, 12, 4: 1–26.

Glaser, B. and Strauss, A. (1967), *The Discovery of Grounded Theory*, Chicago: Aldine.

Glazer, N. (1971), 'Blacks and Ethnic Groups: The Difference, and the Political Difference it Makes', *Social Problems*, 18, Spring: 444–61.

(1975), *Affirmative Discrimination*, New York: Basic Books.

(1983), *Ethnic Dilemmas, 1964–1982*, Cambridge, Mass.: Harvard University Press.

Glazer, N. and Moynihan, D. P. (1963), *Beyond the Melting Pot*, Cambridge, Mass.: MIT Press.

(1975), *Ethnicity: Theory and Experience*, Cambridge, Mass.: Harvard University Press.

Glickman, M. (1972), 'The Nuer and the Dinka: A Further Note', *Man*, NS 7: 586–94.

Gluckman, M. (1956), *Custom and Conflict in Africa*, Oxford: Basil Blackwell.

(1963), 'Bonds Within the Colour Bar', in *Custom and Conflict in Africa*, Oxford: Basil Blackwell.

(1965), *Politics, Law and Ritual in Tribal Society*, Oxford: Basil Blackwell.

Goffman, E. (1959), *The Presentation of Self in Everyday Life*, Garden City, NY: Anchor Books, Doubleday.

Gordon, Milton M. (1981), 'Models of Pluralism: the New American Dilemma', *Annals of the American Academy of Political and Social Science*, vol. 454, March: 178–88.

Gosnell, H. (1935), *Negro Politicians*, Chicago: University of Chicago Press.

Gouldner, A. (1970), *The Coming Crisis in Western Sociology*, New York: Basic Books.

Graburn, N. (1971), 'Introduction' in *Readings in Kinship and Social Structures*, New York: Harper and Row.

Granovetter, M. S. (1974), *Getting a Job: A Study of Contracts and Careers*, Cambridge, Mass.: Harvard University Press.

Green, A. D. (1979), *On the Political Economy of Black Labour and the Racial Structuring of the Working Class in England*, Stencilled Paper No. 62: Birmingham, Centre for Contemporary Cultural Studies.

Hall, P. (1964), *The Industries of London*, London: Hutchinson.

Hall, S. (1977), 'The "Political" and the "Economic" in Marx's Theory' in A. Hunt (ed.), *Class and Class Structure*, London: Lawrence and Wishart.

(1979a), 'Structures in Dominance' in UNESCO, *Race in Sociological Theory*, Paris: UNESCO.

(1979b), 'Pluralism, Race and Class in Caribbean Society' in UNESCO, *Race and Class in Post-Colonial Society*, Paris: UNESCO.

(1980a), 'Racism and Reaction', in Commission for Racial Equality, *Five Views of Multi-Racial Britain*, London: CRE.

(1980b), 'Race, Articulation and Societies Structured in Dominance' in UNESCO, *Sociological Theories: Race and Colonialism*, Paris: UNESCO.

Hall, S. et al. (1978), *Policing the Crisis: Mugging, the State and Law and Order*, London: Macmillan.

Hall, S. et al. (eds.), (1980), *Culture, Media and Language*, London: Hutchinson.

Hamilton, David L. (ed.) (1981), *Cognitive Processes in Stereotyping and Inter-group Behaviour*, Hillsdale, NJ: Lawrence Erlbaum Associates.

Hannerz, U. (1969), *Soulside: Inquiries into Ghetto Culture and Community*, New York: Columbia University Press.

(1980), *Exploring the City*, New York: Columbia University Press.

Hardin, R. (1982), *Collective Action*, Baltimore: Johns Hopkins University Press (for Resources for the Future).

Harré, R. (1979), *Social Being: A Theory for Social Psychology*, Oxford: Basil Blackwell.

Harris, P. D. G. (1980), 'Identity Development in Female Patients Suffering from Anorexia Nervosa and Bulimia Nervosa: An Application of Weinreich's Identity Structure Analysis', M.Psychol. Thesis: University of Liverpool.

(1982), 'Identity Development in Female Anorectic Patients', *10th International Congress of the International Association for Child and Adolescent Psychiatry and Allied Professions*: Trinity College, Dublin.

Hauser, S. T. (1971), *Black and White Identity Formation*, New York: Wiley.

(1972), 'Black and White Identity Development: Aspects and Perspectives', *Journal of Youth and Adolescence*, 1: 113–30.

Heath, A. (1976), *Rational Choice and Social Exchange*, Cambridge: Cambridge University Press.

Hechter, M. (1975), *Internal Colonialism: The Celtic Fringe in British National Development, 1536–1966*, Berkeley: University of California Press.
(1978), 'Group Formation and the Cultural Division of Labour', *American Journal of Sociology*, 84, 2: 293–318.
(1984), 'When Actors Comply: Monitoring Costs and the Production of Social Order', *Acta Sociologica*, 27, 3: 161–83.
(forthcoming), *Principles of Group Solidarity*, Berkeley and London: University of California Press.
Hechter, M. (ed.) (1983), *The Micro Foundations of Macro Sociology*, Philadelphia: Temple University Press.
Hechter, M. and Friedman, D. (1984), 'Does Rational Choice Suffice: Response to Adam', *International Migration Review*.
Hechter, M., Friedman, D. and Appelbaum, M. (1982), 'A Theory of Ethnic Collective Action', *International Migration Review*, 16: 412–34.
Hegel, G. W. F. (1812–16), *Logic*, trans. W. H. Johnston and L. G. Struthers, quoted from *The Philosophy of Hegel*, ed. Carl J. Friedrich, New York: Random House.
(1830), *Hegel's Logic*, trans. W. Wallace, Oxford: Clarendon Press (1975).
Herbstein, J. (1983), 'The Politicization of Puerto Rican Ethnicity in New York: 1955–1975', *Ethnic Groups*, 5, July: 31–54.
Hindess, B. (1984), 'Rational Choice Theory and the Analysis of Political Action', *Economy and Society*, 13, 3: 255–77.
Hirschman, A. O. (1982), *Shifting Involvements: Private Interest and Public Action*, Princeton: Princeton University Press.
Hirschman, C. (1983), 'America's Melting Pot Reconsidered', *Annual Review of Sociology*, 9: 397–423.
Hirschleifer, J. (1977), 'Economics from a Biological Viewpoint', *Journal of Law and Economics*, 20, 1: 1–52.
Hollis, M. (1977), *Models of Man*, Cambridge: Cambridge University Press.
Holloman, R. E. and Arutiunov, S. S. (eds.) (1978), *Perspectives on Ethnicity*, The Hague: Mouton.
Holy, L. and Stuchlik, M. (1983), *Actions, Norms and Representations*, Cambridge: Cambridge University Press.
Hostetler, J. A. (1963), *Amish Society*, Baltimore: Johns Hopkins University Press.
Hughes, E. C. (1931), *The Chicago Real Estate Board*, Chicago: University of Chicago Press.
(1971), *The Sociological Eye: Selected Papers*, Chicago: Aldine.
ICES (International Centre for Ethnic Studies) (1982), Circulation Under Covering Letter from the Chairman, Prof. K. M. De Silva, 16 November 1982.
International Bank of Reconstruction and Development (1981), *World Development Report 1981*, Washington DC: IBRD.
Jackman, Mary R. (1981), 'Education and Policy Commitment to Racial Education', *American Journal of Political Science*, 25, May: 256–69.
Jackman, Mary R. and Senter, Mary S. (1980), 'Images of Social Groups: Categorical or Qualified?', *Public Opinion Quarterly*, 44, Fall: 341–61.
Jackson, P. and Peach, C. (1981), *Social Interaction and Ethnic Segregation*, London: Academic Press.
Jackson, P. and Smith, S. (1981), *Social Interaction and Ethnic Segregation*, London: Academic Press.

Jahoda, M. (1982), *Employment and Unemployment*, Cambridge: Cambridge University Press.

James, W. (1892), *Psychology*, New York: Henry Holt.

Janowitz, M. (1952), *The Community Press in an Urban Setting*, Chicago: University of Chicago Press.

(1966), 'Introduction' in *W. I. Thomas on Social Organisation and Social Personality*, Chicago: University of Chicago Press.

Jeffcoate, R. (1984), 'Ideologies and Multi-Cultural Education', in M. Craft (ed.), *Education and Cultural Pluralism*, Lewes: Falmer Press.

Jenkins, R. (1983), 'Review of *The Ethnic Phenomenon*', *Man*, 18: 430.

Jessop, B. (1982), *The Capitalist State*, Oxford: Martin Robertson.

(1983), 'Accumulation Strategies, State Forms and Hegemonic Projects', *Kapitalistate*, 10: 89–111.

Johnson, C. S. (1934), *In the Shadow of the Plantation*, Chicago: University of Chicago Press.

Johnson, R. (1983), 'What is Cultural Studies Anyway?', Stencilled Paper No. 74, Birmingham: CCCS.

Johnstone, F. (1976), *Class, Race and Gold*, London: Routledge and Kegan Paul.

Joseph, Saud (1983), 'Working-Class Women's Networks in a Sectarian State: A Political Paradox', *American Ethnologist*, 10, Feb.: 1–22.

Kant, I. (1781), *Critique of Pure Reason*, trans. Norman Kemp Smith, London: Macmillan (1929).

Kanter, R. (1972), *Commitment and Community*, Cambridge, Mass.: Harvard University Press.

Kapferer, B. (1969), 'Norms and the Manipulation of Relationships in a Work Context', in C. Mitchell (ed.), *Social Networks in Urban Situations*, Manchester: Manchester University Press.

Karlovic, N. L. (1982), 'Internal Colonialism in a Marxist Society: The Case of Croatia', *Ethnic and Racial Studies*, 5, July: 276–99.

Kasschau, P. L. (1977), 'Age and Race Discrimination Reported by Middle-Aged and Older Persons', *Social Forces*, 55, March: 728–42.

Kelly, G. A. (1955), *The Psychology of Personal Constructs*, New York: Norton.

Keyes, Charles F. (1976), 'Towards a New Formulation of the Concept of Ethnic Group', *Ethnicity*, 3: 202–13.

Keyes, Charles F. (ed.) (1981) *Ethnic Change*, Seattle: University of Washington Press.

Killian, L. (1970), 'Herbert Blumer's Contributions to Race Relations' in T. Shibutani (ed.), *Human Nature and Collective Behaviour*, Englewood Cliffs, NJ: Prentice-Hall.

Killian, L. and Grigg, C. (1967), *Racial Crisis in America*, Englewood Cliffs, NJ: Prentice-Hall (Spectrum).

King, James C. (1981), *The Biology of Race*, Berkeley: University of California Press.

Klass, M. and Hellman, H. (1971), *The Kinds of Mankind*, Philadelphia: J. B. Lippincott Company.

Kosmin, B. A. (1979), 'J. R. Archer (1863–1932): A Pan Africanist in the Battersea Labour Movement', *New Community*, 7, 3: 430–6.

(1982), 'Political Identity in Battersea' in S. Wallman and Associates, *Living in South London: Perspectives on Battersea 1871–1981*, London: Gower/London School of Economics.

Kuhn, Thomas (1962), *The Structure of Scientific Revolutions*, Chicago: University of Chicago Press.

Kuper, L. (1971), 'Political Change in Plural Societies', *International Social Science Journal*, 23, 4: 594–607.

(1974), *Race, Class and Power: Ideology and Revolutionary Change in Plural Societies*, Chicago: Aldine.

Kuper, L. and Smith, M. G. (eds.) (1969), *Pluralism in Africa*, Berkeley: University of California Press.

Kurian, G. T. (ed.) (1982), *Encyclopedia of the Third World*, 3 vols., New York: Facts on File Incorporated.

Lal, B. B. (1982a), '"So Near and Yet so Far": The "Chicago School" of Symbolic Interactionism and its Relationship to Developments in the Sociology of Sociology and Ethnomethodology' in N. Denzin (ed.), *Studies in Symbolic Interaction*, 4, Greenwich CT. Jai Press.

(1982b), 'Robert E. Park's Perspective on Race Relations in Urban America, 1913–1944', Paper presented to the International Conference on the History and Ideology of Anglo-Saxon Racial Attitudes, *c*. 1870–1970, Birmingham, England, September 1982.

(1983), 'Perspectives on Ethnicity: Old Wine in New Bottles', *Ethnic and Racial Studies*, 6, April: 154–73.

(forthcoming), *Robert E. Park and the 'Chicago School' of American Sociology*, London: Routledge and Kegan Paul.

Landa, J. T. (1981), 'A Theory of the Ethnically Homogeneous Middleman Group: An Institutional Alternative to Contract Law', *Journal of Legal Studies*, 10: 349–62.

Lange, A. L. and Westin, C. (1981), *Ethnic Discrimination and Social Identity: A Review of Research and a Theoretical Analysis* (in Swedish), Stockholm: Liber/Publica.

Leach, E. R. (1976), 'Social Anthropology: A Natural Science of Society', *Proceedings of the British Academy*, 62: 157–80.

Leach, E. R. (ed.) (1960), *Aspects of Caste in South India, Ceylon and Northwest Pakistan*, Cambridge: Cambridge University Press.

Lecourt, D. (1980), 'On Marxism as a Critique of Sociological Theories' in UNESCO, *Sociological Theories: Race and Colonialism*, Paris: UNESCO.

Legassick, M. (1974), 'South Africa: Capital Accumulation and Violence' in *Economy and Society*, 3, 3: 253–91.

Legum, C. (ed.) (1981), *Africa Contemporary Record, 1981*, vol. XIII, New York: Africana Publishing Company.

Legum, C. (ed.) (1982), *Africa Contemporary Record, 1982*, vol. XIV, New York: Africana Publishing Company.

LeVine, R. A. and Campbell, D. T. (1972), *Ethnocentrism: Theories of Conflict, Ethnic Attitudes and Group Behavior*, New York: John Wiley and Sons.

Lewis, I. M. (ed.) (1983), *Nationalism and Self-Determination in the Horn of Africa*, London: Ithaca Press.

Lieberson, S. (1980), *A Piece of the Pie: Blacks and White Immigrants Since 1880*, Berkeley: University of California Press.

Liebow, E. (1967), *Tally's Corner: A Study of Negro Street-Corner Men*, Boston, Mass.: Little, Brown and Company

Light, I. (1972), *Ethnic Enterprise*, Berkeley, Calif.: University of California Press.
    (1981), 'Ethnic Succession' in Charles F. Keyes (ed.), *Ethnic Change*, Seattle: University of Washington Press, 54–86.
Lipset, S. M. (1950), 'Changing Social Status and Prejudice: The Race Theories of a Pioneering Sociologist', *Commentary*, 9: 475–9.
    (1959), 'Democracy and Working-Class Authoritarianism', *American Sociological Review*, 24, Aug.: 482–501.
Livingstone, F. (1962), 'On the Non-Existence of Human Races', *Current Anthropology*, 3: 279–81.
Lofland, J. (1970), 'Interactionist Imagery and Analytic Interruptus' in T. Shibutani (ed.), *Human Nature and Collective Behaviour*, Englewood Cliffs, NJ: Prentice-Hall.
Lofland, L. (1980), 'Reminiscences of Classic Chicago, The Blumer-Hughes Talks', *Urban Life*, vol. 9, 3, October: pp. 251–81.
Lopez, David E. (1983), 'Review of *The Ethnic Phenomenon*', *International Migration Review*, 17: 353–4.
Lopreato, Joseph (1984), *Human Nature and Biocultural Evolution*, Boston, Mass.: Allen and Unwin.
Lowenthal, D. (1972), *West Indian Societies*, Oxford: Oxford University Press, Institute of Race Relations.
Lukes, S. (1974), *Power*, London: Macmillan.
Lumsden, C. J. and Wilson, E. O. (1981), *Genes, Mind, and Culture*, Cambridge, Mass.: Harvard University Press.
Lumsden, C. J. and Wilson, E. O. (1983), *Promethean Fire*, Cambridge, Mass.: Harvard University Press.
Lyman, S. (1972), *The Black American in Sociological Thought*, New York: Capricorn Books.
McKay, J. (1982), 'An Exploratory Synthesis of Primordial and Mobilizationist Approaches to Ethnic Phenomena', *Ethnic and Racial Studies*, 5, 4: 395–420.
Magubane, B. (1976), 'The Evolution of the Class Structure in Africa' in P. Gutkind and I. Wallerstein (eds.), *The Political Economy of Africa*, pp. 169–97, London: Sage Publications.
Malinowski, B. (1922), *Argonauts of the Western Pacific: An Account of Native Enterprise and Adventure in the Archipelagoes of Melanesian New Guinea*, London: Kegan Paul, Trench Trubner.
    (1965), *The Dynamics of Culture Change – An Enquiry into Race Relations in Africa*, New Haven, Ct.: Yale University Press.
Marable, M. (1984), *How Capitalism Underdeveloped Black America*, London: Pluto Press.
Marcia, J. E. (1966), 'Development and Validation of Ego-Identity Status', *Journal of Personality and Social Psychology*, 50: 143–52.
    (1980), 'Identity in Adolescence' in J. Adelson (ed.), *Handbook of Adolescent Psychology*, New York: Wiley.
Markovitz, I. (ed.) (1970), *African Politics and Society: Basic Issues of Government and Development*, New York: Free Press.
Marris, P. (1974), *Loss and Change*, London: Routledge and Kegan Paul.
Marshall, R. (1974), 'The Economics of Racial Discrimination: A Survey', *Journal of Economic Literature*, 12, Sept.: 849–71.

Marshall, T. H. (1950), *Citizenship and Social Class*, Cambridge: Cambridge University Press.

Martin, Bernice (1981), *A Sociology of Contemporary Cultural Change*, Oxford: Basil Blackwell.

Martindale, D. (1960), *The Nature and Types of Sociological Theory*, Cambridge, Mass.: Riverside Press.

Marx, K. (1970), *Verker i utvalg*, Bind 3, *Historiske Skrifter*, Oslo: Pax Furlag (originally published 1851–2).

Mason, D. (1982), 'Race Relations, Group Formation and Power: A Framework for Analysis', *Ethnic and Racial Studies*, 5, 4: 421–39.

Masters, R. D. (1983), 'The Biological Nature of the State', *World Politics*, 35, 2: 161–93.

Matthews, F. H. (1978), *The Quest for Community: Robert Park and the Chicago School of American Sociology*, London: McGill – Queen's University Press.

Maxwell, Mary (1983), 'The Genetics of Racism', *The Age Monthly Review*, (Melbourne), 3, 8: 20–1.

Mead, G. H. (1934a), *Mind, Self and Society*, Chicago: University of Chicago Press.

(1934b), *The Social Psychology of George Herbert Mead*, ed. A. Strauss, Chicago: University of Chicago Press.

Meier, A. (1964), *Negro Thought in America, 1880–1915: Ideologies in the Age of Booker T. Washington*, Ann Arbor: University of Michigan Press.

Meiksins Wood, E. (1983), 'Marxism Without Class Struggle?' in R. Miliband and J. Saville (eds.), *The Socialist Register 1983*, London: Merlin.

Meltzer, B. and Petras, J. (1970), 'The Chicago and Iowa Schools of Symbolic Interactionism' in T. Shibutani (ed.), *Human Nature and Collective Behaviour*, Englewood Cliffs, NJ: Prentice-Hall.

Merton, R. K. (1968), *Social Theory and Social Structure*, New York: Free Press.

Michael, R. and Becker, G. S. (1973), 'On the New Theory of Consumer Behaviour', *Swedish Journal of Economics*, 75, 4: 378–96.

Miles, R. (1980), 'Class, Race and Ethnicity: A Critique of Cox's Theory', *Ethnic and Racial Studies*, 3, 2: 169–87.

(1982), *Racism and Migrant Labour*, London: Routledge and Kegan Paul.

(1984a), 'Marxism Versus the Sociology of "Race Relations"?', *Ethnic and Racial Studies*, 7, 2: 217–37.

(1984b), 'The Riots of 1958: Notes on the Ideological Construction of "Race Relations" as a Political Issue in Britain', *Immigrants and Minorities*, 3, 3: 252–75.

Miles, R. and Phizacklea, A. (1984), *White Man's Country: Racism in British Politics*, London: Pluto Press.

Mitchell, J. C. (1966), 'Theoretical Orientations in African Urban Studies' in M. Banton (ed.), *Social Anthropology of Complex Societies*, ASA Monograph No. 4, London: Tavistock.

Montagu, A. (1974), *Man's Most Dangerous Myth: The Fallacy of Race*, 5th edn, New York: Oxford University Press.

Moore, J. W. (1976), 'American Minorities and New Nation Perspectives', *Pacific Sociological Review*, 19, Oct.: 447–67.

Morgan, G. D. (1981), *American Without Ethnicity*, Port Washington, NY: Kennikat Press.

Morgan, G. (1981), 'Class, Theory and the Structural Location of Black Workers', *Insurgent Sociologist*, 10, 3: 21–34.

Morrey, C. R. (1976), *1971 Census: Demographic, Social and Economic Indices for Wards in Greater London*, vol. 2, GLC Research Report, No. 10, London: GLC.
Mugabe, The Hon. R. (1982), 'Socialism in Zimbabwe', An Address Delivered by the Prime Minister, Comrade R. G. Mugabe to a Meeting of the Justice and Peace Commission, Harare: Catholic Commission for Justice and Peace in Zimbabwe, 6 February. Mimeo.
Myrdal, Gunnar (1944), *An American Dilemma*, New York: Harper Brothers.
(1958), *Value in Social Theory*, London: Routledge and Kegan Paul.
(1964), *Challenge to Affluence*, New York: Macmillan.
Nairn, T. (1981), *The Break-Up of Britain*, revised edn, London: New Left Books.
Needham, S. (1984), 'Maternity Blues and Personal Identity Development in First-Time Mothers: An Exploratory Study', Research Dissertation, Diploma in Clinical Psychology: British Psychological Society, Leicester.
Newcomer, P. J. (1972), 'The Nuer are Dinka: An Essay on Origins and Environmental Determinism', *Man*, NS 7: 5–11.
Newman, William M. (1973), *American Pluralism*, New York: Harper and Row.
(1982), 'Review of *The Ethnic Phenomenon*', *Social Forces*, 61: 291–3.
Nikolinakos, M. (1973), 'Notes Towards an Economic Theory of Racism', *Race*, 14, April: 365–81.
Nordhoff, C. (1875) (1965), *The Communistic Societies of the United States*, New York: Schocken Books.
Novak, M. (1972), *The Rise of the Unmeltable Ethnics*, New York: Macmillan.
Nunn, C. A., Crockett, Harry, J. Jnr and Williams, J. Allen Jnr (1978), *Tolerance for Nonconformity: A National Survey of Americans' Changing Commitment to Civil Liberties*, San Francisco: Jossey-Bass.
Offe, C. (1984), *Contradictions of the Welfare State*, London: Hutchinson.
Ohri, A. and Donnelly, L. (1982), 'Alliances and Coalitions in the Struggle for Racial Equality' in A. Ohri *et al.* (eds.), *Community Work and Racism*, London: Routledge and Kegan Paul.
Okely, J. (1979), 'Trading Stereotypes: The Case of English Gypsies' in S. Wallman (ed.), *Ethnicity at Work*, London: Macmillan.
(1983), *The Traveller Gypsies*, Cambridge: Cambridge University Press.
Olson, M. (1965), *The Logic of Collective Action*, Cambridge, Mass.: Harvard University Press.
Olzak, S. (1982), 'Ethnic Mobilization in Quebec', *Ethnic and Racial Studies*, 5, July: 253–75.
Omi, M. and Winant, H. (1983), 'By the Rivers of Babylon: Race in the United States', *Socialist Review*, Part One, 71: 31–65; Part Two, 72: 35–69.
Oppenheimer, Franz (1975), *The State*, New York: Free Life Editions.
Ossowski, S. (1963), *Class Structure in the Social Consciousness*, London: Routledge and Kegan Paul.
Ouseley, H. (1982a), 'A Local Black Alliance' in A. Ohri *et al.* (eds.), *Community Work and Racism*, London: Routledge and Kegan Paul.
(1982b), *The System*, London: Runnymede Trust.
(1984), 'Local Authority Race Initiatives' in M. Boddy and C. Fudge (eds), *Local Socialism?*, London: Macmillan.

Paine, R. (1970), 'Informal Communication and Informal Management', *Canadian Review of Sociology and Anthropology*, 7, 3: 172–88.

(1974a), 'Two Modes of Exchange and Mediation' in B. Kapferer (ed.), *Transaction and Meaning*, Philadelphia: Institute for the Study of Human Issues.

(1974b), *Second Thoughts About Barth's Models*, RAI Occasional Paper, No. 32, London: Royal Anthropological Institute.

Park, R. E. (1913), 'Racial Assimilation in Secondary Groups with Particular Reference to the Negro', *Publication of the American Sociological Society*, 8: 66–83. Reprinted in R. E. Park (1950).

(1916), 'The City: Suggestions for the Investigation of Human Behaviour in the Urban Environment', *American Journal of Sociology*, 20: 577–612. Reprinted in R. E. Park (1952).

(1921), 'Sociology and the Social Sciences', *American Journal of Sociology*, 26: 401–4; 27: 1–21, 169–83. Reprinted in R. E. Park (1955).

(1922), *The Immigrant Press and Its Control*, New York: Harper and Row.

(1923), 'Negro Race Consciousness as Reflected in Race Literature', *American Review*, 1: 505–16. Reprinted in R. E. Park (1950).

(1926), 'The Urban Community as a Spatial Pattern and a Moral Order' in E. W. Burgess (ed.), *The Urban Community*, Chicago: University of Chicago Press. Reprinted in R. E. Park (1952).

(1927), 'Human Nature and Collective Behaviour', *American Journal of Sociology*, 32: 733–41. Reprinted in R. E. Park (1967).

(1928), 'The Bases of Race Prejudice', *American Academy of Political and Social Science Annals*, 140: 11–20. Reprinted in R. E. Park (1950).

(1929), 'The City as a Social Laboratory' in T. V. Smith and L. D. White (eds.), *Chicago: An Experiment in Social Science Research*, Chicago: University of Chicago Press. Reprinted in R. E. Park (1952).

(1934), 'The Negro and His Plantation Heritage', Introduction to C. S. Johnson, *In the Shadow of the Plantation*, Chicago: University of Chicago Press. Reprinted in R. E. Park (1950).

(1935), 'Politics and "the Man Farthest Down" ', Introduction to H. Gosnell, *Negro Politicians*, Chicago: University of Chicago Press. Reprinted in R. E. Park (1950).

(1937), 'Cultural Conflict and the Marginal Man', Introduction to E. V. Stonequist, *The Marginal Man*, New York: Charles Scribner's Sons. Reprinted in R. E. Park (1950).

(1943), 'Race Ideologies' in W. Ogburn (ed.), *American Society in Wartime*, Chicago: University of Chicago Press. Reprinted in R. E. Park (1950).

(1950), *Race and Culture*, ed. Everett C. Hughes, London: Collier Macmillan (Free Press).

(1952), *Human Communities, The City, Human Ecology*, ed. Everett C. Hughes, Glencoe, Ill.: Free Press.

(1955), *Society, Collective Behaviour, News and Opinion, Sociology and Modern Society*, ed. Everett C. Hughes, Glencoe, Ill.: Free Press.

(1957), *Race and Culture*, Chicago: Chicago University Press.

(1967), *On Social Control and Collective Behaviour*, ed. Ralph H. Turner, Chicago: University of Chicago Press.

(1972), *The Crowd and the Public and Other Essays*, ed. Henry Elsner Jnr, Chicago: University of Chicago Press.

Park, R. E. and Burgess, E. W. (1921), *An Introduction to the Science of*

Sociology, Chicago: University of Chicago Press (reprinted 1969).

Park, R. E. and Miller, H. A. (1921), *Old World Traits Transplanted*, New York: Harper and Brothers.

Parkin, F. (1979a), *Marxism and Class Theory: A Bourgeois Critique*, London: Tavistock.

(1979b), 'Social Stratification' in T. Bottomore and R. Nisbet (eds.), *A History of Sociological Analysis*, London: Heinemann.

Parmar, P. (1982), 'Gender, Race and Class: Asian Women in Resistance', in CCCS, *The Empire Strikes Back*, London: Hutchinson.

Parsons, T. (1937), *The Structure of Social Action*, New York: McGraw-Hill.

Patterson, O. (1977), *Ethnic Chauvinism: The Reactionary Impulse*, New York: Stein and Day.

(1983), 'The Nature, Causes and Implications of Ethnic Identification' in C. Fried (ed.), *Minorities: Community and Identity*, Berlin: Springer-Verlag.

Paxton, John (ed.) (1981), *The Statesman's Year Book*, New York: Macmillan.

Peach, C. (1975), *Urban Social Segregation*, London: Longman.

Peach, C. and Smith, S. (1981), 'Introduction' in C. Peach *et al.* (eds.), *Ethnic Segregation in Cities*, London: Croom Helm.

Peach, C., Robinson, V. and Smith, S. (eds.) (1981), *Ethnic Segregation in Cities*, London: Croom Helm.

Pettigrew, T. C. (1978), 'Three Issues in Ethnicity: Boundaries, Deprivations, and Perceptions', in J. Milton Yinger and Stephen J. Cutler (eds.), *Major Social Issues: A Multidisciplinary View*, New York: Free Press, 25–49.

Phillips, M. (1982), 'Separatism or Black Control?' in A. Ohri *et al.* (eds.), *Community Work and Racism*, London: Routledge and Kegan Paul.

Philpott, T. (1978), *The Slum and the Ghetto*, Chicago: University of Chicago Press.

Phizacklea, A. (1983), *One Way Ticket*, London: Routledge and Kegan Paul.

(1984), 'A Sociology of Migration or "Race Relations"? A View From Britain', *Current Sociology*, 32, 3: 199–218.

Phizacklea, A. and Miles, R. (1980), *Labour and Racism*, London: Routledge and Kegan Paul.

Plamenatz, John (1975), *Karl Marx's Philosophy of Man*, Oxford: Clarendon Press.

Poulantzas, N. (1971), *Political Power and Social Classes*, London: New Left Books.

(1978) *State, Power, Socialism*, London: New Left Books.

Prasher, U. (1984) 'The Need for Positive Action' in J. Beynon (ed.)', *Scarman and After*, Oxford: Pergamon Press.

Przeworski, A. (1977), 'Proletariat Into Class: The Process of Class Formation from Karl Kautsky's *The Class Struggle* to Recent Controversies', *Politics and Society*, 7, 4: 343–401.

Rabushka, A. and Shepsle, K. (1972), *Politics in Plural Societies: A Theory of Democratic Instability*, Colombus, Ohio: Merrill.

Rainwater, L. (1970), *Behind Ghetto Walls*, Chicago: Aldine.

Reeves, F. (1982), *The Concept of Prejudice: An Evaluative Review*, SSRC RUER Working Paper 17, Birmingham: University of Aston.

Reich, M. (1981), *Racial Inequality*, Princeton: Princeton University Press.

Resnick, J. and Wolff, R. D. (1982), 'Classes in Marxian Theory', *Review of Radical Political Economy*, 1, 4: 1–18.

Rex, J. (1958), 'The Plural Society in Sociological Theory', *British Journal of Sociology*, 10, 2: 114–24.

(1961), *Key Problems in Sociological Theory*, London: Routledge and Kegan Paul.

(1973), *Race, Colonialism and the City*, London: Oxford University Press.

(1979), 'Black Militancy and Class Conflict' in R. Miles and A. Phizacklea (eds.), *Racism and Political Action in Britain*, London: Routledge and Kegan Paul.

(1981), 'A Working Paradigm for Race Relations Research', *Ethnic and Racial Studies*, 4, 1: 1–25.

(1982a), 'Convergences in the Sociology of Race Relations and Minority Groups' in T. Bottomore, S. Nowak and M. Sokowska (eds.), *Sociology: The State of the Art*, London: Sage Publications, 173–200.

(1982b), 'Social Science Research – A Neo-Kantian Perspective' in M. Cross (ed.), *Social Research and Public Policy*, London: Social Research Association.

(1983a), 'Review of *The Ethnic Phenomenon*', *Ethnic and Racial Studies*, 6, 3: 368–71.

(1983b), Personal Communication.

(1983c), *Race Relations in Sociological Theory*, 2nd end, London: Routledge and Kegan Paul.

Rex, J. and Moore, R. (1967), *Race, Community and Conflict*, London: Oxford University Press.

Rex, J. and Tomlinson, S. (1979), *Colonial Immigrants in a British City – A Class Analysis*, London: Routledge and Kegan Paul.

Reynolds, V. (1980a), Sociobiology and the Idea of Primordial Discrimination', *Ethnic and Racial Studies*, 3, 3: 303–15.

(1980b), 'Sociobiology and Discrimination, A Rejoinder', *Ethnic and Racial Studies*, 3, 4: 482–3.

Rich, P. (1984), *White Power and the Liberal Conscience*, Manchester: Manchester University Press.

Robinson, C. J. (1983), *Black Marxism: The Making of the Black Radical Tradition*, London: Zed Books.

Rose, A. (1971), 'Introduction' in *Human Behaviour and Social Processes*, London: Routledge and Kegan Paul.

Rucker, D. (1969), *The Chicago Pragmatists*, Minneapolis, Minn.: University of Minnesota Press.

Ruse, M. (1979), *Sociobiology, Sense or Nonsense*, Dordrecht: D. Reidel Publishing Co.

(1981), 'Review of *Human Family Systems*', *Social Indicators Research*, 9: 391–2.

Sahlins, M. (1977), *The Use and Abuse of Biology*, London: Tavistock.

Said, Abdul A. and Simmons, Luis R. (eds.) (1976), *Ethnicity in an International Context: The Politics of Dissociation*, New Brunswick, NJ: Transaction Books.

Saifullah Khan, V. (1979), 'Introduction' in *Minority Families: Support and Stress*, London: Macmillan.

(1981), 'Some Comments on the Question of Second Generation', Conference Paper (Mimeo): Linguistic Minorities Project, Institute of Education, University of London.

(1982), 'The Role of the Culture of Dominance in Structuring the Experience of Ethnic Minorities' in C. Husband (ed.), *'Race' in Britain*, London: Hutchinson.

Sargent, L. (ed.) (1981), *Women and Revolution*, London: Pluto Press.

Schermerhorn, R. A. (1970), *Comparative Ethnic Relations*, Chicago: University of Chicago Press.

(1978), *Comparative Ethnic Relations: A Framework for Theory and Research*, 2nd edn, Chicago: University of Chicago Press.

Schuman, H. and Hatchett, S. (1974), *Black Racial Attitudes: Trends and Complexities*, Ann Arbor: Institute for Social Research, University of Michigan.

Schumpeter, J. (1950), *Capitalism, Socialism and Democracy*, New York: Harper.

Schwartz, S. K. and Schwartz, D. C. (1976), 'Convergence and Divergence in Political Orientations Between Blacks and Whites: 1960–1973', *Journal of Social Issues*, 32, Spring: 153–68.

Schwendinger, H. and Schwendinger, J. (1974), *Sociologists of the Chair*, New York: Basic Books.

Schwimmer, E. (1979), 'Symbolic Competition', unpublished manuscript, University of Laval, Quebec.

Sen, A. K. (1977), 'Rational Fools: A Critique of the Behavioural Foundations of Economic Theory', *Philosophy and Public Affairs*, 6, 4: 317–44.

Sen, A. K. and Williams, B. (eds.) (1982), *Utilitarianism and Beyond*, Cambridge: Cambridge University Press.

Shepherd, J. (1983), *Incest, A Biosocial View*, New York: Academic Press.

Sherwood, R. (1980), *The Psychodynamics of Race: Vicious and Benign Spirals*, Brighton: Harvester Press.

Shibutani, T. (1961), *Society and Personality*, Englewood Cliffs, NJ: Prentice-Hall.

Shils, E. A. (1957), 'Primordial, Personal, Sacred and Civil Ties: Some Particular Observations of Sociological Research and Theory', *British Journal of Sociology*, 8: 130–45.

(1967), 'Color, the Universal Intellectual Community, and the Afro-Asian Intellectual', *Daedalus*, 96: 279–95.

(1970), 'Tradition, Ecology and Institution in the History of Sociology', *Daedalus*, 99: 760–825.

Simmel, G. (1969), 'The Metropolis and Mental Life' in R. Sennett (ed.), *Classic Essays on the Culture of Cities*, New York: Appleton-Century-Crofts.

Simpson, G. E. and Yinger, J. Milton (1985), *Racial and Cultural Minorities: An Analysis of Prejudice and Discrimination*, 5th edn, New York: Plenum (1st edn, 1953).

Sithole, M. (1983), 'The Salience of Ethnicity in African Politics: The Case of Zimbabwe', Unpublished Paper (Mimeo): *Journal of Asian and African Studies* (forthcoming).

Sivanandan, A. (1982), *A Different Hunger*, London: Pluto Press.

(1983), 'Challenging Racism: Strategies for the '80s', *Race and Class*, 25, 2: 2–11.

Skidmore, W. (1975), *Theoretical Thinking in Sociology*, New York: Cambridge University Press.

Smith, A. D. (1981), *The Ethnic Revival in the Modern World*, Cambridge: Cambridge University Press.

Smith, A. W. (1981), 'Racial Tolerance as a Function of Group Position', *American Sociological Review*, 46, Oct.: 525–41.

Smith, D. J. (1977), *Racial Disadvantage in Britain. The PEP Report*, Harmondsworth: Penguin Books.

Smith, M. G. (1965), *The Plural Society in the British West Indies*, Berkeley: University of California Press.

  (1969), 'Some Developments in the Analytic Framework of Pluralism' in L. Kuper and M. G. Smith (eds.), *Pluralism in Africa*, Berkeley: University of California Press.

  (1974), *Corporations and Society*, London: Duckworth.

  (1982), 'Ethnicity and Ethnic Groups in America: The View From Harvard', *Ethnic and Racial Studies*, 5: 1–21.

  (1983), 'Ethnicity and Sociobiology', *American Ethnologist*, 10: 364–7.

  (1984), 'The Nature and Variety of Plural Units' in D. Maybury-Lewis (ed.), *The Prospects for Plural Societies: Proceedings of the American Ethnological Society, 1982*, Washington, DC: American Ethnological Society.

Solomos, J. (1982), 'Urban Social Policies, Migrant Workers and Political Authority' in J. Solomos (ed.), *Migrant Workers in Metropolitan Cities*, Strasbourg: European Science Foundation.

Solomos, J. *et al.* (1982), 'The Organic Crisis of British Capitalism and Race: The Experience of the Seventies' in CCCS Race and Politics Group, *The Empire Strikes Back: Race and Racism in 70s Britain*, London: Hutchinson.

Sowell, T. (1975), *Race and Economics*, New York: David McKay.

  (1981), *Ethnic America*, New York: Basic Books.

  (1984), *Civil Rights, Rhetoric or Reality?*, New York: William Morrow.

Spear, A. (1967), *Black Chicago: The Making of a Negro Ghetto, 1890–1920*, Chicago: University of Chicago Press.

Stack, C. B. (1974), *All our Kin: Strategies for Survival in a Black Community*, New York: Harper and Row.

Steinberg, S. (1981), *The Ethnic Myth: Race, Ethnicity, and Class in America*, New York: Atheneum.

Stewart, M. and Whitting, G. (1983), *Ethnic Minorities and the Urban Programme*, Bristol: University of Bristol, School for Advanced Urban Studies.

Stiglitz, J. E. (1973), 'Approaches to the Economics of Discrimination', *American Economic Review*, 63, May: 287–95.

Stone, J. (1977), *Race, Ethnicity and Social Change*, North Scituate: Duxbury Press.

  (1979), 'Introduction: Internal Colonialism in Comparative Perspective', *Ethnic and Racial Studies*, 2, July: 255–9.

Strauss, A. (1970), 'Discovering New Theory From Previous Theory' in T. Shibutani (ed.), *Human Nature and Collective Behaviour*, Englewood Cliffs, NJ: Prentice-Hall.

Symons, D. (1979), *The Evolution of Human Sexuality*, New York: Oxford University Press.

Tajfel, H. (1974), 'Social Identity and Intergroup Behaviour', *Social Science Information*, 13: 65–93.

  (1978), *Differentiation Between Social Groups: Studies in the Social Psychology of Intergroup Relations*, London: Academic Press.

  (1981), *Human Groups and Social Categories*, Cambridge: Cambridge University Press.

(1982a), 'Social Psychology of Intergroup Relations', *Annual Review of Psychology*, 33: 1–39.

Tajfel, H. (ed.) (1982b), *Social Identity and Intergroup Relations*, Cambridge, Cambridge University Press.

Talai, V. (1983), 'Armenians in London: An Anthropological Study of Social Boundary Management', Ph.D. Thesis: University of Manchester.

Taylor, C. L. and Hudson, M. (1976), *World Handbook of Social and Political Indicators*, New Haven, Ct.: Yale University Press.

Taylor, C. L. and Jodice, D. A. (1983), *World Handbook of Political and Social Indicators*, 2 vols., New Haven, Ct.: Yale University Press.

Taylor, M. (1982), *Anarchy, Community and Liberty*, Cambridge: Cambridge University Press.

Taylor, S. (1979), 'The National Front: Anatomy of a Political Movement' in R. Miles and A. Phizacklea (eds.), *Racism and Political Action in Britain*, London: Routledge and Kegan Paul.

TeSelle, S. (ed.) (1974), *The Rediscovery of Ethnicity: Its Implications for Culture and Politics in America*, New York: Harper Colophon.

Thernstrom, S., Orlov, A. and Handlin, O. (eds.) (1980), *The Harvard Encyclopedia of American Ethnic Groups*, Cambridge, Mass.: Belknap Press of Harvard University.

Thomas, W. I. and Znaniecki, F. (1918–20), *The Polish Peasant in Europe and America*, 5 vols., Chicago: University of Chicago Press.

Thurow, L. C. (1969), *Poverty and Discrimination*, Washington: Brookings Institute.

Tobin, J. (1965), 'On Improving the Economic Status of the Negro', *Daedalus*, 94, Fall: 878–98.

Triandis, H. C. *et al.* (eds.) (1980), *Handbook of Cross-Cultural Psychology*, . vols. 1–6, New York: Allyn and Bacon.

Turner, J. H. and Singleton, R. Jnr (1978) 'A Theory of Ethnic Oppression: Toward a Reintegration of Cultural and Structural Concepts in Ethnic Relations Theory', *Social Forces*, 56, June, 1001–18.

UNESCO (1980), *Sociological Theories: Race and Colonialism*, Paris: UNESCO.

United Nations (1979), *Everyone's United Nations*, New York: UN.

(1983), *World Statistics in Brief*, New York: UN.

United States of America State Department (1983), *Background Notes on Countries*, Washington, DC: Government Printing Office.

van Amersfoort, H. and van der Wusten, H. (1981), 'Democratic Stability and Ethnic Parties', *Ethnic and Racial Studies*, 4, 4: 476–85.

van den Berghe, P.L. (1965), *South Africa: A Study in Conflict*, Middleton, Ct.: Wesleyan University Press.

(1967), *Race and Racism: A Comparative Perspective*, New York: Wiley.

(1978), 'Race and Ethnicity. A Sociobiological Perspective', *Ethnic and Racial Studies*, 1, 4: 401–11.

(1979), *Human Family Systems*, New York: Elsevier.

(1980), 'Sociobiology and Discrimination: A Comment on Vernon Reynolds', *Ethnic and Racial Studies*, 3, 4: 475–81.

(1981), *The Ethnic Phenomenon*, New York: Elsevier Press.

(1983), 'Class, Race and Ethnicity in Africa', *Ethnic and Racial Studies*, 6, April: 221–36.

Wallerstein, I. (1974), *The Modern World System*, New York: Academic Press.
   (1977), 'Class and Status in Contemporary Africa' in P. Gutkind and P. Waterman (eds.), *African Social Studies: A Radical Reader*, pp. 277–81, London: Heinemann.
Wallman, S. (1978a), 'Race Relations or Ethnic Relations?', *New Community*, 6, 3: 306–9.
   (1978b), 'The Boundaries of Race: Processes of Ethnicity in England', *Man*, 13, 2: 200–17.
   (1979), 'Introduction: The Scope for Ethnicity' in *Ethnicity at Work*, London: Macmillan.
   (1983a), 'Elnicismo e Localismo: La Relazione Tra Struttura e Cultura in Due Aree di Londra' in A. Signorelli (ed.), *Cultura Popolare e Cultura di Massa*, Milan: *La Ricerca Folklorica*, No. 7.
   (1983b), 'Identity Options' in C. Fried (ed.), *Minorities, Community and Identity*, Dahlem Workshop Reports, No. 27, Berlin, Heidelberg, NY: Springer Verlag.
   (1984), *Eight London Households*, London: Tavistock.
Wallman, S., Dhooge, Y., Goldman, A. and Kosmin, B. A. (1980), 'Ethnography by Proxy: Strategies for Research in the Inner City', *Ethnos*, 45: 1–2.
Wallman, S. and Associates (1982), *Living in South London: Perspectives on Battersea 1871–1981*, London: Gower/London School of Economics.
Ward, R. (1979), 'Where Race Didn't Divide: Some Reflections on Slum Clearance in Moss Side' in R. Miles and A. Phizacklea (eds.), *Racism and Political Action in Britain*, London: Routledge and Kegan Paul.
Warner, S. B. Jnr and Burke, C. B. (1969), 'Cultural Change and the Ghetto', *Contemporary History*, 4: 173–87.
Warner, W. L. (1936), 'American Class and Caste', *American Journal of Sociology*, 42: 234–7.
Watson, J. (1977), 'Introduction' in *Between Two Cultures*, Oxford: Basil Blackwell.
Weber, M. (1947), *The Theory of Social and Economic Organisation*, translated by T. Parsons and A. M. Henderson, Edinburgh: William Hodge & Co.
   (1961), *General Economic History*, New York: Collier Books.
   (1968), *Economy and Society*, vol. 1, New York: Bedminster Press.
Webster, P. (1984), News Report in *The Guardian*, 14 February.
Weigert, A. J. (1983), 'Identity: Its Emergence Within Social Psychology', *Symbolic Interaction*, 6, 2: 183–206.
Weinreich, P. (1969), *Theoretical and Experimental Evaluation of Dissonance Processes*, Ph.D. Thesis: University of London.
   (1977), 'Socialisation and Ethnic Identity Development', *Conference on Socialisation and Social Influence*, Warsaw, Poland: European Association for Experimental Social Psychology and the Polish Academy of Sciences.
   (1979a), 'Cross Ethnic Identification and Self-Rejection in a Black Adolescent' in G. K. Verma and C. Bagley (eds), *Race, Education and Identity*, London: Macmillan.
   (1979b), 'Ethnicity and Adolescent Identity Conflict' in V. Saifullah Khan (ed.), *Minority Families in Britain*, London: Macmillan.
   (1979c), 'Sex-Role Identification, Social Change and Cultural Conflict': British Psychological Society (Northern Ireland Branch) Annual Conference.

(1980), *Manual for Identity Exploration Using Personal Constructs*, London: Social Science Research Council.

(1982), 'A Conceptual Framework for Exploring Identity Development: Identity Structure Analysis and IDEX', *10th International Congress of the International Association for Child and Adolescent Psychiatry and Allied Professions*, Trinity College, Dublin.

(1983a), 'Emerging From Threatened Identities: Ethnicity and Gender in Redefinitions of Ethnic Identity' in G. Breakwell (ed.), *Threatened Identities*, Chichester: John Wiley.

(1983b), 'Psychodynamics of Personal and Social Identity' in A. Jacobson-Widding (ed.), *Identity: Personal and Socio-Cultural*, Atlantic Highlands: Humanities Press Incorporated.

(1983c), 'Ulster's Two Interdependent Identities and their Sociopsychological Maintenance', Symposium: *Ireland: Conflict Dynamics in Ulster*, Annual Meeting of the International Society of Political Psychology: St Catherine's College, Oxford.

Weinreich, P., Carr. I., French, A. and Chivers, A. (1981), *IDEX: Identity Exploration Computer Programme*, rev. edn: Centre for Research in Ethnic Relations, University of Warwick, England and University of Ulster at Jordanstown, Northern Ireland.

Weinreich, P., Harris, P. D. G. and Doherty, J. (1984), 'Empirical Assessment of Identity Syndromes in Anorexia and Bulimia Nervosa', *International Conference on Anorexia Nervosa and Related Disorders*: University College, Swansea.

Williame, Jean-Claude (1970), 'Congo-Kinshasa: General Mobuto and Two Political Generations' in C. E. Welch Jnr (ed.), *Soldier and State in Africa*, Evanston: Northwestern University Press, 124–51.

Williams, R. M. Jnr (1978), 'Competing Models of Multiethnic and Multiracial Societies: An Appraisal of Possibilities' in J. Milton Yinger and Stephen J. Cutler (eds.), *Major Social Issues: A Multidisciplinary View*, New York: Free Press, 50–65.

Wilson, E. O. (1975), *Sociobiology, The New Synthesis*, Cambridge, Mass.: Harvard University Press.

Wilson, W. J. (1978), *The Declining Significance of Race: Blacks and Changing American Institutions*, Chicago: University of Chicago Press.

Wirth, L. (1964a), 'Consensus and Mass Communication' in A. J. Reiss Jnr (ed.), *Louis Wirth on Cities and Social Life*, Chicago: University of Chicago Press (Heritage of Sociology).

(1964b), 'Ideological Aspects of Social Disorganisation' in A. J. Reis, Jnr (ed.), *Louis Wirth on Cities and Social Life*, Chicago: University of Chicago Press (Heritage of Sociology).

Wolpe, H. (1970), 'Race and Industrialism in South Africa' in S. Zubaida (ed.), *Race and Racialism*, London: Tavistock.

(1976), 'The White Working Class in South Africa', *Economy and Society*, 5, 2: 195–240.

(1980), 'Towards an Analysis of the South African State', *International Journal of the Sociology of Law*, 8; 399–421.

Wright, E. O. (1980), 'Varieties of Marxist Conceptions of Class Structure', *Politics and Society*, 9, 3: 323–70.

Wright, H. (1977), *The Burden of the Present: Liberal–Radical Controversy Over South African History*, Cape Town: David Phillip.

Yancey, W. L. and Ericksen, E. P. (1979), 'The Antecedent of Community: The Economic and Institutional Structure of Urban Neighborhoods', *American Sociological Review*, 44: 253–62.

Yinger, J. M. (1965), *Towards a Field Theory of Behavior*, New York: McGraw-Hill.

(1976), 'Ethnicity in Complex Societies' in L. A. Coser and O. N. Larsen (eds.), *The Uses of Controversy in Sociology*, New York: Free Press, 197–216.

(1981), 'Toward a Theory of Assimilation and Dissimilation', *Ethnic and Racial Studies*, 4, July: 249–64.

(1983), 'Ethnicity and Social Change: The Interaction of Structural, Cultural, and Personality Factors', *Ethnic and Racial Studies*, 6, Oct.: 395–409.

(1984), 'Thinking About Assimilation', Unpublished Manuscript.

Young, C. (1976), *The Politics of Cultural Pluralism*, Madison: University of Wisconsin Press.

Young, J. (1983), 'Striking Back Against the Empire', *Critical Social Policy*, 8: 130–40.

Young, K. (1983), 'Ethnic Pluralism and the Policy Agenda in Britain' in N. Glazer and K. Young (eds.), *Ethnic Pluralism and Public Policy*, London: Heinemann.

Young, K. and Connelly, N. (1981), *Policy and Practice in the Multi-Racial City*, London: Policy Studies Institute.

Zablocki, B. (1971), *The Joyful Community*, Baltimore: Penguin Books.

Zakine, D. (1968), 'Class and Class Struggles in Developing Countries', *International Affairs*, 4: 47–55.

Zimbabwe, Government of (1984), *Parliamentary Debates: House of Assembly*, 9, 15, 22 February.

Zubaida, S. (ed.) (1970), *Race and Racialism*, London: Tavistock.

Index

Adam, Heribert, 117–18, 182, 251
affirmative action, 252, 279n3
African states
  ethnic composition, 209–14, *205–7,*
    211–13
  modes of incorporation, 218–23
  political instability, 200–2, 214–18,
    205–7, 211–13
  racial composition, 204–9, *205–7,*
    211–13
  social composition, 203–4, *205–7,*
    211–13
Algeria, 187–225 *passim*
anthropology 227–8, 298
  South African, 184, 186n9
  Soviet, 184, 186n9
  see also social anthropology
anti-racist struggles, 85, 95–7, 108, 131–52
  forms of, 143–52
  marginalisation of, 135–43
anti-Semitism, 48, 191–2
Appelbaum, M., 270–1
attitudes *see* prejudice
Authoritarian Personality, The, 16, 38

Banton, Michael, 3, 4, 12, 13, 14, 65, 80,
    81, 82, 175, 252, 253–4, 257–8,
    259–61, 262n4, 315–16, 316n
Barker, Martin, 50–1, 53
Barth, Fredrik, 64, 173–5, 230, 232, 297
Battersea, 60–3
  compared with Bow, 235–45, *237, 238,*
    239
behavioural ecology, 262n1
Benin, 187–225 *passim*
Ben-Tovim, Gideon, 5, 10, 14, 95–7, 302
Blauner, Robert, 292
Blumer, Herbert, 67, 280–98 *passim*
Boaz, Franz, 297

boundary maintenance, 170–8; *see also*
  boundary process, ethnic boundaries,
  social boundaries
boundary process, 226–45; *see also*
  boundary maintenance, ethnic
  boundaries, social boundaries
Bow *see* Battersea
Burawoy, M., 123–4
Burgess, Ernest W., 280–98 *passim*

Cameroon, 187–225 *passim*
Cape Verde Islands, 187–225 *passim*
capitalism
  and racism in the work of Cox, 42–3
  booty/adventurer, 68
  market, 68, 71, 78
Caribbean, The, 68, 179
categorisation, 8, 9, 177–8, 299
Central African Republic, 187–225 *passim*
Centre for Contemporary Cultural
    Studies, 89–95
Chad, 187–225 *passim*
Chicago Commission on Race Relations,
    285
Chicago School, The, 16, 280–98
  contribution to the study of race
    relations, 285–291, 296–7
  human ecology, 44, 291–2, 296
choice
  as a form of constraint, 17
  see also rational choice, theory
    of
cities, nature of, 281–3
  Chicago as exemplar, 282
class
  economistic concept of, 10, 110–11, 116,
    121–2, 133–4
  relationship to ethnicity, 110–30,
    158–61, 169n4, 256

345